Early Muslim Polemic against Christianity
Abū ʿĪsā al-Warrāq's "Against the Incarnation"

The Muslim thinker Abū ʿĪsā al-Warrāq lived in ninth-century Baghdad. He is remembered for his extensive knowledge of non-Muslim religious communities and his unorthodox views on Islam itself. This book presents an edition and translation of Abū ʿĪsā's *Against the Incarnation*, the second and last part of his *Refutation of the Three Christian Sects*. It is edited and translated by David Thomas and contains the Arabic text alongside the English translation, together with explanatory notes. Dr Thomas' full introduction outlines the pluralist and multi-faith society of medieval Baghdad, and places Abū ʿĪsā in the context of both Muslim theological argument and Christian–Muslim discussions. In this way it demonstrates the author's originality and his influence on later Muslim authors. The book will serve as a companion to the editor's earlier volume, *Anti-Christian Polemic in Early Islam: Abū ʿĪsā al-Warrāq's "Against the Trinity"*, which was published in 1992.

DAVID THOMAS is Senior Lecturer in the Department of Theology and Religion, University of Birmingham. His publications include *Anti-Christian Polemic in Early Islam: Abū ʿĪsā al-Warrāq's "Against the Trinity"* (1992), and *Syrian Christians under Islam, the First Thousand Years* (2001).

University of Cambridge Oriental Publications 59

Early Muslim Polemic against Christianity

A series list is shown at the back of the book

Early Muslim Polemic against Christianity

Abū ʿĪsā al-Warrāq's "Against the Incarnation"

edited and translated by
DAVID THOMAS

CAMBRIDGE
UNIVERSITY PRESS

PUBLISHED BY THE PRESS SYNDICATE OF THE UNIVERSITY OF CAMBRIDGE
The Pitt Building, Trumpington Street, Cambridge, United Kingdom

CAMBRIDGE UNIVERSITY PRESS
The Edinburgh Building, Cambridge CB2 2RU, UK
40 West 20th Street, New York, NY 10011-4211, USA
477 Williamstown Road, Port Melbourne, VIC 3207, Australia
Ruiz de Alarcón 13, 28014 Madrid, Spain
Dock House, The Waterfront, Cape Town 8001, South Africa

http://www.cambridge.org

First published 2002

Printed in the United Kingdom at the University Press, Cambridge

Typeface Monotype Times New Roman 10/12 pt. *System* QuarkPress™ [SE]

A catalogue record for this book is available from the British Library

Library of Congress Cataloguing in Publication data

ISBN 0 521 81132 5 hardback

CONTENTS

PREFACE

Early Islamic religious thought necessarily developed in a context of encounter with other faiths, since large sectors of the population of the Islamic empire held and continued to uphold beliefs that differed from those of their rulers. There were meetings between Muslims and others at all levels of society, in many different circumstances and over many centuries, with the result that important aspects of the religious thought of Islam were deeply shaped by issues and questions introduced from outside. The surviving literature from the long years of encounter provides an excellent insight into the various preoccupations of the different sides, as well as a first-hand record of the arguments they originated in attack and defence. In addition, it provides the basis for reconstructing the development and maturing of theological expression in Islam, and for understanding the progress of society under Muslim rule with its many client communities.

An important part of this literature is devoted to encounters between Muslims and Christians. Here, more acutely than anywhere else, disagreements over fundamental perceptions of God and his relationship with the creation produced fierce debates and exerted immense pressure upon religious exponents to demonstrate the rational character and coherence of the beliefs they advocated. The outcome was a wide range of arguments and forms of explanation that in elegance and sophistication rival any others in the history of interfaith encounters.

In this extensive literature, *The Refutation of the Three Christian Sects* by the third-/ninth-century Muslim Abū ʿĪsā Hārūn b. Muḥammad al-Warrāq stands out as the single most detailed, informed and comprehensive work by a Muslim against Christian doctrines from the whole early period of Islam. No rival for completeness appeared until the eighth/fourteenth century, when Ibn Taymiyya was provoked to write his *Jawāb al-ṣaḥīḥ li-man baddala dīn al-Maṣīḥ*. Abū ʿĪsā's *Refutation* presents a detailed analysis and exposure of the central Christian teachings about the Trinity and the Incarnation as they were held by the main sects active in the early Islamic empire, known as Nestorians, Jacobites and Melkites. It is based upon a deep and wide acquaintance with Christian teachings, as thorough and scholarly as any from a Muslim we know. But it is also fuelled by a passionate concern to maintain belief in the dominant Muslim principle of the absolute oneness of God and his complete distinctiveness from all other forms of existence. The whole work amounts to a stringent and exhaustively full demonstration of the supposed inadequacies of Christian doctrinal formulations, and is a brilliant example of a superior though forgotten mind at the height of its powers.

A few years ago I produced an edition and translation of the first part of Abū ʿĪsā's *Refutation* in *Anti-Christian Polemic in Early Islam, Abū ʿĪsā al-Warrāq's "Against the Trinity"* (University of Cambridge Oriental Publications no. 45, Cambridge, 1992), where I also brought together the known facts about Abū ʿĪsā himself, and attempted to place his work in its intellectual context. At that time I did not consider it necessary to include the second part since this had been edited with a French translation by A. Abel (Brussels, 1949), and was also accessible in E. Platti's edition and French translation of the fourth-/tenth-century Jacobite Yaḥyā Ibn ʿAdī's response (Louvain, 1987), in which the *Refutation* is quoted extensively and thereby preserved. But since Abel's edition is only available in a small number of duplicated copies and has mistakes in the text, and Platti's edition, though immaculate, gives the text as a series of quotations in the Christian work, where the shape and continuity of Abū ʿĪsā's argument cannot be fully appreciated, I have now thought it appropriate to make an edition of the work itself, with an English translation. This has afforded the opportunity to add extra details about Abū ʿĪsā's life to those given in the earlier work, though not to resolve fully the enigma of his attitude towards his own faith, and to place the *Refutation* against the background of contemporary Muslim and Christian debates about the Incarnation and the person of Christ.

In my earlier book I tried to show that by any estimation Abū ʿĪsā was an unusual and exceptional scholar, and that this *Refutation* stands pre-eminent among the surviving records of Muslim–Christian encounters. My respect for him and his achievement remains undiminished, and indeed the further evidence I include in this book will hopefully strengthen this claim.

The preparation of the work has been assisted greatly by the staffs of the Orchard Learning Resources Centre, Selly Oak, Birmingham, and the Bodleian and Cambridge University Libraries, whom I gratefully thank. The Reverend Dr John Davies has read the Introduction and improved its style, while Carol Bebawi has patiently typed the English text and Susan Moore has painstakingly read through everything. I take pleasure in thanking them all for saving me from infelicities and inaccuracies. Those that undoubtedly remain result from my own oversight and lack of precision.

It is my hope that this edition and translation will make more widely available the remainder of the known extant works of a major though neglected scholar, and will contribute towards the deeper knowledge that Christians and Muslims require if they are to learn from their shared history and seek to transcend it.

David Thomas

Introduction

1
Christians and Muslims in early Islamic society

Abū ʿĪsā Muḥammad b. Hārūn al-Warrāq, whose only surviving work is the subject of this book, lived at a time of unprecedented new developments in Islamic thought. He was a contemporary of some of the best-known theologians in Islamic history and, although he is barely remembered among them, he easily measures up as one of the most sophisticated, exciting and surprising minds of early Islam. More than almost any of his contemporaries, he was fascinated by the religions among which Muslims lived, and he subjected the claims they made to some of the most searching interrogations that have survived. We shall see in the next chapter, when we examine his life and thought, how his impartiality towards all religions, including his own, led to misunderstanding about his intentions, and maybe brought imprisonment and execution. But before we consider the surviving details about Abū ʿĪsā himself, we should attempt to say something about the world in which he lived.

The presence of Christians in the world of Islam

Abū ʿĪsā was active in the first half of the third/ninth century, and appears to have spent his whole life in Baghdad. At this time the capital of the Islamic empire was developing culturally and politically into one of the most important cities in the world. It drew immense revenues from an empire that extended from the western Mediterranean to India and the Sahara to Central Asia, a vast area that was more or less united under the rule of some of the most powerful Caliphs in the history of Islam. And from all parts it attracted the talented and ambitious with their different kinds of knowledge and accomplishments, who came in the hope of winning patronage from a noble or even the Caliph himself. It was a city as cosmopolitan as any before it, with a population comprising diverse cultures and religions. Among them none were more prominent than the Christians, who had lived and built their churches and monasteries in the area long before the city was built.

A glimpse of the religious atmosphere of Baghdad in the years that followed its founding in 145/762 is afforded in the report of a debate that supposedly took place in the mid second/eighth century between a Christian leader named Barīha and the Muslim theologian Hishām Ibn al-Ḥakam, who himself had made his way from his native Baṣra to the new city as a market trader.[1] Hishām sets the scene of the encounter as follows:

> While I was seated in my shop at the Karkh gate with people around me reading out the Qurʾan for me, suddenly there appeared a crowd of Christians, both priests and others, about a hundred men all in black with hooded cloaks, and among them was the chief Patriarch Barīha. They stopped around my shop, and my chair was offered to Barīha. He sat on it and the bishops and monks stood around leaning on their staffs, with their hooded cloaks over their heads.[2]

And the two proceed to debate their religious differences, with the Muslim finally getting the better of the Christian. Although the incident probably never took place,[3] this report is significant in showing that in the memory of the fourth-/tenth-century Muslim author who records it, Baghdad in the mid second/eighth century was a city in which Christian priests felt free to appear in public in great, even intimidating numbers, and that discussions about points of religious difference were held in the most public places. Even if the account has no historical basis, it suggests that in later Muslim minds Baghdad in its earliest years was a place of frequent and free encounters between Muslims and Christians.

We shall see in what follows that Christians and the ecclesiastical hierarchy were familiar parts of Baghdad life in the years around the turn of the third/ninth century, and that the churches and monasteries which had long predated the coming of the ʿAbbasids and even Islam to this area became places of gathering for Muslims as well as Christians. The Christian presence in and around Baghdad at this time could not be and was not ignored by the Muslim populace, and it produced an ambivalent response on their part.[4]

Evidence from elsewhere conveys a similar picture to this Muslim account of a religiously pluralist culture in the city and of members of the faiths mixing with comparative freedom. For example, the Patriarch Timothy I, who was leader of the Nestorian Church in the period 164/780–208/823, remarks casually in a letter to a fellow priest that as he was entering the Caliph's court one day, he was accosted by a person "who was well instructed in the thought of Aristotle" and asked to explain aspects of his faith,[5] and in a second, better known, letter to the same priest he describes at length how he managed to defend his faith before the Caliph al-Mahdī.[6] This second letter is an important source of evidence about the form of debates that took place in the years around 200/815, but it is equally significant for the light it casts upon relations between Christians and Muslims. The fact that the ruler of the Islamic empire saw fit to set aside two days to debate with a Christian points to the high value he attached to discussion of specifically religious matters, and also to the political capital he may have seen accruing from being known to treat the Patriarch with so much distinction.

The presence of the Patriarch and a philosopher at the Caliph's court well reflects something of the interest in matters of interfaith that is shown by the frequent debates that were arranged at this time for the Caliph between leading representatives of religions and schools of thought. These were often very elaborate affairs in which a number of scholars and religious leaders took turns to put their case and defend it, while the Caliph and his court looked on. If the surviving examples are anything to go by, the disputants often brought into open discussion points of an extremely technical nature which, while they displayed the mental agility of their authors, must have taxed the minds and patience of any lay person who bothered to follow their finer details.[7] The *majlis* disputation later became such a familiar part of interreligious debate that it was often used by both Christian and Muslim authors as the conventional literary setting for arguments of this kind.[8]

A further detail that illustrates very well the ease with which senior Muslims and Christians mixed in the period of the early ʿAbbasid caliphate occurs in the letter attributed to a certain ʿAbdullah al-Hāshimī. This purports to be a brief invitation from a Muslim noble to his distinguished Christian friend ʿAbd al-Masīḥ al-Kindī to convert to Islam. It is set in the reign of the Caliph al-Ma'mūn (198/813–218/833), to whom the two characters are supposed to be known. There has long been doubt about the authenticity of the letters, and it is now accepted by many that they were both written by the same Christian author some time in the third/ninth century and probably come from a later date than the reign of al-Ma'mūn.[9] For our purposes what is important is that al-Hāshimī is made to say that he has learned a great deal about Christianity from visits to monasteries, hermitages and churches. There he has witnessed the prayers offered through the day, the spiritual exercises performed by the monks, and the extremes of deprivation they endured in their devotion. In addition, he says, he has held discussions with senior priests openly and equitably, without hypocrisy or arrogance but in search of truth,

> Allowing them full freedom to present their arguments and to say whatever they wanted, without wishing to vex them in any way, as do in their discussions the common people, the ignorant and insolent of our religion.[10]

The self-conscious apology at the end of this comment betrays its Christian authorship (or else a disarmingly candid Muslim), though it cannot have totally misrepresented actual situations without revealing the truth of its origins. And so we can take the remark as another indication of the presence of Christians in and around Baghdad, and of their continuing to worship in churches and monasteries as they had before the coming of Islam.

If these incidental references in literary remains from the time of Abū ʿĪsā help us to see that Christians, among followers of other religions, were very much in evidence in Baghdad, and were treated with a measure of respect arising from their piety and learning, other references show even more convincingly how involved the Caliph himself often was with Christians and their religious lives. For example, the fourth-/tenth-century Egyptian author Abū al-Ḥasan ʿAlī al-Shābushtī (d. 388/988) records not only that Muslim nobles were accustomed to visit monasteries on feast days, both to witness the spectacle of the liturgy and enter into the less exalted pleasures of drinking wine and meeting women, but also how the Caliphs al-Maʾmūn and al-Mutawakkil spent enough time in monasteries for the former to become an admirer of the ceremonies performed there, and for the latter to fall in love with a monk's daughter.[11] In addition, the record of the career of the physician and polemicist ʿAlī b. Sahl Rabban al-Ṭabarī, who was a near contemporary of Abū ʿĪsā, shows that despite being a Christian he worked closely under the Caliphs al-Muʿtaṣim, al-Wāthiq and al-Mutawakkil between about 225/840 and 250/864, and retained his faith for most of that time. It was probably only under the persuasion of al-Mutawakkil, who had made him a table companion, that he eventually converted to Islam. Then, in his extreme old age he wrote the two anti-Christian works with which he is associated.[12]

The most instructive contemporary account of Christians living in early third-/ninth-century ʿAbbasid Baghdad and its surroundings is given by the rationalist theologian and *littérateur* Abū ʿUthmān al-Jāḥiẓ (d. 255/869) in a letter which he wrote to some Muslims who had asked for his help against a group of Christians. He prefaces his reply with a wide-ranging exploration of the reasons why Christians are so popular in Islamic society, and offers some fascinating insights into the conduct of Christians under caliphal rule and the response of Muslims towards them.

At one point al-Jāḥiẓ corroborates the details mentioned above when he says that among the Christians "are secretaries to the government, attendants of kings, doctors to the nobility, sellers of perfume and financiers",[13] all positions of influence, intimacy and prestige. He may, in fact, have in mind such figures as ʿAlī b. Rabban al-Ṭabarī himself, or the Nestorian Christian secretaries employed from the monastery of Dayr Qunnā who appear to have influenced state policy in their own favour.[14] And he could hardly be ignorant of the physicians from the Christian Bukhtīshūʿ family who constituted a virtual dynasty of personal medical attendants upon a succession of Caliphs.[15] He might also have added to this list the Christian translators who at the behest of the ʿAbbasid rulers and leading Muslims provided Arabic versions of major philosophical and scientific works from the ancient world.[16] The careful translations of the leading expert in this activity, Ḥunayn Ibn Isḥāq (d. *c.* 265/877), a Nestorian Christian, were so highly prized that the Caliph was prepared to pay for them by weight in gold. According to one anecdote, Ḥunayn capitalised on this by writing in large letters on thick paper, though the Caliph is supposed to have retorted "He thinks he can fool me but I shall gain more than he",[17] as he reflected upon the immense weight of learning he was acquiring.

Uneasy relations between Muslims and Christians

The slight edge of inimicability revealed in this last anecdote echoes another observation in al-Jāḥiẓ's letter about the way in which Christians treat Muslims in debate:

> They choose contradictory statements in our Ḥadīths, our reports that have weak chains of transmitters, and the equivocal verses in our Book, and they take to one side our weak and common people and ask them questions about them. Despite the ideas they have learnt from the heretics and accursed atheists, they often appear innocent before our intellectuals and people of influence. Hence they stir up trouble among the powerful, and cause deception among the weak-minded. And the pity is that each and every Muslim thinks he is an expert in religious matters, and that no one is better at arguing with heretics than anyone else![18]

This depicts the Christians as completely unscrupulous in the way they confused ordinary Muslims by presenting spurious or difficult statements from Muslim scriptural sources, and confuted experts with arguments they innocently passed off as not their own. It is undoubtedly exaggerated, in the same way as the anti-Muslim remark in al-Hāshimī's letter quoted above. But it is important in that it reveals an atmosphere of antipathy between Muslims and Christians, and some hostility. It suggests that despite the frequent meetings and the mutual benefit that both sides might obtain, there was little real liking between the two and no constructive co-operation.

The same point is given acerbity by a complaint that appears slightly earlier in al-Jāḥiẓ's letter:

> [Our judges] take the view that if a Christian accuses the mother of the Prophet (may God bless him and give him peace) of sinning, he should only be reprimanded and chastised. Moreover, they argue that they can say this because the mother of the Prophet (may God bless him and give him peace) was not a Muslim.[19]

The Christians are evidently well informed that whereas they would be severely punished for insulting a Muslim or the Prophet himself, they are legally immune here on the technicality that the Prophet's mother was outside Islam. They are playing games, and preferring to please themselves with a clever manipulation of the law rather than acting responsibly before their Muslim neighbours.

This attitude and its underlying reasons are illustrated at some length in this letter with alarming clarity, as al-Jāḥiẓ describes how Christians ignore the rules that apply to them:

> We know that they ride highly bred horses and camels, play polo . . . wear fashionable silk garments, and have attendants to serve them. They call themselves Ḥasan, Ḥusayn, ʿAbbās, Faḍl and ʿAlī, and also employ these as forenames. They have only now to call themselves Muḥammad, and employ the forename Abū al-Qāsim. And the Muslims adore them!
>
> Many of them have stopped wearing their belts, *zunnār*, while others wear them beneath their clothes. Many of the powerful people among them refrain from paying the poll tax, *jizya*, and although they have the means refuse to give it. They insult those who insult them, and hit those who hit them. And why should they not do this or even more, when our judges, or the majority, consider the blood of a patriarch, metropolitan or bishop to be equivalent to the blood of Jaʿfar, ʿAli, ʿAbbās or Ḥamza?[20]

The first paragraph suggests that many Christians ape Muslim customs of dress and pastimes, but it also intimates that in employing Muslim names and forenames they not only seek to copy their rulers but also to hide the differences between them. This haughty indifference towards conventions is even more evident in the second paragraph, where they are portrayed flouting the laws that pertain to their non-Muslim status.

The place of Christians and others in ʿAbbasid society at this time was in theory governed by the regulations attaching to their client status as *Ahl al-Dhimma* or *Dhimmīs*. These were established upon early precedents that derived from the relations of the Prophet and his immediate successors with non-Muslims who came under their rule. In particular, they were based upon agreements made by the second Caliph ʿUmar Ibn al-Khaṭṭāb and his generals with the representatives of conquered cities. For this reason they were known collectively as the "Covenant of ʿUmar".

It is not clear exactly when this body of regulations reached its full form, and the earliest version which is near complete is given as late as the sixth/twelfth century by Abū Bakr al-Ṭurṭūshī.[21] This compilation is revealing, however, since among its many stipulations, to which the Christians who originally assented to it are supposed to have agreed, are the following:

> We shall show deference to the Muslims and shall rise from our seats when they wish to sit down;
> We shall not attempt to resemble the Muslims in any way with regard to their dress, as, for example, with the *qalansuwa*, the turban, sandals, or parting the hair;
> We shall not speak as they do, nor shall we adopt their forenames;
> We shall not ride on saddles;
> We shall always adorn ourselves in our traditional fashions. We shall bind our belts, *zunnār*, around our waists.
> Anyone who deliberately strikes a Muslim will forfeit the protection of this pact.

(This last clause was supposedly added by the Caliph to the list of concessions made by the Christians.)

We can see immediately that in the passage from his letter just quoted al-Jāḥiẓ is alluding to contraventions of exactly these regulations by Christians who thought themselves above such petty restrictions. The actual misdemeanours of these Christians maybe match the theoretical legislation in the Covenant too closely for anyone to be persuaded that they committed them precisely in this form (unless they were going out of their way to show their contempt for them). But even allowing for literary caricature, there is enough in what al-Jāḥiẓ says to show that Christians, and others, were divided from Muslims by more than religion and customs. The divide was legal and formal, and it must have produced a clear sense of disjunction and dissonance between Muslims and their client peoples.

There are, however, signs that in this early period the regulations were not rigorously enforced. For one thing, the very fact that al-Jāḥiẓ could refer to Christians acting so openly in defiance of them indicates that they might be ignored with some confidence of immunity. And, more significantly, on two occasions in fifty years the Caliphs Hārūn al-Rashīd in 191/807, and al-Mutawakkil in 235/849–50, thought it necessary to issue orders that enforced elements of them in order to curb *Dhimmī* freedoms. Hārūn al-Rashīd's order was intended to ensure that *Dhimmīs* were distinguished from Muslims with respect to their dress and mounts,[22] though al-Mutawakkil went much further, for as well as dress rules he also ordered distinctive signs to be placed on the houses of *Dhimmīs*, the removal of Christian officials from positions of seniority, and other openly discriminatory measures.[23] The necessity to issue orders such as these shows that whatever regulations existed were not at all times applied to the letter. And the fact that al-Jāḥiẓ refers to Christians not even paying the *jizya*, the tax levied on *Dhimmīs* from the earliest times, suggests that conditions must generally have been very lax. But on the other hand, the fact that he can merely mention the regulations without elaboration, and their periodic enforcement, show that people knew they were always there and could be brought into use at any time.

It would appear, then, that Christians and other non-Muslims were permitted in Muslim society, but only on the level of tolerance. They served definite purposes and brought distinctive skills and knowledge for which they were recognised and maybe respected, but they were never welcomed into society as full and equal members. And there was always the fear that their uneasy participation might be suspended as legal restrictions were put in place. It is perhaps no wonder that the Christians about whom al-Jāḥiẓ writes held such an ambivalent attitude, on the one hand wanting to show in their dress, pastimes and refusal to observe marks of distinction that they were no different from Muslim neighbours, while on the other twisting legalities and employing unfair means to poke fun at Muslims and their sensitivities. They exhibit the conflicting attitudes typical of a marginalised group, striving at once to identify with the mainstream culture and to preserve their own separate existence.

Common themes and mutual borrowing

As we noted at the beginning, the early ʿAbbasid period was a time of unprecedented progress in Islamic religious thought. Not only were the main elements of a distinctive theology established at this time, but also the relationship between the teachings of Islam and other faiths. It is fearsomely difficult to talk about the origins of this great surge in ideas, and almost as difficult to plot its development or outline at any given date in this early time. This is because the works that have survived from authors who were active in the third/ninth century and earlier are very few. Indeed, we can only ascertain the teachings of some of the leading thinkers of this time from relatively meagre quotations and mentions found in works from later centuries. The books which they wrote have either perished from neglect or destruction, or may possibly lie unidentified in overlooked corners of libraries. Abū ʿĪsā al-Warrāq's many lost works are only some of the casualties of change in intellectual fashion and the depredations of invading armies.

It will be clear from what we have already seen that Islamic religious thinking developed in a multi-religious milieu. And it is likely that from an early date encounters between Muslims and members of other faiths, prominent among them Christians, raised issues that forced religious thinkers to concentrate on particular questions. It is possible that the record of one of these encounters is represented in the *Disputatio Saraceni et Christiani*, a debate between a "Saracen" and a Christian that is attributed to the Christian theologian John of Damascus (d. *c.* 132/750), who was brought up in the Umayyad court and was for a time a senior official under the Caliph.[24] Although it has survived in a rather disordered form and its authorship is by no means certain, it is generally considered to derive from the mid or late second/eighth century[25] and so can be accepted as a witness of debate from this period.

At the very beginning of the *Disputatio* the difficult question of the relationship between divine omnipotence and human responsibility is raised, and the Christian convinces the Muslim that there must be a measure of human autonomy.[26] Now it is known from elsewhere[27] that this particular problem was being heatedly debated in Islam between those who stressed the scriptural emphasis upon the unassailable omnipotence of God and others who saw in scripture equally important teachings about human responsibility.[28] So here in this debate we may see a Christian taking polemical advantage of an issue that caused disagreement in Islam, and magnifying the problem into an acute challenge.

The reality of the disputational interreligious milieu cannot be denied, though how strongly the emergence and development of theological thinking in Islam was instigated and directed by influences from outside is by no means clear, and scholarly views differ considerably over the issue.[29] Whatever the actual situation may have been, it is certain that before the beginning of the third/ninth century Islamic theological thought had begun to mature into a distinctive systematic discipline with its own methodology. This was known as *kalām*, and it has sometimes been equated with theology in Christianity, though the resemblance is not always close.

In the years before and after the beginning of the third/ninth century the leaders in *kalām* were thinkers known as the Muʿtazila, who were loosely associated into two groups at Baghdad and Baṣra. They became important not only theologically but also politically under the rule of some Caliphs, as their views became officially recognised and in particular their doctrine that the Qurʾan was not eternal but created was used as a test, the *Miḥna*,[30] for anyone serving in public posts.

The Muʿtazila usually called themselves *Ahl al-tawḥīd wa-al-ʿadl*, the People of God's Unity and Justice. This epithet derives from two of the five principles upon which they generally agreed, and it describes the central preoccupations of their theological discourse, the being of God in himself and God's relationship with the world. Of course, these are two of the major themes of the Qur'an, and from what we can tell they were fundamental elements of questioning and debate among Muslims from the earliest times. But the Muʿtazila more than any others brought thinking about them to a point of refinement, and established the lines of discourse on them for centuries to come. With regard to the doctrine of God, they refused to allow any kind of comparison between him and created beings, and they also rejected any description that might involve division or multiplicity within his being. Consequently, he became the equivalent of an unknowable force whose effects were evident to all but whose being in itself was a mystery veiled from human minds. With regard to his justice, they insisted that he gave rewards or punishments for merits or crimes which created individuals themselves deserved. This meant the Muʿtazila conceded that humankind had responsibility for their actions, and so must possess a measure of freedom to perform them. The consequences in this for God's omnipotence produced differences and disputes for centuries afterwards.

These teachings legitimately derive from a reading of the Qur'an, and in this respect the Muʿtazilī thinkers were doing no more than formulating the received learning in a new abstract way. But the context in which they were establishing their principles was one in which Greek and other philosophies were becoming increasingly familiar to Muslims, thanks in large part to the translations made by Christians and to ideas which they were making known. And it is almost certain that these Muslim theologians were explaining and defending their position in this new reality.[31]

An important feature of the Muʿtazilī system of describing the nature of the created world illustrates this point clearly. For them the physical world was composed entirely of atoms, minute material units that combined to make up what is observed and experienced in all its forms. These were the basic blocks, as it were, from which the contingent order was made. They were in themselves all uniform in essence and they were given the characteristics that differentiated them in texture, colour and so on by what were known as accidents. The accidents became attached to atoms and thereby endowed them with the different qualities they acquired. The unceasing changes in combinations of atoms and the appearance of new accidents on them produced in the created order the semblance of movement and continuity.[32]

This method of explaining how the world works enabled the Muʿtazila and others to account for physical phenomena with an impressive degree of completeness and sophistication, though they were not the first thinkers to make use of it. Comparison between this materialist system in Islam and similar systems in Greek and Indian thought suggests that the Muʿtazila were certainly aware of antecedents and maybe borrowed from them.[33] In doing so they were employing language and concepts that allowed them to communicate their ideas in appropriate forms and to defend them in ways that might convince or refute insistent opponents. However, it is important to emphasise that for all the similarities between this physical system and non-Islamic equivalents, one important element distinguishes it. For in the Muʿtazilī conception neither the atoms nor accidents possessed any inherent natures that might make them act in any particular way. Every change that took place, all the combinations of atoms and the additions and subtractions of accidents, were directly caused by God alone. It was a system in which only the one primary cause was active, and there were no secondary causes. And in this respect it was subordinated to the overriding requirement to show how God alone was Controller and Disposer of the world without any associates or rivals.

If this aspect of Muʿtazilī thought betrays traces of their awareness of and possible borrowing from non-Muslim philosophical systems, another shows how closely within the Islamic world itself Muslims and Christians were related in their exposition of the being of God. A major matter of dispute among Muslim thinkers at this time was the divine attributes. It arose from the fact that not only reason but also revelation portrayed God in distinct ways, for example as living, knowing, powerful, and so on. At some quite early stage in the development of debates among Muslims themselves it was acknowledged that these qualities must derive from attributes which God possessed. For example, if God is knowing, he must have knowledge as an attribute from which the quality derives.

This issue was one of the most controversial elements of third-/ninth-century Islamic debate, because the existence of attributes which were related to God's being affected the understanding of how God was understood to be one. Two main interpretations were favoured. The Baṣran Muʿtazilī theologian Abū al-Hudhayl al-ʿAllāf argued that God's attributes were completely identical with his essence, so that in effect he could be said to be knowing, living, powerful and so on by virtue of his own being rather than through a distinct attribute. This explanation safeguarded the absolute oneness of God upon which this group insisted, though it raised major problems concerning his character, since within the prevailing framework of understanding it did not derive his qualities from any specific origin and could not guarantee that they were real. Opponents could thus taunt the Muʿtazila by saying that since God had no attribute of life or knowledge to endow him with the qualities of living and knowing, he must be dead or ignorant.

The other, less widely known, explanation was that the attributes of God were neither identical with his essence nor distinct from it, existing as definite entities which were part of the single being of God. This was more difficult to present clearly, though it had the great advantage of both preserving the reality of the divine attributes and also safeguarding God's unity. It is chiefly associated in this period with the little-known thinker ʿAbdullah b. Saʿīd Ibn Kullāb.[34]

Contemporary Arab Christians who were aware of the Muslim debates over this abstract issue would immediately recognise a similarity with debates in their own tradition over the doctrine of the Trinity. And some appear actually to have employed the logic that underlay the various Muslim positions to clarify their own doctrine in the Islamic milieu. One of them, ʿAmmār al-Baṣrī, who was probably known to Abū al-Hudhayl, consciously employed this logic in order to justify to Muslims the doctrine of the Trinity.[35] His explanation begins as follows:

> Tell me, you who believe in the One, do you say that he is living? If he says: Yes; we say: Is this by an eternal life which he has in his essence, as the soul of a human has in its essence a substantial life which is of it? Or is it by an accidental life, as a body has life which it has received from another, having no life of its own in the essence of its substance? If he says: By an eternal life which he has in his essence; then he agrees with our teaching. If he says: Neither by an essential eternal life, nor by an accidental life; we say: This is as though you will not say "living" in case you should have to affirm that he has a life, whether essential and eternal or accidental. If he says: Yes, we say: Then how, according to you, is he worthy of the name "living"? The name "living" is always derived from "life", because we call a human living as long as life remains in him, but if his living spirit departs from him, we call him dead.[36]

We see here that ʿAmmār takes for granted the relationship between God's qualities and the attributes from which they arise, and also that he finds the denial of attributes unreasonable. He is quite clearly expert in the terms of the Muslim debate and sufficiently involved to take sides against the Muʿtazilī theologians (affirmers of "the One") who refuse to derive God's qualities from essential attributes. To all intents and purposes, he is a Christian *mutakallim* whose language and conceptual framework are no different from those in which Muslim *kalām* debates were conducted.

The one significant difference between ʿAmmār and his Muslim interlocutors is that while in their theology the number of divine attributes extends as far as the Qurʾan and reason allow, in his they are limited to two, the Holy Spirit as Life of the Father and the Son as his Knowledge. Thus ʿAmmār goes on to argue that these two attributes alone are "of the constitution of the essence and of the structure of the substance", and all others depend upon them.[37] But this and similar arguments that he and other Christians employed to defend this limitation never convinced Muslims, and for many years afterwards *mutakallimūn* often took delight in demonstrating how the Christians had misunderstood the whole issue of the divine attributes and had created immense trouble for themselves by recasting their doctrine of the Trinity according to its terms and logic.[38]

We cannot tell the precise circumstances behind ʿAmmār's borrowing of Muslim concepts, though it is hardly likely that the Christians who saw its possibilities were regarded as colleagues or partners in Muslim theological discourse. Instead, they may have been seen by Muslims as interlopers, while they thought of themselves as more than clever in employing Muslim ideas to explain and support a doctrine that was inimical to Islam.

Another example from this time shows the theological rivalry that existed and the distaste produced by clever attempts to overturn accepted beliefs. It occurs in the Letter written by al-Jāḥiẓ which we have referred to above, in a relatively brief argument that clearly exercised both him and many other Muslims. Al-Jāḥiẓ mentions that the group of Christians who were harassing his Muslim correspondents had posed them a question, as follows:

> If God could take, *ittakhadha*, one of his servants as a friend, *khalīl*, could he have taken a human being as a son, *walad*, in the sense of showing him his mercy and love, excellent upbringing and education and the special place he had for him, just as he called a human being friend in the sense of honouring him, showing him esteem, and indicating the special position he had for him?[39]

This may seem reasonable enough. The Qur'an relates: "And God took Abraham as a friend", *wa-attakhadha Allāhu Ibrāhīma khalīlan* (Q 4.125), suggesting that Islamic revelation allows the possibility of an intimate relationship between God and a created being. So it might plausibly be proposed that God could also have taken a human as a son in another intimate form of relationship. And in the way in which the question is formulated there is no apparent threat to the distinction in being between God and his creatures upon which Muslims insisted. For like the human Abraham, the son described here is also a human and becomes son of God only through an act of adoption and not eternal generation.

At first glimpse, then, the parallel between Abraham and Jesus does not appear to raise any difficulties for Muslims. And it may have the advantage of enabling them to acknowledge a basic Christian doctrine, in a step towards reconciliation over the contested issue of whether Jesus was the son of God. But the danger it contains soon becomes obvious. For it requires any Muslim who might sympathise with it to allow what the Qur'an expressly rejects, the claim that God should have taken a son.[40] In effect, the question requires an answer that accepts what the Qur'an denies on the precedent set by the Qur'an itself. If it was meant maliciously it must have been intended to involve Muslims in endless tangles, and if it was meant constructively it expected them to make huge concessions in defiance of their scripture. It is little wonder that al-Jāḥiẓ himself gave a blistering reply to the question, and that for over a century Muslims who came across it found ingenious arguments to refute it, as we shall see in Chapter 3.

This and the previous example of the Nestorian ʿAmmār al-Baṣrī show that there were Christians at the time of Abū ʿĪsā who had considerable knowledge of Islam and made use of it to get their own doctrines accepted in the Muslim milieu, and maybe also to cause irritation to their Muslim neighbours. So it should not surprise us to discover the traces of a rich and sustained polemical literature between the faiths at this time.

Religious encounters between Muslims and Christians

On the Christian side, the earliest polemical account of Islam is given by John of Damascus in the middle of the second/eighth century.[41] This is impressive for the completeness with which it both explains the origins of Islam and condemns it. It occurs at the end of John's *De Haeresibus*, where it is tellingly called "The Heresy of the Ishmaelites", and it portrays the new teachings as nothing more than a jumble which is derived from misunderstood Christian scriptures. John makes use of the Baḥīrā legend, which tells of a meeting between a Christian hermit and Muḥammad as a boy, and the monk's recognition of him as the prophet who is to come.[42] But he turns Baḥīrā into an Arian heretic and portrays Muḥammad as borrowing teachings from him and then presenting them to his countrymen as revelations. The Prophet's purpose was solely to further his own ambitions.

Here John sets the tone of much Christian writing that was to follow by treating Islam as a debased form of Christianity, and its origins as morally suspect. Of course, he was bound to adopt some such view, because as a Christian believing in the finality of Christ and his own revealed scriptures he could not accord any true value to Muḥammad or Islam. Hence it can only be a heresy at best and its founder could only have similar motives to other heretics.

An even more scathing account of Islam is given in the anonymous Letter of ʿAbd al-Masīḥ al-Kindī, which, as we have noted, is set in the time of the Caliph al-Maʾmūn but probably dates from the later third/ninth century.[43] Here the author presents a detailed examination of the Prophet's life and finds him only interested in power and women:

> His one preoccupation and sole thought was to find a beautiful woman to marry or people to raid; he shed their blood, seized their possessions and ravished their women.[44]

Likewise, in the Christian part of another anonymous work from about the same time, that is supposed to have been a correspondence from the early second/eighth century between the Umayyad Caliph ʿUmar II and the Byzantine Emperor Leo III, Qurʾanic justification for polygamy is condemned, and Mecca is exposed as the habitation of demons who entrap Muslims during the annual pilgrimage.[45]

Such surviving comments as these make it abundantly clear that for Christians Islam contained little of value, and Muḥammad was a figure who was widely reviled.

More tactful authors who explained and defended their own doctrines to Muslim audiences, such as ʿAmmār al-Baṣrī and his two contemporaries Theodore Abū Qurra and Ḥabīb Ibn Khidma Abū Raʾiṭa, whom we shall discuss in Chapter 3, wrote against a background such as this and may have subscribed to many of the same attitudes. Their intention may have been to make Christian doctrines comprehensible and acceptable within Islam, but they still argued that Christianity was the supreme religion. Theodore, for example, argues that Christianity fulfils all the conditions required for a universal religion more adequately than any other,[46] while ʿAmmār shows that while religions such as Judaism, Zoroastrianism and Islam rely for their success upon materialistic motivations such as concessions to human desires and ambition, Christianity makes the highest moral demands and so must be heavenly, and therefore superior.[47] In Christian circles at this time there was no welcome for Islam, but rather a total denial of any claims about its divine origins or moral content.

On the Muslim side, popular attitudes become clear by the end of the second/eighth century, in the questions put to the Patriarch Timothy by the Caliph al-Mahdī during their two-day meeting.[48] The main topics fall under three categories. The first is the being of God in himself: for the Caliph the doctrine of the Trinity suggests three distinct beings who can be separated and cannot be equal. The second is the relationship between God and Jesus Christ: for the Caliph this implies that the Father begot the Son physically and that there was a relationship between the Eternal and one born in time, and he objects that Jesus' human traits and actions prohibit his being divine, and that the Divinity came under the control of men when Christ was crucified. The third is the Christian scriptures: the Caliph expects these to contain predictions of Muḥammad, and suspects that they have been corrupted.[49] Other topics he raises are comparatively minor.[50]

Whether or not the Caliph himself argued precisely in the way that Timothy portrays him, the questions attributed to him show the typical concerns among Muslims at this time. They centre very much upon the main teachings of the Qurʾan concerning Christianity, and upon Muslim debates over the oneness and distinctiveness of God and the authenticity of the Bible.

Among Muslim *mutakallimūn* in this period the refutation of other faiths appears to have been an integral part of the activity of *kalām*. We do not have much detailed knowledge of the substance of their attacks since these have been lost apart from a few comparatively minor works (and, of course, Abū ʿĪsā's major examination of Christian doctrines). But we can gather some information from the lists of titles of these theologians' writings that appear in later authors. Thus we know that several leading Muʿtazilīs devoted works to other faiths, including Ḍirār Ibn ʿAmr, Ḥafṣ al-Fard, Bishr Ibn al-Muʿtamir,[51] Ibrāhīm al-Naẓẓām[52] and Abu Jaʿfar Muḥammad al-Iskāfī.[53] And furthermore we are told that ʿĪsā b. Ṣubayḥ al-Murdār wrote an attack on the Christian Theodore Abū Qurra,[54] and that Abū al-Hudhayl al-ʿAllāf of Baṣra attacked a certain ʿAmmār the Christian, who is plausibly the Nestorian ʿAmmār al-Baṣrī whom we have mentioned above.[55]

A little light is cast on the contents of Muslim attacks such as these by the few surviving refutations of Christianity from the early third/ninth century. These include the philosopher Abū Yūsuf Yaʿqūb b. Isḥāq al-Kindī's demonstration that according to the logic of Aristotelian philosophy the doctrine of the Trinity is untenable,[56] and the convert ʿAlī al-Ṭabarī's exposure of the inconsistencies between Gospel teachings and the Nicene Creed in his *Radd ʿalā al-Naṣārā*,[57] and his elaborate proof on the basis of his own fresh readings that the Bible predicts Muḥammad in his *Kitāb al-dīn wa-al-dawla*.[58] But ʿAlī al-Ṭabarī is atypical of Muslim debate because of the deep knowledge of Christianity he brought with him when he converted, and al-Kindī applies philosophical rather than theological methods of inquiry. So their works are of only limited use in discerning common Muslim attitudes at this time.

A more helpful surviving tract and maybe the earliest extant Muslim refutation of Christianity is the *Radd ʿalā al-Naṣārā* of the Zaydī theologian al-Qāsim Ibn Ibrāhīm (d. 246/860),[59] which he may have written as early as 210/825.[60] It comprises three well distinguished parts: at the beginning an explanation of why God is unique and cannot have partners in his divinity; then a detailed exposition of the doctrines promoted by the main Christian sects in the Muslim empire; and thirdly a refutation of the two doctrines of the Trinity and divinity of Christ, the former by means of theological arguments,[61] and the latter by means of a re-reading of Christian scripture to prove Christ's humanity.[62] The contents of these sections aside, it is immediately obvious that the chief preoccupations of the refutation reflect the Caliph al-Mahdī's in his debate with Timothy, namely the Trinity, the divinity of Christ and indirectly the correct interpretation of Christian scripture (with which, incidentally, ʿAlī al-Ṭabarī is also concerned in his *Kitāb al-dīn wa-al-dawla*). This is made particularly acute by the presence in the *Radd* of a full and detailed account of Christian beliefs concerning the atonement, but no further references at all to these in the subsequent arguments against Christian doctrines. We must assume that this central Christian belief did not provoke curiosity because it had no bearing upon Islamic beliefs themselves.

Al-Qāsim Ibn Ibrāhīm's preoccupation with some Christian beliefs and not others suggests a possible trend in Muslim anti-Christian polemic in the third/ninth century. The doctrines of the Trinity and divinity of Christ both presented direct competition to the Muslim doctrine of the oneness and distinctiveness of God, which, as we have seen, the Muʿtazila were promoting with particular acuity at this time. It could well be that part of their own activity in refining the doctrine of *tawḥīd* comprised examinations and refutations of rival formulations, so that they could prove the correctness of what they believed not only through positive arguments of their own, but also through demonstrations that competing accounts of the nature of God were inadequate.

We must be careful not to build too much upon the evidence of one work. But this suggestion does receive support from elsewhere. There is, of course, Abū ʿĪsā's own *Radd*, which as we shall see comprises a full exposition of Christian doctrines, and then refutations only of the two doctrines of the Trinity and the Incarnation or divinity of Christ. And from later in the century the fragmentary refutation of the Muʿtazilī Abū ʿAlī al-Jubbāʾī has the same structure, of an exposition and refutations of the same two doctrines.[63] Most impressively, the encyclopaedic compendium *Al-mughnī* of the fourth-/tenth-century Muʿtazilī ʿAbd al-Jabbār includes at the conclusion of its first section on the being and attributes of God, which occupies the first five volumes, a long and detailed exposition of Christianity, together with refutations of these two doctrines and no others.[64] As we shall see in Chapter 4, this shows signs of being indebted to Abū ʿĪsā's *Radd*.

It seems undeniable from this evidence that as the practice of anti-Christian refutations settled into a tradition, the two doctrines that most challenged the Muslim doctrine of *tawḥīd* became the primary focus of attack, irrespective of the beliefs and doctrines that Christians themselves emphasised. So it is not unreasonable to suppose that even in the early ʿAbbasid period this same pattern was coming into being.

The inference we may draw is that even in this early period many Muslim theologians were not so much interested in Christianity for what Christians themselves believed as for the doctrines in which they most starkly diverged from the main beliefs of Islam. And these theologians used the deficiencies they detected in those doctrines to support their own doctrine of the absolute oneness and distinctiveness of God. ʿAbd al-Jabbār's strategic placing of his refutation of Christianity, together with attacks on the beliefs of dualist sects, at the conclusion of his section on God's oneness in the *Mughnī* provides graphic evidence that by the time he was active anti-Christian polemic had become a constituent part of Muslim theology and was subordinated to this broader purpose of showing, through a comparison of inadequacy, that of all known versions only the Muslim doctrine of the absolute oneness of God stood up to intellectual scrutiny.

This in its turn suggests that just as Christians recognised in Islam only a heretical form of their own faith, Muslims saw in Christianity little more than a deviant version of their own beliefs. Either side was conditioned by its own scriptures and doctrines to fashion its own construction of the other. In the written records of encounters, which would be removed at least one stage from actual meetings, we find little to suggest that authors were investigating one another's beliefs at first hand, but rather this tendency to portray the other without question in terms of the particular author's own faith.

This judgement should be tempered in some individual circumstances, not least that of Abū ʿĪsā, whom we shall see in Chapter 3 approaching Christianity with unnervingly accurate and complete knowledge, and unfailingly keen logic. And it does not wholly apply to certain authors who seem in part to have shown interest in the faiths known in the Islamic world mainly because they existed and were curious and strange.

Among the lost works from the early ʿAbbasid period which we only know from their titles are some that appear to have been descriptive accounts of non-Islamic faiths.[65] There is, for example, the *Milal al-Hind wa-adyānuhā* (*The Confessions and Faiths of India*) of the second-/eighth-century author Abū Muḥammad Ibn al-Muqaffaʿ (d. *c.* 140/757), and from the third/ninth century there is the *Adyān al-ʿArab* (*The Faiths of the Arabs*) of Abū al-

Mundhir Ibn al-Kalbī (d. *c.* 206/821),[66] the *Adyān al-ʿArab* (*The Faiths of the Arabs*) and *Kitāb al-aṣnām* (*The Book of Idols*) of Abū ʿUthmān al-Jāḥiẓ (d. 255/869), the *Kitāb al-milal wa-al-duwal* (*The Book of Confessions and Powers*) of Abū Maʿshar Jaʿfar al-Balkhī (d. 272/886), and the *Risāla fī waṣf madhāhib al-Ṣābiʾīn* (*The Letter describing the Groups of the Sabians*) of Aḥmad b. al-Ṭayyib al-Sarakhshī (d. 286/899). There are also the *Kitāb al-maqālāt* (*Book of Opinions*) of Abū Yaʿlā Muḥammad al-Mismaʿī, known as Zurqān (*fl.* mid-third/ninth century), which presented the teachings of Aristotle and the beliefs of the Muslims, the people of Ḥarrān, the Sabians, the Hindus and the Buddhists,[67] and the *Kitāb al-maqālāt* of Abū al-ʿAbbās al-Irānshahrī (*fl.* late third/ninth century) which included the teachings of the Jews, the Christians, the Manichaeans, the Hindus and the Buddhists.[68] While we cannot on the whole say what these works were like, it seems probable from their titles and what we know of their contents that they were largely descriptive in character. This points to the fact that those who wrote them and those for whom they were written exhibited a lively curiosity in what was not Islamic,[69] maybe just because it was different.

It is possible to say a little more about this genre of religious literature on the basis of what can be reconstructed of a lost work of Abū ʿĪsā al-Warrāq himself. This was probably his major single composition, and it was recognised as an important source of information about non-Islamic faiths for many centuries after Abū ʿĪsā's death. He followed the fashion by calling it *kitābunā alladhī waṣafnā fīhi maqālāt al-nās wa-ikhtilāfahum* ("the book in which we have described people's opinions and their differences"), and it was known to others as *Kitāb maqālāt al-nās* or simply *Kitāb al-maqālāt*.[70] It was best known for its descriptions of the dualist religions, including the Manichaeans, the Mazdakians, the Daysanites, the Marcionites and the Zoroastrians; these were used by a number of later authors, whose quotations from the work make up the longest extant portions.[71] But it also contained descriptions of Jewish beliefs, including sectarian differences over the religious calendar,[72] of Christian beliefs, including maybe as many as seventy minor sects,[73] of Shīʿī Muslim beliefs,[74] and maybe of pre-Islamic Arabian beliefs.[75] It does not appear to have contained any arguments concerning the validity of these beliefs, but to have been expressly a detailed and impartial guide. And it did not simply outline the main features of these religions, but appears to have explored relatively minor differences between groups with the same precision that is evident in the description of Christian beliefs which we can see at first hand at the beginning of the *Radd ʿalā al-Naṣārā*.[76]

It is difficult to avoid the conclusion that Abū ʿĪsā was interested in the faiths he investigated for themselves, as phenomena that made up the record of human religious experience. And maybe in showing this interest he was sharing the curiosity of the other authors of the lost contemporary works on non-Islamic religions which we have listed. But it would be inaccurate to regard this interest as entirely antiquarian in character or as unrelated to belief in Islam. For we see in the case of Abū ʿĪsā that his accounts in the *Kitāb al-maqālāt* extended only to those major religions that competed within the Islamic empire and might therefore constitute real threats to the absolute monotheism that he himself espoused, and also that within the known corpus of his works were attacks on most of the religions he describes in this work.[77] So the *Kitāb al-maqālāt* may have been written in order to bring together accounts of beliefs which Muslims should be aware of and resist, and also to provide the raw information upon which Abū ʿĪsā 's refutations of other religions were based. So even though it may exhibit true curiosity in what was other than Islam, this was governed by a concern to relate it to Islam itself and show its flaws and deficiencies.

If this example of Abū ʿĪsā and his major lost work is at all representative, we see that at this time even writers of apparently descriptive explorations of religions outside Islam were in the last analysis interested in their curious features for what these might reveal about the superiority of Islam. Their openness to the other was tempered by continuing loyalty to their own beliefs.

Conclusion

These are some of the main features of the religious context in which Abū ʿĪsā lived and wrote, a world in which Christians and others were accepted among Muslims but only grudgingly, where they might be discriminated against perfunctorily, and might find the law enforced against them unexpectedly. For their own part, Christians participated in Islamic society as far as this benefited them, and they took advantage where they could get away with it. They enriched society with the intellectual heritage and talents which they brought, and they themselves were enriched by ideas they could borrow and ways of thinking in which they saw advantage.[78] There was a great deal of discussion and disputation over matters of faith, and the flourishing of a polemical literature in which the respective positions became set and developed in detail and sophistication.

Abū ʿĪsā himself participated fully in these encounters and religious disputes, and as we have just seen produced notable writings to fuel them. We should now turn to the man himself, and attempt to understand him and his individualistic attitude to all matters of religion, including his own.

2

Abū ʿĪsā al-Warrāq and the study of religions

Fragments of Abū ʿĪsā's life

From all that we can tell about him, Abū ʿĪsā Muḥammad b. Hārūn b. Muḥammad al-Warrāq was a complicated and maybe misunderstood individual. Brief details about him in early Muslim sources and surviving fragments from his own works suggest opposing opinions that prohibit any easy judgement concerning his religious attitudes and his approach to the question of religious truth.

It seems safe to say that Abū ʿĪsā lived and was active in the early or mid third/ninth century, was a native of Baghdad, wrote notable works on non-Islamic faiths, and held views that others found difficult to categorise. Beyond this we know nothing for certain, except that his refutation of Christianity and the few fragments of his extant writings make it important to discover more about him.[1]

The earliest mention of Abū ʿĪsā is made by Abū al-Ḥusayn ʿAbd al-Raḥmān al-Khayyāṭ in the *Kitāb al-intiṣār*, which he completed in about 269/882. There he connects Abū ʿĪsā with the arch-heretic Ibn al-Rāwandī,[2] and calls him the latter's teacher and predecessor, and the instigator of his desertion from the Muʿtazila.[3] He also adds that Abū ʿĪsā was originally a Muʿtazilī with Shīʿī sympathies but became a Manichaean dualist, and expressed great hatred for the Caliph ʿAlī Ibn Abī Ṭālib on account of all the blood he had shed.[4] At about the same time as this, Abū ʿAlī al-Jubbāʾī (d. 303/915) condemns Abū ʿĪsā as a dualist and a Shīʿī who, together with Hishām Ibn al-Ḥakam and Ibn al-Rāwandī, sought to revile religion.[5]

These details of information are challenged a few decades later by Abū ʿAlī's former pupil Abū al-Ḥasan al-Ashʿarī (d. 324/935) in his *Kitāb maqālāt al-Islamiyyīn*. He says that Abū ʿĪsā and Ibn al-Rāwandī embraced Shīʿism and wrote works about the Imamate, and he acknowledges Abū ʿĪsā as a source of information about the views of the second-/eighth-century Shīʿī thinkers Hishām Ibn al-Ḥakam (d. *c.* 179/795–6) and Hishām b. Sālim al-Jawālīqī, and about dualist teachings.[6] Here Abū ʿĪsā's move to Shīʿism is acknowledged, but his association with dualism is made no stronger than acknowledging him as an authoritative source.

More substantial information is given later in the fourth/tenth century by Abū al-Ḥasan ʿAlī al-Masʿūdī (d. 345/956). In his *Kitāb murūj al-dhahab* he associates Abū ʿĪsā closely with the Shīʿa, both in beliefs and writings, and adds the first biographical facts about him, that he was a native of Baghdad and died in the Ramla quarter in 247/861, leaving many impressive works, among them the *Kitāb al-maqālāt.*[7] We will list the titles of all the works mentioned by him and other authors at the end of this chapter.

Ibn al-Nadīm (d. *c.* 385/995), writing in the *Fihrist*, gives a list of eleven works by Abū ʿĪsā, and includes him among the Muʿtazila and Murjiʾa as an associate of Ibn al-Rāwandī and a brilliant Muʿtazilī who mingled teachings so much that he was accused of dualism. In a brief mention elsewhere in the work, Ibn al-Nadīm groups him among the recently professed *zindīq*s who were Manichaeans.[8]

It appears that by the late fourth/tenth century, about a hundred years after Abū ʿĪsā's active life, there was growing uncertainty about him. His attraction to Shīʿī beliefs is accepted, and a number of his works in favour of Shīʿism support this judgement. But he is also linked with Manichaeism or some form of dualism, and there is doubt as to whether this was an intellectual interest or full personal profession.

This uncertainty continues in later centuries. ʿAbd al-Jabbār (d. 415/1025) repeatedly calls Abū ʿĪsā a *zindīq* or *mulḥid*, condemns him as a Shīʿī and the corrupter of Ibn al-Rāwandī, and remarks that he made criticisms of the Prophet Muḥammad in order to enhance the position of the Shīʿī Imams.[9] In contrast, ʿAbd al-Jabbār's opponent, the Shīʿī author ʿAlī b. al-Ḥusayn al-Sharīf al-Murtaḍā (d. *c.* 436/1044) explains in his *Kitāb al-shāfī fī al-Imāma* that the accusation of dualism was, surprisingly, levelled by Ibn al-Rāwandī, who was Abū ʿĪsā's enemy, and that he and others found support in this from Abū ʿĪsā's own thorough and appreciative account of dualism in his *Kitāb al-maqālāt.*[10] In the same sympathetic vein, the two fifth-/eleventh-century Shīʿīs Aḥmad b. ʿAlī al-Najāshī and Abū Jaʿfar Muḥammad al-Ṭūsī both unquestioningly associate him with the Shīʿa, the former mentioning refutations of some of his works by Shīʿī scholars[11] and the latter giving him a full biographical notice, though without adding any substantial details, and appending a list of his works.[12] And then in the sixth/twelfth century, the heresiographer Abū al-Fatḥ Muḥammad al-Shahrastānī (d. 548/1153) calls him a Majūsī, "who knew these people's views",[13] and Ibn al-Jawzī (d. 597/1200) includes among events in the year 298 AH a report attributed to Abū ʿAlī al-Jubbāʾī that the authorities sought to arrest Ibn al-Rāwandī and Abū ʿĪsā, and while the former escaped they put Abū ʿĪsā in prison, where he died.[14]

These short and diverse fragmentary references produce little about Abū ʿĪsā that is clear, apart from situating him in the third/ninth century and identifying him as a Shīʿī who may have come over from the Muʿtazila. They are ambivalent about his relationship with Ibn al-Rāwandī and also about his attitude towards dualist beliefs. And they do not even agree about the precise period of his activities or the date of his death. These two matters call for further discussion.

When was Abī ʿĪsā active?

On the matter of dates there is evidence to suggest that Abū ʿĪsā was active mainly in the second quarter of the third/ninth century. Most significantly, al-Ashʿarī in about 300/912 reports him speaking with a companion of the Shīʿī theologian Hishām Ibn al-Ḥakam, *baʿḍu aṣḥāb Hishām ajābahu marratan.*[15] Since the latter died in about 179/795–6,[16] and the companion can hardly have survived him by more than fifty years, this meeting must presumably have taken place before about 230/844–5. In addition, al-Khayyāṭ, writing before about 269/882, repeatedly links Abū ʿĪsā with Abū Ḥafṣ al-Ḥaddād, who is known from the early third/ninth century,[17] and implies that the two were contemporaries.[18] And most specifically, al-Masʿūdī in the early fourth/tenth century states that Abū ʿĪsā died in the Ramla quarter of Baghdad in the year 247/861.[19] He does not give any authority for this, but its precision of both place and date suggests that he bases it on some certain knowledge.

When these details are taken together, they suggest that Abū ʿĪsā was active in writing and debate approximately between 220/835 and 250/865.[20] But other items of information appear to point to a rather later period in the third/ninth century.

One of these is the date 298/910–11 given by Ibn al-Jawzī as the year in which the events that led to Abū ʿĪsā being imprisoned took place.[21] This would suggest he was active in the latter half of the third/ninth century. However, we should be cautious about accepting what Ibn al-Jawzī says, because the actual report about Abū ʿĪsā, which is a self-contained paragraph given on the authority of Abū ʿAlī al-Jubbāʾī, contains no reference in itself to any date, and it actually appears in a later author, who is discussing the conflicting evidence about Ibn al-Rāwandī's death, without any association with a particular year.[22] So whatever reason Ibn al-Jawzī had for placing the report in this year comes from somewhere else, and is no more reliable than any other information.

A second item of evidence that might indicate a late date comes at the end of an account of Manichaean teachings given by al-Shahrastānī in the *Kitāb al-milal wa-al-niḥal* on the authority of Abū ʿĪsā. Here a Manichaean leader refers to the year 271/884–5.[23] Clearly, if this passage was part of Abū ʿĪsā's original then he must have written his account after this date. But it is by no means certain that Abū ʿĪsā himself was responsible for this reference.

Parallel with al-Shahrastānī's account of these teachings is the earlier account given by ʿAbd al-Jabbār on the authority of Abū Muḥammad al-Nawbakhtī from Abū ʿĪsā. The two differ in some incidental details, and significantly in the absence from ʿAbd al-Jabbār's version of anything other than the teachings of Mānī. So, either ʿAbd al-Jabbār removed from his source all that was not directly from Mānī himself, or al-Shahrastānī made additions, including the remark from the later Manichaean which contains this date.[24] This difference raises at least the possibility that the passage was not part of Abū ʿĪsā's original report, and removes it from the sure evidence that might support a late date.

The third item of related information is rather less tractable than either of these, and suggests that Abū ʿĪsā was still active in the middle of the century at least.

This information occurs in an unpublished manuscript work, the *Kitāb sharḥ ʿuyūn al-masāʾil fī ʿilm al-uṣūl* of the fifth-/eleventh-century author Abū Saʿīd al-Muḥsin b. Muḥammad al-Jushamī al-Bayhaqī (d. 494/1101). It was first brought to light by W. Madelung,[25] and it comprises a brief passage eight lines long which details some beliefs of the Jārūdiyya, a sub-sect of the Zaydiyya. It begins abruptly with: "Abū ʿĪsā al-Warrāq mentioned and said: the Jārūdiyya differ among themselves . . .", and then gives brief details of their belief in the return from the dead of three ʿAlids named as Muḥammad b. ʿAbdullah, Muḥammad al-Qāsim al-Ṭāliqānī and Yaḥyā b. ʿUmar Ṣāḥib al-Kūfa, adding the comment that the Zaydiyya in general repudiate these ideas. It concludes with the remark, "The source, *aṣl*, of this report is Abū ʿĪsā, though he was a dualist undoubtedly, and so this report of his should not be relied upon."

Clearly, by the middle of the fifth/eleventh century Abū ʿĪsā was routinely denounced, while at the same time being acknowledged as a significant historical source no matter how dubious. But this brief entry is important mainly as an indication of dating. The same details about the three ʿAlids are given without mention of any source by al-Ashʿarī,[26] who goes on to explain that they each raised rebellions in early ʿAbbasid times, Muḥammad b. ʿAbdullah during the reign of al-Manṣūr, Muḥammad al-Qāsim al-Ṭāliqānī under al-Muʿtaṣim, and Yaḥyā b. ʿUmar in the reign of al-Mustaʿīn.[27] The last was killed in 250/864,[28] which suggests that if Abū ʿĪsā was the author of this report, he survived for some time afterwards.

This reference in al-Jushamī seems conclusive, though some slim measure of doubt is cast on its authenticity by the fact that although al-Ashʿarī, who lists Abū ʿĪsā as a Rāfiḍī author only a few pages before he gives his unattributed version of these Jārūdī beliefs,[29] and al-Masʿūdī, who names Abū ʿĪsā as an authority on Zaydī sects, among them the Jārūdiyya,[30] both know of his close literary connection with Shīʿism, they do not mention him in connection with their reports of Yaḥyā b. ʿUmar's rebellion.[31] Of course, their silence proves little, and it is difficult to set them as challenges against al-Jushamī. But given the almost chronic confusion that attended everything about Abū ʿĪsā in the centuries following his death it is at least possible that someone who knew he was an authority on Shīʿī, and among them Zaydī, sects should link with him this trio of eccentric beliefs, which appears to have circulated as an independent pericope from early times.

These three items of information, then, provide substantial though not irrefutable evidence for Abū ʿĪsā's period of activity having been in the later third/ninth century. Al-Shahrastānī's date is not strong, though al-Jushamī's is, and must be placed against the evidence in favour of an earlier period, and especially al-Masʿūdī's date of 247/861 for his death. So, with the usual qualifications that seemingly have to be made in connection with Abū ʿĪsā, we might think of him at his most vigorous in the decades before and maybe just after the middle of the third/ninth century, without specifying any more than this.

What did Abū ʿĪsā believe?

While there is a degree of lingering uncertainty about the period of Abū ʿĪsā's main activity, it is even more difficult to be clear about his religious stance. In some reports he is called a Muʿtazilī with Rāfiḍī-Shīʿī sympathies, as we have seen, while in others he is habitually condemned as a *mulḥid*, *zindīq*, Manichaean and even Zoroastrian. The facts are confused and their interpretation can only be hypothetical.

On the one side, some authors who give reports on Abū ʿĪsā's authority say only that he was no more than a Shīʿī. Al-Ashʿarī, in about 300/912, says that he embraced Rāfiḍism, wrote works about the Imamate and transmitted dualist views,[32] and a little later al-Masʿūdī calls him a Shīʿī and employs his works as sources for Shīʿī teachings.[33] In the fifth/eleventh century al-Sharīf al-Murtaḍā defends him against the accusation of dualist,[34] while Aḥmad b. ʿAlī al-Najāshī gives him a full notice in his Shīʿī biographical work, with no mention of any doubt about his standing.[35]

On the other side, al-Khayyāṭ in the late third/ninth century condemns Abū ʿĪsā as a one-time Rāfiḍī who became a Manichaean and promoted dualist teachings,[36] while Abū ʿAlī al-Jubbāʾī is reported as saying he was obviously a dualist.[37] In the later fourth/tenth century Ibn al-Nadīm includes him in a list of self-professed *zindīq*s who were Manichaeans,[38] while at about the same time ʿAbd al-Jabbār calls him a *zindīq* and *mulḥid.*[39] Further, in the sixth/twelfth century Ibn al-Jawzī calls him a *mulḥid*,[40] and al-Shahrastānī says he was a *Majūsī.*[41] These latter references are lent great weight by the assertions of Ibn al-Rāwandī, who is repeatedly associated with Abū ʿĪsā as his pupil,[42] that Abū ʿĪsā followed Mānī's precepts and urged people to do the same.[43] Even more emphatically, he quotes Abū ʿĪsā condemning the Imam ʿAlī because of the blood he caused to be shed.[44]

It is not easy to make sense of these conflicting labels. One of the simplest solutions would be to say that Abū ʿĪsā was a dualist and those who regarded him as no more than a Shīʿī did not know all the details about his life. But the facts do not seem to allow any clear-cut answer. In the first place, at least two of his known works were refutations of dualist groups. These are no longer extant, but their titles are enough, the *Kitāb iqtiṣāṣ madhāhib aṣḥāb al-ithnayn wa-al-radd ʿalayhim* (which can be translated as either *The Book of Facts about the Beliefs of the Dualists and the Refutation of Them*, or *The Book of Reprisal against the Beliefs of the Dualists and the Refutation of Them*) and the *Radd ʿalā al-Majūs*.[45] So, certainly at the time or times when he wrote these he could not have been sympathetic to dualism.

In the second place, there is evidence that his name was purposely blackened. It seems that the earliest surviving sources of the accusation that Abū ʿĪsā was a dualist or Manichaean are al-Khayyāṭ in his *Kitāb al-intiṣār* and Abū ʿAlī al-Jubbāʾī quoted in al-Sharīf al-Murtaḍā. But both of these wrote refutations of works by Ibn al-Rāwandī[46] and so cannot be assumed to have remained neutral about either him or his associates, least of all the man who was regarded as his teacher. In order to strengthen their case, they might eagerly have made the most of hints that Abū ʿĪsā was dabbling in dualism in order to condemn Ibn al-Rāwandī by association.

But the story does not end with them. For they may have been transmitting information already circulated by Ibn al-Rāwandī himself, who according to al-Māturīdī attributed Manichaean beliefs to Abū ʿĪsā.[47] His word would appear to be decisive, though there is good reason to doubt it since we know that the one-time master and pupil became enemies at some point in their lives. Al-Sharīf al-Murtaḍā states that Ibn al-Rāwandī was the foremost among the Muʿtazila to make the false accusation, *qadhf*, of dualist against Abū ʿĪsā "because of the hostility that lay between them", *li-ʿadāwa kānat baynahumā*,[48] while Ibn al-Jawzī refers to mutual accusations between them over the authorship of a book,[49] and Ibn al-Rāwandī's arguments preserved by al-Māturidī appear to be from a work in which he was quoting and then refuting Abū ʿĪsā.[50] In view of what seems to be a bitter break in their relationship, it is plausible to think of the pupil casting his former teacher in the harshest light and letting it be known that any concern he had for dualist beliefs or indication that he admired anything about them originated from personal involvement rather than mere intellectual interest.[51]

It is, then, at least possible that the tradition of accusing Abū ʿĪsā of heresy, *ilḥād*, and dualism, *zandaqa*, *thanawiyya*, etc., derives from hostile scandalmongering against him. But it could be that he himself was not entirely free from some unwitting responsibility for this. The fact that his writings on dualism constitute one of the main sources used by later Muslim authors[52] suggests that he was widely regarded as a leading exponent in Arabic of dualist beliefs. And so it may not have been entirely clear that he himself did not necessarily subscribe to the teaching he explained so fully. In fact, al-Sharīf al-Murtaḍā feels compelled to explain that Ibn al-Rāwandī and other people's doubts about his dualism spring from "the very positive way in which he presented their views in his *Maqālāt* and his over-detailed account of their vague teachings", *ta'kīd Abi ʿĪsā li-maqāla al-thanawiyya fī kitābihi al-maʿrūf bi-al-Maqālāt wa-iṭnābuhu fī dhikr shubhatihim.*[53]

So maybe he took some pride in his knowledge about dualism. And he may even have used this to expose certain logical weaknesses in Islam. For if we refer to Ibn al-Rāwandī's statements about him in al-Māturidī we see that his intention was to show that Manichaeism was more rational than Islam. In the clearest of these statements he questions the validity of a saying from the Prophet Muḥammad on the grounds that it conflicted with the common views of Jews and Christians, the principle being that, as Mānī had taught, a single utterance, even from a prophet, cannot take precedence over the consensus of rational minds. In another statement he again places the teaching of Mānī above proclamations of the Prophet, causing Ibn al-Rāwandī to object that while the latter are supported by proofs, the former are irrational.[54]

We cannot know the original context in which these isolated comparisons were made, nor be sure of how much bias Ibn al-Rāwandī has given them. They certainly seem to challenge fundamental tenets of Islam (we will say more about this below), and to approve of the teachings of Mānī, though maybe the real truth is that Abū ʿĪsā was not so much endorsing Manichaeism as applying the rational methods he saw in its system to challenge consensual certainty about the beliefs of Islam.

We have a complicated picture, and one that is obviously incomplete. On the one hand, Abū ʿĪsā was known as an expert on dualist sects, with so much knowledge and apparent sympathy that many were uncertain about him and some who were hostile classed him with the dualists. And he himself may have fuelled the accusation by making criticisms of Islamic beliefs from a somewhat detached position. On the other hand, however, his known writings indicate that he not only described and explained dualism but also attacked it, and that he retained at least an interest in Shīʿī Islam throughout his writing career. The evidence that should tip the balance in favour of his Muslim sympathies occurs in his main surviving work, the *Radd ʿalā al-Naṣārā*. Throughout this text he repeatedly emphasises beliefs about God that mark him as a staunch monotheist, and is constantly on guard against appearing to be compromising God's unity and distinction from all other beings. Examples in the part of the text presented in this volume include paras. 216, 218, 231, 236, 251 and 351, and also his reference to Jesus "whom *we* call ʿĪsā" in para. 203. The occurrence of such exclamations and denials in the middle of proofs, wherever the unity of God seems to be under threat, indicates that this belief was not something formal and hollow in Abū ʿĪsā's mind, but part of his whole understanding of the groundwork of reality.

This evidence and the general lack of clarity about Abū ʿĪsā's true religious affiliation notwithstanding, S. Stroumsa feels confident in identifying him as an undoubted Manichaean. She rejects the possibility that the dualist utterances associated with him were reports from others with which he may not necessarily have agreed, and overlooks both the works in which he attacked dualism and others in which he showed clear loyalty to beliefs that are at least consistent with Islam. In their place she brings forward the single item of the title of his lost *Al-gharīb al-mashriqī*, pointing out that the figure of the

"Eastern stranger" to which it alludes "carried a definite meaning in Manichaean mythology". From here she proposes that this book might support the claim that Abū ʿĪsā was himself a Manichaean.[55] But a title alone hardly provides sufficient grounds on which to establish a theory and reject other items of evidence that point to other possibilities. Stroumsa's claim, which she herself comes to accept as fact,[56] cannot be entertained seriously while it refuses to take into account the whole body of available evidence. It may even overlook the possibility that any Manichaean symbols behind this title are literary allusions which do not reflect the author's real conviction.

So it seems on balance that Abū ʿĪsā subscribed to the fundamental Muslim belief in the oneness of God and probably regarded himself as some sort of Muslim. But he cannot have been orthodox in either his views or interests, for in both his attitude to traditional Islam and his investigations into non-Muslim beliefs he proceeded in such a way as to cast a shadow of doubt in many minds.

Abū ʿĪsā's criticisms of Islam

We do not know much about Abū ʿĪsā's attitude to the teachings of Islam, since everything that has survived is in the form of isolated fragments. It is a precarious procedure to try and impose order upon the thinking they contain, though the following general points seem reliable.[57]

In the first place he refused to accept that the claims to prophetic status and inspiration of Muḥammad or anyone else could be based upon miraculous acts or insights. Generally speaking, the acts that prophets performed may have been interpreted as miracles by people whose knowledge was limited, when they may really have been no more than tricks.[58] And in the specific case of Muḥammad, the claim that he was divinely inspired to know that the Jews would not seek for death when he challenged them to do so in the face of their assertion that the Hereafter was reserved for them alone (Q 2.94f.), or that he was inspired to recite stories identical with those in the Bible because he was not able to read any previous scriptures in order to copy from them (Q 29.48), can easily be explained without having recourse to the miraculous.[59] Most significantly, the inability of Muḥammad's opponents to imitate the style of the Qurʾan was not because of its miraculous origins but because they had different standards of literary style, or were too busy fighting him, or were not learned people, or even because Muḥammad had special literary gifts, which were his by nature and not divinely endowed.[60]

In these remarks Abū ʿĪsā argues that the accepted claims are not impregnable, and it is possible to offer alternative explanations that weaken the miraculous basis of Islam, or any prophetic religion. This being so, the prophet becomes just like any other human being, and there is no incontrovertible reason to accept his utterances as unique or divine in origin. In fact, there is good reason not to do this because, as Abū ʿĪsā argues in another characteristically neat proof, if prophets called humankind to follow teachings which did not conform to logic, these could only be accepted by changing the foundation of understanding from reason to arguments provided by God, which would lead to the collapse of human discourse: *wa-fī dhālika zawāl al-khiṭāb*.[61]

This last point is clearly of great significance for Abū ʿĪsā. The independent exercise of the mind in judging religious claims and teachings leads him to prefer materialist philosophical maxims about mundane reality against the premises of religion,[62] and to side with the Manichaeans in resisting the authority of revelation.[63] In fact, he suggests that reason alone can provide the criteria for moral conduct.[64] And as can be seen from his attack on the Christian doctrine of the Incarnation in the text and translation below, he finds irrational thinking repugnant and only fit for sarcasm.

It is important to remember, of course, that these views are preserved by al-Māturīdī in very fragmentary form, and are taken not directly from one of Abū ʿĪsā's works but from Ibn al-Rāwandī, who appears to have been refuting them.[65] And so it is not easy to judge whether Abū ʿĪsā was expressing them from his own personal conviction or whether he was using them to show that revealed religions, and among them Islam, cannot be accepted on the grounds alone that they appear to be beyond rational inquiry.

If Abū ʿĪsā considers the accepted teachings about the status of the prophets, and Muḥammad in particular, wanting in many respects, he appears also to find the Qur'an deficient. As we have seen above, he questions its miraculous nature and also some of its statements about Muḥammad's inspired wisdom and independence from accounts in earlier scriptures. And as if to underline this attitude, he argues that the Qur'an must be inconsistent if in one place it urges those who are unclear about the prophets before Muḥammad to ask the People of the Reminder (Q 16.43, 21.7), while in others it accuses these people of concealing the truth (Q 3.71, 2.42),[66] and also mockingly asks why, if it declares that angels were with Muḥammad at the victory of Badr (Q 8.9 and 12), they were not present at the defeat of Uḥud.[67]

It is difficult to imagine a conventionally minded Muslim making remarks of this kind even as part of an intellectual exercise. However Abū ʿĪsā may have intended them, we can see why others who heard or read them concluded that he was a dangerous heretic. But if he remained a Muslim of sorts, as the majority of the evidence from his surviving writings seems to show, and did not become a dualist or any other kind of believer, what was he?

Abū ʿĪsā's search for certainty in religion

The simple answer to this question might seem to be that he was more a religious sceptic than anything else, interested in religion but finding faults in all its historical embodiments. Such an inference might suggest that he was lacking in seriousness, but nothing in fact could be further from the truth. For when we turn to examine Abū ʿĪsā's knowledge of and attitude towards the non-Islamic religions he knew, we quickly come to see that he both immersed himself in their histories and teachings, and retained the detachment to demonstrate the shortcomings they possessed.

Abū ʿĪsā's major work on religions, and probably his single most important writing, was the book he called *Kitāb maqālāt al-nās wa-ikhtilāfihim*. We have already discussed this at the end of Chapter 1. As we said there, it appears to have focused on the main religions known in the Islamic world, and especially those that challenged the Islamic doctrine of strict monotheism. An examination of references to it and its extant fragments indicates that the *Maqālāt* went far beyond portraying only the main outlines of each faith it depicted. Rather, it gave both details of their teachings and the differences in interpretation held by the various sects within them.[68] With respect to the dualists, for example, the book described the beliefs of the Manichaeans, the Mazdakians, the Daysanites, the Marcionites, and the Zoroastrians among others, and also the views of the Manichaeans on the relationship between light and darkness, accidents and bodies and the actions of the two fundamental forces.[69] If such details are characteristic of the work as a whole, then it must have been a major compendium of religious teachings and views, much like Abū al-Ḥasan al-Ashʿarī's slightly later *Maqālāt al-Islamiyyīn*, which treats varieties of Muslim faith in immense and apparently impartial detail.

The two features of Abū ʿĪsā's *Maqālāt*, its concern with the major faiths and its interest in their details, allow us to infer that in this major work Abū ʿĪsā was maybe making a close analytical survey of the forms of belief in God that vied as alternatives to one another in the regions directly known to him and in his time. If so, the work must have been the outcome of an attempt to discover about them and find out precisely what they taught. And even more, it was the product of an exhaustive, maybe objective, study of the intricacies of their teachings which went beyond the immediate requirements of argument and refutation and investigated them for their own sakes.

Of course, we know the *Maqālāt* only in fragments and so cannot be at all definite about its full contents or intention. But from what it does tell us, we can safely conclude that its author was not only keen to know about the different versions of faith but also passionately interested in their inner workings. It becomes easier now to see why al-Sharīf al-Murtaḍā was forced to admit that many who read the account of the dualist sects contained in the work were left in doubt about Abū ʿĪsā's own religious loyalties.[70]

Another feature of the fragments and references relating to the *Maqālāt* is that all of them point to the work as a descriptive account of religious teachings rather than a polemic against them. Thus it may have comprised no more than its title indicates, the views held by people and the differences between them. That this was indeed the case is indicated by a statement at the beginning of the *Radd ʿalā al-Naṣārā*, where Abū ʿĪsā excuses himself from going into the identity and teachings of minor Christian sects, partly because this particular work is devoted to the three main sects, and partly because "We have previously given descriptions of the reasons for the distinctions between their beliefs and the proofs employed by each group in the book in which we have described people's views and the differences between them."[71] The relationship implied here is between a descriptive work and a polemic which depends upon it for most of its factual information. The same may also have applied in the case of Abū ʿĪsā's polemics against the Jews, *Radd ʿalā al-Yahūd*, the dualists, *Kitāb iqtiṣāṣ madhāhib aṣḥāb al-ithnayn wa-al-radd ʿalayhim* and *Radd ʿalā al-Majūs*, and maybe Muslims, *Al-gharīb al-mashriqī*, *Kitāb al-ḥukm ʿalā sūra: Lam yakun*, and others.[72] If these lost works resembled the refutation of Christian doctrines at all closely, they will similarly have built searching and thorough arguments upon firm bases of evidence derived from the one main source.

On the one hand, then, we see Abū ʿĪsā showing passionate interest in some of the main faiths of his day and apparently studying them with sensitivity and sympathy. On the other, he composed detailed refutations of what they taught, involving hostile arguments that, at least in the case of Christianity, he pursued to their logical limits. In this he showed a meticulousness and seriousness that prohibit any imputation of religious indifference or lack of concern. Rather, he seemed to be immersed in the deepest search into religious truth, or maybe truth about the nature of divinity, and was prepared to extend his questioning into all the versions of faith he knew in order to find it. His stance may perhaps appear to be sceptical and over-critical, but behind that his intention was to conduct the fullest inquiry into what the faiths presented and any coherence they possessed.[73] We shall see this carried out with almost painful thoroughness in the refutation of the Incarnation.

Abū ʿĪsā's religious outlook

If, then, Abū ʿĪsā was not an orthodox Muslim, and was also critical of other bodies of religious teaching, it becomes difficult to know exactly what he was, as many of his contemporaries and those who came later discovered. He may well have found most understanding and sympathy for his views from others who challenged the consensus of the day. And that could be why he was regarded as a Rāfiḍī.

While it is not entirely clear what this designation meant in the early third/ninth century,[74] it is accurate to say that the Rāfiḍiyya were supporters of ʿAlī and his descendants whose main distinction was that they rejected Abū Bakr and ʿUmar in the belief that ʿAlī had been designated as Imam by the Prophet himself. They were not generally associated with exaggerated claims about the superhuman characteristics of the Imams.

The point of greatest significance about the Rāfiḍiyya with respect to Abū ʿĪsā is that they appear to have held unusually open and radical views about the nature of faith. According to one of the earliest accounts of them, given by Abū al-Ḥasan al-Ashʿarī, they entertained a range of challenging possibilities: they argued that since God existed and so must be a thing, he could be described in human terms; they questioned whether his attributes were eternal and whether he could change his will; they wondered whether the Qurʾan had been added to or reduced; some thought the Imams were superior to prophets and even angels; they allowed that while the Prophet might sin, the Imams could not; and they pondered the possibility that knowledge of the Imam freed believers from observing the religious law.[75] Individuals and groups expressed differing views about these points, suggesting that there were lively discussions about fundamental issues to do with Islam.

Abū ʿĪsā clearly was also interested in Shīʿism. Among his lost works, the *Kitāb ikhtilāf al-Shīʿa* may have been a descriptive account of their political and doctrinal differences, and the *Al-imāma*, in longer and shorter versions, and *Kitāb al-saqīfa*, named after the hall of the Banū Sāʿida in Medina where the succession after Muḥammad was decided in favour of Abū Bakr, were probably discussions about the legitimate leadership of the community.[76] If he also wrote the *Naqḍ al-ʿUthmāniyya*, which would have argued against the superiority of the Umayyads over the ʿAlids, his support of the Shīʿī Imams seems decided.[77] ʿAbd al-Jabbār confirms his loyalty when he concedes that Abū ʿĪsā's reason for attacking the Prophet in the ways we have seen above was to enhance the status of the Imams.[78] Whether this is an accurate explanation or a rationalisation based upon incomplete information (he also accuses Abū ʿĪsā of being a dualist) is unclear.

Abū al-Ḥasan al-Ashʿarī seems quite certain. As we saw at the beginning of this chapter, he states that Abū ʿĪsā together with Ibn al-Rāwandī embraced Rāfiḍism and wrote books in support of the Imamate, and gives some backing to this when he reports that Abū ʿĪsā passed on a statement from a companion of the leading Rāfiḍī theologian Hishām Ibn al-Ḥakam.[79] He is confident that Abū ʿĪsā was not only sympathetic towards Shīʿism but actually became a Rāfiḍī.

It appears from al-Ashʿarī that the searching inquiries into basic matters of faith we have just listed were pursued by the Rāfiḍiyya almost alone in the decades following the start of the third/ninth century. The logic behind their challenging questions would be that the Imam was given leadership in the community in matters of teaching and faith, and the fact that the first followers of the Prophet did not recognise this meant that they could not be accepted as reliable, even the Ten Blessed Companions with the Caliphs Abū Bakr and ʿUmar among them.[80] It followed that the teachings transmitted by the latter had no decisive authority, and even the text of the Qurʾan was not beyond doubt. The Imam alone was the voice of final discrimination, whether he relied on his own wisdom or followed the guidance of the religious law.[81] At the same time this meant that authority in Islam was at this time not fixed and unchanging in an irrecoverable past, but was present and responsive to events.

This may have been the source of attraction of the Rāfiḍiyya for Abū ʿĪsā. Their rejection of what appeared to be set and non-negotiable sources of faith in favour of the more immediate and on-going exegesis and statements of inspired teachers may have represented to him the possibility that access to understanding the mystery of the divine lay in a continuing examination of religious claims and a preparedness to leave nothing untouched. Their approach may have fitted well with his own wide-ranging investigations into the variety of beliefs about God and all the shortcomings they showed.

Yet even among the Rāfiḍiyya Abū ʿĪsā may have not been entirely comfortable. The scathing remark about ʿAlī as a man tainted with spilling blood which he is supposed to have privately made to Ibn al-Rāwandī[82] suggests that he thought the Imam's judgement was fallible and his actions questionable. It shows that he ruled out entirely ideas that the Imams were perfect and therefore beyond criticism.

So, as far as our sources allow us, we see a truly complicated figure. He wrote works which showed such understanding of dualism that people thought he was a dualist, while he had such a thorough knowledge of Christian doctrines that he could show how one interpretation might lead into another or become heresy.[83] And yet he attacked these and other statements of faith with searching rigour. He also turned his questioning onto Islam itself and joined in others' criticisms of the person of the Prophet and the reliability of the transmitted text of the Qurʾan. At the same time, he remained passionately interested in questions of faith throughout his life, and quite probably retained belief in the reality of one God.

Maybe Abū ʿĪsā found it easier to ask questions than to subscribe to readily identifiable credal positions. While remaining, in his own mind, a monotheist and a Muslim, his challenges to accepted beliefs apparently made it difficult to find congenial and supportive colleagues. He may have discovered those who were called Rāfiḍīs easiest to get on with, though even against their preferences for a presently available source of authority over others which were locked in the past he struck some critical notes. We will probably never know for certain, and we should be warned by the over-simplified labels of heresiographers against imagining we can understand a mind from a distant time about whom our immediate sources are so sparse.

Abū ʿĪsā's works

Before we turn from questions connected with Abū ʿĪsā's biography, we should list his known works in order to underline the extent of his interests in religious matters. None of these is extant and most of them are only known from their titles. Of the few from which fragments survive, only the *Radd ʿalā al-thalāth firaq min al-Naṣārā* has come down in a condition more substantial than a few paragraphs.

The sources from which the works are known are all given in the introduction to our edition of Abū ʿĪsā's refutation of the Trinity.[84] In the following list the titles are grouped thematically, and a few details of information which have been discovered since that edition are added. The numbers preceding the titles are those of the alphabetical list in the work on the Trinity.

Works on non-Islamic religions:

8. *Kitāb maqālāt al-nās wa-ikhtilāfihim*, one of Abū ʿĪsā's major works, and possibly the source of information he employed for his refutation of the beliefs of the major religions he knew. It contained accounts of pre-Islamic Arabian beliefs, Jewish sects, dualist sects, Christian beliefs and Islamic beliefs,[85] and may have been a primarily descriptive work.

16. *Radd ʿalā al-Yahūd*.

7. *Kitāb iqtiṣāṣ madhāhib aṣḥāb al-ithnayn wa-al-radd ʿalayhim*.

12. *Radd ʿalā al-Majūs*.

13,14,15. *Radd ʿalā al-Naṣārā*, in short, medium and long versions, of which the text preserved in Yaḥyā Ibn ʿAdī's response comprising attacks on the Trinity and Incarnation, from its length, is presumably the latter.

19. A refutation of minor Jacobite and other Christian sects, planned as a completion of the *Radd ʿalā al-Naṣārā*.

These refutations were probably based upon the information gathered in the *Maqālāt*.[86]

Works on aspects of Shīʿī beliefs:

4. *Kitāb ikhtilāf al-Shīʿa*.

5, 6. *Al-Imāma*, in longer and shorter versions.

17. *Kitāb al-saqīfa*, referring to the shelter in Medina where the succession to the Prophet was decided in the absence of ʿAlī.

9. *Kitāb al-majālis*, containing a debate in which the Rāfiḍī Hishām Ibn al-Ḥakam appeared, and hence maybe a record of intra-Muslim disagreements.

11. *Naqḍ al-ʿUthmāniyya*, against the claim that the Umayyads were superior to the ʿAlids, though not definitely attributable to Abū ʿĪsā.

Some of these works may be dependent upon the Shīʿī parts of the *Maqālāt*, while others are defences of the Imams.

Works critical of Islam:

3. *Kitāb al-ḥukm ʿalā sūra: Lam yakun*, probably a discussion about passages omitted from *Sūra* 98, the opening words of which are: *Lam yakun alladhīna kafarū*, which are thought to have referred unfavourably to members of the Quraysh including some who became Muslims.[87]

18. *Kitāb al-zumurruda*, maybe an attack on the Prophet, though of dubious attribution; S. Stroumsa suggests that Abū ʿĪsā did not write such a work, but that the work of this name by Ibn al-Rāwandī was "the fruit of his discussions with al-Warrāq".[88]

1. *Al-gharīb al-mashriqī*, Abū ʿĪsā's most notorious work, containing criticisms of the Prophet and Islamic teachings; many later Muslim authors attacked it, and al-Sharīf al-Murtaḍā in his apology for Abū ʿĪsā awkwardly suggests it came from a dualist author and not Abū ʿĪsā.[89]

20. *Al-nawḥ ʿalā al-bahāʾim*, listed by Ibn al-Nadīm directly after the preceding title as *fī al-nawḥ ʿalā al-ḥayawān*, suggesting it may have been a description of *Al-gharīb al-mashriqī*. But al-Sharīf al-Murtaḍā refers to it separately by the title given here,[90] and it is also named in a marginal gloss in the MS of al-Jushamī's *Sharḥ ʿuyūn al-masāʾil*,[91] to which we referred in connection with Abū ʿĪsā's dates. What exactly the "lament over animals" was occasioned by remains obscure, though it was evidently anti-Muslim since al-Sharīf al-Murtaḍā dissociates it from Abū ʿĪsā in the same sentence as *Al-gharīb al-mashriqī*. In light of the two facts that Abū ʿĪsā is known to have attacked various aspects of the Prophet's career, as we have seen above, and that the *Kitāb al-zumurruda*, with which he was closely associated, attacked aspects of the *ḥajj*,[92] it might be suggested that it contained criticisms of the logic in slaughtering animals on ʿĪd al-Aḍḥā.

These four works, if actually written by Abū ʿĪsā, indicate his detachment from accepted Islamic beliefs. Their contents were clearly known to a wide audience, though since they were almost completely suppressed they must have presented irritating and distasteful criticisms of dearly held Muslim beliefs.

Works concerned with questions of *kalām*:

2. *Al-ḥadath*.

10. *Masʾala fī qidam al-ajsām maʿ ithbātihi al-āʿrāḍ*, possibly part of a longer work.

These may have been contributions to the developing debate over the nature of the contingent order and the process of change.

The last two works suggest that Abū ʿĪsā participated in his own way in the kind of discussions that were current among third-/ninth-century *mutakallimūn*. But on the whole, this list of titles suggests that he was less interested in questions raised within the context of Islamic self-understanding, than in questions about the justification for believing at all. Hence his painstaking surveys of the major religious traditions he knew, and his inquisitive examinations of all religious claims, including those of Islam. It is these for which he was generally remembered, and his most durable influence was on Muslim attitudes towards Christianity and dualist sects. But maybe the works that meant most to him personally were his expositions and investigations of the Shīʿī groups who provided him with some intellectual refuge. Of course, we cannot be confident that he found any set of beliefs congenial, or that his unceasing inquisitiveness made him welcome.

One thing we can be confident about. Abū ʿĪsā's mind was as sharp as any other we can encounter in the early period of Islam. As he turned its power onto the Christian doctrine of the Incarnation he produced decisive arguments which later Muslims borrowed and Christians found difficult to answer. The way in which his arguments fit into contemporary disputations between Muslims and Christians is our concern in the next chapter.

3
The doctrine of the Incarnation in the time of Abū ʿĪsā

The picture presented in Chapter 1 suggests that during the first ʿAbbasid century Christians socially and economically fared reasonably well under Islamic rule. While in theory they occupied specific and confined positions in society, set apart from their Muslim neighbours by dress codes, constraints upon public conduct and restrictions upon worship, in practice they seem largely to have escaped legal sanctions, and in some ways profited from a position which allowed them access to Muslim society but denied them full participation in it. In intellectual relations, there was evidently a complicated relationship between theologians from the two religions. On the level of method they influenced and stimulated one another, and, as we saw, some Christians evidently felt little compunction in taking from their Muslim counterparts concepts to help explain the Trinity. But as we shall see in this chapter, on the level of actual ideas and doctrines there was little progress in understanding, and, in the third/ninth century at least, no easy way of accepting one another. This, of course, was because the elements of the respective beliefs were irreconcilable, and the only approach toward the other faith worthy of consideration was confrontation. In consequence the surviving records comprise brief refutations and a few discursive demonstrations of the deficiencies in the other's position.

With respect to the doctrine of the Incarnation, which is the focus of this study, the position was that Christians were forced to explain and defend it according to whatever sectarian interpretation they themselves followed and with whatever means they could mobilise. The Muslims in turn sought to deny it, and employed an ingenious variety of arguments to show its insufficiency. Among these latter, we shall see that Abū ʿĪsā's has claim to be the most thorough and penetrating. A continuing difficulty was to find a method of discussing the several aspects of the doctrine that the other side would accept. This was a recurrent challenge, as the surviving attempts clearly illustrate.

The earliest Muslim reactions to the Incarnation

Turning first to the Muslim side, we know of a great many works written against elements of Christian beliefs in the period with which we are concerned. In fact, as we saw earlier,[1] most of the best-known theologians of the day can be credited with one or more refutations. And some, if not all, almost certainly concentrated on problems arising from Christian claims about Jesus. Among these, ʿĪsā b. Ṣubayḥ al-Murdār's (d. *c.* 226/841) *Kitāb ʿalā Abi Qurra al-Naṣrānī*[2] and Abū al-Hudhayl al-ʿAllāf's (d. *c.* 226/840) *Kitāb ʿalā ʿAmmār al-Naṣrānī fī al-radd ʿalā al-Naṣārā*[3] must be presumed to have included arguments against the Christological explanations put forward by the Christians named in their titles.

As they responded to the teachings of the Christians, Muslims were, of course, influenced and informed by the Qurʾan, in which the primary emphasis upon the oneness and distinctiveness of God excludes the possibility of a close relationship between him and any creature. In the Qurʾan one of the main ways in which this emphasis is expressed is in the repeated denial that Jesus was God's son. So, for example, it calls Jesus the son of Mary and no more than a servant of God (e.g. Q 5.75), it depicts his birth as a creation which has nothing to do with any communication of God's being (Q 19.35 = 3.59, 4.171), it refers to his miracles as being performed with God's permission (Q 5.109f.), and it depicts him denying that he possesses divine attributes (Q 5.116f.). It says nothing about any atoning or redeeming action on his part, and in the denial of the crucifixion (Q 4.157) removes any grounds for suggesting this.

This teaching about the createdness of Jesus and rejection of his divinity or divine sonship was the most important influence upon Muslim attitudes towards the Incarnation. As we might expect, it determined the almost unanimous rejection of the doctrine throughout the early centuries, and it often provided Muslims with the framework for their actual arguments against Christian teachings.

The strong influence of the Qurʾan is evident very early in the history of encounters between Christians and Muslims. Towards the end of the second/eighth century, for example, the Caliph al-Mahdī in his questioning of the Nestorian Patriarch Timothy I assumes that Christians believe God had intercourse with Mary to produce a son, that since Jesus worshipped and prayed he must have been human, and that he was not crucified.[4] And in general he makes the assumption that the indications that Jesus was human rule out his divinity. When the Patriarch tries to distinguish between human and divine characteristics according to his own beliefs about the two natures of Jesus, the Caliph rejects his words,[5] revealing that his own understanding of what Christians believe about Jesus comes mainly from the Qurʾan rather than from any explanation about their doctrines he may have received from Christians or informed Muslims.

The same understanding can be seen in the two longest surviving Muslim refutations of Christian teachings about Jesus from the time of Abū ʿĪsā. Despite the fact that their authors were fully aware of the details of contemporary doctrines of the Incarnation, they showed less concern for these than for aspects of the belief that could be understood and attacked along Qurʾanic lines.

The *Radd ʿalā al-Naṣārā* of the Zaydī Imam al-Qāsim Ibn Ibrāhīm (d. 246/860), as we saw in Chapter 1, comprises three proofs: an elaborate explanation of the Islamic doctrine of God and reasons why he cannot be related to other beings and especially a son; an account of Christian teachings about the Trinity and the nature of Christ; and then a refutation of the Trinity and a proof based mainly on the Gospels that Jesus was not divine. It continues with a long series of quotations from the Gospel of Matthew, meant to show that Jesus made no claims about being divine, and comes to a sudden end with the conclusion probably lost.

Al-Qāsim's arguments against the divinity of Christ occur in two groups in the *Radd*. The first follows his opening demonstration that God is one and distinct. While the points he makes here have logical consistency, they are clearly inspired by the Qurʾan, as some of the most important among them show. For example, the proof that a son would be equal in power to God and so would hinder him, rendering both incapable of creating,[6] is derived from such verses as Q 21.22 and 23.91, while the argument against the eternity of both Father and Son, that if God took, *ittakhadha*, a son the latter would have to be contingent,[7] is based upon such verses as Q 18.3–5, and ignores any Christian defences of what eternal begetting might be.

Contrary to his dependence on the Qurʾan here, and his apparent indifference towards Christian doctrines themselves, al-Qāsim shows later that he knows Christianity very thoroughly. He goes on to give an account of what Christians believe where, after describing the Trinity,[8] he relates how one of the Persons took a veil and covering from Mary and through her became a body which was perfect in all its humanity, *tajassada minhā bi-jasadin kāmilin fī jamīʿ insāniyyatih*, giving himself up for crucifixion as a mercy to humankind. Then he distinguishes between the teachings of the Melkites (whom he calls *al-Rūm*) that the Son took from Mary a nature and so the Messiah was two natures, *ṭabīʿa*, in one hypostasis, *uqnūm*; of the Jacobites that the divine and human became one when the Son became a body from Mary, *tajassada bihi*; and of the Nestorians that the Son became a body which was perfect and complete in its nature and hypostasis, and so the Messiah was two natures and hypostases. The purpose of this action was in order to free humankind from the power of Satan, which the Son accomplished through the stratagem of the cross.[9]

Despite the fact that al-Qāsim's poetical language incorporates rhymes and redundancies, this account of the three major Christologies is remarkably precise. In his summary of the Melkite teaching, for example, he says that the eternal divine hypostasis "took [from Mary] a nature without hypostasis and became a hypostasis to the nature from her", *fa-akhadhā minhā ṭabīʿatan bi-ghayri uqnūmi fa-kāna li-tabīʿatihā uqnūm*. In a similar way, he sums up the Jacobite teaching that the divine and human became a simple character in the extremely apt phrase "they became completely one", *fa-ṣāra jamīʿan wāḥidan*. The only other Muslim account which can be compared with this accurate detail is that of Abū ʿĪsā.

Nevertheless, for all the intimate knowledge which he shows in this description, in the refutation of the divinity of Christ that follows al-Qāsim ignores completely the information he has set down. Instead, he goes back to the books of the Bible, which he says Christians claim as the source of their doctrines about the Messiah,[10] and his main argument becomes the question of what is the appropriate interpretation of these books.[11] The first criterion he proposes is the witness of the characters directly connected with the person of the Messiah, and so he quotes from the Gospels words from angels, Mary, Jesus himself, his disciples and God, all of which either show that he was not divine or else contain insufficient attestation that he was.[12] These must be the controls upon any other parts of the Bible which may appear to support the divinity of the Messiah, and in order to enforce this point al-Qāsim quotes at length words of Jesus from the Gospel of Matthew that point to his station as a prophet and servant.[13]

The impression al-Qāsim leaves in this examination of the divinity of Christ is that there is a serious disjunction between the contemporary teachings of the churches on the one hand, and on the other any rational understanding of the divine nature of God and a fair reading of the very scriptural sources to which Christians refer. He does not see any need to discuss his opponents' actual doctrines, because in his mind these depart sadly from what reason can tell about God and from the truth of scripture itself (it is incidentally important to his argument for him to accept the integrity of the Bible in principle).[14]

In this attack al-Qāsim's indebtedness to the Qur'an is clear, both in his first group of arguments, where his logical objections are inspired by its teachings, and in his second group, where his appeal to the Christian scripture seems modelled on the view that revelation as given by God is superior to human speculation. Here he finds a commonly acceptable criterion, and his appeal not so much to the New Testament or even the Gospels in general but to precise witnesses preserved within them, seems difficult to counter. In this respect his ingenious and economical refutation differs from the more direct approach of Abū ʿĪsā, who does engage with the Christological formulas which al-Qāsim summarises and then ignores. However, both theologians share the attitude that the Christians of their day are out of touch with the wider perceptions of what can be ascertained about the nature of God and what is reasonable and unreasonable to say about him.

This is also true of the attack made by the convert from Christianity ʿAlī b. Rabban al-Ṭabarī.[15] He worked for many years among Muslims of the highest rank, though he only embraced Islam when he was seventy, in about 235/850. At this time he wrote his *Radd ʿalā al-Naṣārā* as a sort of recantation[16] and a concentrated attempt to expose the weaknesses in Christian doctrines.

ʿAlī al-Ṭabarī's approach in this work is in the main to show how contemporary beliefs among Christians either do not agree with reason or are irreconcilable with the Bible. For example, in the second of his seven *Muskitāt*, "the Silencers", questions intended to rule out any response, he asks whether what the Messiah said about himself was reliable or not. If his opponents reply that it was only reliable in part they insult him, but if they say that it was completely reliable they acknowledge that according to his own words he was sent from God and subject to him, and so they contradict the Creed which states that he is true God from true God.[17] Similarly, in the last of these seven questions he forces the Christians to agree that Christ lived in one place and at one time, as the Gospels relate, and then to admit that since this makes him limited and so created, it contradicts the words of the Creed that Christ is creator of all things.[18]

These are typical of the tight logical conundrums that ʿAlī al-Ṭabarī is able to make up on the basis of his Christian, probably Nestorian,[19] experience. He proceeds from a fundamental understanding that contemporary Christian beliefs do not square with the teachings of their scripture, and in essence show a casualness in interpreting its contents. In fact, he says, the Gospels and letters of Paul contain about twenty thousand verses which refer to the Messiah as human, although Christians, such as the Fathers of the Council of Nicea, interpret these in the light of a mere ten unclear statements, *kalimāt mushkilāt*.[20] So for him Christian doctrines about Christ have nothing to do with the origins of Christianity itself.

ʿAlī al-Ṭabarī clearly knows the various formulas of the main Christian sects and he refers to them in passing, though understandably he sees no need to describe and explain them. And he does not discuss them or refute them, since for him the starting point is scripture and the objection that Christians have departed from it. Here he agrees with al-Qāsim Ibn Ibrāhīm, and he shows the same indebtedness to the Islamic emphasis upon scripture being the standard of religious thinking as well as its origin. So he undercuts Christian beliefs by arguing that they have no basis in Christian tradition itself, and therefore lack the seriousness that might merit attention.

Both these refutations are radical criticisms of the whole legitimacy of the Christological elaborations which Christians in the third-/ninth-century Muslim world were defending and presumably living by. So one wonders how effective the attacks they contain might be. The two authors take the majority witness of the Gospels and other Biblical texts as the test of true teaching, and have in their minds a conception of God which emphasises his transcendence and otherness.[21] And so in principle Christians might have to acknowledge the force of their arguments. But in practice they are so far away from much of what Christian theologians were saying about the nature of Christ that their arguments may have been considered irrelevant. The terms in which they argued hardly met those in which Christians themselves thought.

If al-Qāsim Ibn Ibrāhīm and ʿAlī al-Ṭabarī have a certain amount in common in their attacks, the third extant work from this period containing arguments against the divinity of Jesus is quite different. It was written by the polymath Abū ʿUthmān al-Jāḥiẓ (d. 255/869), whose *Radd ʿalā al-Naṣārā* was abridged sometime before the beginning of the fifth/eleventh century.[22] In the surviving parts there are two arguments about the divinity of Christ worthy of note in addition, of course, to the invaluable comments about the social standing of Christians in Muslim society which we referred to in Chapter 1.

We have already mentioned the first of these arguments concerning Christ.[23] It was evidently a well-known question both in al-Jāḥiẓ's own time and later. As he states it, the Christians say: If God took one of his servants as a friend, *khalīlan*, then could he have taken one of his servants as a child, *waladan*?[24] This is a skilfully constructed question based on the teaching in the Qur'an that Abraham was God's friend (Q 4.125). It deceptively encourages agreement by acknowledging that the one he might take as a child is a human servant like Abraham, though at the same time it threatens the consistency of the Qur'an by compelling acceptance of a relationship denied there by means of an analogy with a relationship condoned there.

This adoptionist concession on the part of the unknown Christian group may seem surprising, but it is rivalled by the response of the anonymous theologians which al-Jāḥiẓ recounts (*ra'aytu min al-mutakallimīn man yujizū dhālika*). These presumably Muslim thinkers go on to say that there is no real difference between taking a son, in the sense of adopting, and taking a friend, in the sense of caring, because in their view titles, *al-asmā'*, are only useful in a specific social context, and are applied to meet particular circumstances.[25] They appear to be suggesting that revelation assumes different forms to suit changes of conditions and, more radically, that none of these is more authentic than any other. They also hint at the notion that language, and hence the language of the Qur'an, is fitted to particular situations where its meaning can be best understood, and so there is nothing absolute about it. This is why they can go on to argue that in the Muslim context God has allowed certain terms to be used of him but not their synonyms: thus *mu'min* but not *muslim*, and *raḥīm* but not *rafīq*.[26] Such startling ideas, which threaten some of the claims of Islam to any uniqueness, seem to anticipate the pluralist thinking of later times, although they do not seem to have had any immediate influence that can be detected from the surviving literature.

Another response to the comparison between Abraham and Jesus quoted in the same context by al-Jāḥiẓ is that of his teacher Ibrāhīm al-Naẓẓām, which he says is also that of the Muʿtazilīs. According to this, the term *khalīl Allāh* is the equivalent of *ḥabīb*, *walī* or *nāṣir Allāh*, and by extension also of *walad*, in the sense of adoption, because all convey the same concept of God's compassion for a creature.[27] Again, these Muʿtazilī thinkers have no objections to language being used in a loose sense, so long as when using the term "child of God" all ideas of physical paternity are excluded.

Al-Jāḥiẓ himself disagrees completely with the two views he has summarised. He goes on to argue that the title *khalīl* is not derived from *khulla*, "friendship", as the others suppose, but from *khalla*, "need", and that it designates Abraham's unique experiences in his wanderings and sufferings, just as titles given to other prophets designate theirs.[28] And he also contends that the comparison between "friend" and "child" does not admit the general use of language which the other theologians he quotes employ so creatively. He maintains that if Jesus is called child of God no matter how it is intended, God must be called father, and so all the other names of family ties become possible for him. And more seriously, if God were to elevate a servant to the position of son he would unavoidably lower himself to some extent, and this is ludicrous.[29]

This question, which continued to attract the attention of theologians for over a century,[30] is an instance of Muslims being put on the defensive over the person of Jesus. Its careful formulation shows a Christian who thought the Qurʾan might be made to support the divine sonship of Jesus in some form, and the positive responses given by al-Jāḥiẓ's contemporaries suggest he succeeded in part. Al-Jāḥiẓ himself, however, sees the danger both to the authority of the Qurʾan and to the doctrine of God, and rejects the terms in which the question is stated.

Later in the *Radd* al-Jāḥiẓ turns the tables on those Christians who have been causing trouble with these questions about the nature of the Messiah, and attacks the two-natures Christologies with scathing directness.[31] There are three alternatives, he says: the Messiah was either human and not divine, or divine and not human, or divine and human. Logically speaking, he could not be divine without any humanity because of all the human traits he bore; and if he was human but was called divine at points when divinity, *al-lāhūt*, was in him, then at these points the Divinity became a body, which entails anthropomorphism.[32] So the Messiah can only have been human.

Here al-Jāḥiẓ reduces the Christian formulas to three logical alternatives and destroys the two that conflict with his own Muslim beliefs by showing that the Messiah could not have been divine entirely and that a combination of divine and human would implicate the divine in corporeality. His penetrating arguments bear the same bleak elegance of al-Qāsim Ibn Ibrāhīm's rebuttals, and the questions which al-Jāḥiẓ himself quotes from the Christians earlier in the *Radd*. The trouble is that while the conclusions he quickly draws may have satisfied him and other Muslims, they fail to take into account all the painful attempts made by Christians to meet the objections he raises. So we must wonder how effective they could have been in any encounters with actual Christian beliefs. But they were possibly never intended for real debates. Al-Jāḥiẓ displays a deep dislike for Christians and their ways in this letter, as we saw in Chapter 1, and here he maybe shows his disgust most decisively in his peremptory dismissal of their doctrines.

As we shall see, Abū ʿĪsā focuses on exactly these same Christological formulas, but exposes their deficiencies in much more detail and at greater length. It could be that his approach to the subject reflects a less popular audience or his own interest in the questions of how a major religious group could seriously believe that God was related intimately to human nature. Whatever the case, when we turn from al-Jāḥiẓ, and also al-Qāsim Ibn Ibrāhīm and ʿAlī al-Ṭabarī, to the much more elaborate discussions of Abū ʿĪsā's *Radd*, we leave arguments that are the products of an almost impatient disregard for what Christians may be trying to say, and encounter an altogether more thorough exploration.

Later Muslim reactions to the Incarnation

Naturally, we do not know whether any other Muslim works written in the early third/ninth century adopted the same considered approach of Abū ʿĪsā. With so many known refutations lost, it is difficult to make a proper judgement on the relative merits of his work against its background. However, a little more light is shed on the issue by attacks on Christian beliefs that appeared slightly later, and these tend to confirm the impression that most arguments against the Incarnation from the third/ninth century were comparatively slight.

The *Kitāb al-awsaṭ fī al-maqālāt* of the Muʿtazilī theologian known as al-Nāshiʾ al-Akbar (d. 293/905–6)[33] contains a detailed exposition and arguments against the two major Christian doctrines of the Trinity and Incarnation which indicate that the author had considerable knowledge of Christian thinking. On the Incarnation he begins by describing the position of "the majority" of Christians as follows: the Son who is the Word inhered, *ḥalla*, in a complete and perfect man by good will, *al-masarra*, not substance, composition or mingling, and so this man was called son, just as iron is called fire when fire inheres within it; the title Messiah applied to both substances and both individuals, although the two individuals were one entity, *maʿnā*, in the being of the Messiah, and they had one action and one will; some matters are specific to the Messiah in his human nature, others in his divine nature, and others to both together, arising from God's acting through the human.[34]

This very succinct account, which particularly reflects Nestorian Christology in its reference to the inhering of the divine in the human and the combining of the two natures and individuals,[35] is followed by brief accounts of the Christologies of twenty-one other groups, including the Melkites and Jacobites. Al-Nāshiʾ presents them all without comment in what appears as a very full and impartial description.[36]

The purpose that may have been served by this catalogue of Christologies is not clear, for in the surviving parts of the *Awsaṭ* al-Nāshiʾ makes no further mention of them. In his attack on the Incarnation, he argues first against those Christians who claim to derive their doctrine about Christ from the Gospels, that there is no proof there that Jesus is the Son of God in a unique sense, and no support from a source outside Christianity for a doctrine of uniting in any form.[37] Then, turning to points based on reason, he argues that if the divine and human are fixed in their beings they cannot be transformed into each other, and it is unreasonable to think that the Creator and a contingent being can be transformed. Christians show their ignorance of these principles when they say such things as "It united with him and became him", even though they disapprove of such statements as "The Creator mixed with the contingent", not realising that the act of uniting is more extreme than mixing.

On the question of the death and burial of the Messiah, in the first place the Christians cannot say that the Creator died if they do not mean to include the divine in the death of the Messiah. And it is no defence to say that the Messiah died in his human nature, for however he died death affected him in himself in some way, and so both human and divine were involved.[38]

Rather than focusing on one particular Christian sect, in these responses al-Nāshiʾ seems to gather up all the different interpretations of the Incarnation; he suggests that no matter how they express the doctrine they do not overcome the problems that it has no basis in scripture, that there is no reasonable explanation of a true uniting of divine and human, and there is no escape from implicating the divine in the Messiah's death. He raises real difficulties here, similar to those of which Abū ʿĪsā makes so much.[39] And his reasoning derives from the same origin as that of earlier Muslim polemicists, that the distinction between the divine and created is complete and the two cannot be associated. He does not see it as necessary to go into more detail, because for all their explanations the Christians have compromised this principle.

It is noteworthy that as far as these arguments indicate, al-Nāshiʾ is interested mainly in the two-natures doctrine as opposed to the question of the Messiah being Son of God or of God having a son, which are closer to the form of objection in the Qurʾan. In this respect he concurs with Abū ʿĪsā, in meeting the doctrine as he understands it directly from the Christians.

The same generalised approach is taken by al-Nāshiʾ al-Akbar's younger contemporary Abū ʿAlī al-Jubbāʾī (d. 303/915–16), the leader of the Baṣra Muʿtazilīs at the end of the third/ninth century. Like the writings of almost all the other Muslims we have discussed, his arguments against Christianity have not survived in their entirety. ʿAbd al-Jabbār quotes points he makes, and these probably derive from the refutation of Christianity he is known to have written,[40] though most represent only a sample of his total attack on the Incarnation.[41]

According to the fragments preserved by ʿAbd al-Jabbār, Abū ʿAlī al-Jubbāʾī's refutation comprised an initial exposition of Christian beliefs, followed by an attack on the Trinity, a discussion of the question first mentioned by al-Jāḥiẓ in which Jesus as Son is compared with Abraham as friend of God, and then an attack on the two-natures Christology.[42]

In his exposition, Abū ʿAlī says that the Word of God is the Son and was the Messiah who appeared in the body, *jasad*, which was on earth. Some use the title Messiah of the Word and the physical form, *jism*, when the one had united with the other, others use it of the Word and not the body, and others use it of the body, saying that the Word became a contingent body when it entered Mary's womb and appeared to people.[43]

This brief account seems to be a schematisation of the Christologies associated with the three main Christian sects, and with considerable simplification. The first statement may be that of the Melkites, who are made to say that the divine and human united though were not confused, the second that of the Nestorians, who say that the two characters were sufficiently distinct for only the divine to be called Messiah, and the third that of the Jacobites, who hold that the divine and human became fused into one. This is the most abstract and compressed Muslim account of the different interpretations of the Christians we have so far encountered, and it suggests that Abū ʿAlī may have known the Christological models themselves only at second hand, and more seriously that he was mainly interested in their theological significance rather than the attempts at explanation they represented.

In the few brief arguments concerning the person of Christ that are quoted from Abū ʿAlī, he exhibits the same peremptory style of treatment. In response to what by this time must have been the well-known comparison between Abraham as friend of God and Jesus as Son of God, he asserts that the force of the title given to Abraham arises from the revelation, *waḥy*, and favour, *karāma*, given to him. So whether it derives from *khulla*, "friendship", or *khalla*, "need", it is used of Abraham because of his particular circumstances. But the term "Son of God" must always mean one born from the Father, *mawlūdan min al-Ab*, and so can never be used where God is involved.[44]

Here Abū ʿAlī rejects al-Jāḥiẓ's earlier arguments, which are based upon the derivation of *khalīl* from *khulla*, as irrelevant and insists that you cannot really draw a comparison: *khalīl* shows God's favour on a prophet, but *ibn* would show God's generation of a being from himself. In his haste, Abū ʿAlī ignores the carefully inserted condition that Jesus might be regarded as son by adoption and favour rather than generation, and so misses the point of the question, though he would presumably reply that there can only be one meaning of *ibn* when used in relation to God.[45]

In a further ramification of this, Abū ʿAlī later defends the difference between calling Jesus word and spirit of God, as the Qurʾan states (Q 4.171), and Son of God by arguing rather weakly that people were guided by Jesus as by a word and were given life in their religion by him as they are given life by the spirits in their bodies, but there is no warrant for calling him Son of God.[46] Again he maintains the principle that God cannot be related to any other being.

It would be useful to know more of Abū ʿAlī's reasoning on these points, though we can infer that this dogmatic principle about the distinction between God and other beings is his basic criterion which determines the meaning he both reads in the Qurʾan and gives to terms in general. So the considerations about the consistency of the linguistic usage which are embodied in these two comparisons with which he disagrees are not of primary importance to him.

The third set of arguments preserved from Abū ʿAlī criticise the Christian doctrine more directly. In the severely summarised form in which most of them are preserved, they are: firstly, Christians must admit that the Messiah worshipped himself if at the uniting he as a human and the divine Son became one thing, even though one cannot worship oneself just as one cannot show gratitude to oneself; secondly, the action of the divine nature must have been identical with the action of the human nature, meaning that the two had the same power, and hence the human nature must have had power to act by virtue of its own essence, *qadara al-nāsūt li-dhātih*, like the divine nature, and their existences must have been similar; and thirdly, the other two divine hypostases in the Trinitarian Godhead must have been able to unite with a human in the same way as the Word because they have the same substance, though if uniting is possible for only one of them they must be distinct from one another.[47]

The first and third of these are simple logical deductions from the two doctrines they attack. They are very much in the same scathing style as Abū ʿĪsā, and in fact the third is more or less identical with a point he makes at the beginning of his attack on the Uniting of the divine Word with the human.[48] However, the second argument is more involved than these two. It brings in the understanding that while the power to act in God is through an eternal attribute which is identical with his essence (to which as a Muʿtazilī Abū ʿAlī would subscribe), in humans this power is endowed by accidental attributes which are external to the essence of the being itself, and so is not permanent. But if the divine and human natures in the Messiah had a single mode of action, then the power to act in the human must have been of his own essence, and so permanent. Therefore, the human must have been transformed into the divine, which nullifies the doctrine of two different natures.

This argument suggests that Abū ʿAlī's original refutation may have employed many more *kalām*-based points like it, as is the case with his attack on the Trinity.[49] Maybe by this time in the latter part of the third/ninth century the logic he is using here was shared by both Muslims and Christians. Whether it was or not, this is an example of an approach which appears to make no allowance for the ways in which the opponents presented and tried to explain their views. To his mind, their doctrine conflicts with Islamic teaching and so deserves nothing more than a brief retort.

Of course, we cannot tell how long Abū ʿAlī's complete attack on the Incarnation originally was, though it is likely that ʿAbd al-Jabbār would have included more arguments if there had been any greater variety than he represents here. So it appears that, like the other fragmentary works which have survived from the decades before and after Abū ʿĪsā was writing, this attack was relatively brief and not primarily concerned with Christian doctrines as representatives of the various Christian sects discussed them.

Summing up these surviving polemical works from various points in the third/ninth century, we can see that they show considerable knowledge of the Christologies promoted by at least the major Christian groups. But then, as they respond to Christians, they tend to focus upon the person of Jesus as a single individual, arguing that the Gospels give no support to his divinity but rather point to his many human traits, or that the divine character must have been changed when it became one with the human. Maybe this apparent indifference towards the Christological formulations shows a certain lack of understanding of what they were trying to express. After all, if a Christian used such terms as *ittaḥada bihi fa-ṣāra huwa huwa* "[the divine] became one with it [the human] and it became it", as al-Nashiʾ al-Akbar intimates,[50] a Muslim might be forgiven for taking them at face value and assuming they meant something like a fusion or confusion of natures and then concluding this was all nonsense. But, as we have said, this indifference more strongly stems from the influence of the Qurʾanic discourse, where the issue between Christians and the truth is their insistence that the man Jesus was the Son of God. The strength of this influence was understandably greater than any explanation from a Christian, especially when the latter frequently seemed not to make sense.[51]

It should also be added that a number of motifs in the polemical texts, among them the comparison of the miracles of Jesus and those of other prophets to show that they do not single him out as divine,[52] and the question about the comparison between Abraham as friend of God and Jesus as Son of God which we have examined in certain instances above, suggest that some Muslim authors may have been putting up defences against advances from Christians: al-Jāḥiẓ for one wrote his refutation in order to help a group who felt beleaguered by Christians. In circumstances where the debate was brought to Muslims they would understandably fall back on their own source teachings rather than get involved in the web of logic related to Christological formulations.

But Abū ʿĪsā al-Warrāq did precisely that. He mastered Christian teachings in the many details over which they differed. To what extent he was more forceful than other Muslims in making the Christians recoil is maybe indicated by the fact that his arguments, rather than anyone else's, drew a Christian response from Yaḥyā Ibn ʿAdī within a century, and were later employed by Muslims themselves. We shall see this in the next chapter. First it will be helpful to see what Christians who wrote in Arabic were trying to say about the Incarnation at the time when he was writing.

The Incarnation in Arab Christian thought

Christians who lived in the Islamic empire were put on the defensive from very early times, as their Muslim neighbours applied the teachings of the Qurʾan to make them explain what they believed about God and how they regarded the person of Jesus Christ. It soon happened that these and other questions based upon interpretation of the Qurʾan became the main points of contention between Christians and Muslims.

The first signs of this process are evident in the records of some of the earliest exchanges between Christians and Muslims that have survived. For example, in the meeting between John I, the Jacobite Patriarch of Antioch, and a Muslim leader, which may have taken place as early as 18/639,[53] the main questions raised are: how Christians can disagree among themselves if there is only one Gospel; whether the Messiah was God; how creation was governed when God was in the womb; whether Abraham and Moses agreed with Christian beliefs; and how reason and scripture can be made to support the claim that the Messiah was God, born of the Virgin, and that God had a son.[54] These all derive entirely from Qurʾanic teachings that God could not have a son, that the Messiah was human and denied that he was Son of God, and that earlier messengers anticipated the coming of Muḥammad, together with possible inferences from it that the Gospel has been corrupted and that Jesus' infancy and his lordship over creation are incompatible.[55] As might be expected in the circumstances, the Muslim directs the course of the discussion entirely, and any possibility of the Christian explaining why God became incarnate, what the act of redemption involved, or how the Christ was both divine and human does not arise.

This shaping of discussion is even more pronounced in the debate that took place between the Nestorian Patriarch Timothy I and the ʿAbbasid Caliph al-Mahdī soon after 164/780.[56] They met on two possibly consecutive days, but even so the Patriarch was given little opportunity to explain his own position on the person of Christ. Questions about Jesus arise through the course of the first day and, in fact, the Caliph begins the whole exchange by asking how Christians can believe that God would marry and have a son (echoing the teaching of Q 6.10), and forcing the Patriarch to distinguish between the eternal generation of the Son as Word of God and his human birth from Mary. This leads into the main discussion about the nature of Christ, which is a set of explanations of how the Messiah was one being, although both eternal and temporal.

Timothy is hard pressed to make the Caliph fully understand his beliefs about the two natures of Christ. He begins by giving the accepted Nestorian description that the one nature was clothed in the other. But as soon as al-Mahdī insists that this is duality he resorts to metaphorical explanations: a man is one although he has body and soul, the Caliph is one although he is an individual man and the outward appearance of sovereignty, and in the same way the Messiah was one person although he had two distinct natures.

Al-Mahdī is not convinced by this and refers to Jesus' words to his disciples, "I am going to my God and to your God",[57] which suggest that he considered himself other than God. Timothy tries to explain that these words indicate the humanity of Jesus looking on God as his God, while Jesus' words immediately preceding, "I am going to my Father and your Father", indicate his divinity looking on God as his Father. Again al-Mahdī is not satisfied, and in a further attempt at explanation Timothy coins the metaphor of the Caliph writing words, of which he can be thought father, on papyrus, of which he can be thought owner. Just as something generated from the Caliph becomes one with something manufactured, so the Son who is begotten of the Father becomes one with the human who is created, and so can regard God as both Father and Deity.[58]

The aptness and elegance of these metaphors are masterful, but the fact that Timothy has to employ them shows how difficult he finds it to explain himself in this situation, and how reluctant he might be to use other terms. Al-Mahdī argues from the premise that Jesus was created, and his first concern is then to get Timothy to admit that the human Messiah cannot be Son of God, an approach fully determined by the Qur'an. Timothy on the other hand comes from the entirely different context in which the Son is accepted as divine and his Incarnation is understood as the instrument of God's redemptive act. So he is concerned to show in reason how the divine could become one with the human. They both share the belief that divinity and humanity are opposites, but they defend this in entirely different forms according to the larger bodies of teachings they each follow. And it is the Caliph who dictates the kind of discussion that takes place on this occasion, while the Patriarch has little opportunity to set out his teachings in a way that might make them appear less abstruse. His plea at the outset, that he cannot and should not presume to explain the mysteries of God, hints at the whole apophatic tenor of his thinking. But it goes unheeded.[59]

Timothy's resort to metaphors rather than more concrete interpretations is maybe a sign that he and other Christians in the Islamic empire were perceiving the pressure of having to respond to a new challenge. The main Christological debates with which they had been preoccupied among themselves, concerning the mode of relationship between the divine and human in Christ, were only relevant in interdenominational disputes. Now Muslims were questioning the fundamental possibility of the Divinity being related to a human at all, rather than the modalities of the union, and Christians were required to produce new explanations and defences. It is possible to see this process of changing emphasis in works written at about the time of Abū ʿĪsā's main activity. The appearance of arguments in favour of God having a son or becoming incarnate, alongside expositions of the two-natures doctrine, show how Christians were responding to the Qur'anic agenda with which they were confronted. And this change on their part adumbrates the singularity of Abū ʿĪsā's approach. Far from mobilising elements of the Qur'anic discourse, he attempts to enter into the world of Christian Christological reasoning and to address it within its own logical structure. An examination of Christian works from his time will show this change and give emphasis to his originality.

The *Fount of Knowledge* of John of Damascus is one of the major compendiums of philosophical and doctrinal teaching of the Eastern Church. It was written towards the middle of the second/eighth century and was intended for a Christian, Greek-reading audience.[60] John would have been vividly aware of

Muslims and their faith, of course, since like his father and grandfather he had worked in the caliphal service in Damascus. And, indeed, he includes the earliest sustained Christian account of Muslim beliefs, the well-known Chapter 100/101 on the Ishmaelites, in the second part of this work, the *On Heresies*.[61] But there are no signs that he was addressing anyone other than Christians when he wrote, and the work can be taken as an attempt to set out orthodox beliefs, and defend and distinguish them from heretical Christian alternatives.

The third part of the work, *On the Orthodox Faith*, comprises one hundred chapters in a single progression which shows the shape of Christian thinking in the century before Abū ʿĪsā.[62] It begins with an account of God in himself (1–14), and of creation, the human individual and free will (15–44), then explains the need for salvation and how this was effected by the Son being made flesh, how this union of divine and human subsisted and can be explained (45–81), and finally how the Christian appropriates this salvation through the sacraments and the life of the Church (82–100). Here, the discussion of the union fits in as God's response to the historical reality of human sin, "the most fitting solution for this most difficult problem",[63] and develops as an explanation of how the divine and human remained separate and unconfused, yet were in reality united in order to accomplish the act of redeeming humankind and winning back obedience. The discussion of how the two natures united yet remained distinct is necessarily long, over a third of the entire length, because it includes demonstrations of how Monophysites, Nestorians and others are wrong, and exactly how the two natures existed together, acted in unison, and so on.

What John does not need to argue at length in this treatise intended for a Christian readership is the fact that the Word of God who was God himself became incarnate, or that the united divine and human can be called Messiah and by extension Son of God. These are agreed between all Christians and so can be stated more or less in passing. Of course, for Muslims they constituted major problems.

The same is true of a brief confession of faith written by the Melkite Theodore Abū Qurra,[64] one of the first Christians who wrote extensively in Arabic, and possibly the best known Christian *mutakallim* in Muslim circles. He lived from some time in the mid-second/eighth century to around 215/830.[65] The work itself contains no indications to help dating, but its editor I. Dick suggests that it may have been a statement which Theodore made when he was consecrated bishop, and suggests some time around 180/795.[66] If this is true, it was composed about half a century before Abū ʿĪsā was writing.

The confession is concerned only with the Trinity and Incarnation, and the latter is given much the more detailed attention.[67] After explaining what is correct and what is incorrect belief about the Trinity, Theodore continues that the eternal Son came down from heaven "for our sake and for our salvation", took flesh, *tajassada*, and became human, *ta'annasa*.[68] And then, for the rest of the short work he expounds the correct belief about the union of the Son with the human, and shows where he himself differs from such known heretics as Nestorius, Eutyches and Severus "the ass".

Like John of Damascus' work, Theodore's also focuses on the problem of the mode of the Incarnation rather than the fact, because the latter is agreed by all Christians while the former has produced disagreements and anathemata for centuries. In fact, he hardly expands upon the form given in the Creed when referring to the Son descending and being born. And it is maybe worth noting in passing that he seems to consider the two verbal forms *tajassada* and *ta'annasa* familiar enough to stand alone without comment or paraphrase.

These two expositions by leading Christian scholars in the Islamic world from the second/eighth and early third/ninth centuries indicate the main preoccupations of Christians about the doctrine of the Incarnation.[69] The fact of the union of divine and human was not an issue of contention, though the specific mode in which the two natures really and actually formed the one Messiah while retaining their separate status and identity caused intense disagreement.

Arab Christian theologians on the Incarnation

When we turn to other works of Theodore, however, we find a rather different approach. Some of his brief tracts are evidently written in reply to Muslims, and here we see the issue of God becoming incarnate and having a son occupying the centre of attention, and producing some innovative arguments from Theodore. In his *Fī al-radd ʿalā man yunkiru li-Allāhi al-tajassuda wa-al-ḥulūl*[70] the main point is that if it can be accepted, presumably by the opponent, that God appeared in a cloud or is seated on the throne (as Jews and Muslims acknowledge in their respective scriptures), there is no reason why in principle his appearing in the flesh should not be allowed.[71] It is the fact of the Incarnation that clearly causes problems here, and Theodore attempts to overcome these by showing that all traditions, and particularly Islam, admit comparable intimate connections between God and created things.

There are also two tracts by Theodore in reply to those who deny that God could have a Son. In the first, *ʿAlā sabīli maʿrifati Allāhi wa-taḥqīqi al-ibni al-azalī*, Theodore's argument in response to an anonymous opponent, *al-jāhid li-al-ibn,*[72] is that if God were unable to beget a Son, something which humans can do, then he would be weak, and if he has begotten a Son he himself is not earlier in time than his Son since, unlike humans, God's willing to have a Son is identical to his act of begetting.[73] In the second, *Maymar yuḥaqqiqu anna li-Allāhi ibnan huwa ʿidluhu fī al-jawhar*, he argues slightly differently that God must have mastery, *riʾāsa*, but that this cannot be over anything so inferior as a creature and so must be over an equal who is of the same nature as himself and hence a son.[74]

The arguments in these two tracts appear as part of a proof of the Trinity in Theodore's *Maymar fī wujūdi al-khāliqi wa-al-dīni al-qawīm*,[75] a work also written with Muslims in mind.[76] And they seem to have achieved a certain notoriety among Muslims. For in the early fourth/tenth century the Baghdad Muʿtazilī Abū al-Qāsim ʿAbdullah b. Aḥmad al-Balkhī (d. 319/931) made fun of them,[77] while later in the same century the Muʿtazilī master ʿAbd al-Jabbār (d. 415/1025) summarised the second, mentioning "Qurra the Malkī" by name and reproducing many of its key terms, and refuted it.[78]

The point for our purpose is that the emphasis falls upon the possibility of God having a Son rather than the nature of this Son. The Islamic surroundings seem to shift the central question away from the traditional Christian debate about the two natures of Christ. But there may also be another feature in these arguments which is evoked by the new context of thinking. Theodore's proofs indicate not only that God may have a Son, but that if he is God he must have a Son, a necessity quite contrary to contemporary Muslim argumentation. This may be the start of a new form of exposition of doctrine in a polemical context, and it is possibly why Muslim theologians took notice and refuted it.[79]

We begin to see what may be a new direction in Christian writing about Christ, in which the involved interpretation of how divine and human subsisted together as Messiah, instanced in John of Damascus and Theodore Abū Qurra's confession of faith, is complemented by defences of the divine Sonship of Christ and the Incarnation of the divine, exemplified in the two brief tracts from Theodore and the Patriarch Timothy's glittering metaphors.[80] A survey of some of the other Arab Christians writing on the person of Christ at about this time will show how this new direction was common to those who felt compelled to take the sensitivities and objections of their Muslim neighbours into their own thinking.

One of the most creative Arab Christian authors who was active in the early third/ninth century is ʿAmmār al-Baṣrī. We know virtually nothing about him, except that he was a Nestorian,[81] and since he evidently wrote in reply to questions and objections from Muslims, he can reasonably be identified as the ʿAmmār al-Naṣrānī against whom the Baṣran Muʿtazilī Abū al-Hudhayl al-ʿAllāf wrote one of his lost works.[82] This places him in the early part of the third/ninth century, and since Abū al-Hudhayl may not have been active after about 215/830 (he died in about 226/840), then some of ʿAmmār's major works, together with the Muʿtazilī's responses, must have appeared before this time. Such a date fits the internal evidence of ʿAmmār's works, where in particular his proof of the Trinity is set directly against precisely the doctrine of divine attributes proposed by Abū al-Hudhayl.[83] But as we shall see, ʿAmmār may have had not only Abū al-Hudhayl in mind when writing, because some of his main points correspond closely to matters discussed by Abū ʿĪsā.

Two of ʿAmmār's works have survived in partial form, each of them covering a range of theological and doctrinal topics in a loose rational structure which is reminiscent of Syriac antecedents, but with clear Muslim correspondences.[84] They are both addressed to Muslim audiences, and they include extensive defences of the Incarnation.

In the *Kitāb al-Burhān* ʿAmmār begins his defence of the belief that the Messiah was the Son of God by showing in some detail that fatherhood and sonship within the Godhead are not comparable with their human equivalents and are of such a form that they do not violate God's unity or transcendence.[85] And he further prepares his ground by arguing, with reference to the Qurʾanic teaching that God has not begotten or been begotten (Q 112.3), that only the lowest things in the observable world do not beget, and that in fact generation is a sign of superiority, and it should therefore be attributed to God.[86]

These initial arguments establish the possibility that God could have a son, and suggest that as God it is actually necessary for him to do so, in a way similar to Theodore Abū Qurra's brief tracts. And they reflect the same polemical preoccupation to defend a position rather than to explain it, explicitly with Muslim sensitivities in mind.

From here, ʿAmmār turns to defend the Incarnation itself. He begins by showing that God's act of creation demonstrates his grace and generosity, and from this basis he argues successively: that God's appearance in a human was his supreme act of communication and the culmination of his generosity towards creation; that this appearance in a body was his response to humankind's desire to see him; that by this he became visible to those whom he would judge on the last day and who therefore had a right to see him; and that his appearing in this form opened the way for humans to have supremacy over all things, including the world to come.[87]

In these four stages ʿAmmār emphasises that the Incarnation was the most direct way in which God could communicate with creation. It was both the culmination of the generous regard he had shown from the start, and the promise of an eternal future for humankind after death. So there was something natural and inevitable about it, since it continued an established process and provided the supreme means by which God could complete the instruction he had begun beforehand and show his generous nature.

In this Christology of divine communication there is little about the Incarnation as a means of ransoming souls or winning them from the devil, as some other Christians at this time taught.[88] We may suspect that ʿAmmār intentionally avoided such notions in order to anticipate objections that God's plan had somehow gone wrong and required rectification. The net outcome is certainly that his interpretation resembles more closely the Muslim conception that God has given guidance through revelations imparted to successive messengers, and that his relationship with humankind is effected through an appeal to intelligence and understanding.

ʿAmmār does not make this resemblance explicit at all. But his care to point out that in the act of incarnate communicating God was not implicated in physicality but united with the human only *bi-al-tadbīr*, "by control",[89] shows respect for the belief that God is absolutely distinct from created being. And his remark at one point that God addresses creation directly *bi-ghayri rasūlī baynahu wa-baynahum*, "without any messenger between him and them",[90] suggests that he considers his interpretation of the Incarnation to be the supreme instance of the kind of communication that was sent through the line of prophetic messengers.

Of course, ʿAmmār can hardly omit altogether any mention of Christian teachings about the two natures of Christ. But he explains away sectarian differences by simply saying that while there is disagreement about whether the Messiah's human body was one hypostasis or two, Christians are unanimous that God cannot be seen or confined.[91] This remark, more than anything, exemplifies his concern to maintain the inviolability and distinctiveness of God in the Incarnation. Together with his assertion that the Incarnation was God's generous act of communication with creation, it shows his awareness of the context in which he was writing, and of the need to explain why God should appear in a bodily form and how, when he did this, he avoided entanglement in physicality. As with the writings of Theodore Abū Qurra examined above, the emphasis here is upon the possibility of Incarnation rather than its exact mode, and also upon the distinction throughout between God and the created order. But ʿAmmār goes further than his contemporary. He takes the argument to his opponents by showing that God's direct communication through a human is the inevitable culmination of his relationship with humankind, and furthermore that it is more direct than any other kind of communication and therefore superior.

ʿAmmār's other work is the *Kitāb al-masāʾil wa-al-ajwiba*, which as its title suggests is in simple question-and-answer form, with an opponent who is not named but must be a Muslim asking the questions to which ʿAmmār gives answers.[92] The fifty-one questions in the part of the work concerned with the Incarnation move through a roughly logical order, from the uniting of the divine and human and the birth of the Messiah (1–19), to the reason for the Incarnation (20–31), the death of the Messiah (32–42) and the consequences of his resurrection (43–51). Whether they were, in fact, asked spontaneously by a Muslim is unlikely, given the fairly smooth order in which they successively cover the various aspects of the doctrine of atonement as a Nestorian might hold it. But as we shall see later, some of them could have been asked by Abū ʿĪsā himself, and show how he and ʿAmmār were participating in the same general discussion about the nature of Christ. So while the Muslim protagonist is probably fictional, the kinds of questions he asks derive from real debates. For our purposes, questions 1–19 demand closest attention since they deal with the actual manner in which the divine and human united.

The questions begin with the problem of how the divine and human retained their respective identities while uniting in reality (1)[93] and how the Messiah could be one entity, *maʿnā wāḥid*, but not either totally eternal or totally contingent (2). This introduces a series of problems about the identity of the Messiah and the being who was born of Mary, and whether both natures are called Son of God (3–10), which issues into discussions about the way in which God himself may have been affected (11–14). In turn, this leads into two questions concerning the involvement of the other Persons of the Godhead in the act of uniting (15–16), and then into more problems about the possibility of the divine remaining unaffected while in reality becoming one with the human (17–19).[94] A brief summary does little justice to the subtlety and complexity of the arguments on either side, though it is maybe enough to show that the main emphasis is upon the issue of God's distinctiveness and separateness from contingent beings, and how this can be preserved in the Incarnation. There is little about the manner in which the two natures subsisted in union together.

Although there are no signs that the Muslim questioner was anything more than a convenient literary device for ʿAmmār, some of the questions he asks are similar to matters discussed in Abū ʿĪsā's *Radd*. In particular, it is striking that questions 15 and 16 raise the same difficulty as Abū ʿĪsā does in the opening paragraphs of his attack on the Incarnation. This is, that if the three Persons of the Trinity are equal, why did only the Son unite rather than the Father or the Holy Spirit?[95] It is attractive to suppose from this that Abū ʿĪsā may be at least connected with the questions which prompt ʿAmmār in this whole part of the *Masāʾil*, though since the contemporary Jacobite theologian Abū Rāʾiṭa was also aware of this particular question,[96] we are maybe safer in saying that all three theologians were joining in a common debate in which a recognised set of problems would be raised.

This being said, the approach of the Muslim in asking the questions in this section has the same clear-cut precision as Abū ʿĪsā's. We can see this to good effect in question 8, where the opponent begins by saying: Since the Messiah comprised the two united substances, then because Mary gave birth to the Messiah and he ate, drank, walked and underwent changes, Christians must say that Mary gave birth to the two united substances, and they both ate, drank and changed. ʿAmmār replies by comparing the two natures of the Messiah with the body and soul of a human, and arguing that only the former undergoes these physical experiences.[97] The question forces ʿAmmār into the awkward position of trying to show how the Messiah was born and grew as a full human, but also how the divine was not implicated, and he resorts to the suitable but rather strained comparison with the soul, which he depicts as somehow detached from the body.

This kind of arguing is characteristic of Abū ʿĪsā's method, and for this reason ʿAmmar's *Kitāb al-masāʾil wa-al-ajwiba* is an important witness to the fact that there were Christians who participated in the kind of encounter presupposed by Abū ʿĪsā's *Radd*, and that the form of questions and objections he raises were part of a wider debate. The evidence mentioned above, that ʿAmmār was probably targeted by the leading Muʿtazilī Abū al-Hudhayl, suggests that he expressed himself in forms that Muslims found accessible and with a force they found it impossible to ignore. So he constitutes a prime instance of a Christian who cast his theology to suit a polemical context which demanded new forms of Christological exposition.

The last Christian theologian from this period we shall discuss is the Jacobite Ḥabīb Ibn Khidma Abū Rāʾiṭa. It seems clear he was active at the beginning of the third/ninth century, because he is listed among those who took part in a Synod at Rosh ʿAinā in 212/827–8, attending presumably as Bishop of Takrit, a title he is accorded in later authors.[98] And he probably knew Theodore Abū Qurra, since he wrote about a meeting between the latter and an Armenian prince which took place sometime between 197/813 and 201/817.[99] His works also reflect awareness of questions discussed by theologians from this time.

Abū Rāʾiṭa gives his main account of Christology in the letter entitled *On the Incarnation*.[100] This follows on from his letter *On the Trinity* and continues the same question-and-answer form, in which opponents, *mutakhālifūnā*, who are earlier identified as People of the South, *ahl al-tayman*,[101] Muslims, are made to introduce each stage of the argument with a new inquiry. The letter includes discussions about many aspects of the doctrine, including the purpose of the Incarnation and Biblical texts which seem to undermine it. For our purposes paragraphs 1–11 are most pertinent.

The first set of problems raised here is concerned with the involvement of the divine in the act of becoming flesh. The Muslims indicate their difficulties at the start by suggesting that the Messiah must have been three hypostases if the triune God was involved, to which Abū Rāʾiṭa replies that it was not the whole Godhead but only the Son who became flesh (2). The Muslims are clearly not satisfied and provocatively ask whether the act of becoming flesh was performed by the Word alone, in which case do the hypostases each act separately? Abū Rāʾiṭa responds that just as Muslims say that God's attributes are separate from one another, so the hypostases within the Godhead are separate (3–7).

This question of the involvement of the whole Godhead is also referred to by ʿAmmār al-Baṣrī, as we have noted, and is Abū ʿĪsā's first topic for interrogation in the part of his *Radd* on the Incarnation. So we shall discuss it in full in the next chapter in order to see whether there are any signs of direct links between the three theologians. It is an inevitable inference in Muslim minds from the double Christian claim that the Godhead is three and the divine united with a human. Its prominence at the beginning of Abū Rāʾiṭa's discourse on the Incarnation illustrates the importance he attaches to responding to Muslim conceptions of the doctrine.

In a further step, the discussion now moves to the issue of how exactly the divine and human subsisted together in the Messiah. If this was by the divine coming to rest, *sakana*, in the human, with which Abū Rāʾiṭa agrees, the Muslims fear that the body must surround the divine and so restrict it. But Abū Rāʾiṭa argues that the divine is not to be understood in the same way as physical objects but rather as surrounding the body, just as fire in a piece of coal or the sun's light in the eye surround these bodies and are not restricted by them (8–10). This leads to the objection that there can thus be no difference between the way in which the divine is in this body and in all other bodies, which Abū Rāʾiṭa counters by arguing that this body is unique in being made one with the divine (11).

Whether Abū Rāʾiṭa's replies provide any satisfying solutions may seem doubtful, when, for example, he says that the Word always remains the Word and the body a body, although their combination is one hypostasis, which is the true becoming flesh of the divine, true man, one and not two.[102] But what is more important for us is that the major emphasis in his argument is upon countering any accusation that the divine may have connected in any way with the human, rather than the mode in which they continued in union. Although he does state his distinctive Jacobite Christology, Abū Rāʾiṭa is fully aware that he must argue the point with which Muslims disagree most acutely, and this becomes the main element in his demonstration.

Conclusion

As we examine the Christological explanations of these Christian authors who wrote in the Islamic world around the beginning of the third/ninth century, we can detect elements in the structure of their thought that appear to be sensitive towards the Qurʾanic portrayal of God and criticisms built upon it. They respond by presenting their teachings about the person of Christ in new ways. Alongside the particular Christological formulas and explanations they themselves advocate against other Christian sects, they now seek to defend points of belief that were not previously given prominence. Chief among these are the impossibility of God having a Son, and the illogicality of the divine changing when it became human in the act of uniting. While we cannot go as far as to say that in the Islamic context new Christologies were fashioned, we cannot avoid noticing the new emphases and configurations that were given to traditional explanations, which in consequence assumed distinctive forms. At the same time, Christian sects continued to express their beliefs in the Incarnation, and among themselves actively debated the varying interpretations of exactly how this uniting of divine and human had taken place.

On the Muslim side, the great majority of polemicists were concerned to challenge the doctrine of the Incarnation over the threat it contained to the oneness and distinctiveness of God. For them the whole notion of God having a Son was ruled out because it implied sharing of divinity and so loss of uniqueness. And, as they saw it, the very idea of the divine and human coming into contact, however this was explained, implied anthropomorphism. Such ideas were anathema in the Muslim milieu, where the doctrine of *tawḥīd* was being debated with vigour, and the Muʿtazila were leading the effort to distinguish between God and the created order.

There might have been a risk that theologians of opposing sides would talk past one another as they sought to promote their own concerns, the nature of the incarnate God for Christians, and the separateness between divine and human for Muslims. But as we have noted, Christians who wrote in Arabic became aware of the requirement to relate their doctrines to Muslim concerns, as far as was possible. And as we will see in the next chapter, Abū ʿĪsā al-Warrāq was one of the few Muslims at this time who took the discussion into the field of Christian concerns by examining and criticising the prevailing Christologies of his day as the major sects presented them to themselves and one another.

We have seen already that Abū ʿĪsā was remarkable for his independence of mind with regard to matters of faith. Certainly, he did not feel constrained to accept the traditional beliefs of Islam uncritically, and he acquired so much knowledge of dualist beliefs that he was both accused of dualism and employed by later Muslim authors as the single most influential authority on dualist sects. So his thorough knowledge of the details attaching to the doctrine of the Incarnation and his method of refuting it should not surprise us. What maybe should strike us as unusual is the very difference between him and other Muslims. We may not be able to say exactly why he was so independent in his approach and so extremely dedicated in his exploration of Christian doctrines. But these features of his work single him out as a uniquely intriguing and significant theologian.

4
Abū ʿĪsā's refutation of the Incarnation

Abū ʿĪsā's interest in religions which challenged Islam in their teachings about God is arguably unsurpassed in the period in which he lived, and is hardly rivalled at any time in the history of Islam. It seems to have been a passion, and as we have seen it contributed towards the misunderstanding and condemnation that bedevilled him and his reputation.[1] The result was some of the best informed accounts and arguments ever composed by a Muslim theologian, which despite his controversial authorship fed later polemical works and helped form the character of continuing attitudes towards non-Muslim religions.[2] In this chapter we shall examine his refutation of the Incarnation in order to see what it can tell us about Abū ʿĪsā and his method of studying and criticising Christianity as one non-Islamic religion. And we shall also see how information and arguments from this part of the *Radd* were employed by later authors as fundamental constituents of their own refutations of this religion which they rejected as an erroneous form of their own.

The integrity of the *Radd ʿalā al-Naṣārā*

It is important to keep in mind that this refutation of the Incarnation was part of an all-embracing refutation of the doctrines of Trinity and Incarnation as they were held by the major Christian sects of Melkites, Nestorians and Jacobites. In its original form, the *Kitāb al-Radd ʿalā al-thalāth firaq min al-Naṣārā* comprised three main sections: firstly an introductory account of various aspects of Christian teachings about the two doctrines (paras. 1–15 in the present work), then arguments against the Trinity (paras. 16–150 in *Anti-Christian Polemic in Early Islam*), and thirdly arguments against the Incarnation (paras. 151–351 in the present work). They were all tightly bound together by cross-references and structural correspondences in the two main attacks, and references back to the descriptive account upon which they are largely based. A. Abel argues that the two attacks were actually separate works.[3] But the only support he adduces comes from small differences in Yaḥyā Ibn ʿAdī's responses to the arguments against the Trinity and the Incarnation, rather than Abū ʿĪsā's work itself, and his claim is contradicted by the two simple facts that the descriptive account which precedes and introduces the refutation of the Trinity clearly anticipates the present refutation of the Incarnation as well, and that there are repeated echoes and mentions in this third part of the two parts which precede it.[4] There is, in fact, no convincing reason to doubt that in its original form the *Radd* consisted of an introductory account of Christian doctrines, followed by two attacks, the whole comprising an ambitious attempt to show that the explanations and interpretations of the leading Christian sects were logically flawed and incoherent. We will say more of this a little later.

Of course, the *Radd* is no longer extant in this original form. It has come down as part of Yaḥyā Ibn ʿAdī's *Tabyīn ghalaṭ Muḥammad Ibn Hārūn*,[5] where it is split into the three hundred and fifty-one or so paragraphs which form the targets for this Jacobite theologian's comments and counter arguments. So we cannot be completely sure that the entire *Radd* survives. However, a number of indications suggest that if anything has been omitted it must have been of only minor importance in the original. In the first place, Yaḥyā appears to have preserved even parts of the work that could not materially serve his purpose of replying to what he saw as errors and misunderstandings. These include Abū ʿĪsā's invocation at the opening and his description of Christian doctrines (paras. 1–15). In the second place, there is no easily detectable break in the continuity of arguments from Abū ʿĪsā, as the edition presented here demonstrates, and no obvious omission that leaves a gap in the plan which Abū ʿĪsā implicitly signals in his Introduction when he describes elements of the Trinitarian and Incarnational beliefs. And in the third place, Yaḥyā presents himself as a careful, and even fussy, respondent to his opponent's views. Maybe a single example will make this point clearly. It comes at the end of Abū ʿĪsā's arguments against the Nestorians' and Jacobites' explanations of the two natures in the Messiah, where he acknowledges that he has gone into a great many details, but says he will not prolong this section since he has already covered many of its aspects earlier (para. 273). Yaḥyā replies as follows:

> We do not have to consider or examine what is contained in this section, since it is information about what he has done, and description of the matter he has discussed. It does not contain any argument which requires us to go into its correctness or otherwise.[6]

The effectiveness of his work would not have been impaired if he had left out this admission and explanation of Abū ʿĪsā. His own relieved response shows that he is keen to answer everything his opponent sets down, and gives a clear indication that he cannot have omitted anything that has the least interest or importance.

Such comments give reassurance that the body of Abū ʿĪsā's *Radd*, including the attack on the Incarnation, has not been edited or cut in any important way. The close correspondence between the main arguments this latter part contains and the outline descriptions of beliefs about the Incarnation in the

Introduction to the whole work, paras. 9–15, which we shall discuss shortly, tends to confirm this. And there can be no serious doubt about the integrity of the beginning of this part, since the first set of arguments, paras. 151–60, which are concerned with the issue of why the Son alone united and not the other two hypostases, forms a smooth bridge passage between the earlier attack on the Trinity and the main attacks on the expressed Christian teachings about the uniting of divine and human that follow.

There is, however, uncertainty about the ending of the *Radd*, since in the extant text what appears to be a conclusion is followed by another set of arguments and then a second conclusion. In P167, the oldest manuscript, the sequence is as follows: at the end of the last major set of arguments against the Jacobites concerning their description of the Messiah and a concluding exclamation of praise (para. 345 below), the author states his intention to refute the minor groups connected with this sect. But this suddenly breaks off, and Yaḥyā interrupts at this point that the rest of this statement is to be found in his preferred copy of the text, and then he says: "From the start of this passage, *min awwal hādhā al-mawḍiʿ*, to the passage, *al-mawḍiʿ*, above which is this sign ✣ is not found in the preferred correct copy" (para. 345 end); this is followed by a declaration from Abū ʿĪsā that his arguments against the Jacobites are concluded (where the ✣ sign appears), and a set of brief arguments against all three sects and another exclamation of praise (paras. 346–51); then lastly Yaḥyā indicates that at the end of some (or one) of the manuscripts of the book at its conclusion come words of Abū ʿĪsā to the effect that he will begin to refute minor Christian groups, eleven of which he names, in a separate book (para. 352).

There is obviously confusion about this ending, and since Yaḥyā himself is fully aware of it, it must have occurred at an early stage in the manuscript history. There appear, in fact, to be two distinct conclusions. The first is at the end of para. 345:

> Exalted is God the one like whom there is nothing, and he is the all-hearing, all-seeing. ◎[7] *Tamma al-kitāb*, the book against the Nestorians, the Melkites and those from the Jacobites whose teachings we have described is complete. All praise to God the Lord of the worlds.
>
> We shall start to refute those who are attached to the Jacobites, such as the Julianists and the followers of Eutyches – the rest that follows this to the end of what is in this copy is contained in the preferred copy [the last clause is obviously Yaḥyā's explanatory comment].

The second conclusion occurs after the brief arguments directed at all three sects at the end of para. 351 and in para. 352:

> This argument, though it shows the errors in the teachings of all three sects, is most serious and compelling against the Jacobites and Melkites. May God the one, the self-subsistent be praised, nothing resembles him, who has never begotten nor been begotten, none is like him.

[Yaḥyā continues: I have found something at the end of some copies of this book, after its conclusion and close, of which this is a copy; I have recorded it here, and these are its very words:]

We shall start to refute those who are attached to the Jacobites, such as the Julianists and the followers of Eutyches, and other Christian divisions, such as the Maronites, the Sabellians, the Gregorians, the followers of Macedonius, the followers of Apollinaris, the Arians, the followers of Eunomius, the followers of Photinus, and the Paulicians, the followers of Paul of Samosata, in a separate work, if God the exalted wills. There is no strength except by God the most high, the most great.

This second conclusion is clearly a fuller and more complete form of the first, which Yaḥyā appears to have cut in consideration of the same text being repeated later. The Christian obviously knew different manuscripts in which the two endings appeared, and for him the longer, which includes the arguments in paras. 346–51, was superior, *al-nuskha al-ṣaḥīḥa al-mukhtāra*. But we have to allow the possibility that both endings were composed by Abū ʿĪsā.

Considering the first ending, it is certainly characteristic of Abū ʿĪsā in its brevity and in its careful mention of only some Jacobites, which refers back to the same point in the descriptive Introduction to the *Radd*.[8] But the second is also typical of him, in its equally brief closing remark about the particular difficulty which his argument holds for the Jacobites and Melkites, and its apt allusion to Q 112.2–4, which summarises the thrust of the whole work in its rejection of plurality in God and denial of his involvement in generation. So what we may have is both a first version of the *Radd*, and then a second version in which Abū ʿĪsā added the short series of general arguments which he had discovered or made up himself, paras. 346–51. Yaḥyā considered the second version to be the better, but in his conservative way he preserved both endings, taking the trouble to point out that the best manuscript contained the same statement by Abū ʿĪsā of his intention to refute minor sects as the first, but now following the series of brief arguments, which is understandable. His rather unclear reference at the end of para. 345 to a particular section, *mawḍiʿ*, of the work not appearing in the best version may be taken to indicate the passage which starts at the end of para. 345 with *tamma al-kitāb*, following the two-concentric-circles sign ◎ which is used throughout MS P167 to indicate a major section break, and continues to *inqaḍā al-kalām* with the cross mark above it at the beginning of para. 346.[9] It was the longer and presumably later version of the *Radd* that Abū ʿĪsā wished to circulate, comprising the whole of the text that follows, with the exception of the concluding lines of para. 345. We shall refer to this in our discussion of the work.[10]

The structure of the refutation of the Incarnation

The structure of the attack on the Incarnation and the progression of its arguments are reasonably easy to follow. There are two main parts, the first on particular moments in the human experience of the Messiah, and the second on the manner in which the two natures united within him, together with the supplementary set of questions which we have suggested above Abū ʿĪsā added after he had composed his main attacks. Their contents correspond loosely to the topics outlined in the paragraphs on Christology in the descriptive introduction to the *Radd*, paras. 9–15.

The first part, paras. 151–219, is headed "The argument against them about the Uniting and the Birth", *al-kalām ʿalayhim fī al-ittiḥād wa-fī al-wilād*. It falls into two sections. The first, paras. 151–60, centres on the Trinitarian question as to why only the Son was the subject of an act of uniting, and whether this was an act of all three hypostases or just one. Abū ʿĪsā discusses the issue in general terms, paras. 151–6, before turning to the particular difficulties of each of the three sects, paras. 157–60, in what constitutes an elegant transitional passage from the main attack on the Trinity earlier in the *Radd* to the detailed investigation into the various teachings about the Incarnation that follow.

The second section of this first part, paras. 161–219, which is much longer, is concerned with issues arising from the uniting of the divine and human natures at the birth and death of the Messiah. In arguments against each of the three sects, Abū ʿĪsā teases out the problems connected with the involvement of the divine nature firstly in the foetus in Mary's womb and Jesus' growing up, paras. 161–75, and secondly in the crucifixion and death, entombment and revival, paras. 176–86. And then he discusses the same problems with respect to the specifically Melkite teaching that the divine united not with an individual human but with the universal human nature, paras. 187–219. This part focuses upon these particular moments in the life of the Messiah in order to expose the difficulty of implicating the divine nature in experiences that are impossible for God, or of sustaining the claim that the uniting was a reality at these times.

The second part, paras. 220–345, is indicated clearly by the words "Next chapter" *bāb akhar*.[11] Here Abū ʿĪsā turns from particular moments in the Messiah's human experience to the explanations offered of how the divine and human natures united within him. In the first section, paras. 220–9, he examines and refutes the metaphors of uniting employed by the various groups, showing how their application to the divine nature raises embarrassing difficulties. Then in the second section, paras. 230–345, indicated by the heading "The Declaration against them about their Description of the Messiah", *al-qawl ʿalayhim fī waṣfihim al-Masīḥ*, which is the other major set of arguments against the Incarnation, he attacks the attempts of the three groups to show how the two natures were united. Against the Nestorians, he asks how the Messiah could be both God and human, paras. 230–42, and how the action, paras. 243–7, and will, paras. 248–73, of the two natures could be one. Against the Melkites, he questions some of their statements about the relationship between the substances of the divine and human natures, paras. 274–9, and then shows the weaknesses in other teachings concerning the uniting of the divine with the universal human, paras. 280–303. And thirdly against the

Jacobites, which is indicated by the heading "The Argument against the Jacobites", *al-kalām ʿalā al-Yaʿqūbiyya*,[12] he asks firstly how the one being could be both eternal and contingent, paras. 304–28, secondly how exactly the divine and human could become one at the uniting, paras. 329–40, thirdly how the divine nature could share in the bodily experiences of the Messiah, paras. 341–3, and lastly whether analogies with physical objects adequately serve to explain this teaching, paras. 343–5.

The arguments in the second section of this part touch upon many of the same issues as the second section of the first part, as Abū ʿĪsā repeatedly says.[13] But whereas there they are concerned with the problems raised for the divinity and to some extent humanity as distinct natures, here they focus upon the logical coherence of the doctrinal formulas and models which the sects promote.

The third main part of the *Radd*, paras. 346–51, which is introduced with the words "The argument against the Jacobites is concluded, and it may be said to these three sects", *inqaḍā al-kalām ʿalā al-Yaʿqūbiyya wa-yuqālu li-hādhihī al-firaq al-thalāth*, is much briefer and has almost the character of an afterthought. Its two main arguments are against the Messiah participating in his own creation as a human, paras. 346–8, and the consequences of the Messiah being the father of a child, paras. 350f. This part does not correspond to anything in the descriptive introduction of the *Radd*, and it differs from other parts in not being based upon anything Christians themselves have said.

Emilio Platti suggests a structure to the work which differs in a few details from this.[14] He acknowledges exactly the same main divisions, but separates our second section, paras. 220–345, into two chapters, on the metaphorical expressions used by Christians to explain the doctrine of uniting, paras. 220–9, and the three sects' descriptions of the divine and human within the Messiah, paras. 230–345. There is not much to choose between this and the structure followed here, though perhaps the decisive *bāb akhar*, at para. 220, which is the clearest surviving indication of a new subject in the whole *Radd*,[15] shows that what follows all holds together as different parts of one thematic attack against the actual doctrinal statements and explanations of the three sects.

This easy progression of arguments against the many aspects of the Incarnation has the same comprehensive character as the earlier arguments in the *Radd* against the Trinity. Abū ʿĪsā's double approach and attention to all three Christian sects ensures that few, if any, points of doctrine are left unexamined. His knowledge of the Christological formulas used by the different groups, which is rivalled only by al-Qāsim Ibn Ibrāhīm among contemporary Muslim polemicists,[16] together with his own inventiveness of thought, enable him to draw out implications in doctrines and relate consequences to root principles in ways that compel admiration and invite us to wonder why he took so much trouble to acquire this degree of intimacy with beliefs which were not his own. But, as we have seen, he seems to have repeated this with dualist religions[17] and presumably with other forms of belief as well. If he ever completed the refutation of minor Christian sects he was planning (paras. 345, 352), then he must also have demonstrated the same encyclopaedic knowledge there, and caused considerable embarrassment to Christians.[18]

Abū ʿĪsā's method

The method of attack which Abū ʿĪsā employs is virtually identical to his approach in his refutation of the Trinity. There are three main kinds of argument. The first seeks to show that a doctrinal statement or a clear implication of a statement is either inconsistent within itself or contradictory to a major Christian teaching. A good example of the former technique occurs early on where Abū ʿĪsā argues that if, as the Christians maintain, the uniting was effected by all three divine hypostases for the Son alone, then the Son must have something which the Father and Holy Spirit do not, *li-al-ibn fī dhālika al-fiʿl . . . mā laysa li-al-ab* (para. 156). If the Son has no distinction, then why should only he, and neither the Father nor the Spirit, participate in the uniting? The problem here, as Abū ʿĪsā identifies it, is that although Christian teachings insist that the Son is not different from the other hypostases, he is distinct as the sole subject of the Incarnation. The inconsistency could only be resolved, in the terms set, by the Christians conceding that the Son is unique in some way and so abandoning the principle that the hypostases are equal in all respects.

An example of the latter technique of showing how a doctrine is contradictory to a major teaching occurs in his arguments against the Jacobites' Christology (paras. 329f.). He begins by establishing a number of doctrinal points: the Messiah became Messiah at the moment of uniting; the uniting occurred between a human individual and the divine hypostasis; he was Messiah at this moment, and the Messiah is one substance from two and one hypostasis from two. These are all in accordance with Jacobite teachings. But, he continues, the consequence must be that when the divine and human were on the point of uniting at the moment he was two hypostases he was also one, at the moment he was two substances he was also one, and at the moment he was divine and human he was also a third entity which was neither divine and human in distinction nor divine and human combined. His argument is that at the precise point of uniting the two subjects were neither in their previous state of being separate nor in their subsequent state of being combined, as the Jacobite Christological model requires. But if it was at this very point that the Messiah became Messiah, then at this moment the Messiah must have been a *tertium quid*. This, Abū ʿĪsā declares, is clear and manifest contradiction, and this matter would be sufficient even if there were no others against his opponents. He argues further that if the Jacobites try to wriggle out of this difficulty by saying that the Messiah became Messiah after the moment of uniting, then they oppose their own teaching by denying that the uniting caused the Messiah to be Messiah.

This clinically methodical progression shows how he was able to propel the issue to the point where the opposition had either to admit they were indeed inconsistent (it is an excellent illustration of this technique), or were simply in danger of contradicting their own teachings.

The second kind of argument is very similar to this, though it brings the discussion to the point where it threatens to contravene plain, generally admitted logic. An example occurs in Abū ʿĪsā's examination of the metaphorical explanation of the relationship between the human and divine as the Word appearing to creation through the human, though without indwelling or mingling with the human body of the Messiah. If this means that the Word did this by control over the Messiah's body, he retorts, then since God's control extends throughout creation, the Word must have united with prophets, other humans, animals, plants and even inanimate matter. This is why, he finally observes, it contains fallacy and faultiness all through it (para. 227). There is no need for Abū ʿĪsā to pursue this argument to its conclusion because he has shown graphically that the metaphor cannot safeguard the distinction between the divine uniting specifically with the Messiah and with any other entity in creation. Those with reasonable minds will see the logical weakness without his having to prove it.

Appeals to agreed forms of logic that both Christians and Muslims might readily be expected to acknowledge are less frequent in this part of the *Radd* than in the earlier arguments against the Trinity, though this is largely explained by the nature of the subjects under scrutiny. For while in his attack on the Trinity Abū ʿĪsā often appeals to shared theological principles about the nature of God in himself, here in his attacks upon the notion of God uniting with a human and becoming implicated in a creaturely life he can appeal to the more straightforward distinction between the human and divine.

This is his third main kind of argument, and it is understandably the most common employed by Abū ʿĪsā against the Incarnation. It appears as a precept to show that a Christian statement is wrong in a number of forms. For example, in the response to the claim that the act of uniting occurred before the Messiah's birth, Abū ʿĪsā simply indicates that this means the divine nature was carried in Mary's womb, born, brought up, nourished, ate and drank (para. 167). He does not need to take the argument further since his point is made by simply referring to these creaturely experiences which the divine undergoes. It also appears less straightforwardly in jibes and shows of mock horror at Christian excesses. For example, in his argument against the metaphor for the uniting of the divine and human as mixing and mingling, when his opponents claim that the Word mingled with the human in a unique way, he responds that it must also then have touched and separated from the component elements of the human in a unique way, and must have moved and rested, been happy and suffered in a unique way (para. 222). He means that if they can apply physical terms in a way made meaningless by the non-physical character of the Word, he can do the same with other terms, and so ridicule the whole reality of the Divinity participating in the experiences of the Messiah's life. His concluding remark in this paragraph shows his pretended shock at such enormities: "This issue and all its consequences are too great and vast for us to gather together in a book."

In all these arguments, Abū ʿĪsā is acutely concerned to prove his opponents wrong in terms they cannot easily question. So he includes no explicit references to the Qur'an or Islamic teachings, but rather attempts to argue from within the Christian positions themselves, drawing inferences from the logic of their statements alone, and making observations on the sole basis of the individual teachings and their wider Christian contexts. This presupposes considerable knowledge of Christian teachings and understanding about the implications of these, and it is the major respect in which Abū ʿĪsā stands out from the majority of his Muslim contemporaries.

Abū ʿĪsā's sources

It is more or less impossible to be certain about Abū ʿĪsā's sources, since he is silent about any authorities he used. But we can feel confident that he made use of his own *Kitāb maqālāt al-nās wa-ikhtilāfihim*, his lost account of the beliefs held by the major religions of the Arab domains.[19] For he refers to this in his Introduction to the *Radd* as a work in which he describes the Christian sects, including "some of the reasons for the distinctions between their beliefs and the proofs employed by each group".[20] Although he does not cite it directly in the course of his work, the *Maqālāt* quite probably underlies the description of Christian doctrines with which the work begins. Beyond this, the rest of the attack appears to be derived from the basic teachings outlined at the start, informed by an impressive accumulation of knowledge about them. We may surmise that Abū ʿĪsā made the same thorough investigation into the main Christian sects and minor groups[21] as he did into dualists and others, for which he was renowned.[22] And we may also suppose that he derived his information from a range of sources in order to obtain full knowledge of each of the Christian groups he targets.[23]

We come a little closer to discovering Abū ʿĪsā's sources, and his own methods, by considering the two arguments in the attack on the Incarnation that have clear parallels in other works of the period. The first of these is his allusion to the comparison between the miracles of Jesus and those of other prophets, a well-known motif in Muslim polemical literature that can be traced from the beginning of the third/ninth century for hundreds of years.[24] In its typical form this comparison comprises references by the Muslim author to one or many miracles of Jesus which might be taken as showing his unique powers, followed by similar miracles of Old Testament prophets or occasionally the Prophet Muḥammad to prove through the comparison that such feats cannot be taken as proof of Jesus' uniqueness and hence his divinity. Many other authors devote much space to such comparisons and describe the rival miracles in some detail. Abū ʿĪsā, however, does little more than refer to the comparison, in a way that makes the motif entirely his own. A brief examination will show how he treats it.

He mainly employs this argument in his discussion about the metaphorical explanation of the uniting of the divine Word with the human as "It controlled [the creation] through him", *dabbara ʿalā yadih*. If, he contends, Christians mean by this that the Word caused miracles to appear through the human Jesus, they should recall that according to their beliefs it did the same through earlier prophets, some of whose miracles were greater than his, so if this is uniting then the divine being must have united with countless prophets (para. 226).[25] Here Abū ʿĪsā appears to be fully aware of the practice of making comparisons between miracles, and thus indicates his knowledge of contemporary polemical modes, and maybe his indebtedness to an argumentative tradition. But at the same time he strips the motif of everything except its central principle that comparisons between miracles rebut claims of Messianic uniqueness, and offers no illustrations from the miracles of Jesus and Old Testament equivalents. And rather than employing it as a substantive component in his *Radd*, as other Muslim authors of the time often did, he reduces it to a single response appropriate to the Christian claim that Jesus' actions have some sort of unique quality and significance. If Abū ʿĪsā was as fully aware of the motif of comparisons as this argument suggests, then his indifference towards it shows the severely abstract approach he favours. Further, his decision to avoid the scriptural quotations that he would have to give, tells us something about his attitude to these texts themselves. We shall return to this point shortly.

The second argument which Abū ʿĪsā employs in common with other authors is the first in his attack on the Incarnation, namely the problem of how only one hypostasis could become incarnate when all three are supposed to be identical in every respect. This argument is set out elsewhere most fully in one of the letters of the Jacobite Ḥabīb Ibn Khidma Abū Rāʾiṭa, who as we saw in the previous chapter was active at about the same time as Abū ʿĪsā in the early decades of the third/ninth century.[26]

In the second letter of his surviving works, on the Incarnation, Abū Rāʾiṭa's opponents, *mukhālifūnā*, whose polemical preoccupations and own interests identify them clearly as Muslims,[27] raise the issue of the identity of the divine subject of the Incarnation. They say: If the one who participated in the Incarnation, *al-mutajassid*, was divine then it must have been the three hypostases, for how can the Christian say it was one of them and not all three?[28] The point underlying this compressed argument is that if God in his fullness is three hypostases, as Abū Rāʾiṭa has earlier acknowledged in his first letter on the Trinity, and it is God who participates in the Incarnation, then the Christian claim that the Son became incarnate but not the other two hypostases is self-contradictory.

Abū ʿĪsā employs a very similar argument, though he makes more of it. In a question to the Jacobites and Nestorians he asks: If the three hypostases effected a single act of uniting for the Son, why could they not do the same for the Father? If they could, there would have been a second Messiah, and also a third if the Spirit were made incarnate, entailing Messiahs who were related as father and son. A further consequence would be that the Father may have united with a human at an earlier time, or may do so in the future.[29] While there is a slight shift in emphasis, the main point is the same as in Abū Rāʾiṭa, that if it is God himself who is concerned in the act of uniting then it is possible for all three hypostases to become incarnate.

A second argument reported by Abū Rāʾiṭa from his opponents concerns the action of the Godhead: Is the Incarnation of the Word in the body an action of the Word alone, *fiʿl min huwa*? And if it is an action of the three hypostases, do they have a single joint action or does each of them have its own particular action?[30] Whatever argument underlies this has been truncated by Abū Rāʾiṭa, but the point seems clear, that there is some inconsistency in claiming either the Word alone effected the Incarnation for itself, or the three hypostases effected it for the Word alone. If the former, the single hypostasis would appear to have unique characteristics, and if the latter it is strange that all three hypostases should effect an action in which only the Word was involved.

Abū ʿĪsā's corresponding argument has close resemblances: If the act of uniting was an action of all three hypostases, why was it an action for the Word alone, and why was the Word alone united when there was no difference between it and the other hypostases in the act of uniting, *wa-laysa la-hā fī fiʿl al-ittiḥād mā laysa la-humā*? But if it was an action of the Word alone, then the Word must have an action of its own, and so also may the Father and Holy Spirit, so that each hypostasis may control its own creation or become incarnate itself. Alternatively, if all three hypostases effected the act of uniting for the Son alone, there is still a difference between the Son and the other hypostases because he alone united with the human.[31] The central issues are that if the three hypostases are equivalent, as Christians claim, then it is not possible to single out one of them as the doctrine of the Incarnation requires.

There are clear resemblances between these questions of Abū Rāʾiṭa's Muslim opponents and Abū ʿĪsā's forceful mockery. Is it possible that the Christian actually knew these contents of the *Radd*? It would be attractive to link the two, and not unreasonable in the circumstances that alone among Muslim polemicists of this time Abū ʿĪsā seemed alive to hard-hitting arguments which addressed the logical entail of the Trinity and Incarnation. But the evidence does not allow us to go further than entertaining the possibility, and strictly speaking to consider that the Christian and Muslim may in their own ways have been employing the same source. This latter likelihood is increased by the fact that the early third-/ninth-century Nestorian ʿAmmār al-Baṣrī also knew of the same question from Muslims,[32] and that signs of it can also be detected in debates between the Nestorian Patriarch Timothy I and Muslims from the latter part of the second/eighth century.[33] So it appears that the point was well-known by the time of Abū ʿĪsā. It also occurs later in the third/ninth century in arguments reported from the Muʿtazilī Abū ʿAlī al-Jubbāʾī.[34]

Even if we cannot point to any direct indebtedness, we may nevertheless infer from these correspondences that Abū ʿĪsā was touching issues which Christians found sensitive and were under pressure to explain. Here, and presumably at many other places in the *Radd* where lack of information prevents us from identifying similarities, he was discussing matters of acute importance to his opponents, and so must have been very much aware of the main issues raised between Christians and Muslims at this time.

It is very difficult to go further than this on the question of sources. In the first part of the *Radd* against the Trinity Abū ʿĪsā gives hints that he may have picked up some of his information and practised some of his arguments in direct exchanges with Christians, but in this second part he is rather more reticent.[35] A single note of advice reveals his experience of debates, when he says:

> Anyone who asks them in this argument . . . must not be satisfied with any term from them which has no meaning. For they of all communities have terms which have no meaning when they explain these beliefs of theirs. He must ask them the meanings, to distinguish between what they say and what can be said in response to them. (para. 292)

This plea for clarity maybe shows how frustrated Abū ʿĪsā became when he was attempting to make his interlocutors conduct a meaningful discussion in the language of common currency. He is clearly referring back to at least one dissatisfying occasion, and we may imagine that he is recalling times when he may have learnt directly something of what Christians believe, as well as opportunities to try out some of his own arguments.

This rather fragmentary information about Abū ʿĪsā's sources is enough to show that he was acquainted with current arguments in both Christian and Muslim circles, and participated in exchanges with all the misunderstandings they produced. And this brings us to the question of what his intentions in writing were, whether he composed his *Radd* as an arsenal for debaters, or as a more considered response to the Christian articulations he examines, or as something else.

The purpose of the *Radd ʿalā al-Naṣārā*

Abū ʿĪsā does not state his intentions, of course, at least not in any of the surviving parts of the *Radd*. The evidence we do find suggests that one main part of his design was to amass such a comprehensive collection of arguments against every aspect of the doctrines he had chosen that they would prove unanswerable by any Christian who tried. This is clear from almost every part of the work, where point is piled upon point, and it is underlined in an aside at the end of the progression of arguments against the Nestorian characterisation of the Messiah, where Abū ʿĪsā says:

> We have produced enough questions for these groups on this matter, and the argument against them on it is considerable. So we will cease for fear of prolonging it, though much of what we have asked them on the uniting can be put to them on the Messiah. (para. 273)

This acknowledgement gives the impression that he is concerned not to leave any aspect unattended, even at the risk of being prolix. We can only conclude that he was intending to produce arguments suitable for Muslim colleagues to use.[36]

If the *Radd* was intended to serve this immediate purpose – and some of its more forceful knock-down arguments fit in with it well – there is also a rather wider intention evident in the larger emphasis detectable throughout the work. This is more theological in nature, and it indicates Abū ʿĪsā's deeper concerns in composing this polemic.

When we consider the nature of the arguments in the *Radd* we notice that almost without exception they focus on aspects of one central issue, which is that of the Divinity becoming implicated in human or creaturely characteristics and experiences. Every one of the major sections of the refutation of the Incarnation deals with a main aspect of the issue, in turn the events of the Messiah's birth and human life, the metaphorical explanations of the relationship between the two natures, and the precise form in which the sects understood the divine and human natures to have united together. The overwhelming emphasis is upon the ontological structure of the Messiah, and within that upon any threat to the divine nature's distinctiveness and separateness. Christians are required to explain how the Divinity is safeguarded from being caught up in the experiences of humanity, and it quickly emerges that Abū ʿĪsā considers that any suspicion it may have been involved in the foetal stages or birth of Jesus, in his upbringing and then his death, is equivalent to invalidating the doctrine.

This single preoccupation is underlined by Abū ʿĪsā's almost complete lack of interest in exploring the meaning or significance of the crucifixion of Jesus. He certainly knows about the Christian understanding of the event, since at various places in the *Radd* he reports Melkites and Jacobites saying that the Divinity died "for us" *min ajlinā*,[37] and refers to the Melkite belief that the Word cannot have united with a single body, since if it had it would have come into the world only in order to save this body alone, *innamā jaʾat bi-khalāṣi dhālika al-jasadi dūna ghayrih*.[38] But nowhere does he discuss the atonement or show any concern about it except to question the probity and logic of the divine nature of the Messiah having to die.[39] He does not argue with his Christian opponents over the purpose of this and seems particularly incurious about what it could mean that the Messiah's death may have been representative or salvific.

The conclusion to be drawn must surely be that in the main Abū ʿĪsā was not interested in Christian doctrines as such. He was interested in them insofar as they rivalled and threatened the doctrine of the oneness of God. All his polemical efforts are directed towards demonstrating that the deviations they contain are logically unviable, but he seems to have no time for the doctrines as they form part of Christian beliefs about the relationship between God and humankind.[40]

Of course, it is possible that Abū ʿĪsā was not confronted with the doctrines he attacks in a full account of Christian beliefs, but rather as separate arguments about such topics as a triune Godhead or an incarnate deity. In this case, he might have known the kind of occasional apologetic writings that were composed for Muslims by Theodore Abū Qurra and other contemporary Christians, which often centred on individual points. But this idea is not very likely, for the major reason that Abū ʿĪsā appears to know about such key Christian beliefs as the atonement, as is clear in his passing references mentioned above, and in his summary of the Nicene Creed, in which he relates the agreed Christian belief:

> The Son came down from heaven and took a body from Mary of the seed of David and clothed himself in it; he appeared to humankind, was crucified, killed and buried; and after three days he rose again and ascended into heaven.[41]

He may not say very much about this doctrine, nor indeed about the doctrine of the Holy Spirit, of which he is also clearly aware,[42] but his hints are enough to indicate that he knows it is part of Christian beliefs. And anyway it is inherently unlikely that, with his avid concern to discover about Christianity, Abū ʿĪsā would have left the full range of their beliefs uninvestigated.

So it is much more probable that he had some good reason to concentrate upon his two target doctrines and did so by choice, than that he had no knowledge of the totality of Christian beliefs or the reason why his opponents held the unacceptable teachings they did. Although it is impossible to know this reason with certainty, it would appear to spring from the concern he seems to have shown in many of his works for defending the doctrine of the oneness of God.

We have seen above that Abū ʿĪsā's arguments against the Trinity and uniting form varied aspects of the central desire to separate God from any creaturely characteristics. We can go further and say that his attacks are all intended to demonstrate that there is no rational basis or logical coherence to doctrines which deviate from this central axiom. From this it follows that the *Radd* would appear to be an extended apologetic exposure of challenges to the fundamental teaching of Islam.

At the risk of speculating further, it might not be improbable that this attack against Christian doctrines formed part of a major project in which Abū ʿĪsā attempted to show, almost by default, that the doctrine of the oneness and distinctiveness of God was the only viable form in which divinity could be conceived. We know that he composed attacks on the Jews, the *Radd ʿalā al-Yahūd*, and upon the dualists, the *Kitāb iqtiṣāṣ madhāhib aṣḥāb al-ithnayn wa-al-radd ʿalayhim* and the *Radd ʿalā al-Majūs*, in addition to three attacks on the Christians.[43] And we also know that the work for which he was usually remembered, the *Kitāb maqālāt al-nās*, contained extensive descriptions of the beliefs of these religions as well as some others known within the Islamic world.[44] From the fact that we know only of descriptions of beliefs in this work, we may conclude that it contained the results of Abū ʿĪsā's researches into the beliefs of religionaries whose faiths resembled and rivalled Islam.[45] We know from the *Radd* that the *Kitāb maqālāt al-nās* was written earlier,[46] and can assume it was a major source. So maybe we can go on to infer a similar relationship between the polemics against other faiths and this great descriptive compendium, and conclude that these related works formed a joint presentation and individual refutations of the beliefs which were alternatives to Islam. As the shortcomings and excesses of each of these faiths were brought out, so gradually it would emerge that only the belief which asserted that God was absolutely one and organically unrelated to the created order had conviction.

If these lost works did together constitute a project to defend a version of Islamic belief (of course, we have had to assume that like the *Radd ʿalā al-Naṣārā* the other lost refutations concentrated on the teachings about God in the respective faiths), then it would appear that Abū ʿĪsā's primary intention was to support monotheism in its strictest form. Refutation of alternative explanations of Godhead is part of this, though in themselves the arguments against Christianity and other faiths are not systematic demolitions of their doctrines as such. In a sense, refutation is apologetic.

It is important at this point to recall that Abū ʿĪsā did not exclude Islam from his polemics.[47] As we saw above, his arguments against the veracity of Muḥammad and the consistency of the Qurʾan are biting. And although they have come down in fragmentary form,[48] their uncompromising directness makes it clear that Abū ʿĪsā did not accept traditional Islam without question, and indicates that his beliefs were more likely a form of rational monotheism than immediately recognisable Islam.

We have come some distance from the arguments against the Incarnation in the *Radd*. But maybe we can now see why this doctrine causes so much concern and fascination to Abū ʿĪsā. He is employing it in part to test and define his own beliefs and to support his own doctrines by showing that any alternative is unviable. And so he approaches it in the detached forensic way of reducing it to propositional formulas and testing these to breaking point. The reason why Christians express their beliefs in such a doctrine, and the relationship between this and other teachings they hold are of minor importance for him. His concern is to refute what may seem facile modes of defining deity, so that his own philosophically stringent insistence upon the one God is left as the only acceptable form of belief.

The influence of Abū ʿĪsā's arguments

This underlying motive for examining the doctrine of the Incarnation (and, of course, the Trinity in the earlier part of the *Radd*) at such length springs from Abū ʿĪsā's insistence upon the oneness of God. On this point he is entirely in agreement with traditional Islam, even though he may have rejected other elements of received teachings. But despite the comprehensive manner in which he counters Christian claims and the patently monotheistic principles on which he does so, it is not easy to see exactly how among Muslim authors who came after him his *Radd* influenced the course of anti-Christian polemic.

Few of the surviving later third-/ninth-century discussions of the Incarnation are at all detailed, and none of them compares with Abū ʿĪsā's *Radd*.[49] From the latter half of the century, two of the fragments from the Baghdad Muʿtazilī Abū al-Qāsim ʿAbdallah b. Aḥmad al-Balkhī's (known as al-Kaʿbī) (d. 319/931) *Awāʾil al-adilla fī uṣūl al-dīn* indicate that the original work contained some points about Christian beliefs concerning Christ.[50] And we can perhaps assume that the lost works on Christianity attributed to Abū al-Ḥasan al-Ashʿarī (d. 324/935), Abū Hāshim al-Jubbāʾī (d. 321/933), Abū ʿAlī Muḥammad Ibn Khallād (d. *c.* 326/938) and Abū Bakr Aḥmad b. ʿAlī Ibn al-Ikhshīd (*fl.* early fourth/tenth century) did so as well.[51] Unfortunately, none of the arguments from these important theologians have come down in presently traceable forms.

Our main information about the character of Muslim attacks against beliefs about the person of Christ at the end of the third/ninth century is provided by lengthy fragments from the works of two Muʿtazilī theologians we have already encountered. These are enough to suggest, if not confirm, that Abū ʿĪsā's approach may have begun to exert an effect upon Muslim treatments of Christianity.

The first of these is Abū al-ʿAbbās ʿAbdallah, al-Nāshiʾ al-Akbar (d. 293/905–6), one of the Muʿtazila of the Baghdad school, whose *Kitāb al-awsaṭ fī al-maqālāt* was a critical presentation of the main religious groups of his time. Included among these were the Christians, and the doctrines they hold which attract his attention are the Trinity and Incarnation. He both describes these and refutes them, as we briefly mentioned in Chapter 3.[52]

Al-Nāshiʾ begins by describing the Christologies of a main group, who appear to be the Nestorians, and also of about twenty subsidiary groups, showing detailed knowledge of differences in their beliefs. Then, without further reference to these variations, he argues against the doctrine on the basic grounds that the divine and human characters involved in the act of uniting could not change into each other, and that the divine could not be involved in the Messiah's death and burial. His intention is clearly to centre on the key principles at stake in the Incarnation, and his long presentation of the many different Christological details presumably serves to show that all Christian teachings are variants of the same fundamental belief that the divine became implicated in human experiences.

There is no obvious connection between these arguments and anything in Abū ʿĪsā's *Radd*, except that they are each concerned with the same issue of possible confusion between the divine and human. And there is no equivalent in Abū ʿĪsā to al-Nāshiʾ al-Akbar's list of Christian sects.[53] But there does seem to be a similarity in approach: both polemicists summarise their opponent's teachings accurately and from Christian sources, and both argue against what they perceive to be central points of weakness in the doctrine as these are understood from the Muslim perspective of the complete distinction between the human and divine. It should also be added that both Muslims direct their attacks at the doctrines of the Incarnation and Trinity.

The same is true of the other late third-/ninth-century theologian whose attack has been preserved in fragmentary form. This is Abū ʿAlī Muḥammad b. ʿAbd al-Wahhāb al-Jubbāʾī (d. 303/915–6), the leader of the Baṣra Muʿtazila. He is recorded as having written a refutation of Christianity,[54] and some brief arguments attributed to him are preserved in the fourth-/tenth-century Muʿtazilī ʿAbd al-Jabbār's *Mughnī*, though there is no clear indication that all these latter came from the same work. Again, we examined his arguments in Chapter 3.

The fragments begin with a short description of Christian doctrine, which includes a schematised account of Christological teachings, to the effect that the title Messiah according to some opinions should be applied to both divine Word and human body, according to others to the Word alone, and according to others to the body, since the Word became a body.[55] These cryptic alternatives correspond respectively to the interpretations of the Melkites, the Nestorians and the Jacobites.

The first two of the subsequent arguments against the Incarnation which ʿAbd al-Jabbār summarises from Abū ʿAlī concern verses from the Qurʾan. One is a reply to the comparison cited earlier by al-Jāḥiẓ, that if Abraham could be God's friend (Q 4.125), Jesus could be his son;[56] the other is a response to the related question, if it is acceptable for God to call Jesus his word and his spirit (Q 4.171), why is it not acceptable for him to call Jesus his son in the Gospel?[57]

Abū ʿAlī's main arguments against the Incarnation are quite different in tone from these, with the same quality of contradictory reductionism as Abū ʿĪsā's criticism. In them Abū ʿAlī forces Christians to acknowledge that the Messiah must have worshipped himself, if he was both human and divine; and similarly that the action of the divine must have been identical with that of the human, which means that they had the same power to act, *qudra*, and that the divine nature employed the power of the human nature, *qadara al-lāhūt bi-qudrati al-nāsūt*.[58] He goes on to argue that the other two hypostases must have been able to unite in the same manner as the Word since their substance was one; that the hypostases must have been different since only one united; and that the Son must have united with Mary because Jesus was part of her.[59]

Even though they are severely abbreviated, the style of these arguments is very reminiscent of Abū ʿĪsā's and the contents of two of them are very similar indeed: the argument about the single act of the two natures recalls points which Abū ʿĪsā addresses to Nestorians and Jacobites,[60] though without reference to the distinctively Muslim *kalām* consequence of a single attribute of power; and the argument about the uniting of the Father and Holy Spirit and the difference between the hypostases is so close to the opening section of Abū ʿĪsā's *Radd*[61] that, if Abū ʿAlī did not actually know it, he must have been very familiar with a version closely related to it.

As with al-Nāshiʾ al-Akbar, we see in these fragments from Abū ʿAlī an exposition of Christian beliefs followed by arguments against them, chiefly with respect to the way in which they compromise divine unity and distinctiveness. And the arguments exhibit a confidence and sureness that suggest the author is clear about the main point of his attack, which is not the articulation of the Christian sects as such, but the underlying principles which in Muslim eyes they subvert.

These correspondences between the works of the two late third-/ninth-century polemicists and Abū ʿĪsā are suggestive, though it is difficult to be sure of what. Maybe their structure and method, as far as we can identify these from their fragmentary form, represent developments of Abū ʿĪsā, and greatly reduce his long, drawn-out examinations. Direct connections cannot be established (though in their present incomplete state we should maybe not expect them), but the point remains that the structure of both later works can plausibly be explained in terms of the earlier model.

Moving on to the fourth/tenth century,[62] there is a much clearer line of dependence between Abū ʿĪsā and two major theologians, the Ashʿarī Abū Bakr Muḥammad al-Bāqillānī (d. 403/1013), and the Muʿtazilī ʿAbd al-Jabbār b. Aḥmad al-Hamadhānī al-Asadābādī (d. 415/1025). They each knew fully the information about Christian doctrines which he presents,[63] and also made some use of his arguments against the Incarnation. They were by no means injudicious in their selection of material from his attack, and the more sophisticated form of argument they generally employed suggests that they may have found Abū ʿĪsā dated and somewhat simple. But there can be little doubt that they had access to Abū ʿĪsā's original work in some form.

Al-Bāqillānī was the leading exponent of Ashʿarī thinking in the fourth/tenth century,[64] and his *Kitāb al-tamhīd* is the earliest surviving substantial presentation of Ashʿarī *kalām*.[65] Among its discussions about aspects of Islamic belief and refutations of groups and individuals from inside and outside Islam, it includes an attack on the Christian doctrines of the Trinity and Incarnation for which al-Baqillānī made clear though unacknowledged use of Abū ʿĪsā. The relationship between the two authors was indicated some years ago by A. Abel, who rightly draws attention to points of similarity between the *Kitāb al-tamhīd* and the *Radd*.[66] This is by no means simple, however, and calls for some explanation.

Al-Bāqillānī begins his refutation of the Incarnation[67] by listing various attempts to explain the mode of uniting: the Word inhered, *ḥallat*, in the Messiah's body; the uniting was a mixing and mingling, *ikhtilāṭ wa-imtizāj*; the Jacobites say the Word was changed into flesh and blood; the Jacobites and the Nestorians say it was like the mixing of water with wine or milk, it was the taking by the Word of the body as a habitation and location and its directing matters, *tadbīr al-ashyā'*, and appearing through it alone; some interpret this appearing and the taking of the body like a cover, *iddirā'uhā lahu*, as mixing, while others say it was like the appearance of a face in a mirror or the imprint of a seal in wax; one said that the Word inhered in the Messiah as God inheres in heaven or the intelligence in the soul; the Melkites say that in the uniting two became one.[68]

Clearly there are resemblances between some of these analogies and those given by Abū ʿĪsā in his introductory description of Christian doctrine, where he lists: mixing and mingling, *al-imtizāj wa-al-ikhtilāṭ*; the Word taking the human as a habitation and location, *haykalan wa-maḥallan*; its putting on the body as a cover, *iddara'at al-jasada iddirā'an*; its inhering in him and controlling affairs through him, *ḥallat fīhi fa-dabbarat bihi*; its controlling affairs and appearing through him but not by indwelling or intermingling; its appearing like the imprint of a seal appears in clay; its appearing like a man's face appears in a mirror.[69] Use of the same technical terms and phrases, and the close correspondence in analogies, together with the general order of listing them, all indicate that al-Bāqillānī took his list from a source very close to Abū ʿĪsā's *Radd*.

But we cannot say that al-Bāqillānī simply followed the *Radd* directly without question. For he attributes some of his analogies to particular Christian groups, which Abū ʿĪsā does not, and adds the interpretation of the individual Christian, who was maybe Theodore Abū Qurra,[70] which does not appear in Abū ʿĪsā. So it would seem that if he was employing the *Radd* directly, he was adding quite specific information of his own.[71]

Al-Bāqillānī's responses to these explanations bear few resemblances to Abū ʿĪsā's, and are more indebted to the thought of his own time.[72] The closest is his argument against the uniting as mixing and mingling, which he says must lay the eternal Word open to contingent characteristics such as disclosure and concealment, movement and rest, distance and nearness, *al-ẓuhūr wa-al-kumūn, wa-al-ḥaraka wa-al-sukūn, wa-al-bu'd wa-al-qurb*.[73] Abū ʿĪsā's equivalent argument is that anything which mixes with a body must have a surface of an equivalent size and the parts of the one must come into position opposite (*bi-izā'*) the parts of the other, which entails the eternal Word being limited in size and divided into parts.[74] Here it is possible to see the later theologian taking his predecessor's idea and re-expressing it in more appropriate terminology.

The closest correspondence between the major arguments presented by the two authors can be seen in the next section of al-Bāqillānī's work, where he discusses the involvement of the Godhead in the act of uniting.[75] His argument is that since there must be an agent of the act of uniting, if this agent was the substance, or the hypostases, or all of them together, they must all have united. But if it was the Son alone, then the substance and other hypostases may have been responsible for worlds and actions in isolation, *yanfaradu kullu uqnūm min al-aqānīm bi-ʿawālim wa-afʿāl lā yafʿaluhā al-ākhiru*, bringing them into mutual obstruction and opposition, *jāza an tatamānaʿu wa-takhtalifu.*[76] This recalls the opening arguments of Abū ʿĪsā's attack on the Incarnation in the *Radd*,[77] where he first shows that if the uniting was an act of all three hypostases it must involve all of them, and then that if it was an act of the Word alone, the other hypostases may also have performed acts alone as well, and so may be responsible for controlling a world in isolation, *jāza an yanfaradu kullu wāḥid minhā bi-tadbīr ʿālam dūna ṣāḥibīhu*, or making a creation.[78] He continues with other similar arguments which expose the difficulties which arise from the Son alone uniting.

It seems clear here that al-Bāqillānī has seized the same idea as Abū ʿĪsā and developed it along similar, though rather simpler, lines. In fact, it is easy to see him taking Abū ʿĪsā's actual arguments and abbreviating them.

Other features of the *Tamhīd*, and particularly references to the Melkite doctrine of the universal human, *al-insān al-kulī*, being born of the individual Mary,[79] and the union of divine and human continuing in death unless the human who died alone was not the Messiah,[80] clearly indicate a close relationship with the *Radd*. But al-Bāqillānī hardly ever reproduces any more than single terms or brief phrases, and he rejects or cuts down arguments at will. So we might conclude that while he had extensive knowledge of Abū ʿĪsā's attack, he used it as he pleased, extracting only what he thought useful and setting it out to his own design, together with material from other sources which form the rest of his discussion about the Incarnation.[81] The fact that he makes use of the *Radd* as a major source demonstrates its significance, though his changes to arguments and rejection of so much of the work reveals how techniques may have developed in the century between Abū ʿĪsā and himself. And these also reveal the singular nature of the *Radd*, directed so fully towards the details of Christian doctrine that it maybe seems irrelevant to many Muslim purposes.

The case seems to be the same with respect to the other major fourth-/tenth-century theologian who used Abū ʿĪsā, the Muʿtazilī ʿAbd al-Jabbār.[82] He was the leading exponent of the Muʿtazilī *madhhab* in his time, and his main work the *Al-mughnī fī abwāb al-tawḥīd wa-al-ʿadl* is the single most important surviving treatise on their thought. This great twenty-part compendium took twenty years to complete, between 360/971 and 380/990, and in the course of dictating it ʿAbd al-Jabbār incorporated ideas from numerous authors, including Abū ʿĪsā.

It is past questioning that ʿAbd al-Jabbār made use of the earlier theologian's refutation in his chapter on Christianity,[83] which forms part of volume V of this work. But he does not mention Abū ʿĪsā by name at all here, and earlier in this volume he shows signs of knowing Abū ʿĪsā's statements about dualist religions through the late third-/ninth-century Shīʿī Abū Muḥammad al-Ḥasan b. Mūsā al-Nawbakhtī, who takes these from Abū ʿĪsā's "book", almost certainly his *Maqālāt al-nās.*[84] So we should be warned against assuming a direct link with the *Radd*.

Unlike al-Bāqillānī, and following Abū ʿĪsā and the two later third-/ninth-century Muʿtazilīs Abū ʿAlī al-Jubbāʾī and al-Nāshiʾ al-Akbar, ʿAbd al-Jabbār structures his attack in three parts, namely an exposition of doctrine and attacks on the Trinity and the Incarnation. In the exposition he first gives the points on which Christians agree and then those on which they disagree. They agree that the Son united with the individual they call the Messiah, and that this individual appeared to people, was crucified and killed. Then, on points of disagreement, the Nestorians say the Messiah was divine and human, Anointer and anointed, who became one Messiah through the uniting. The Messiah was two substances and two hypostases, the divine substance being the Son and the human substance Jesus, Yashūʿ, born of Mary. Instead of "it united" they sometimes say "it took flesh" or "it became human" or "it became composite".[85] This closely corresponds to Abū ʿĪsā's account of the Nestorians in the *Radd*, where he too refers to Anointer and anointed, two substances and two hypostases. However, the earlier polemicist presents the synonyms of the action of uniting elsewhere in this account as terms employed in common by all Christians.[86]

ʿAbd al-Jabbār goes on to say that the Melkites, whom he calls *al-Malkāniyya*, think that the Messiah was two substances, one eternal and the other contingent, and that according to the majority of the Jacobites he was one substance from two, the eternal Divinity and the human who became one substance and hypostasis; some say one nature.[87] The brief account of the Melkite Christology is different from Abū ʿĪsā's version, and so is ʿAbd al-Jabbār's term for them at this point,[88] but the statement attributed to the Jacobites is very close to Abū ʿĪsā's words that according to them the Messiah was a substance from two, a hypostasis from two, which in the uniting became one thing, nature, hypostasis and volition.[89]

ʿAbd al-Jabbār next presents metaphorical explanations of the mode of uniting: it was a mingling, *imtizāj*; the divine took the human as a habitation and location; the divine inhered in the human and controlled by him and through him; it was like the appearance of a face in a mirror; it was like the imprint of a seal in wax.[90] These are so close in wording and order to Abū ʿĪsā's list[91] that they could have been quoted from it.

All these and other correspondences in ʿAbd al-Jabbār's exposition[92] suggest strongly that he had access to Abū ʿĪsā's description, and preserved its key terms in what was a summary of the rather longer earlier version.

ʿAbd al-Jabbār's subsequent refutation of the Incarnation is divided into eight sections according to various propositions about the doctrine which he identifies from his exposition.[93] Some of these are concerned with the metaphorical explanations listed above, though on the whole the arguments contained in them are rather remote from anything in Abū ʿĪsā.

Among the few incidental correspondences is ʿAbd al-Jabbār's brief argument at the beginning of his attack, that either the Son or the substance, which is the hypostases together, must have united with Jesus, and if the former then the Christians must say that Jesus is Creator, though they say the Creator is God, who is the Father.[94] The issue here is that if the Son was involved in the act of uniting then he must have been the agent of the act and so, as agent of all acts, the Creator; but this contradicts the teaching that God the Father is Creator. Abū ʿĪsā's similarly placed opening argument against the Incarnation, which involves the principle that if the Son alone was involved in the uniting then he must be different from the other Persons,[95] may be the originating inspiration for this point.

Another correspondence is ʿAbd al-Jabbār's argument against the uniting as mingling, that if the Word mingled with Jesus and so came into adjacency with him, it must have done the same with other prophets since Jesus is no different from them,[96] which echoes Abū ʿĪsā's same point in response to the explanation that the Word controlled affairs through Jesus and appeared in him like an image in a mirror.[97]

It must be said that ʿAbd al-Jabbār presents these arguments in severely abbreviated form. So if he was using Abū ʿĪsā's *Radd* directly, he was only taking the gist of some of arguments without respect for the work as a whole.

Looking at the entire attack, we can see distinct points of dependence in ʿAbd al-Jabbār upon Abū ʿĪsā but little to link the *Mughnī* directly to the *Radd*. He may have scoured his predecessor's attack for points he thought telling, and discovered that the information in it about Christian beliefs was its main value. On the other hand, he may have had no direct knowledge of the *Radd* but found information from it in an intermediary work, remaining unaware that his source was a figure whom he reviled.[98]

Summing up, it appears that by the latter part of the fourth/tenth century Abū ʿĪsā's *Radd* had become an important source of information about Christian beliefs, and to some extent of arguments against them. Whether later theologians used it directly or through other sources, they recognised its value though saw no compelling reason to respect its integrity or even acknowledge its authorship.

We come back to suggestions raised earlier, that the style of arguments employed by Abū ʿĪsā did not appeal any longer to Muslim theologians, who may have thought him outdated. And, more significantly, they felt confident enough in their own principles of theology to employ these against all opponents, whether Muslim, Christian or any of the other religions they refuted in the course of their works. So neither al-Bāqillānī nor ʿAbd al-Jabbār may have seen any attraction or relevance in Abū ʿĪsā's painstaking efforts to present arguments established on objective logic and reason.

Nevertheless, these later masters clearly reveal in the use they made of their predecessor how important his work was in the history of Muslim–Christian exchanges. Over a century after Abū ʿĪsā composed it, the *Radd* was still recognised as one of the important Muslim refutations of Christian doctrines. While Abū ʿĪsā himself disappeared in a cloud of insinuation, his research into Christian beliefs and some of his arguments were still valued as accurate and cogent. It is sad that later Muslims took fewer pains than he did, and allowed misrepresentations to foul his reputation and so rob him of the respect and stature he rightly deserves.

The edition of Abū ʿĪsā's refutation of the Incarnation

The edition and translation below follow very much the same lines as those on which our edition of Abū ʿĪsā's refutation of the Trinity are based. The Arabic appears on one page and the English translation facing, with Abū ʿĪsā's text ordered according to Yaḥyā Ibn ʿAdī's quotations from the Muslim original, each unit numbered 151 onwards following on from the sequence of the first part of the *Radd*. The translation is divided into paragraphs as appropriate and suggested by the division markers given in the text and in the copy preserved in the earliest MS P167, while for the sake of convenience headings and subheadings are introduced where the text no longer contains them. Headings that do remain are reproduced as part of the translation, while the ones supplied are put within square brackets.

As will be remembered, Abū ʿĪsā's *Radd* does not survive as an independent work, but only in the extensive quotations of Yaḥyā Ibn ʿAdī's reply, his *Tabyīn ghalaṭ Muḥammad Ibn Hārūn*. This, as he tells us,[99] was his second version, in which he made some changes and additions to an earlier attempt. And it is this second version which forms the basis of all the known copies of the work.

Among these copies, three are particularly important for establishing the text of the *Radd*.[100] The earliest and best of them is Paris 167, kept in the Bibliothèque Nationale in Paris, which was made in the monastery of St Philotheus near Cairo in 624/1227 by Yūsuf b. Kuwayl b. Jurja b. Abi al-Fakhr, Anbā Mikhā'il bishop of Ṭuwwa and Ṭantā.[101] As its scribe tells us, it was copied from a very old original in Iraqi script. In the textual footnotes this MS is referred to as ب (Paris). Vatican 114, made by Abū Saʿīd Ibn Abi Faḍl in 712/1312, is a faithful copy of it.

The second important MS is Vatican 113, in the Vatican Library, made by al-Amjad Abū al-Majd in the monastery of St Anthony in the Wādī ʿAraba in 626/1229. This is referred to as ف (Vatican) in the textual notes below. Paris 168, of which some parts date from the fourteenth century or earlier, is largely a restored copy of this MS.

The third significant MS is Cairo 506, kept in the Library of the Coptic Patriarchate in Cairo. It was made in 638/1241. We showed in our edition of Abū ʿĪsā's attack on the Trinity[102] that Cairo 506 is actually a copy of Vatican

113, a fact that is corroborated by the apparent repetition of the name of the scribe of Vatican 113 in its colophon.[103] So for the present edition we have only made use of it in a few places to confirm readings, when we have referred to it as ق (Cairo).

We have based this edition and translation on Paris 167 and Vatican 113, and have compared it with Platti's edition of Yaḥyā Ibn ʿAdī's work, which we refer to in the textual notes as ل (Louvain).

It is clear that all the main MSS are very closely related. We have argued elsewhere[104] that there is some slim evidence to indicate that Vatican 113 shows knowledge of Paris 167 and may be a copy of it. In the course of preparing this part of the *Radd* we have not found any evidence to strengthen this and nothing to contradict it. So we let it stand. Platti takes the contrary view, suggesting that the two MSS are independent copies of the same original, though he presents no evidence to support this view.[105] For practical purposes it is not important whether the two are independent or not, since their differences are very few indeed, and hardly raise any notable problem for reading the Arabic. Our hope is that the work of this important third-ninth-century master may be made available to an English-speaking readership so that his innovative scholarship can be properly appreciated and he may be recognised for the leading theologian he undoubtedly was.

In the Arabic text that follows archaic spellings have been modernised where they give a clearer reading (though some instances such as the omission of *alif* in *thalath* and *salam* have been left), and orthographic forms have been commented on in the accompanying endnotes. Significant variants in the MSS employed are listed in the textual footnotes, where the || symbol indicates the MS reading that has been preferred: e.g.

ب || ف :

(reading from right to left, of course) means "The text here follows Paris 167 || Vatican 113 has the variant reading: . . ."

Since the parts of Abū ʿĪsā's descriptive Introduction that deal with the Incarnation give an outline of many of the topics he discusses, these are reproduced from the published edition of his refutation of the Trinity with the paragraph numbers of Yaḥyā's text, nos. 9–15,[106] included.

الردّ على الاتّحاد
الجزء الثاني من كتاب الردّ
على الثلاث فرق من النصارى

The refutation of the uniting
The second part of the refutation
of the three Christian sects

الردّ على الاتّحاد
الجزء الثاني من كتاب الردّ
على الثلاث فرق من النصارى

١. قال خصم النصارى، بعد حمده اللّه على ما مَنَّ به عليه من معرفة توحيده، ومَسئلته ايّاه المعونة على من ألحدَ في دينه، وإقراره بأن لا حول به ولا قوّة إلاّ باللّه:[١]

٩. ثمّ زعمت النسطوريّة وأكثر اليعقوبيّة أنّ الابن الذي هو الكلمة اتّحد[٢] بإنسان محدث مولود من مريم،

١٠. وزعمت الملكيّة أنّ الابن اتّحد بالانسان المحدث. ذهبت النسطوريّة وأكثر اليعقوبيّة بقولهم «إنسان» إلى إنسان واحد شخص واحد، لأن الابن عندهم إنَّما اتّحد بإنسان جزئي لا كلّي؛ وذهبت الملكيّة بقولها «الإنسان» إلى الجوهر الجامع لأشخاص الناس، وذاك أن الابن عندهم إنَّما اتّحد بالإنسان الكلّي لا الجزئي ليخلّص الكلّ، زعموا. قالت الملكيّة: ولو كان اتّحد بإنسان واحد لكان إنّما أراد تخليص ذلك الواحد لا الكلّ. فلاِختلافهم في وصف المتّحديّة اختلفوا في قولهم «إنسان» و «الإنسان»، وربّما تسهّلوا جميعاً في العبارة عند من يعرف معناهم، فجعلوا مكان قولهم «إنسان» «الإنسان» ومكان قولهم «الإنسان» «إنساناً». والأصل الذي يرجعون إليه هو ذلك التحديد الذي وصفناه عنهم قبلُ. وربّما جعلوا مكان «اتّحد» «اتوحد» ومكان قولهم «اتّحاد» «اتوحاد»،[٣] ومعنى هاتين اللفظتين عندهم واحد، يذهبون بذلك إلى أنّه صار من اثنين واحد. وربَّما قالوا «تأنّس»، وربَّما قال بعضهم «تجسّد»، وبعضهم يقول «تركّب»،[٤] ويستسهل أن يقول «التركيب» مكان

١٦. ف، ب تصحيح || ب في النصّ: سهلوا.

[The refutation of the uniting The second part of the refutation of the three Christian sects

1 THEIR TEACHINGS ABOUT THE UNITING]

After giving praise to God for bestowing upon him knowledge of his oneness, imploring his help against those who have erred in their faith, and affirming that all his strength and power come from God, the enemy of the Christians said:[1]

9 The Nestorians and the majority of the Jacobites claim that the Son,
10 the Word, united[2] with *a* temporal human being born of Mary, | and the Melkites claim that the Son united with *the* temporal human being. When they say "*a* human being" the Nestorians and the majority of the Jacobites mean one human being and one individual, because according to them the Son in fact united with a particular human being, and not the universal. And when the Melkites say "*the* human being" they mean the substance which is common to all human individuals. This is because, according to them, the Son in fact united with the universal human, and not a particular, in order to save everyone, as they claim. The Melkites say: If it had united with one human being then it could only have intended to save this individual and not everyone. Thus, their differences over the description of the action of uniting cause them to disagree over the terms "*a* human being" and "*the* human being", although according to those acquainted with their ideas they all tend to apply the explanations loosely, interpreting "*the* human being" as "*a* human being" and *vice versa*. The principle they seek to maintain is this definition which we have given from them above.

Sometimes they interpret "it united" as "it became one", and "uniting" as "oneness",[3] the meaning of the two words being the same for them, that one resulted from two. Sometimes they say "it became human", sometimes some of them say "it became flesh", and others "it became composite",[4] thinking it easy enough to substitute "composition" for

قوله «الاتِّحاد» لعادة قد جَرت له بتلك اللفظة؛ وكلّهم مُجمع على صحّة لفظ الاتِّحاد.

١١. وأجمعوا جميعاً أنّ الاتِّحاد فعْل حادث به صار المسيح مسيحاً. ثُمّ اختلفوا في ذلك الفعل: ما هو، وعلى أيّ وجه كان، وكيف صار من الاثنين واحد.[٥] فزعم بعضهم أنّ الكلمة اتّحدت بذلك الإنسان على طريق الامتزاج والاختلاط منها به؛ وقال بعضهم: بل اتّخدته هيكلاً ومحلاً؛ وقال بعضهم: بل ادّرعت الجسد ادّراعاً؛[٦] وقال بعضهم: بل حلّت فيه فدبّرت به وعلى يديه؛ وقال بعضهم: لم تحللْ فيه ولكنّها دبّرت على يديه وظهرت منه لهذا الخلق لا على الحلول ولا على المخالطة؛ وزعم بعضهم أنّها ظهرت فيه كما يظهر نقش الخاتم في الطينة المطبوعة، لا على أنّ نقش الخاتم انتقل فحلّ في الطينة ولا خالطها ولا زال عن موضعه. وقال بعضهم: ليس على شيء من ذلك كلّه ولكن على معنى أنّ الكلمة ظهرت في ذلك الجسد كما تظهر صورة الإنسان ويُرَى وجهه في المرآة المجلوّة النقيّة؛ فعلى هذا الوجه زعموا كان الاتِّحاد لا على غيره.

١٢. وزعم أكثر اليعقوبيّة أنّ الاتِّحاد ليس على وجه من هذه الوجوه، ولكن على معنى أنّ الجوهرين صارا جوهراً واحداً وأنّ الأقنوم[٧] الذي هو الكلمة والأقنوم الذي هو الإنسان المحدَث صارا أقنوماً واحداً.[٨] وإنَّما قلنا «أكثر اليعقوبيّة»، ولم نذكر في هذا الموضع كلّ اليعقوبيّة لأنّ في اليعقوبيّة صُنوفاً أُخَر تخالف هؤلاء في الاتِّحاد وفي معنى المسيح. ولها ألْقاب أُخر لم نسمّها بها ولم نذكر أقاويلها في هذا الكتاب، ولا أقاويل غيرها من صُنوف النصارى، كالمارونيّة والأُليانيّة والسباليّة والأريوسيّة والبوليّة أصحاب بولي السمساطي وغير هؤلاء من فرقهم؛[٩] لأنّا إنَّما كتبنا هذا الكتاب على جمهور هذه الفرق الثلث لا غير.[١٠] وقد أتينا على وصف صنوف النصارى وألْقابها وأسماءها، وذكرنا بعض العلل التي فرّقت

١٧. ب || ف: ولكن على أن الجوهرين صار جوهراً واحداً.
٢١–٣٠. ب || ف: في الاتحاد في معنى المسيح.

"uniting" because of the familiar usage of the term. They all agree that the expression "uniting" is correct.

11 They all quite agree that the uniting was an action occurring at a particular time by which the Messiah became Messiah. Then they differ over this action, what it was, the way it happened, and how two could become one.[5] Some of them claim that the Word united with the human in the sense of mixing and mingling with him; others that it took him as a habitation and location; others that it put on the body as a garment;[6] others that it came to dwell in him and controlled its affairs through and by means of him. Some say it did not come to dwell in him but controlled affairs by means of him and appeared to mankind through him, though not by indwelling or intermingling; others that it appeared in him as the imprint of a seal appears in impressed clay, for the imprint is not transferred to inhere in the clay or mix with it, nor does it move from its place. Others say it has nothing to do with any of these at all, but means that the Word appeared in this particular body just as a man's form appears when his face is seen in a clean, polished mirror. They claim that the uniting occurred in this way and no other.

12 The majority of the Jacobites claim that the uniting did not occur in any of these ways, but in the sense that the two substances became one substance, and that the hypostasis[7] which was the Word and the hypostasis which was the temporal human being became one hypostasis.[8]

We say only "the majority of the Jacobites", and we shall not discuss all the Jacobites here because among the Jacobites there are other divisions which differ from these over the uniting and who the Messiah was. They have other titles, but we shall not state these or discuss their views in this book, nor the views of other Christian divisions such as the Maronites, the Julianists, the Sabellians, the Arians, the Paulicians, followers of Paul of Samosata, or any other of their sects.[9] For we have written this book specifically about the majority of these three sects and not others.[10] We have previously given descriptions of the Christian divisions, their titles and names, and reported some of the reasons for the distinctions

بين أديانها واِحتجاج كلّ فرقة منها لقولها في كتابنا الذي وصفنا فيه مقالات الناس واختلافهم.(١١) فجميع ما أضيفُه في كتابي هذا إلى اليعقوبيّة فإِنَّما أعني به الأكثر منهم لا تلك الصنوف التي تميّزت عن معظمهم.

١٣. الحرف المنقوط في السباليّة بآء حرف بين البَاء والفَاء اِلاّ أنّه إلى الباء أقرب. والحرف المنقوط بآء في البوليّة حرف تحيد به البَاء ونغمة أخرى ليست في العربيّة يقارب مخرجها مخرجاً بين البَاء والفَاء. كثير ممّن يكتب هذا الاسم يكتب هذا الحرف فاَء وهو إلى البَاء أقرب، وليس من جنس الحرف الذي في السباليّة.(١٢) وقد كان لجمهور النصارى قول متقدّم في التثليث والاتّحاد قبل اِفتراق اليعقوبيّة والملكيّة والنسطوريّة، اجتمعوا عليه لمّا أظهر أريوس الخلاف في التثليث ودعا إلى نِحلته. واجتمع أساقفتهم ورؤساءوهم وأظهروا البرأة منه، وكتبوا قولهم الذي اجتمعوا عليه يومئذٍ.(١٣) وكان الذي كتبوا من ذلك واجتمعوا عليه أن زعموا: أنّ الإله القديم جوهر واحد يعمّ ثلثه أقانيم، أباً والداً غير مولود، واِبناً مولوداً غير والِد، وروحاً منبثِقاً بينهما؛ وأنّ الابن نزل من السماء واتّخذ جسداً من مريم من زرع داوود فتدرَّع به؛ وظهر للناس وصُلب وقُتل ودُفن؛ وقام بعد ثلثة أيّام وصعد إلى السماء. وكتبوا ذلك الكتاب نسخاً وبثّوه في أكثر مدنهم وأمصارهم. فكانت هذه جملتهم إلى أن حدثت الاختلافات بعد ذلك.(١٤)

١٤. فأمَّا قولهم في المسيح، فإِنّ هذه الفرق الثلث اختلفت فيه.(١٥) فزعمت النسطوريّة أنّ المسيح ماسح وممسوح إله وإنسان، يعنون بالماسح الكلمة وبالممسوح الإنسان الذي ولدته مريم. وزعموا أنّه جوهران قنومان مشيئة واحدة، جوهر قديم هو الكلمة وجوهر محدث هو الإنسان المولود من مريم، أقنوم قديم هو الكلمة وأقنوم محدث هو الإنسان الذي ولدته مريم. وربَّما قال بعضهم «طبيعتان

٦. ق || ب: تحتذ به || ف: نحد به.
١٦–١٧. ب || ف: منبثقاً بينهما واتخذ من مريم.

between their beliefs and the proofs employed by each group, in the book in which we have described people's views and the differences between them.[11] So, everything I attribute to the Jacobites in this book I intend only as from the majority and not these divisions which are separate from the main body.

13 The letter in Sabellians written as "b" is a letter between "b" and "f", though it is closer to "b". And the letter written as "b" in Paulicians is a letter which is a shade like "b" and another sound not found in Arabic which lies somewhere between "b" and "f". Many of those who write the name write this letter as "f" though it is closer to "b". It is not the same kind of letter as that in Sabellians.[12]

The majority of Christians already possessed a view about the Trinity and the Uniting before the split into Jacobites, Melkites and Nestorians. They agreed upon it when Arius initiated a controversy about the Trinity and called people to follow him. Their bishops and leaders met together and published a repudiation of this man, setting down the views upon which they had agreed that day.[13] And the claims they set down and agreed upon are:

The eternal Divinity is one substance comprehending three hypostases,
the Father who is generating and not generated,
the Son who is generated and not generating,
and the Spirit which pours forth from them both.
The Son came down from heaven
and took a body from Mary of the seed of David,
and clothed himself in it;
he appeared to mankind, was crucified, killed and buried,
and after three days he rose again and ascended into heaven.

They made copies of this book and sent them to the majority of their towns and cities. This comprised everything they held until the differences arose in later times.[14]

14 Concerning their views about the Messiah, the three sects differ between themselves.[15] The Nestorians claim that the Messiah was both Anointer and Anointed, divine and human, meaning by "Anointer" the Word, and by "Anointed" the human who was born of Mary. They claim that he was two substances and two hypostases with one will: an eternal substance, the Word, and a temporal substance, the human born of Mary; an eternal hypostasis, the Word, and a temporal hypostasis, the human who was born of Mary. Some of them may say, "two natures

وأقنومان» و«طبيعة» و«جوهر» هاهنا واحد. وزعم بعض الملكيّة أنّ المسيح جوهران أقنوم واحد مشيئتان، جوهر قديم هو الكلمة وجوهر محدث هو الإنسان الكلّي، وأقنوم قديم هو الكلمة لا غير. وإنَّما نفوا أن يكون له أقنوم محدث لأنّ الكلمة عندهم اتّحدت بالإنسان الكلّي لا الجزؤي؛ قالوا: والإنسان الكلّي ليس بأقنوم إذ ليس بشخص؛ فلذلك زعموا أنّ المسيح أقنوم واحد. وكثير منهم يقولون: المسيح أقنوم واحد ذو جوهرين وذو مشيئتين. وعلّة هؤلاء في أنّه أقنوم واحد علّة أولئك، واحتجاجهم واحد. وزعم أكثر اليعقوبيّة أنّ المسيح جوهر من جوهرين وأقنوم من أقنومين، يذهبون بذلك إلى أنّ جوهر الكلمة وجوهر الإنسان المأخوذ من مريم صارا بالاِتّحاد شيئاً واحداً طبيعة واحدة أقنوماً واحداً ومشيئة واحدة. قالوا: ولو كان المسيح أقنومين أو جوهرين لكَان العدد لم يسقط بالاِتّحاد. ومثلوا ذلك بالفحمة تُلقى في النار فتصير جمرة. قالوا: فالجمرة ليست بنار مفردة ولا فحمة مفردة، وإنَّما صارت جمرة زعموا لاِتّحاد النار بالفحمة. وزعموا أنّ ذلك الإنسان صار إلهاً ولا يقولون صار الإله إنساناً، كما يقال صارت الفحمة ناراً إذا صارت جمرة ولا يقال صارت النار فحمة، كما يقال زعموا الدينار المحمَّى إذا غلب عليه ضياء النار وحرارتها وتلهُّبها صار الدينار ناراً ولا يقال صارت النار ديناراً.[١٦]

وزعمت هذه الفرق الثلث أنّ المسيح صُلب وقُتل، ثُمّ اختلفوا في
١٥. الصلب والقتل، بمَنْ وقعا على الحقيقة، ومَن المصلوب في الحقيقة. فزعمت النسطوريّة أنّ المسيح صُلب من جهة ناسوته لا من جهة لاهوته، وأنّ الصلب والقتل إنَّما وقعا على الإنسان المولود من مريم دون الإله، لأنّ الإله لا يناله قتل ولا صلب ولا ألَم. يعنون بقولهم «ناسوته» إنسانيته وبقولهم «لاهوته» إلاهيّته. يذهبون بإلاهيّته إلى الكلمة المتّحدة بإنسانه. وزعم كثير من الملكيّة أنّ

and two hypostases", though in this instance "nature" and "substance" are identical.

Some of the Melkites say that the Messiah was two substances and one hypostasis with two wills: an eternal substance, the Word, and a temporal substance, the universal human; an eternal hypostasis, the Word, and nothing more. They deny that he had a temporal hypostasis precisely because, according to them, the Word united with the universal human not a particular. They say: The universal human is not a hypostasis since it is not an individual. Hence they claim that the Messiah was one hypostasis. Many of them say: The Messiah was one hypostasis possessing two substances and two wills, having the same reason for saying that he was one hypostasis as those above, and employing the same argument.

The majority of the Jacobites claim that the Messiah was one substance from two substances and one hypostasis from two hypostases, meaning that the substance of the Word and the substance of the human taken from Mary became through the uniting one thing, one nature, one hypostasis and one will. For, they say, if the Messiah had been two hypostases or two substances then their number would not have been eliminated by the uniting. They compare this to a lump of coal which when placed in the fire becomes an ember. The ember, they say, is not fire alone and not a lump of coal alone, for it has become an ember, they claim, through the uniting of the fire with the lump of coal. They say that this particular human being became a Divinity, but do not say that the Divinity became a human being, just as the lump of coal can be said to have become fire by virtue of becoming an ember, but the fire cannot be said to have become a lump of coal. Likewise, they claim, if the brightness, heat, and flames of a fire take hold of a heated dinar then the dinar is said to become fire, but the fire is not said to become a dinar.[16]

15 The three sects claim that the Messiah was crucified and killed, but then they differ over the crucifixion and killing, concerning whom in reality these things affected and who in reality the crucified was. The Nestorians claim that the Messiah was crucified with respect to his human nature but not his divine nature, and that the crucifixion affected the human being born of Mary but not the Divinity, since the latter cannot be harmed by crucifixion, killing or suffering. By their expression "his human nature" they mean his humanity, and by "his divine nature" his divinity, the latter signifying the Word which united with the human in him.

Many of the Melkites claim that

الصلب والقتل وقعا على المسيح بكماله بذلك الجسد، والمسيح بكماله هو اللاهوت والناسوت. وكثير منهم يقولون: إنّ المسيح هو ذو الجوهرين اللذين أحدهما لاهوت والآخر ناسوت، لا كما قالت النسطوريّة أنّه إنَّما صُلب من جهة ناسوته. قالت الملكيّة: وإذا كان ناسوت المسيح ناسوتاً كليّاً ليس بأقنوم ولا شخص لم يجز عليه الإنفراد في صلب ولا في غيره، ولا القيام بنفسه مفرداً دون غيره. قالوا: وإذ كان الأمر كذلك فقد وجب أن يكون القتل والصلب إنَّما وقعا على المسيح بكماله. قالوا: ولو كان اللاهوت مفرداً من الناسوت غير متّحد به، لما جاز على اللاهوت قتل ولا صلب ولا نالته أيدي المخلوقين. وكثير منهم يزعم أنّ الصلب والقتل والألم كلّ ذلك إنَّما نال الإله، تعالى الإله، بالتدبير(١٧) لا بالحسّ والمباشرة. وزعم أكثر اليعقوبيّة أنّ الصلب والقتل وقعا بالمسيح الذي جوهر من جوهرين. قالوا: ولو كان الصلب والقتل إنَّما وقعا بأحد الجوهرين لكان قد بطل التأنّس وانتقض الاِتّحاد، ولكن الصلب والقتل إنَّما وقعا على ما ليس بمسيح، لأنّ كلّ واحد من الجوهرين على الإنفراد ليس بمسيح. ويقولون مع ذلك: صُلب الإله من أجلنا، أي ليخلّصنا.(١٨) وقولهم «صُلب الإله» على نحو قولهم «صار الإنسان إلهاً» لا يذهبون بذلك إلى تجويز وقوع الصلب والقتل باللاهوت لو كان مفرداً غير متّحد، ولكنّه إنَّما جاز ذلك عليه عندهم لاتّحاده بالناسوت. ولو كان غير متّحد به لم يجز عليه قتل ولا صلب ولا ألم.

فهذه جوامع أقاويل النسطوريّة والملكيّة ومَن أومأتُ إليه من اليعقوبيّة. وأنا مبتدىء في النقض عليهم إن شاء الله تعالى؛ وباللّه ذي الحول والقوّة استعين.(١٩)

٧. ب || ف: وإذا كان الأعم

the crucifixion and killing affected the Messiah in his entirety in the body, "the Messiah in his entirety" being the divine nature and the human nature. Many of them say that the Messiah possessed two substances one of which was the divine and the other the human nature, unlike the Nestorians who say that he was crucified with respect to his human nature. The Melkites say that since the human nature of the Messiah was the universal human nature and not a hypostasis or an individual, its isolation during the crucifixion or anything else was not possible, and neither was its resurrection in isolation and alone. They say: This being the case, the killing and crucifixion must have affected the Messiah in his entirety. They say: If the divine nature had been isolated from the human nature and not united with it, then death and resurrection would not have been possible for it and neither could human hands have harmed it. Many of them claim that the crucifixion, killing and suffering all harmed the Divinity, may he be exalted, by control[17] not by any physical constraints.

The majority of the Jacobites claim that the crucifixion and killing affected the Messiah who was one substance from two. They say: If the crucifixion and killing had only affected one of the substances then the incarnation would have been ruined, the uniting dissolved, and the crucifixion and killing would have affected one who was not Messiah, since each of the two substances alone was not the Messiah. Hence they say: The Divinity was crucified for us, that is, to save us.[18] Their expression "the Divinity was crucified" is like their expression "the human became divine": they do not mean to suggest by it that the crucifixion and killing could have affected the divine nature if it were isolated and not united. For in their view this could only happen to it because it united with the human nature; if it had not done so then the killing, crucifixion and suffering could not have happened to it.

These, then, are the main views of the Nestorians, the Melkites, and those Jacobites I have specified. I shall now begin my refutation of them, if God the exalted one wills. To God, Lord of power and strength, I appeal for help.[19]

(بسم الله الرحمن الرحيم وبالله استعين:

الجزء الثاني من تبيين يحيى بن عدي بن حُميد بن زكريّا غلط محمّد بن هرون المعروف بأبي عيسى الورّاق في الجزء الثاني من كتابه في الردّ على الثلث الفرق من النصارى، وهم اليعقوبيّة والنسطوريّة والملكيّة، وهو من أوّل الكلام في الاِتّحاد إلى آخر الكتاب.)

١٥١. الكلام عليهم في الاتّحاد وفي الولاد.[٢٠] يقال لهم[٢١] جميعًا:
أخبرونا عن اتّحاد الكلمة بالإنسان الذي اتّحدت به؛ أهو فعل
١٥٢. للكلمة دون الأب ودون الروح أم فعل للأقانيم الثلثة؟[٢٢] | فإن
زعموا أنّ الاتّحاد فعل للأقانيم الثلثة، قلنا: فلِم كان اتّحاداً للكلمة
١٥٣. دون الأب ودون الروح، | ولِم كانت الكلمة هي المتّحدة دونهما
وليس لها في فعل الاتّحاد ما ليس لهما؟

١٥٤. وإن زعموا أن الاتّحاد فعل للكلمة دون الأب ودون الروح،
أثبتوا للاِبن فعلاً غير فعل الأب وغير فعل الروح، وخصّوه بصُنع
صَنَعه لم يصنعه الأب والروح. وإذا جاز أن ينفرد واحد منها بفعل
دون باقيها، جاز ذلك في كلّ واحد من الأقنومَين الآخرَين؛ وإذا
جاز ذلك جاز أن ينفرد كلّ واحد منها بتدبير عالَم دون
صاحبَيه وبخلق بَريّة دون صاحبَيه. وهذا هو الخروج من قولهم.[٢٣]

٨. ب || ف: فعل الكلامة.
٩. ب || ف: فعل الأقانيم.
١٠. ب || ف: فعل الأقانيم الثلثة.
١٠. ب || ف: فلم كان الاتحاد للكلمة.
١٣. ب || ف: فعل الكلمة.

(In the name of God the Compassionate, the Merciful. To God I appeal for help.

The second part of Yaḥyā b. ʿAdī b. Ḥumayd Ibn Zakariyya's demonstration of the error of Muḥammad b. Hārūn, known as Abū ʿĪsā al-Warrāq, in the second part of his book on the refutation of the three Christian sects, the Jacobites, the Nestorians and the Melkites. It runs from the beginning of the argument about the uniting to the end of the book.)

151. THE ARGUMENT AGAINST THEM ABOUT THE UNITING AND THE BIRTH[20]

[The Trinity and the Uniting]

Say to them[21] all together: Tell us about the uniting of the Word with the human being with whom it united. Was this an action of the Word and not of the Father or the Spirit, or was it an action of the three hypostases?[22]

152 If they claim that the uniting was an action of the three hypostases, we say: Then why was it the uniting of the Word and not of the Father
153 or the Spirit? | And why was it the Word that united and not either of the others, although it had no part in the action of uniting that they did not have?

154 And if they claim that the uniting was an action of the Word and not of the Father or the Spirit, they acknowledge an action of the Son which is other than the action of the Father or the Spirit. And they single him out in carrying out an act which the Father and Spirit did not. But if it is possible for one of them to act alone without the others, this is possible for each of the other two hypostases. And if this is possible, it is possible for each of them alone to control a world without its two companions, and to create a creature without its two companions. This is a departure from their teachings.[23]

١٥٥ . على أنّه إذا كان جائزًا أن تنفرد الكلمة بفعل يكون اتّحادًا لها دون الأب ودون الروح، لم يكن منكرًا أن يبتدئ الأب اتّحادًا لنفسه قبلها فيكون هو المتّحد دونها؛ وكذلك الروح أن فعلت اتّحادًا لنفسها قبلهما كانت هي المتّحدة دونهما.

١٥٦ . فإن كرهوا هذا وقالوا: بل الاتّحاد فعل فعلته الأقانيم الثلثة اتّحادًا للابن وحده، قلنا: للابن في ذلك الفعل الذي هو الاتّحاد ما ليس للأب؛ فإن قالوا: لا، قلنا: فكيف كان اتّحادًا للابن دون الأب وما معنى قولكم «فعلته الأقانيم الثلثة اتّحادًا للابن دون الأب» إذ كان ليس للابن فيه ما ليس للأب؟ وكذلك القول في الروح. ولِم لا كان الأب هو المتّحد به دون الابن إذ ليس للابن فيه ما ليس للأب، أو لِم لا كانت الروح هي المتّحدة به دون الابن إذ لم يكن للابن في فعل الاتّحاد ما ليس للروح؟

١٥٧ . فإن اعترض معترض من الملكيّة فزعم أنّ الاتّحاد ليس فعلاً للأقانيم ولا لِواحد منها ولكنّه فعل للجوهر والجوهر غير الأقانيم،(٢٤) قلنا: فقد أخرجتَ الأب والابن والروح من ذلك الفعل، وإذا وجب ذلك في فعل واحد وجب في كلّ الأفعال ووجب أن يكون لا فعل للأقانيم ولا لواحد منها وإنّما يكون الفعل للجوهر. فالأب عندك على سياق هذا القول لا يخلق شيئًا ولا يصنع شيئًا، وكذلك الابن وكذلك الروح فرّقتَهم في اللفظ أم جمعتَهم. وكذلك الأب على هذا القياس لا يَقدر على شيء ولا يعلم شيئًا ولا هو إله ولا رب

٣. ب || ف: فيكون هذا المتحد.

155 Now if it is possible for the Word to act alone in uniting without the Father or the Spirit, it cannot be denied that the Father might have effected a uniting for himself before this, so that he was the one who united without the Word; and likewise the Spirit, if it had made a uniting for itself before either of them, it would be the one who united without
156 either of them. | But if they object to this and say: But the uniting was an action which the three hypostases performed as a uniting for the Son alone, we say: In this action of uniting the Son had what the Father did not have. And if they say: No, we say: Then how was it the uniting of the Son and not the Father, and what is the meaning of your statement, "The three hypostases performed it as a uniting for the Son and not the Father", if the Son had nothing in it that the Father did not have? The argument concerning the Spirit is the same. And why did not the Father unite rather than the Son, if the Son had nothing in it that the Father did not? Or why did not the Spirit unite rather than the Son, if the Son had nothing in the action of uniting that the Spirit did not have?

157 If a Melkite opponent objects and claims that the uniting was not an action of the hypostases or of one of them, but was an action of the substance, which is other than the hypostases,[24] we say: Then you have excluded the Father, Son and Spirit from this action. And if this must be so in one action it must be so in all actions, and there can be no action of the hypostases nor of any one of them, but only of the substance. So, according to you, on the basis of these words the Father creates nothing and performs nothing, and likewise the Son and the Spirit, whether you separate them in what you say or group them together. Similarly, according to this reasoning the Father has no power over anything, has no knowledge of anything, is not a Divinity, Lord,

ولا قـــديم، وكذلك الابن ولا الـروح جمعتَهـم في الوصـــف والتسـميّة أم فرّقتَهم في ذلك. وإنّما القــادر العــالم الإله القــديم الحـــيّ على أصـلِك هو الجـوهر، فمَن عَبَد واحـداً من هؤلاء الثلثـة أو الثلثـة جمعًا فقد عبد ما الإله غيره. وإنما قلنا «فقد عبد ما الإله غيره» ولم نَقُلْ «فقد عبد غير الإله» لأنّهم لا يسمحون بأن يكون الأقانيم غير الجوهر وإن كان الجوهر عندهم غير الأقانيم. فإذا كانوا كذلك فهم محْدَثون مربوبون لا يقدرون ولا يعلمون وليســوا بأحياء ولا ناطـقين. على أنّه متى زعـم أنّ الفعل للجوهر الذي هو غير الأقانيــم الثلثة لا للأقانيم ولا لواحد منها فقد نفى عن المســيح الفعـل لأنّ المسـيح عنده هو ليس الجوهر الذي هو غير الأقانيم بل هو عنـده واحــد من الأقانيم الثلثة[٢٥]. وإذا نفى المسيح الفعل وجب عليه أن ينفي عنه القدرة والعلم والحياة على ما أصَّل. وهذا خلاف نصرانيّتهم، بل نفيه عن المسيح الفعل وحده دون نفي العلم والقدرة خلاف نصرانيّتهم. وليس ذلك بمنجي صـاحب هذا المقالة من أن يزعم أنّه قد كان جائزًا أن يفعل الجوهر اتحادًا واحدًا يكون اتّحادًا للأب دون الابن ودون الروح وبـدلاً من اتّحـاد الابن، كمـا فعل في زعمـه اتّحــادًا واحـدًا كان اتّحــادًا للابن دون الأب ودون الـروح، وأنّه ليـس واحد من الأقانيم بأولى بجواز ذلك فيه من الأقنومَين الآخَرين. إذا سِيم ذلك ولا يمتنع منه بحجّة.

٧. ب || ف: وإذا كانوا.
١٩. ب || ف: ذلك منه من.

or eternal, and similarly the Son and the Spirit, whether you describe and identify them together or separately. According to your principle, the one who is powerful, knowing, Divinity, eternal and living is the substance alone, and whoever worships one of these three or the three together is worshipping one who the Divinity is not. We say, "He is worshipping one who the Divinity is not", and not "He is worshipping one who is other than the Divinity", only because they will not concede that the hypostases are other than the substance, even though in their view the substance is other than the hypostases. So, if they are like this they are temporal and subordinate, they have no power and do not know, they are not living or speaking. Hence, in claiming that the action is of the substance, which is other than the three hypostases, and not of the hypostases or one of them, he denies action to the Messiah, since for him the Messiah is not the substance, which is other than the hypostases, but for him is one of the three hypostases.[25] And if he denies action to the Messiah, he must deny him power, knowledge and life according to the principle he has set. And this is contrary to their Christianity, though his denial of action to the Messiah alone, apart from denying knowledge and power, is contrary to their Christianity.

And this does not release the one who takes this view from having to claim that the substance may have been able to effect a single uniting which would have been for the Father and not the Son or the Spirit and instead of the uniting of the Son, just as in his claim it performs a single uniting which is for the Son and not the Father or the Spirit, or that there is no particular one of the hypostases rather than the two others for which it is possible. If this is set forth, there is no argument to disallow it.

١٥٨ . ويقال لليعقوبيّة والنسطوريّة خصوصًا: إن جاز أن يفعل الأقانيم الثلثة اتّحادًا واحدًا يكون اتّحادًا للابن دون الأب ودون الروح، فلِم لا يجوز أن تفعل الأقانيم الثلثة اتّحادًا واحدًا يكون اتّحادًا للأب دون الابن ودون الروح فيكون الأب متّحدًا بإنسان كما كان الابن متّحدًا بإنسان؟ فإن أبوا ذلك سُئلوا الفرق، ولا فرق لهم ما تمسّكوا بقولهم وأجروا علّتهم.

١٥٩ . وإن سوّوا بينهما وأجازوا ذلك ولزموا القياس، قيل لهم: أفليس لو فعلت الأقانيم ذلك بالأب لَكان يكون للناس مسيح آخر، وكذلك لو فعلته بالروح كان لها مسيح ثالث، فيكون أحد المسحاء في قولكم هذا ابنًا لمعبودكم ويكون المسيح الآخر أبًا لمعبودكم ويكون المسيح الثالث روحًا له، ويكون أحد المسحاء ابنًا للآخر وأحدهم أبًا للمسيح الذي هو إبنه فيكون مسيح بن مسيح ومسيح أبا مسيح؟ وهذا خلاف قولهم ومنكر عندهم ولا بدّ منه ما تمسّكوا بأصلِهم.

ويقال لهم: إن كان هذا جائزًا فما يدريكم لعلّ الأب قد اتّحد فيما تقدّم من الزمان بإنسان أو سوف يتّحد به فيما يستقبل؟

فإن زعموا أنّهم لا يدرون لعلّ ذلك كذلك، فارقوا قولهم لأنّ المعروف من قولهم كراهة ذلك والامتناع منه. وإن ادّعوا أن ذلك لم يكن ولا يكون، سُئلوا الحجّة ولا حجّة عندهم

٢١ . ب || ف: لم يكن ولا يكن.

158 And say especially to the Jacobites and Nestorians: If the three hypostases were able to perform one uniting which was a uniting for the Son without the Father or the Spirit, why could not the three hypostases have performed a single uniting which would be for the Father and not the Son or the Spirit, so that the Father would be united with a human just like the Son? If they reject this, they should be asked what is the difference, though there is no difference between these as long as they hold onto their teaching and insist upon their reasons.

159 But if they regard both of these as the same, allow that this may have been possible and concede the comparison, say to them: If the hypostases had performed this for the Father, would there not have been another Messiah for the people? And similarly if they had done it for the Spirit, would there not have been a third Messiah for them? Then, in this teaching of yours, would not one of the Messiahs have been son of the being you worship, another father of the being you worship, and the third spirit to him? And would not one of the Messiahs have been son of the other, and one of them father to the Messiah who was his son, so there would have been Messiah son of Messiah and Messiah father of Messiah? This is contrary to their teaching and denied among them, though it is unavoidable as long as they hold onto their principles.

Say to them: If this is possible, then how can you know whether the Father may not have united with a human in time past, or will not unite with one in time to come? If they claim that they do not know whether this might happen, they separate themselves from their teaching, because their accepted teaching condemns this and rejects it. And if they maintain that this has never been and will not be, they should be asked for the proof; though they have no proof

فيه لأنّ ذلك لا يعلم على أصولهم إلاّ بخَبَر وليس لهم في هذا خبر أنّه لم يكن ولا يكون. ومتى ادّعى مدّعٍ منهم في ذلك خبرًا جاز لمخالفيهم أن يُعارضوهم بالأخبار التي تنفي كون الإتّحاد كلّه وكلّ ما اتّصل به.[٢٦] وهذا ما لا يجدون إلى دفعه سبيلاً.

١٦٠. فأمّا الملكيّة فإن سُئلوا عن ذلك فقيل لهم: ما تنكرون أن تفعل الأقانيم أو يفعل الجوهر اتّحاداً للأب كما فعلت أو فعل اتّحادًا للابن؟ فلعلّهم أن سيقولوا: إذا كان الابن متّحدًا بالإنسان الكلّي وليس بعد الإنسان الكلّي إنسانيّة، فبأيّ شيء يتّحد الأب؟[٢٧] قيل لهم: إن شئتم اتّحد بالإنسان الكلّي في حال ما الابن متّحد به، وإن شئتم اتّحد به في زمان آخر دون الابن كما كان الابن متحدًا به في بعض الأزمان دون الأب، وإن شئتم اتّحد الأب بإنسان جزئي، وإن شئتم كان الأب متّحدًا بالكلّي وكان الاِبن متّحدًا بالجزئي، وإن شئتم اتّحدا جميعًا بإنسانين جزئيّين؛ إذ ليس يمكنكم أن تدفعوا شيئًا من هذه الأقسام من طريق الإحالة وألا تُخرجوا شيئًا منها من القدرة،[٢٨] وإذ لم يكن ممتنعًا في القدرة أن يتّحد أحدهما ثم يَخرج من ذلك الاتِّحاد ويبطل ذلك الفعل ويتّحد الآخر. وأنتم وإن اِدّعيتم أنّ الاتِّحاد لا يُبطل أبدًا ولا ينتقض فليس يمكنكم أن تخرجوا نقضه من قدرة الإله الذي فعله، وإنّما تعوّلون في أدّعائكم أنّه لا يبطل ولا ينتقض

١٦. ب || ف: ولا تخرجوا.

for it, because in their principles this is not known except by report, and they have nothing in the report that it has never been and will not be. And should anyone among them maintain that there is a report on this, their opponents could respond to them with reports that deny the uniting entirely and everything connected with it.[26] And this is something that they will not find a way of rejecting.

160 As for the Melkites, if they are asked about this and we say to them: Why do you deny that the hypostases or the substance performed a uniting for the Father in the same way that they or it performed a uniting for the Son? maybe they will then say: If the Son united with the universal human and there is no humanity apart from the universal human, then to what could the Father have united?[27] Say to them: If you wish, he could have united with the universal human at the moment when the Son united with it. Or if you wish, he could have united with it at another time without the Son, just as the Son united with it at one time without the Father. Or if you wish, the Father could have united with an individual human. Or if you wish, the Father could have united with the universal and the Son with the individual. Or if you wish, they could both have united with individual humans. You cannot reject any of these alternatives as impossible without excluding one of them from power,[28] for in respect of power there is no reason why one of the two could not have united, and then have left this uniting and cancelled this action, and for the other to have united. And although you maintain that the uniting was never cancelled or destroyed, you cannot exclude its being destroyed from the power of the Divinity who performed it. So you can only really say in your claims that it has not been cancelled or destroyed

على قول بعض أسلافكم أو على ظنّ قَدَّرتموه في أنفسكم. وأذا لم يمتنع ذلك ولم يخرج من القدرة توجّه عليهم أكثر ما ألزمناه اليعقوبيّة والنسطوريّة في هذا الباب؛ والسؤال على الملكيّة في اِتّحاد الروح كالسؤال في اِتّحاد الأب. وبعد فلو تجافينا لهم عن هذا وسوّغناهم الاِمتناع من اِطلاقه في المستقبل لِما تهيّأ لهم أن يقولوا بحجّة: «لم يكن جائزًا في الأب أو في الروح قبل اِتّحاد الاِبن أو بَدَلاً من اِتّحاد الاِبن» فإن تجاسر منهم متجاسر على منع ذلك في الأب أو في الروح قبل اتّحاد الاِبن أو بَدَلاً من اتّحاد الاِبن، عُورض بِامتناعه في الاِبن كما امتنع في الأب وفي الروح. وإذا امتنع في الأب والروح امتنع في غيره لاستواء القضية وإذا امتنع في الاِبن امتناعه في غيره لاستوا القضية بطل الاتّحاد كلّه ولم يجدوا إلى تثبيته سبيلاً.

١٦١. ويقال لليعقوبيّة والنسطوريّة: متى اتّحدت الكلمة بالإنسان المأخوذ من مريم[٢٩]، أقبل الولاد أم بعد الولاد أم في حال الولاد؟

١٦٢. فإن قالوا: قبل الولاد، قلنا: قبل الولاد وقبل الحَمْل أو قبل الولاد وذلك المولود حَمْل؟

١٦٣. فإن قالوا: قبل الولاد وقبل الحمل، وزعموا أنّه قد اتّحد به قبل أن يكون إنسانًا سويًّا، وقبل أن يُصَوّر ويُؤَلّف، وإذا كان ذلك كذلك فسد قولهم «اتّحد القديم بإنسان تامّ» لأنّه لم يكن تامًّا إذ ذاك؛ وفسد قولهم «اتّحد

٢–٣. ب || ف: الزمناه لليعقوبيّة.
٣. ب || ف: وفي هذا الباب.
٤. ب || ف: فلو تحامينا.
٥. ب || ف: الامتناع في اطلاقه.
٩. ب: هامش || ف: كما امتنع في الاب. وفي الروح واذا امتنع في الابن (ل *pace*).
١٠. ب: لاستواء القصة

according to a teaching of one of your predecessors or a supposition that you have made yourselves. And if this is not ruled out and not excluded from power, they are faced with more than we have forced upon the Jacobites and Nestorians in this section. The question to the Melkites about the uniting of the Spirit is like the question about the uniting of the Father.

Further, if we were to pass over this and grant them that it cannot be severed in the future, they have no way of saying with any proof: "It was not possible for the Father or the Spirit before the uniting of the Son or in place of the uniting of the Son." And if any foolhardy person among them is presumptuous enough to deny it for the Father or the Spirit before the uniting of the Son or in place of the uniting of the Son, reply to him that it was impossible for the Son, just as he says it was impossible for the Father and the Spirit. And if it was impossible for the Father and the Spirit, it was impossible for others because the proposition is the same; and if it was impossible for the Son since it was impossible for others because the proposition is the same, then the whole uniting is cancelled, and they will not find any means of affirming it.

161 [The uniting and the human experiences of the Messiah

1. *Against the Nestorians and Jacobites*

i. *The conception and birth*]

And say to the Jacobites and Nestorians: When did the Word unite with the human taken from Mary,[29] before the birth, after it, or at the moment
162 of the birth? | If they say: Before the birth, we say: Before the birth and before the pregnancy, or before the birth when what was born was still a
163 foetus? | If they say: Before the birth and before the pregnancy, and claim that it united with him before he was a full human and before he was shaped and put together; if this is so, their teaching that the eternal united with a complete human is false, because he was not complete at the time. And their teaching that it united with an individual human is false,

بإنسان جزئي » لأنّ الإنسان الجزئي إنّما كان إنسانًا جزئيًا لمّا صار مصورًّا بشريًا.

١٦٤. وهذا الموضع على النسطوريّة أشدّ منه على الصنف الآخر، وذاك أنّه يلزمُهم أن يزعموا أنّ اللاهوت قد كان حملاً مع الناسوت تسْعَة أشهر أو نحوها من مُدَد الحمل مُقيمًا معه في الموضع الذي يُحمل فيه الجَنين ثمّ وُلدا جميعًا، وهو خلاف قولهم إنّ المسيح وُلد من جهة ناسوته لا من جهة لاهوته.[٣٠]

١٦٥. وهذا أيضًا ينقض قول مَن زعم أنّ الاتّحاد هو الاِختلاط والاِمتزاج[٣١] لأن الاِتّحاد على هذه المقالة قد وقع قبل تمام الصورة وقبل البشريّة. فكيف يكون اِختلاطًا أو اِمتزاجًا بالإنسان المولود والإنسان المولود لَمّا يكن إذ ذاك؟ وينقض أيضًا قول مَن زعم أنّ الكلمة اتخذته هيكلاً ومحلاً، وقول مَن قال إنّ الكلمة ادّرعته اِدّراعًا، وقول مَن قال: اِتّحادها به هو أن حلّت فيه فدبّرت به وعلى يديه، وقول مَن قال: ظهرت منه لهذا الخلق لا على الحلول ولا على المخالطة، وقول مَن قال: ظهرت فيه كما يظهر نقش الخاتم في الطينة المطبوعة، وقول مَن قال: ظهرت في ذلك الجسد كما يظهر صورة الإنسان في المرآة النقيّة؛ لأنّ هذا كلّه لا يُتوهّم وقوعه ولا وقوع شيء منه قبل الحمل بالإنسان وقبل تمام صورته.

٥. ب || ف: الحبل.
١١. ب: (نص) || ب (هامش): لم؛ ف: لما لم يكن؛ ل: لم يكن.
١٢–١٣. ب || ف: من قال ادرعته.

because the individual human is an individual human only when it becomes formed as a man.

164 This matter is more difficult for the Nestorians than for the other group. This is because it forces them to claim that the divine nature was a foetus together with the human nature for nine months or so through the period of pregnancy, remaining with it in the place in which the embryo is carried, and that then they were born together. And it is contrary to their teaching that the Messiah was born with respect to his human nature but not with respect to his divine nature.[30]

165 This also invalidates the teaching of the one who claims that the uniting was a mingling and mixing,[31] because according to this view the uniting took place before the complete shaping and before he was man. For how could it be a mingling or mixing with the human who was born, when the human who was born did not yet exist at this point? It also invalidates the teaching of the one who claims that the Word took him as a habitation and location; of the one who says that the Word put him on as a garment; of the one who says that its uniting with him was that it dwelt within him and controlled its affairs through him and by means of him; of the one who says: It appeared through him to humankind neither through indwelling nor through mingling; of the one who says: It appeared in him like the imprint of a seal appears in impressed clay; and of the one who says: It appeared in this body as the shape of a person appears in a polished mirror. This is because the occurrence of any of these, and the occurrence of anything to do with them, cannot be imagined before the human was conceived or before its form was complete.

١٦٦ . ويلزم اليعقوبيّة فيه أيضًا أن يزعموا أنّه كان جوهرًا من جوهرين قبل الحمل وفي حال الحمل وفي حال الولاد وأنّ مريم لم تلد إنسانًا على الحقيقة ولا إلهًا على الحقيقة، لأنّها إن كانت ولدت إنسانًا فتمّ جوهر الإنسان وأقنومه وإن كانت ولدت إلهًا فتمّ جوهر الإله وأقنومه. وهذا ينقض قولهم: المسيح جوهر واحد أقنوم واحد. وبعض ما يقولونه في جواب هذه المسئلة يُفسد بعضًا.

١٦٧ . وإن قالوا: اتّحد به وهو حمل صورة تامّة، قلنا لهم: فقد كان اللاهوت إذن حملاً قبل الولاد وإذا جاز أن يُحمل جاز أن يُولد، ولا يتهيّأ على أصولهم فرق بين أن يُولد وأن يُربّى ويُغذّى ويأكل ويشرب. ويلزمهم في هذا أيضًا أكثر ممّا لزمهم إن زعموا أنّ الاِتّحاد به كان قبل الحمل.

١٦٨ . وإن قالوا إنّ الاِتّحاد في حال الولاد، قلنا: كان في حال الولاد على أنّ الولاد اشتمل على الكلمة أو إنّما حصل الولاد للإنسان وحده؟ فإن كان الولاد لم يحصل إلّا للإنسان وحده والإنسان ليس بمسيح عندكم كان هذا نقضًا لقولكم «مريم ولدت المسيح». وإبطالاً لما في الكتب التي زعمتم أنّها أخبرت أنّ إمرأة تلد إلاهًا.[٣٢]

١٦٩ . وإن كان الاِتّحاد قد اِشتمل على الكلمة فقد ولدت مريم الكلمة إذًا ولادًا صحيحًا، والكلمة عندكم إله، فالإله إذًا قد ولدته مريم. فإن قالوا: نعم، على ما أعطوا، قلنا: فإذا جاز

٩. ب || ف: ويغتذي.
١٠. ب || ف: ألزمهم.
١٢. ب || ف: (هامش): إن كان الاِتّحاد.
١٩. ب || ف: عندكم إلها.

166 On this as well the Jacobites are forced to claim that he was one substance from two before the pregnancy, during the pregnancy and during the birth, and that Mary did not give birth to a human in reality or to a Divinity in reality, because if she had given birth to a human then the substance and the hypostasis of a human would have resulted, and if she had given birth to a Divinity the substance and hypostasis of a Divinity would have resulted. And this invalidates their teaching that the Messiah was one substance and one hypostasis. One part of what they say in reply to this question falsifies another.

167 And if they say: It united with him when he was a completely formed foetus, we say to them: So the divine nature was a foetus before the birth, and if it could be carried then it could be born. But according to your principles there is no actual distinction between being born and being brought up and nourished, eating and drinking. In this also they are forced to acknowledge more than if they claim that the uniting with him was before the pregnancy.

168 And if they claim that the uniting was at the moment of the birth, we say: It may have been at the moment of the birth, though did the birth include the Word or did the birth only happen to the human alone? For if the birth only happened to the human alone, and the human was not the Messiah in your view, this invalidates your teaching that Mary gave birth to the Messiah. And it nullifies what is in the books which you claim report that a woman will give birth to a Divinity.[32]

169 And if the uniting included the Word, then Mary gave birth to the Word as a true birth. In your view the Word is a Divinity, and so Mary actually gave birth to the Divinity. If they say: Yes, according to what they have received, we say: Then if he could

أن يُولد فلِم لا يجوز أن يكون حملاً؟ فإن أجازوا ذلك لم يمكنهم أن يفرقوا على أصولهم بين أن يكون حملاً وبين أن يُربّى ويُغذّى ويأكل ويشرب. فإن أجازوا ذلك أيضًا لم يمكنهم أن يجعلوا بين الإله والإنسان فرقًا. وإن لم يجيزوه، قلنا: وما الفرق على أصولكم بين أن يُولد وبين أن يُربّى ويُغذّى ويأكل ويشرب؟

١٧٠. وإن قالوا: لم يكن الاِتّحاد قبل الولاد ولا في حاله وإنّما كان بعد الولاد، قلنا: فإنّما صار المسيح مسيحًا بعد الولاد، وهذا أيضًا نقضًا لقولكم أنّ مريم ولدت المسيح لأن المسيح عندكم ليس هو الإنسان وحده، وإبطال لما في الكتب التي زعمتم أنّها أخبرت أنّ إمرأة تلد إلهًا. فإن كانت هذه المرأة قد ولدت إلاهًا فقد كان الاِتّحاد قبل الولاد.

١٧١. ولا بُدّ لنسطوريّتهم إذا زعموا أنّ المسيح جوهران جوهر قديم وجوهر مُحدَث، ثم زعموا أنّ مريم ولدت المسيح، من أن يزعموا أنّ مريم قد ولدت هذين الجوهرين اللذين هُما عندهم المسيح. وإذا ولدتهما وأحدهما عندهم إله فقد ولدت إلاهًا قديمًا، ولا يجوز أن تلد أيضًا إلاّ ما كان محمولاً فهذا يوجب أنّها قد كانت حاملةً لذلك الإله. وكذلك إذا زعموا أنّ المسيح صُلب وقُتل ودُفن لزمهم أن يزعموا أنّ ذلك كلّه وقع بالجوهرين اللذين هما عندهم المسيح، لأنّه متى وقع شيء من ذلك بأحد الجوهرين

١٤. ب || ف: مريم قد ولدت المسيح.
١٥. ب || ف: مريم ولدت هذين.

be born, why could he not be a foetus? And if they allow this, then according to their principles they will not be able to distinguish between being a foetus and being brought up and nourished, eating and drinking. And if they allow this also, they will not be able to make any distinction between the Divinity and the human. And if they do not allow it, we say: Then according to your principles what is the distinction between being born and being brought up and nourished, eating and drinking?

170 If they say: The uniting was not before the birth or when it happened, but was actually after the birth, we say: So the Messiah became Messiah only after the birth. And this too is an invalidation of your teaching that Mary gave birth to the Messiah, because according to you the Messiah was not the human alone. And it nullifies what is in the books which you claim report that a woman will give birth to a Divinity. And if this woman did bear a Divinity, the uniting took place before the birth.

171 And the Nestorians among them, since they claim that the Messiah was two substances, eternal and temporal, and then claim that Mary gave birth to the Messiah, cannot avoid claiming that Mary gave birth to these two substances which in their view were the Messiah. And if she gave birth to them, and in their view one of them was a Divinity, then she gave birth to an eternal Divinity. And of course, she could only have given birth to what was carried, which means that she must have carried this Divinity. Likewise, if they claim that the Messiah was crucified, killed and buried, they must claim that all this happened to the two substances which, according to them, were the Messiah. For if any of this happened to either of the two substances,

وأحد الجوهرين ليس بمسيح على الإنفراد فإنّما صُلب وقُتل ودُفن ما ليس بمسيح.

١٧٢. وكذلك يلزم مَن زعم من الملكيّة أنّ المسيح جوهران جوهر قديم وجوهر مُحدث. فأمّا الذين زعموا منهم أنّه أقنوم قديم ذو جوهرين فذلك عليهم أغلط وأشدّ لأنّه لا بُدّ لهم إذا زعموا أنّ المسيح أقنوم قديم لاهوتي وزعموا أنّ مريم ولدت المسيح على الحقيقة وِلادًا صحيحًا من أن يزعموا أنّ المولود من مريم هو الأقنوم اللاهوتي. ولا تلد المرأة إلاّ ما كان حملاً؛ فالأقنوم اللاهوتي هو المحمول، وكذلك هو المصلوب وهو المقتول وهو المدفون إلاّ ألاّ يكون لما يذكرون من الولاد والصلب والقتل والدفن حقيقة ولا صِحّة، أو يكون الذي وقع به ذلك كلّه غير المسيح. فهذا خلاف دينهم.

١٧٣. ولا بُدّ ليعقوبيّتهم إذا زعموا أنّ المسيح جوهر من جوهرين أحدهما قديم والآخر مُحدَث من أن يزعموا أنّ مريم لم تلدْ إلهًا قديمًا ولا إنسانًا لأن الإله القديم عندهم ليس جوهرًا من جوهرين والإنسان ليس جوهرًا من جوهرين أحدهما قديم والآخر مُحدَث. وهذا كلّه إختلاط من قائليه وتهويس لقابليه.

١٧٤. ويقال لليعقوبيّة والنسطوريّة أيضًا متى زعموا أنّ الاتّحاد كان قبل الولاد وفي حال الحمل: أخبرونا عن اللاهوت، أكان يزيد بزيادة

١١. ب || ف: إلا أن لا.

and either of the two substances alone was not the Messiah, then the one who was crucified, killed and buried would not actually have been the Messiah.

172 It is decisive against the particular Melkite who claims that the Messiah was two substances, eternal and temporal. And as for those of them who claim that he was an eternal hypostasis which possessed two substances, this leads to more serious error for them, because if they claim that the Messiah was an eternal divine hypostasis, and that Mary gave birth to the Messiah in reality in a true birth, they cannot avoid claiming that the one born of Mary was the divine hypostasis. And a woman gives birth only to what has been a foetus; so the divine hypostasis was carried, and was likewise crucified, killed and buried, unless there is no validity or truth in what they say about the birth, crucifixion, death and burial; or else the one to whom all this happened was not the Messiah. But this is contrary to their religion.

173 And the Jacobites among them, if they claim that the Messiah was a substance from two substances, one eternal and the other temporal, cannot avoid claiming that Mary did not give birth to either an eternal Divinity or a human, because according to them the eternal Divinity is not a substance from two substances, and the human is not a substance from two substances, one of them eternal and the other temporal. All this is jumbling on the part of those who say it, and confusion for those who accept it.

174 And say to the Jacobites and Nestorians as well, since they claim that the uniting existed before the birth and during the pregnancy: Tell us about the divine nature, did it grow with the growth

أجزاء المحمول في البطن وينموا مع نموّ أعضائه، أم لم يكن اللاهوت ينموا ولا يزيد؟ فإن لم يكن ينموا ولا يزيد فالاتّحاد إذن إنّما وقع ببعض أعضاء الإنسان وبعض أجزائه دون بعض، وأكثره ليس متّحدًا به وإنّما اتّحد منه إذن بأقلّ من عشره في حال بلوغه. فبعضه على هذا القول مسيح وأكثره ليس بمسيح.

١٧٥. وإن زعموا أنّ اللاهوت كان يزيد مع زيادة أجزائه وينموا مع نموّ أعضائه أوقعوا على اللاهوت الزيادة والنقصان وجعلوا الاتّحاد متجدّدًا وقتًا فوقتًا. وهذا يوجب عليهم أن يزعموا أنّه لم يستكمل الاتّحاد إلى أن تناهت زيادة أجزائه، وينبغي إن كانت أجزائه نقصت بعلّة أو بضعف أو بخفّة بَدَن أن يكون اتّحاده منتقصًا على قدر ذلك.

١٧٦. ويقال لهم: ما تقولون في حال الصلب وحال القتل وحال الدفن، أكانت الكلمة في تلك الأوحال متّحدة به أم كان الاتّحاد قد انتقض وبَطل؟ فإن كان الاتّحاد قد انتقض وبطل فليس هو إذًا في تلك الأحوال مسيحًا، وينبغي على هذا القول أن يكون الاتّحاد عاوده بعد قيامه من القبر أو يكون حَدَث بعد قيامه من القبر اتّحادًا ثانٍ متجدّد. ويلزمكم معه أن تزعموا أنّ المسيح قد كان في وسط من أمره لا مسيحًا ولا إلاهًا ولا ابنًا لله. ويلزمكم أيضًا على هذا القول أن تزعموا أنّ الذين قتلوه نقضوا اتّحاده وأن الخلق نقضوا اتّحاد الخالق.

٧. ف || ب: والنقضان.
٩. ب، ف || ل: زيادة الاجزائه.
١٢. ب || ف: تقولون فيه في.
١٧. ب || ف: ويلزمهم معه أن يزعموا.
١٨. ب || ف: ويلزمهم.
١٩. ب || ف: يزعموا.

of the parts of what was being carried in the womb, and did it increase with the increase of its limbs? Or did the divine nature not grow and increase? And if it did not increase and grow, then the uniting only involved some of the limbs and parts of the human and not others, and the majority of him was not united with it, and so it was united only with less than a tenth of him in his maturity. According to this teaching, some of him was Messiah but most of him was not.

175 And if they claim that the divine nature did grow with the growth of his parts, and increase with the increase of his limbs, they impose increase and decrease upon the divine nature, and they make the uniting something renewed from time to time. This compels them to claim that the uniting was not completed until his parts had finished growing. And if his parts decreased through sickness or weakness or because his body grew slighter, then its uniting with him would necessarily have decreased accordingly.

176 [ii. *The crucifixion and death*]

Say to them: What do you say about the moment of crucifixion, the moment of killing and the moment of burial? Was the Word united with him at these moments, or had the uniting been destroyed and obliterated? If the uniting was destroyed and obliterated, then at these moments he was not Messiah, and according to this teaching the uniting must necessarily have returned to him after his resurrection from the tomb, unless it began after his resurrection from the tomb as a second renewed uniting. In addition to this, you have to claim that in the middle of his existence the Messiah was not Messiah, or Divinity, or Son of God. Further, according to this teaching you must claim that those who killed him destroyed his uniting, and that creatures destroyed the uniting of the Creator.

١٧٧. وإن زعموا أنّه كان في أحوال القتل والصلب والدفن مسيحًا وكان الاتّحاد في تلك الأحوال ثابتًا، قلنا: أفكان حيًّا في تلك الحال، حال القتل وحال الدفن، أم كان ميتًا؟ فإن زعموا أنّه كان فيها حيًّا كابروا العِيان وأثبتوه مقتولاً حيًّا ومدفونًا حيًّا ناطقًا إلاهًا مُدبّرًا. وهذا على النسطوريّة أغلظ منه على اليعقوبيّة.[٣٣]

١٧٨. وإن زعموا أنّه كان في تَينك الحالين ميتًا لا حيًّا، قيل لهم: فقد أوقعتم الموت على المسيح بكماله إذ كان الموت لم ينقض اتّحاده فأدخلتم اللاهوت مع الناسوت في الموت والقتل والصلب[٣٤] والدفن. فإن كَرَه ذلك منهم كارِه ورجع إلى أن يقول: لم يقع شيء من ذلك إلا على الإنسان المتّحد به دون اللاهوت، قلنا: والإنسان وحده ليس بمسيح عندكم، فإنّما صُلب وقُتل ودُفن ما ليس بمسيح. وفي هذا الكلام أيضًا ما يوجب انتقاض الاتّحاد ويردّكم إلى الشيء الذّي منه هربتم.

١٧٩. ويقال للنسطوريّة: أرأيتم، إن كان الاتّحاد لم يُنتقض ولم يبطل في حال الموت، أفليس الكلمة عندكم في تلك الحال متّحدة بإنسان ميت لا حيّ فالإله عندكم متّحد بالمَوتى؟

١٨٠. وبعد، فلا يخلو المسيح في تلك الحال من أن يكون إلاهًا أو ليس بإله؛ فإن زعموا أنّه في تلك الحال ليس بإله كفروا بإلاهيّته، وأقلّ ذلك أن يزعموا أنّ إلاهيّته قد بطلت عنه بالموت. وإن زعموا أنّه في تلك الحال إله أثبتوا إلاهًا ميّتًا.

٣. ب || ف: أم ميّتًا.

177 If they claim that he was Messiah at the moments of killing, crucifixion and burial, and that the uniting remained constant at these moments, we say: Was he living at this moment, the moment of killing and the moment of burial, or was he dead? If they claim that he was living during them, they ignore the obvious and attest that he was killed living and buried living, speaking, divine and controlling. This is more embarrassing for the Nestorians than for the Jacobites.[33]

178 If they claim that in these two moments he was dead and not living, say to them: Then you have imposed death upon the whole of the Messiah since death did not destroy uniting in him, and you have implicated the divine nature with the human nature in death, killing, crucifixion[34] and burying. If any of them finds this objectionable and goes back to saying: All of this happened only to the human who was united with, and not the divine nature, we say: But the human alone was not the Messiah in your view. So then the one who was crucified, killed and buried was not the Messiah. In this argument also is what causes the collapse of the uniting, and brings you back to the thing from which you have fled.

179 And say to the Nestorians: What is your view? If the uniting was not destroyed or obliterated at the moment of death, then according to you was not the Word united with a man who was deceased and not living, so that in your view the Divinity was united with the deceased?

180 Furthermore, at this moment the Messiah must have been either divine or not divine. If they claim that he was not divine at this moment they disbelieve in his divinity, let alone claiming that divinity was obliterated by death. And if they claim that he was divine at this moment, they acknowledge that the Divinity was deceased.

١٨١. ويلزمهم على هذا القول أيضًا أن يزعموا أنّ المسيح مرّةً إله وإنسان حيّ ومرّةً إله وإنسان ميت.

١٨٢. وقد زعمت هذه الفرق الثلث أنّ المسيح مات. فيقال لهم جميعًا: إن كان المسيح مات فمَن أحياه بعد الموت؟ فإن قالوا: هو أحيا نفسه، قيل لهم: فالمَوتى إذن يُحيون أنفسهم، وكيف يُحيي نفسه مَن لا تدبير له ولا عِلم ولا قدرة؟

١٨٣. وإن قالوا: أحياه غيره، فقد أقرّوا بأن غير المسيح يُحيي الموتى وثبت أنّه هو لا يُحيي الموتى. فيجب على أصلهم حينئذٍ أن يكون المسيح ليس بإله وأن يكون غيره هو الإله.

١٨٤. وإن زعموا أو زعم منهم زاعم أنّ لاهوته أحيا ناسوته، قلنا: سألناكم عن المسيح الميت في زعمكم، مَن أحياه؟ ولم نسألكم عن الناسوت، من أحياه؟ لأن الناسوت وحده عندكم ليس بمسيح. فدعوا ما لم تُسئَلوا عنه وأجيبوا عمّا سُئلتم عنه.

١٨٥. ويقال لهم: إذا كان اللاهوت وحده عندكم ليس بمسيح والناسوت وحده عندكم أيضًا ليس بمسيح فإنّما قلتم: مَن ليس بمسيح أحيا مَن ليس بمسيح. ونحن إنّما سألناكم عن الميت الذّي هو عندكم مسيح فأجبتمونا عن ميت ليس بمسيح، وهذا ظلم في الكلام.

١٨٦. ويقال للملكيّة واليعقوبيّة: زعمتم أنّ الإله مات من أجلكم؛

١٠. ب || ف: زعم زاعم منهم.

181 According to this teaching they are also forced to claim that the Messiah was at one time Divinity and human living, and at another time Divinity and human deceased.

182 These three groups claim that the Messiah died. So say to them all: If the Messiah died, then who revived him after death? If they say: He revived himself, say to them: So the deceased revive themselves. But how can someone with no control, knowledge or power revive himself?

183 If they say: Another revived him, they attest that some other than the Messiah revives the deceased, which is to acknowledge that it is not he who revives the deceased. But according to their principles it then follows that the Messiah was not divine and that the Divinity was another than him.

184 And if they or one of them claim that his divine nature revived his human nature, we say: We have asked you about the deceased Messiah in your claim, who revived him? We have not asked you about the human nature, who revived him? For the human nature alone, as you say, was not the Messiah. Leave aside what you have not been asked, and answer what you have been asked.

185 Say to them: If the divine nature alone, in your view, was not the Messiah, and the human nature alone, in your view, was likewise not the Messiah, then you are effectively saying that one who was not the Messiah revived one who was not the Messiah. We asked you only about the deceased one who, as you see it, was the Messiah, but you have answered us about a deceased one who was not the Messiah. This is unfair arguing.

186 Say to the Melkites and the Jacobites: You claim that the Divinity died for your sakes.

أفهو إلى الساعة ميت أو قد حيّ؟ فإن قالوا: ميت، قيل لهم: فمتى يكون حشر هذا أو نشره؟ على أنّه إذا كان ميتًا فلا تدبير له ولا علم ولا قدرة. وإن قالوا: قد حيّ، قلنا: فمَن أحياه؟ فإن قالوا: هو أحيا نفسه، قلنا: فالمَوتى إذن يُحيون أنفسهم. وهذا كالذي قبله. وكيف يُحيي الميت نفسه والميت لا علم له ولا قدرة؟ وإن قالوا: أحياه غيره؛ قلنا: فالذي أحياه إله أم ليس بإله؟ فإن قالوا: إله، أثبتوا إلاهًا ثانيًا غير الميت أقدر على إحياء الموتى من الإله الذي زعموا أنّه مات، فهو حينئذٍ أولى بالعبادة مِن الذي مات، إن يكلّموا على أصولهم وعلى حقائق دينهم. ويلزمهم في ذلك أيضًا أن يزعموا أنّ لهم إلهَين أحدهما حيّ والآخر ميت. ولا بدّ مع ذلك من أن يكونوا يعبدونهما أو يعبدون أحدهما دون الآخر، فإن عبدوهما جميعًا فقد عبدوا الحيّ والميت. وإن عبدوا الحيّ وحده وأنكروا عبادة الميت منهما وأبوها كانوا قد أنكروا عبادة إلاههم وأمتنعوا منها، ولا سيّما لما مات من أجلهم واحتمل المكروه ليُخلّصهم بزعمهم. فعند ذلك تركوا عبادته وأنكروها وقد كانوا يعبدونه قبل احتماله الموت في جَنب خلاصهم ونفعهم. ويقال لهم: أخبرونا عنه، أيستحقّ العبادة وهو ميت أم لا يستحقّها؟ فإن قالوا: يستحقّها، فقد زعموا أنّ الميت يستحقّ العبادة وألزموا أنفسهم عبادة ميت إذ كان مستحقًّا

١٩. ب || ف: أم لم.

Is he still dead or has he revived? If they say: Dead, say to them: When will his resurrection take place? But of course, if he is deceased he has no control, knowledge or power. And if they say: He has revived, we say: Who revived him? And if they say: He revived himself, we say: Then the deceased can revive themselves; and this is like the one preceding. And how can the deceased revive himself, when the deceased has no knowledge or power? And if they say: Another revived him, we say: Who revived him, a Divinity or not? If they say: A Divinity, they affirm a second Divinity other than the deceased, more able to revive the deceased than the Divinity who they claim died. And this one will deserve worship more than the one who died, providing that they speak according to their principles and the truths of their faith. In this circumstance they must also claim that they have two divinities, one living and the other dead. And in consequence they cannot avoid worshipping both of them, or one of them alone. If they worship both of them together, they worship the living and the deceased. And if they worship the living alone and refuse to worship the deceased and scorn it, they have refused worship to their Divinity and have turned away from it. And this despite the fact that he died for them and endured adversity in order to save them, as they claim. At that time they abandoned worship of him and denied it, even though they had worshipped him before he accepted death in order to save and benefit them.

Say to them: Tell us about him, was he worthy of worship when he was dead, or not? If they say: He was worthy, they claim that the deceased are worthy of worship, and they commit themselves to worshipping the deceased, if in their view he was worthy

ذاك عليهم. وهذا يكفي صاحبه من أن يُزاد عليه شناعة أخرى أو يكسر قوله بأكثر مما جرى على لسانه. وإن زعموا أنّه لا يستحقّ العبادة فقد زعموا أنّ إلاهًا لا يستحقّ العبادة، وهذا أيضًا من ذلك النحو الذي يكتفي في كسره بما يظهر على لسان صاحبه. على أنّه إذا لم يستحقّ شيئًا من العبادة كثيرًا ولا قليلاً لم يستحقّ أن يُعظّم تعظيم الإله ولا أن يمدح مدحه ولا أن يُوصف بصفاته، ولم يصلح توجيه شيء من ذلك إليه. وإذا لم يستحقّ العبادة أيضًا فقد أثبتوا إلهَين أحدهما يستحقّ العبادة والآخر لا يستحقّها. وإن زعموا أنّ الذّي أحياه ليس بإله، زعموا أنّ مَن ليس بإله يحيي الإله؛ وهذا مع فساده قول أرعن لا يقوله مَن به مسكة.

١٨٧. ويقال للملكيّة: أتخلو مريم، عليها السلم، من أن تكون ولدت الكلمة والإنسان الكلّي والإنسان الجزئي على الحقيقة، أو تكون ولدت الكلمة والإنسان الكلّي دون الجزئي، أو تكون ولدت الكلمة والإنسان الجزئي دون الكلّي، أو تكون ولدت الإنسان الكلّي والإنسان الجزئي دون الكلمة، أو تكون ولدت الكلمة وحدها دونهما، أو تكون ولدت الإنسان الكلّي وحده دون الكلمة ودون الإنسان الجزئي، أو تكون ولدت الإنسان الجزئي دون الكلمة ودون الإنسان الكلّي على الحقيقة الولاد

١. ب || ف: ذلك عليهم.
١. ف، ب (تصويب) || ب (نصّ) علمه.
١٢. ب || ف: ويقال لهم اعنى الملكية.

of it. The proponent of this view has said quite enough, without adding any further horrors about him or saying any more than has already passed his lips. If they claim that he was not worthy of worship, they claim that a Divinity is not worthy of worship. And this too is the kind of thing that is enough to shatter all that passes its proponent's lips. However, if he is not worthy of any worship great or small, he is not worthy of being accorded the majesty of divinity or being given its glory or being ascribed its attributes; it is not fitting to address any of this to him. Also, if he is not worthy of worship, they affirm two Divinities one of whom is worthy of worship and the other is not. And if they claim that the one who revived him is not divine, they claim that one who was not divine revived the Divinity. Apart from its falseness, this is a rash statement; no one with any control would make it.

187 [2. *Against the Melkites*

i. *The conception and birth*]

Say to the Melkites: Is it possible for Mary, on whom be peace, to have done otherwise than give birth to the Word, the universal human, and the individual human in reality; or give birth to the Word and the universal human without the individual; or give birth to the Word and the individual human without the universal; or give birth to the universal human and the individual human without the Word; or give birth to the Word alone without the other two; or give birth to the universal human alone without the Word and without the individual human; or give birth to the individual human without the Word and without the universal human in reality as an authentic

الصحيح؟ ودَعَوْا تعليق الألفاظ التي لا حقائق لها ولا محصول عند التفتيش والمواقفة[٣٥]. فإن زعموا أنّها ولدت الكلمة والإنسان الكلّي والإنسان الجزئي، كان في هذا منهم تثبيت أنّها قد ولدت الإله القديم ولادًا صحيحًا وأنّه كان في بطنها قبل الولاد وأنّه اِبنها إذ كان وَلَدها. فالقديم على هذا القول بن مريم على التصحيح وابن آدم. والذي هو عندهم ابن الله، تعالى الله، قد صار ابنًا لمريم وآدم بالولاد. وإذا جاز عليه الولاد الصحيح والكون في البطن في موضع الجَنِين ثمّ خرج من ذلك الموضع إلى غيره فقد لزمته صفات الأجسام المحدودة المحاط بها المنتقلة من مكان إلى مكان. فإذا كان هذا حُكم أقنوم واحد من أقانيم القديم لزم الأقنومين الآخرين هذا الحكم لاِتفاقهم في الجوهريّة، أعِني حكم الأجسام المحدودة. وهذا يبطل زعمهم أنّ القديم جوهر ليس بجسم ولا محدود ولا في مكان دون مكان ولا يحاط به،[٣٦] مع غير ذلك من وجوه النقض لأقاويلهم من أقاويلهم يفتحها عليهم هذا القول.

١٨٨. وفيه أيضاً عليهم أنّهم إذا أثبتوا الإنسان الكلّي مولودًا من مريم، وجب أن يكون اِبنها إذ كان وَلَدها، فيصير الكلّي اِبنًا للجزئي ويصير الجوهر ابن أقنومه.[٣٧] ويجب إذا كان الجوهر الكلّي ابنها وولدها أن تكون أقانيمه وأشخاصه كلّها أَبنأَها وأولادها، فيلزم على هذا القول أن يكون آدم وما ولد كلّهم

١٠. ب || ف: وإذا.
١٦. ب || ف: عليهم إذا.

birth? They utter forms of words which contain no reality and which do not yield any result when examined or scrutinised.[35] For if they claim that she gave birth to the Word, the universal human and the individual human, then in consequence they make the acknowledgement that she gave birth to the eternal Divinity in an actual birth, and that he was in her womb before the birth, and that as her child he was her son. So according to this statement the eternal was son of Mary in actuality and son of Adam. So the one who for them was Son of God almighty became a son to Mary and Adam through birth. And if actual birth and being in the womb, the place of embryos, and then coming out of this place to another was possible for him, then he must have had the attributes of limited, circumscribed physical bodies which can be transferred from place to place. If this is a judgement which applies to one of the hypostases of the eternal, it must apply to the other two hypostases because of their congruence in being substance – I mean the judgement of limited physical bodies. And this destroys their claim that the eternal is a substance and not a physical body or limited or in one place or circumscribed,[36] as well as opening other possibilities for contradicting their statements.

188 Part of what is against them is also that if they affirm that the universal human was born of Mary, it must have been her son since it was her child. So the universal would have become son of the individual, and the substance become son to its hypostasis.[37] And if the universal substance was her son and child, then all its hypostases and individual beings must have been her sons and children. According to this teaching, Adam and all whom he procreated must have been

بنيــها وأولادهــا على الصحّة وعلى حقيقة الولاد والبنوّة، وأن تكون هي بنت نفسها إذ كانت عندهم أقنومًا من أقانيم الجوهر الكلّي وشــخصًا مـــن أشـخاصـــه؛ فتــكون هـــي أمّ نفســـها وبنت نفســها ووالدة لنفسـها ومولودة من نفسها: فأقنوم واحد والد مولود بنت أمّ أب اِبن لا على التثنية ولا على الإضافة. وإذا كانت أيضًا قد ولدت الإنسان الكلّي فقد كان في بطنها قبل الولاد ثمّ خرج بالولاد، وهذا يثبته شخصًا محدودًا محاطًا به متنقلاً من مكان إلى مكان. وكونه شخصًا يخرجه على أصولهم من حُكم الجواهر الكلّية إلى حكم الأقنوم الجزئي فهو حينئذٍ أقنوم جزئي شخص واحد لا جوهر كلّي. فنقول لهم في هذا أيضًا: وكيف يلدُ الجزئي الكلّي، وهل تُولَد الكلّيات والجواهر العاميات أو إنّما تولد الجزئيات والأشخاص الأقنوميات؟ فإن قالوا: لم تلد مريم الكلّي بالكلّية فيلزم ما قلتم، وإنّما ولدته بمعنى أنّها ولدت الإنسان الجزئي الذي هو أقنوم من أقانيمه، وذلك الأقنوم هو الإنسان الكلّي بالجوهر؛ فإذا ولدت الأقنوم الذي هو هو بالجوهر فقد ولدته على هذا الوجه لا على أنّها ولدت الجوهر الكلّي بكلّيته، قلنا: ففي هذا كلّ الذي ألزمناكم وقد زدتمونا على أنفسكم شيئًا آخر أو أشياء أُخر: إذا كانت قد ولدته على هذا الوجه وكان ذلك ولادًا صحيحًا فهو اِبنــها وولدها على هــذا الوجــه وقد صـــار الكلّي اِبنًا للجــزئي من هــذا الطريق، مــع توابع هذه القضــية إلى آخر ذلك الكلام

٥. ب، ف || ل: التشبيه.
٢٠. ب || ف: من هذه.
٧–٨. ب || ف: محاطا به من مكان.

her sons and children in actuality and through the reality of birth and sonship. It also means that she must have been her own daughter, since according to them she was one hypostasis and one individual of the universal substance. So she must have been her own mother, daughter, parent and offspring; and one hypostasis was parent, offspring, daughter, mother, father and son, but not in a comparative or relative manner. Also, if she gave birth to the universal human then this was in her womb before the birth and emerged at the birth. And this confirms that it was an individual who was limited, circumscribed and transferred from one place to another. According to their principles, its being an individual removes it from being judged like universal substances to being judged like an individual hypostasis, and thus it becomes an individual hypostasis, a single being, and not a universal substance.

We also say to them on this: How could the individual give birth to the universal, and are universals and general substances generated, or are only the partial, individual and hypostatic generated? If they say: Mary did not give birth to the universal as universal, necessitating what you say, but she gave birth to it only in the sense that she gave birth to the individual human who was one of its hypostases, and this hypostasis was the universal human in substance; if she gave birth to the hypostasis which as substance was it itself, then she gave birth to it in this way not in the sense of giving birth to the universal substance in its universality, we say: In this is everything we have compelled you to accept. And you have added for us a few other things against yourselves: if she gave birth to it in this way and if this was an actual birth, then it was her son and child in this respect, and the universal became son of the individual in this way, with all the consequences of this proposition, to the end of this argument

الذي قدّمنــا ذكره. وأيّ وجـه ما صرفتم إليه ولادتها إياه فذلك كلّه لاَحِق به من ذلك والجه الذي لحقته منه الولادة. وفيه أيضًا أنّها على هذا القول إذا ولدت الشيء فقد ولدت غير ذلك الشيء لأنّ الجوهر الكلّي عندكم غير الأقنوم. وإذا كان الشيء الواحد اِبنها فغير ذلك الشيء اِبنها، وهذا عجيب.[٣٨] وأخري، وهي أنّها إن كانت قـد ولـدت الإنســان الكلّي على هذا الوجه فكلّ إمـرأةٍ ولدت مولودًا فقد ولدت الإنسان الكلّي على هذا الوجه. ووجه آخر أيضًا، وهــو أنّه إذا كان ولاد الجـزئي ولادًا للــكلّي فكلّ امــرأة ولدت إنسانًا ذكرًا أو أنثى في وقت الاتّحــاد وبعد الاتّحاد فقد ولدت الإنسان الكلّي والأقنـوم القديم المتّحـد به إذ كان ذلك الأقنوم القديم قد صار هو والإنســان واحدًا بالاتّحاد. فبالمسـيح على واجــب هذا الكلام ابن كلّ امرأة ولدت إنسانًا في وقت الاِتّحاد وبعد الاِتّحاد. وإلاّ فأثبتوا لنا مريم، عليها السلم، فيما تدعون من وِلادتها الأقنوم القديـم أو الانسان الكلّي بوِلادتها الجزئي من سائر الوالدات في ذلك الوقـت، وأثبتوا ولادتها من ولادة كلّ واحدة منهُن في ولادتها الجزئي والكلّي لا في دعوى أخرى تدعونها تُضيفونها إلى هذا ليست من ولاد الجزئي والكلّي في شيء. ولَن تجدوا إلى إبانتها وإبانة ولادتها في ذلك سبيلاً إذ لم يكن الإنسان في الشـخص الذي ولدته مريم أخـصّ منه في غيره من الأشــخاص

٥. ب || ف: عجب. ١٥. ب || ف: الوادات، ف (هامش): الولادات.
١٣. ب || ف: فبينوا (ف (هامش): الاصل، فابينوا).
١٤. ب || ف: من ولادها للأقانيم. ١٥. ب || ف: وأبينوا ولادها.
١٤. ب || ف: بولادها الجزئي. ١٦. ب || ف: في ولادها.

which we have mentioned above. And no matter how you look at the matter, it was this she gave birth to and so all of this attaches to it in the same way that the birth attaches to it.

Another point is that, according to this teaching, if she gave birth to the thing she must also have given birth to something other than this thing, because according to you the universal substance is other than the hypostasis. If the one thing was her son, then the thing other than this was her son, which is amazing.[38] And again, if she did give birth to the universal human in this respect, then every woman who has given birth to a child has given birth to the universal human in this respect. There is another point also, which is that if an individual parent was parent of the universal then every woman who has given birth to a male or female baby at the time of the uniting or since has given birth to the universal human and the eternal hypostasis which united with it. This is because this eternal hypostasis and the human became one in the uniting. So, by the force of this argument, the Messiah is son of every woman who has given birth to a baby at the time of the uniting and since. Otherwise, demonstrate to us that Mary, upon whom be peace, according to what you proclaim gave birth to the eternal hypostasis or the universal human through giving birth to the individual, alone among all the births of that time. And demonstrate that her giving birth was alone among all those births, in that she gave birth to the individual and the universal, and not because of another claim which you make in addition to this which has nothing to do with the birth of the individual or universal. You will not find a way to separate her or to separate her giving birth, because the human in the individual whom Mary bore is no more particular than in other individuals,

وإذ لم يكن لذلك الشخص في الإنسانيّة ما ليس لغيره. وإذا كان ولاد الجزئي أيضًا هو ولاد الكلّي على هذا الوجه فتربية الجزئي هي تربية الكلّي على هذا الوجه ونشوء الجزئي هو نشوء الكلّي وتغذّي الجزئي هو تغذّي الكلّي وتحرّك الجزئي وتنقّله في الأماكن وتصرّفه وزيادته ونقصانه وسِمَنه وهزاله ومرضه وصحّته وحياته وموته كلّ ذلك فهو تحرّك الكلّي وتنقّله في الأماكن وتصرّفه وزيادته ونقصانه وسمنه وهزاله ومرضه وصحّته وحياته وموته، فكلّما وُلد الجزئي وُلد الكلّي وكلّما تربّي هذا ونشاء وأكل وشرب وزاد ونقص ومرض وصحّ وحيى ومات فقد تربّى الكلّي ونشأ وأكل وشرب وزاد ونقص ومرض وصحّ وحيى ومات على ذلك الوجه. وإذا كان هذا حُكمه على التحقيق لا على المجاز فالكلّي يزيد وينقص ويأكل ويشرب ويسمن ويهزل ويذهب ويجيء ويمرض ويصحّ ويموت ويحيا وتَحَلّه الأعراض والأحداث. فهل نفيتم من وصف الشخصيّة شيئًا إلاّ ألحقتموه به؟ ويلزم أيضًا أن يكون الجزئي متى فعل فقد فعل الكلّي ومتى أحسن وأساء فقد أحسن الكلّي وأساء، وكذلك متى صدق وكذب وأطاع وعصى وآمن وكفر ومتى أمر ونهى، على أنّ المطيع لا يكون مطيعاً إلاّ وهو مأمور والعاصي لا يكون عاصيًا إلاّ وهو مُنهى. وإذا كان بعض أقانيم الكلّي متحرّكًا وبعضها ساكنًا في حال واحدة وبعضها مؤمنًا وبعضها كافرًا في حال فالكلّي في تلك

٥. ب || ف: هزالته. ١٥. ب || ف: ويلزمهم. ١٩. ب || ف: وإذ.

and because this individual person has no quality of being human that others do not have.

Further, if the birth of the individual was the birth of the universal in this respect, then the upbringing of the individual was the upbringing of the universal in this respect, the growing of the individual was the growing of the universal, the eating of the individual was the eating of the universal, the motion of the individual, his movement to different places, his behaviour, his increase and decrease, his fatness and thinness, his sickness and health, his life and death, all these were the motion of the universal, its movement to different places, its behaviour, its increase and decrease, its fatness and thinness, its sickness and health, its life and death. For when the individual was born the universal was born, when he was brought up, grew, ate, drank, increased, decreased, was sick, was healthy, lived and died, the universal was brought up, grew, ate, drank, increased, decreased, was sick, was healthy, lived and died in the same manner. If this verdict about him is real and not metaphorical, then the universal increased and decreased, ate and drank, grew fat and thin, went and came, was sick and healthy, died and lived, and accidents and events affected it. Have you withheld any description of individuality which you have not laid upon it? It also follows that when the individual acted the universal acted, and when he was good and bad the universal was good and bad, and similarly when he was honest and dishonest, when he was obedient and disobedient, when he believed and disbelieved, when he ordered and forbade, except that one who is obedient is only obedient when ordered and the disobedient is only disobedient when forbidden. And if some of the hypostases of the universal were in motion at one moment and some of them were not, some believing and some not, then at this moment the universal

الحال متحرّك ساكن ثابت في المكان زائل عنه مؤمن كافر مصدّق مكذّب مقرّ بالشيء منكر له في حال واحدة. وإذا كان بعض أقانيمه عندكم مأمورًا بشيء وأقنوم آخر مأمور بخلاف ذلك الشيء وضدّه في حال واحدة فالكلّي مأمور بالشيء وبضدّه في حال واحدة وبأخذه وبتركه في وقت واحد؛ وهذا مع فساده في نفسه ذمّ شديد للأمر الناهي إذ يأمر المأمور بأن يفعل الشيء وضدّه في حال واحدة وبأن يأخذه في حال ما يتركه ويتركه في حال ما يأخذه. وهذا تكليف ما لا سبيل إليه وما لا يجوز وقوعه ولا الوصول إليه بوجه من الوجوه.[٣٩] وأنتم تهربون مما هو أقلّ من هذا وتفزعون من تكليف ما لا يطاق مما قد يجوز أن يطاق، وموضع فزع لعمري واستقباح، فكيف بتكليف ما لا يجوز أن يطاق ولا يوجد إليه سبيل أبدًا ولا يمكن على وجه من الوجوه؟ فكذلك يلزمهم في الصلب والقتل والدفن والألم أن يكون كلّ ذلك قد وقع بالكلّي إذ وقع بالجزئي وحلّ في الكلّي إذ حلّ في بعض أقانيمه. ولا أرى هذا، أعني وقوع الصلب والقتل والألم به، إلاّ أسْهَل عليكم من بعض ما تقدّم ذكره إلاّ أنّ ذلك كلّه يؤدّي إلى تصيير الكلّي شخصًا تحلّه هذه الأحداث ويحسّها ويجدها وتُرى قائمةً به. وكذلك يلزم أن تكون الأبصار متى أدركت الجزئي فقد أدركت الكلّي، وكذلك سائر الحواسّ والمشاعر، ومتى نالته الأيدي فقد نالت الكلّي. ففي هذا أنه يُرى

١٨. ب: يحدها.

was in motion and at rest, stationary in a place and leaving it, believing and unbelieving, trustworthy and lying, asserting something and denying it, all in one moment. And if one of its hypostases, in your view, was ordered to do a thing and another hypostasis was ordered to do something different from and opposite to this at one moment, then the universal would have been ordered to do a thing and its opposite in one moment, with undertaking it and not undertaking it at one time. Apart from the inherent incorrectness in this, it is a strong censure of the one who orders and forbids, since he orders the one who is ordered to do a thing and its opposite in one moment, and to undertake it in the moment he should abandon it and abandon it in the moment he should undertake it. This is an imposition which cannot be fulfilled, which should not be given, and which cannot be achieved in any way.[39] But you are turning away from rather less than this, for you are dismayed at the imposition that is not fulfilled although it can be. This is most definitely a reason for dismay and revulsion. How can something be imposed that cannot be fulfilled, nor a way of doing this ever be found, nor any possibility at all?

In the same way, with respect to the crucifixion, killing, burying and suffering, they have to accept that all this happened to the universal since it happened to the individual, and that it affected the universal since it affected one of its hypostases. And I do not see that this, I mean the occurrence of the crucifixion, death and suffering, will be any easier for you than some of what has been mentioned earlier, unless it all leads to the universal becoming an individual being to whom these events happened, which he felt and experienced, and they were happening to him. It also follows that when eyes perceived the individual they beheld the universal, and likewise the other senses and feelings. And when hands seized him, they seized the universal. And this means that he was seen

بالأبصــار ويُدرك بالحواسّ على التحقيق كما رأت الجزئي وأدركته على التحقيــق. ورؤية الأبصار وأدراك المشـاعر لا تقــع في شيء منه مجـاز ولا تعليق، وإنّما هو وجود ومشاهدة ومعاني ثابته حقيقيّة. وهذا خلاف قولكم في الجوهر الكلّي لأنّ الجوهر الكلّي عندكم لا يُرى بالأبصـار ولا يُدرك بالحــواسّ. ويلزم أيضاً أن يكون الاتّحاد بالجزئي اتّحادًا بالكلّي إن لو وقع اتّحاد بالجزئي، إذ كان الجزئي هو الكلّي بالجوهر، كما كان ولاد الجزئي ولادًا للكلّي لهذه العلّة على ما فسّـرتم وشرحتم. وإذا كان الاتّحاد بالجزئي اتّحادًا بالكلّي فيما يدفعون أن تكون الكلمة إنّما اتّحدت بالكلّي على هذا الوجه ومن هذا الطريق لا غير كما ولدته مريم على هذا الوجه ومن هذا الطريق لا غير؟ وإذا كان ذلك كذلك سقط الخلاف بينكم وبين اليعقوبيّة والنســطوريّة في حقيقة الاتّحاد بالكلّي في قولكـــم وبالجزئي في قولهــم لأنّ الأمر حينئذٍ يؤول إلى معنىً واحــد وإن اختلفت الألفاظ وإن زدْتم عليهم في العبارة ذكر الكـلّي. وهذا إذا حصّــل عليــكم وردّ إلى ما يُوجبه الكـلام على مذاهبكم لم يحصل منه غير الاتّحاد بالجزئي كما لا يحصل الولاد والبنوّة إلاّ للجزئي.

١٨٩. ونقـــول لكـــم أيضـــًا: إذا كان الاتّحـــاد عنـــدكم هـــو أنّه صـــار من الاثنين واحـد، فكيف صـار من الكلمـة والإنســان الكـلّي واحـد، اَختلطـا اَمتزجـا تشـابكا أم لا، وصـارا واحـــدًا

٥. ب || ف: بالحواس على التحقيق. ١٤. ب || ف: زدْتم عليهما. ٢٠. ب || ف: واحداً.

by eyes and felt by sensations in reality, just as they saw and perceived the individual in reality. Being seen by the eyes and perceived by the senses is not something that occurs metaphorically or conditionally; it exists, is visible and is an established, actual reality. But this is contrary to your teaching about the universal substance, because in your view the universal substance cannot be seen by the eyes or perceived by the senses.

It also follows that the uniting with the individual must have been a uniting with the universal, if indeed the uniting affected the individual, since the individual was the universal as substance; and also that the birth of the individual was the birth of the universal for this reason, according to what you have explained and set out. And if the uniting with the individual was the uniting with the universal, how can they reject the possibility that the Word could have united with the universal only in this respect and manner and no other, and also that Mary could have given birth to it in this respect and manner and no other?

And if the matter is like this, the difference between you and the Jacobites and Nestorians about the actuality of the uniting with the universal in your teaching and the individual in your teaching disappears, because in this circumstance the matter reverts to one significance even though the words differ, and even though you go further than them in explanation of the mention of the universal. If this strikes home to you and answers what is necessitated by the argument concerning your doctrines, nothing remains from it except the uniting with the individual, and similarly there is no more than the birth and sonship of the individual.

189 We also say to you: If in your view the uniting was two becoming one, then how did the Word and the universal human become one? Did they mingle, mix and intertwine or not? Did they become one

في الجـوهرّية أم في الشـخصيّة والأقنـوميّة؟ فإن كانـا اختلـطا أو امتزجا أو تشابكا، فهذه صفات الأشخاص لا صفة الجوهر الكلّي الذي ليس بشخص. معما في الاختلاط والامتزاج والتشابك من إيجاب تحديد المختلطين والممتزجين والمتشابكين واستغراق أحدهما صاحبه.[٤٠]

١٩٠. وإن كانا أيضًا صارا واحدًا في الجوهريّة فقد انقلبت جواهرهما جميعًا أو جوهر أحدهما إلى جوهر الآخر. وإن انقلبا جميعًا عن جواهرهما فقد خرجا من جوهر القديم وجوهر الحديث؛ وإن كان انقلب جوهر أحدهما إلى جوهريّة الآخر فقد صار المُحدَث إذًا قديمًا أو القديم مُحدَثًا.

١٩١. وإن كانا صارا واحدًا في الشخصيّة والأقنوميّة فقد صار الجوهر الكلّي إذن شخصًا واحدًا أقنومًا واحدًا؛ وفي هذا عليكم ضروب من الفساد والنقض لما أصّلتم في وصف الجواهر الكليّة والأقانيم قديمها وحديثها. وإذا بطل هذان الوجهان في قولهم «صار من الاِثنين واحد» فقد بطل الاتّحاد بالكلّي وبقي الاتّحاد بالجزئي، وهذا قول يعقوب ونسطور وفيه من الفساد ما فيه،[٤٠] ولا بُدّ لهم منه أو طَرْح الاتّحاد كلّه، فهذا خلاف دينهم.

١٩٢. وإذا ولدت مريم، عليها السلم، أيضًا الكلمة والإنسان الكلّي والإنسان الجزئي فقد ولدت جوهرين أقنومين جوهر اللاهوت

٢. ب || ف: لا صفات الجوهر.
١١. ب || ف: قنومًا واحدًا.
١٤–١٥. ب || ف: من الاثنين واحدا.

in substantiality, or in individuality and hypostaticity? Maybe they mingled or mixed or intertwined, but these are attributes of individual beings not an attribute of the universal substance, which is not an individual being. At the same time, mingling, mixing and intertwining entail the two things which mingle, mix and intertwine being limited, and the one being absorbed by its companion.[40]

190 Also, if the two became one in substantiality, then either the substances of both were transformed together or the substance of one of them was transformed into the substance of the other. If they were both transformed together from their substances, they would depart from the substance of the eternal and of the temporal. And if the substance of one of them was transformed into the substantiality of the other, the
191 temporal would become eternal or the eternal temporal. | And if they became one in individuality and hypostaticity, the universal substance would then become one individual being and one hypostasis. In this lie forms of error and contradiction for you, considering the characterisation of universal substances and eternal and temporal hypostases by which you stand.

If both of these alternatives are abandoned when they say, "Two became one", then the uniting of the universal is destroyed and only the uniting of the individual remains. This is the teaching of Jacob and Nestorius, with the error contained in that.[41] They must accept this or reject the whole uniting, though it is contrary to their religion.

192 Also, if Mary, upon whom be peace, gave birth to the Word, the universal human and the individual human, then she must have given birth to two substances and hypostases, the substance of the divine nature

وجوهر الناسوت الكلّي أقنوم اللاهوت الذي هو ذلك الجوهر الخاصّي وهو الكلمة[٤٢] وأقنوم الناسوت الذي هو الإنسان الجزئي. وهذا في الولاد كقول النسطوريّة في المسيح أنّه جوهران أقنومان. ويزيد عليهم في ذلك ذكر الإنسان الكلّي، فهذا ما يدخل في ذلك القسم.

١٩٣. وإن زعموا أنّها ولدت الكلمة والإنسان الكلّي دون الجزئي فكلّ ذلك الكلام الذي قدّمنا ذكره لازم لهم إلاّ ما لحقهم فيه بولادتها الجزئي مع الكلّي ومع الكلمة. فلا خلاف بين جوابهم هذا وأوّل جوابهم ذاك إلاّ أنّهم زادوا في ذاك قولهم أنّها ولدت مع الكلمة والإنسان الكلّي ذلك الإنسان الجزئي. ووِلادة الإنسان الجزئي لا تُنكر ولا تدفع أيضًا عنهم ما لزمهم في تثبيتهم ولادتها الكلمة والإنسان الكلّي متى أجابوا بذلك.

١٩٤. وإن زعموا أنّها ولدت الكلمة والإنسان الجزئي دون الكلّي فجميع ما لزمهم بولاد الكلمة في الجواب المتقدّم يلزمهم هاهنا.

١٩٥. ويقال لهم مع ذلك: إن كانت لم تلد الإنسان الكلّي فكيف ولدت الكلمة المتّحدة به وقد صارت الكلمة بزعمكم وذلك الذي لم تلده واحدًا لاِتّحادها به؟ إلاّ أن تزعموا أنّها ولدت الكلمة قبل الاتّحاد فتكون قد ولدتها مجرّدة لا متّحدة، وهذا خلاف أصولكم.

٩. ب، ف || ل: جوابهم ذلك.
٩. ب || ف، ل: زادوا في ذلك.
١٠. ب || ف: وولاد الإنسان.
١٠–١١. ب || ف: لا ينكر ولا يدفع.
١١. ب || ف: ما الزمهم.
١١. ب || ف: ولادتها للكلمة.
١٤. ب || ف: ما الزمهم.
١٦. ب: نزعموا (غير منقوطة)؛ ف، ل: يزعموا.

and the substance of the universal human nature, the hypostasis of the divine nature which is the specific substance and the Word,[42] and the hypostasis of the human nature which is the individual human. With regard to the birth, this is like the teaching of the Nestorians about the Messiah, that he was two substances and two hypostases. We can add in this a reference to the universal human against them, because it is what comes into this section.

193 And if they claim that she gave birth to the Word and the universal human without the individual, all of the argument which we have presented above applies to them except what affects them concerning her bearing of the individual together with the universal and the Word. And there will be no difference between their answer here and their first answer on this, except that they will add in what they say that she gave birth to this individual human together with the Word and the universal human. And as long as they answer in this way, the birth of the individual human cannot be denied or rejected by them either, since it is implied in their affirmation that she gave birth to the Word and the universal human.

194 If they claim that she gave birth to the Word and the individual human without the universal, everything that applies to them concerning the
195 birth of the Word in the preceding answer applies to them here. | As well as this, say to them: If she did not give birth to the universal human how could she give birth to the Word which was united with it, when according to your claim the Word and this which she did not bear became one through its uniting with it? Your only alternative is to claim that she gave birth to the Word before the uniting, and so she gave birth to it separately and not united. And this is contrary to your teaching.

١٩٦ . ويلزمكم أيضًا على هذا أن تزعموا أنّ مريم لم تلد المسيح على الصحّة إذ كان المسيح جوهرين أحدهما الإنسان الكلّي، أو كان أقنومًا ذا جوهرين أحدهما الإنسان الكلّي، لأن الأقنوم القديم إن ذُكِر مجرّدًا فليس بذي جوهرين وإنّما هو إذ ذاك أقنوم واحد ذو جوهر واحد.

١٩٧ . وإن أبوا إلاّ الإدّعاء فقالوا: قد ولدت الأقنوم اللاهوت متّحدًا بالإنسان الكلّي ولم تلد الانسان الكلّي، قلنا: فمن أدنَى ما في هذا عليكم أنّكم قد رجعتم إلى مُعارضة قول النسطوريّة، فأثبتم المسيح مولودًا من جهة لاهوتة لا من جهة ناسوته كما أثبتوه مولودًا من جهة ناسوته لا من جهة لاهوته. وهذا هو التعليق الذي تنكرونه عليهم لأنّهم لم يحقّقوا عندكم أنّها ولدته إذ زعموا أنّها ولدته من جهة الناسوت دون جهة اللاهوت. وأنتم أيضًا فلم تحقّقوا وِلادتها إيّاه متى زعمتم أنّها ولدته من جهة لاهوته دون جهة ناسوته. بل قولكم في ذلك أعجب: وقول النسطوريّة، وإن لم يكن فيه تحقيق لِولاد المسيح على الصحّة، أقرب إلى ما يتوهّم كونه في الولاد لأِنّ الذي يحصل للنسطوريّة إذا حقّق هذا عليها ولاد الإنسان الجزئي وحده لا ولاد المسيح الذي هو عندهم إله وإنسان. وأنتم إذا حقّق هذا عليكم حصل لكم إدّعاء

١. ب || ف: ويلزمهم.
١. ب || ف: على هذا أن مريم.
١٠. ب || ف: التعلق.
١٢–١٣. ب || ف: لم تحققوا.

196 But according to this you are also forced to claim that Mary did not give birth to the Messiah in actuality, since the Messiah was two substances, one of them the universal human, or he was a hypostasis which possessed two substances, one of them the universal human. For if the eternal hypostasis is considered separately, it is not the possessor of two substances, but in such a circumstance is only one hypostasis which possesses one substance.

197 And if they reject anything but the claim and say: It was the hypostasis of the divine nature united with the universal human which she gave birth to, not the universal human, we say: The very least against you in this is that you will end up with the opposite to the teaching of the Nestorians, for you affirm that the Messiah was born in respect of his divine nature but not in respect of his human nature, just as they affirm that he was born in respect of his human nature but not in respect of his divine nature. This is the form of expression which you deny them, because in your view they cannot affirm that she gave birth to him, since they claim that she gave birth to him in respect of his human nature without the divine nature. And neither can you affirm that she gave birth to him when you claim that she gave birth to him in respect of his divine nature without his human nature.

But your teaching on this is more surprising. For although there is no confirmation in the teaching of the Nestorians of the birth of the Messiah in actuality, it is closer to what one could imagine happened in the birth, because if this is affirmed against them, the result for the Nestorians is the birth of the individual human alone, not the birth of the Messiah who for them was divine and human. But if this is affirmed against you, the result for you is the claim

ولاد الأقنوم اللاهوتي دون الإنسان الكلّي. فولاد الإنسان الجزئي من الإنسان أقرب في التوهّم من ولاد الإله من الإنسان لأن الإنسان إذا ولد إنسانًا فإنّما ولد ما هو من جنسه. وإذا ادّعي مُدّعٍ أنّ الإنسان ولد إلاهًا، كان قد أوجب الإنسان ولاد أبعد الأشياء عندكم من جنسه. وبعد، فلو أرَدتم أن تقولوا «ولدت الأقنوم اللاهوتي مجرّدًا غير متّحد» هل كان يمكنكم أن تأتوا بغير زعمكم أنّها ولدت الأقنوم اللاهوتي ولم تلد الإنسان الكلّي؟ ولو توهّمتموها أو توهّمها متوهّم قد ولدت الكلمة مجرّدة، هل كان يتوهّم غير هذا؟ فتعليقكم ذكر الاتّحاد بالإنسان الكلّي في حال الولاد أو قبل الولاد مع نفيكم عنه الولاد لا معنى له.

١٩٨. ونسألكم أيضًا ونقول لكم: كيف ولدت مريم الكلمة دون الأب ودون الروح إلاّ أنّ الكلمة انفصلت من الأب ومن الروح فصارت في بطن مريم ومولودة منها؟ فإن كانت انفصلت فقد انقطعت منهما وباينتهما وصارت عنهما بمَعزل. وفي هذا إيجاب التبعيض والتجزّؤ والتحديد والخروج من مكان إلى مكان. وإن كانت لم تنفصل من الأب ولا من الروح ولا يجوز ذلك عليها عندكم، فكيف صارت إلى تلك المواضع دونهما، وكيف صارت هي والإنسان الكلّي واحدًا دونهما؟

٢. ب || ف: الوهم.
١٣. ب، ف || ل: مولوده منها.

that it was the birth of the divine hypostasis without the universal human. And the birth of the individual human from a human would be easier to imagine than the birth of the divine from a human, because if a human gives birth to a human it only gives birth to the same kind as itself, but if someone alleges that the human gives birth to the divine, he necessarily affirms that the human can give birth to things which in your view are furthest from its kind.

Again, if you wanted to say, "She gave birth to the divine hypostasis separately and not united", could you state something different from your claim that she gave birth to the divine hypostasis and not to the universal human? And if you imagine, or someone imagines that she gave birth to the Word alone, how could he imagine something different from this? So your persistence in saying that the uniting with the universal human was at the moment of birth or before the birth, despite your denying that it was born, is meaningless.

198 And we also question you and say to you: How did Mary give birth to the Word without the Father and without the Spirit unless the Word was separated from the Father and Spirit, came into Mary's womb and was born from her? And if it was separated it was cut off from them, parted from them and was isolated from them. In this is entailed division, fragmentation, limitation and moving from place to place. But unless it was separated from the Father and the Spirit, this could not have happened to it, as you see it. So how could it enter these conditions without them, and how could it and the universal human become one without them?

١٩٩. وإن قالوا: لم يصرْ في بطن مريم ولا في مكان من الأماكن، قلنا: فأي شيء معنى قولكم «ولدتها مريم»، وقولكم «مريم ولدت الإله»؟ وهل تلد المرأة إلاّ ما كان حملاً وكان جنينًا في بطنها مَسْتورًا، إلاّ أن يتكلّموا على غير الحقائق فيلحقوا بأهل التجاهل؟

٢٠٠. وإن زعموا أنّ مريم ولدت الإنسان الكلّي والجزئي دون الكلمة تركوا المعروف من قولهم وادعائهم في الأصل أنّها ولدت إلهًا، وأوجبوا أنّها لم تلد المسيح على الحقيقة إذ كان المسيح عندهم إمّا جوهرين أحدهما الكلمة وإمّا أقنومًا قديمًا له جوهران كما يقولون كثيرًا. فإذ لم تلد الأقنوم القديم على القولين جميعًا فلم تلد المسيح.

٢٠١. ويلزمهم أيضًا في ولادتها الإنسان الكلّي جميع ما ألزمناهم في ذلك من قبل.

٢٠٢. ويكونوا أيضًا كمن زعم أنّ المسيح وُلد من جهة ناسوته لا من جهة لاهوته، وهذا القول عندهم من عظيم الخطاء.

٢٠٣. وإن زعموا أنّها ولدت الكلمة وحدها دونهما، لزمهم في ذلك ما ألزمناهم متى زعموا أنّها ولدت الكلمة مجرّدة لا متّحدة بالإنسان الكلّي. وقد مرّ الكلام في هذا على أنه متى زعم زاعم أنها لم تلد إنسانًا كلّيًا ولا جزئيًا فقد دفع الوجود وكابر العِيان في دفعه ولادها ذلك الإنسان الجزئي. ولأنّ مريم، عليها السلم، عندهم قد ولدت يسوع الذي نسمّيه نحن عيسى، على عيسى

٢. ب || ف: فبأي.   ٢–٣. ب || ف: ولدت الإله.   ١١. ب || ف: في ولادها.

199 If they say: It was not in Mary's womb or in any place, we say: Then is there any scrap of meaning in your statement, "Mary gave birth to it", or your statement, "Mary gave birth to the Divinity"? And can a woman give birth to anything except what she has carried and what has been an embryo hidden in her womb, unless they argue contrary to reality and place themselves among the ignorant?

200 And if they claim that Mary gave birth to the universal human and the individual without the Word, they abandon what is accepted in their statement and what they assume in the principle that she gave birth to a Divinity. They make it impossible for her to have given birth to the Messiah in reality, because in their view the Messiah was either two substances one of which was the Word, or an eternal hypostasis with two substances, as they generally say. But if she did not give birth to the eternal hypostasis, following either statement, she did not give birth to the Messiah.

201 They are also forced to accept with regard to her giving birth to the universal human all that we have forced them to accept here.

202 They are like the one who claims that the Messiah was born with respect to his human nature, but not with respect to his divine nature,[43] although this statement is for them the most serious error.

203 And if they claim that she gave birth to the Word alone without the other two of them,[44] they are forced to accept on this what we have forced them to accept when they claimed that she gave birth to the Word separately not united with the universal human. The argument about this continues with saying that as long as anyone claims that she did not give birth to a universal or individual human, he rejects what actually is and disbelieves what is evident in rejecting that she gave birth to this individual human. For according to them Mary, on whom be peace, gave birth to Jesus whom we call ʿĪsā, upon ʿĪsā be

السلم،[٤٥] ودفعهم هذا أيضًا خروج من دينهم.

٢٠٤. وإن زعموا أنّها ولدت الإنسان الكلّي وحده دون الكلمة ودون الإنسان الجزئي تركوا قولهم ودفعوا الوجود والعِيان في دفعهم ولادتها يسوع الذي نسمّيه نحن عيسى، على عيسى السلم، وانسلخوا من دينهم. ولزمهم أيضًا في ولادتها الكلّي ما ألزمناهم في ذلك من قبل، وصاروا مع ذلك إلى أن يزعموا أنّ مريم إنّما ولدت المسيح من جهة ناسوته فقطّ.

٢٠٥. وإن زعموا أنّ مريم إنّما ولدت الإنسان الجزئي دون الكلمة ودون الإنسان الكلّي فقد صرّحوا بأنّها لم تلد المسيح قطّ بوجه من الوجوه لأنّ المسيح عندهم غير الإنسان الجزئي من جميع الجهات. كذلك حقيقته عند من قال منهم «المسيح جوهران، جوهر قديم هو الكلمة وجوهر حديث هو الإنسان الكلّي»، وعند من قال منهم «المسيح أقنوم واحد ذو جوهرين». والجوهر القديم والأقنوم القديم والإنسان الكلّي كلّ هذا عندهم غير الإنسان الجزئي. ومتى زعموا أيضًا أنّ مريم لم تلد إلاّ الإنسان فقد فارقوا أصولهم وانسلخوا من دينهم.

٢٠٦. ولن يقولوا بأكثر هذه التقاسيم، ولكن الاستقصاء لهم وعليهم في الكلام والشرح لهذه القصّة ولِما فيها أدّى إلى ذكر هذه الوجوه. وأردنا أيضًا ألاّ يتعلّق متعلّق منهم بشيء منها متى ضاق عليه الكلام في هذا الباب إلاّ وجد المحِقّ ما يدفعه عن تعلّقه.

٤. ب || ف: ولادها يسوع.
٤. ب || ف: على عيسى أفضل السلم.
٥. ب || ف: في ولادها الكلي.
٥. ب، ف || ل: ما لزمناهم.

peace.[45] And their rejection of this is also a departure from their religion.

204 And if they claim that she gave birth to the universal human alone without the Word or the individual human, they abandon their teaching, and reject what actually is and what is evident in rejecting her giving gave birth to Jesus whom we call ʿĪsā, upon ʿĪsā be peace, and they cast off their religion. And with regard to her giving birth to the universal they are also forced to accept what we have forced them to accept above, and in addition they begin to claim that Mary gave birth to the Messiah only with respect to his humanity and no more.

205 If they claim that Mary gave birth only to the individual human without the Word or the universal human, they declare that she did not give birth to the Messiah at all in any way, because in their view the Messiah is different from the individual human in all respects. The real case is the same for the one among them who says, "The Messiah was two substances, an eternal substance which is the Word, and a temporal substance which is the universal human", and for the one among them who says, "The Messiah was one hypostasis possessing two substances." The eternal substance, the eternal hypostasis and the universal human, all these, according to them, are different from the individual human. And as long as they claim also that Mary gave birth only to the human, they separate themselves from their principles and cast off their religion.

206 They do not refer to most of these divisions. But close investigation in argument, whether for or against them, and explanation of this matter and what it contains lead to an enumeration of these aspects. And we do not want any of them to be able to cling to a single one of these points when the argument on this subject becomes difficult for him, without finding the truth that will prise him away from clinging to it.

وتحميل الكلام جميع ما يحتمله من الوجوه أشفى وأبلغ في الإنصاف وأكثر في البيان وأحسم لطمع الحائد عن سُنن الكلام وطريق الحجّة.[٤٦]

٢٠٧. وليس بعد هذه الأقسام شيء يتعلّقون به في هذا الباب ولا لهم وجه غيرها يعوّلون عليه في قصّة ولاد المسيح. وإذا دخل هذه الأقسام من الخلل والفساد ما دخلها تعطّل عليهم الولاد والاتّحاد ولم يمكنهم أن يزعموا أنّ المسيح مولود من مريم ولا أنّه ابنها بوجه من الوجوه يثبت لهم طرفة عينٍ، ولا بُدّ لهم من التعلّق ببعض هذه الوجوه الفاسدة أو ترك قولهم.

٢٠٨. ويُسألون فيقال لهم: أتخلو الكلمة من أن تكون اتّحدت بالإنسان الكلّي في ذلك الجسد المولود من مريم أو في جسد آخر هو غيره أو لا في جسد من الأجساد البتّة؟[٤٧] فإن كانت اتّحدت به في ذلك الجسد المولود من مريم فقد أحاط ذلك الجسد بهما، أعني بالكلمة وبالإنسان الكلّي، وحصرهما، وقاما به واشتمل عليهما إذ كان اتحادهما فيه لا في غيره من الأجساد. وإذا كانا أيضًا قد اتّحدا فيه وهو حَمْل في بطن مريم فقد أحاط به وبهما بطن مريم، عليها السلم وعلى ابنها. وهذا يوجب تحديد اللاهوت وصغر شخصه إذ أحاط به البطن. ويُوجب أيضًا أنّ الإنسان الكلّي محصور في موضع الجنين.

١٢. ب || ف: آخر غيره.

To amass together everything that may possibly be contained in an argument is more demonstrably and fully just; it makes for more clarity and is a strong disincentive against ignoring the norms of argument and the ways of debate.[46]

207 Other than these divisions there is nothing to which they can cling on this issue, though they have no other aspect with which to support themselves on the matter of the birth of the Messiah. And if fault and error have entered into these divisions, the birth and uniting are rendered useless for them, and they cannot claim that the Messiah was born of Mary, and the fact that he was not her son in any respect is confirmed to them as quickly as blinking, although they must continue to cling to some of these erroneous alternatives or else abandon their teachings.

208 Question them and say to them: Could the Word have united with the universal human in any other way than in this body born of Mary, in another body different from it, or in no body at all?[47] If it united with it in this body born from Mary, then this body contained them both, I mean the Word and the universal human, and confined them; they were situated upon it and it surrounded them, since their uniting was in it and not in any other body. Also, if they united in it and it was a foetus in Mary's womb, then her womb contained it and both of them, peace be upon her and her son. This entails the limitation of the divine nature and decrease of it as an individual since the womb contained it. It also entails the universal human being contained in the place of the embryo.

٢٠٩. وإن زعمتم أنّهما لم يكونا فيما هناك ولم يشتمل عليهما فلم يكن الاتّحاد إذن قبل الولاد ولا كان اتّحادهما في ذلك الجسد المحمول وهو محمول. على أنّه لو كان الاتّحاد أيضًا بعد الولاد لم يكن بين إحاطة الجسم الذي اتّحدا فيه بهما وجواز إحاطة البطن بهما فرْق في هذا المعنى لأنّه لا يحاط إلاّ بمحدود ولا تجوز الإحاطة إلاّ بمحدود.

٢١٠. وإن قالوا: اتّحدت الكلمة بالإنسان في جسد آخر غير المولود من مريم، فارقوا أصولهم وأوجبوا أنّ ذلك الجسد الآخر هو جسد المسيح لا الجسد المولود من مريم.

وصيّروا المسيح ابن إنسان آخر وابن امرأة أُخرى إن كان مولودًا. وإن لم يكن مولودًا، فذاك أبعد من مذاهبهم. ويلزمهم في ذلك الجسد من ذكر التحديد والإحاطة أيضًا ما لزمهم في هذا.

٢١١. وإن زعموا أنّها اتّحدت به لا في جسد من الأجساد ولا في مكان من الأماكن، قلنا: فأدنى ما في ذاك أنّه ليس ابن مريم، ولا ذلك الجسد المولود من مريم جسدًا له، ولا بينه وبينه سَبَب بوجه من الوجوه أكثر من أنّه خلقها بزعمكم وخلق ولدها. فأما أن يكون بينه وبينها سبب بالمسيحيّة أو بالاتّحاد أو بالولاد فلا.

٢١٢. ويبطل على هذا الجواب وعلى قول من قال «اتّحدت الكلمة بالإنسان في جسد آخر غير المولود من مريم» إن قال ذلك قائل

١. ب || ف: فإن زعموا.
١٤. ب || ف: في ذلك.

209 And if you claim that these two were not in that place and it did not contain them, then the uniting could not have taken place before the birth and could not have been in this body which was carried while it was being carried. However, if the uniting had taken place after the birth there would be no difference in this context between being confined within the body in which they united and the possibility of being confined in the womb, because only what is limited can be confined and confinement always implies limitation.

210 If they say: The Word united with the human in another body other than the one born of Mary, they separate themselves from their principles, and require that this other body should be the body of the Messiah and not the body born of Mary. They make the Messiah the son of another man and woman, if he was born. And if he was not born, that is even further from their beliefs. They also have to say the same things with regard to restriction and being confined about this body as they do of that.

211 And if they claim that it united with it in no body nor in any place, we say: The least we can say about this is that he was not the son of Mary, the body born of Mary was not his body, nor was there any greater relationship between him and it than that he created her, as you claim, and created her child. As for any relationship between him and her in Messiahship, the uniting and birth, there was none.

212 According to this answer and according to the statement of the one who says, "The Word united with the human in another body other than the one born of Mary", if anyone says this

وأجاب به مجيب، قول من زعم منكم أنّ الصلب والقتل والألم كلّ ذلك نال المسيح بكمالِه بذلك الجسد ـ نال الصلب والقتل عندكم جوهرَيْه جميعًا أو أحد جوهرَيه ـ لأنّه إذ لم يكن متّحداً بذلك الجسد ولا في ذلك الجسد لم يجز أن يُصلب بذلك الجسد ولا أن يُقتل بذلك الجسد ولا أن يناله الألم بذلك الجسد. ولا قسم أيضًا في هذا الباب غير هذه الأقسام الثلثة وكلّ واحد منها ينقض عليهم أصلاً من أصولهم أو أصولاً من أصولهم.

٢١٣. ويُقال لهم: أخبرونا عن الصلب والقتل والألم، بمَن حلّ كلّ ذلك، أبجسد المسيح دون لاهوته أم بلاهوته دون جسده أم بجسده ولاهوته جميعًا؟ فإن زعموا أنّ ذلك حلّ بالجسد دون اللاهوت صاروا إلى قول النسطوريّة. وقُلنا لهم أيضًا: والمسيح عندكم غير الجسد لأنّ المسيح عندكم هو الكلمة والإنسان الكلّي أو الأقنوم القديم ذو الجوهرين، وذلك الجسد جزئي لا كلّي ولا هو الأقنوم القديم. فإنّما حلّ ذلك كلّه بما المسيح غيره من كلّ الجهات.

٢١٤. وإن قالوا: حلّ ذلك باللاهوت دون الجسد، تركوا أيضًا قولهم ودفعوا العيان والوجود عند أنفسهم وأصحابهم،(٤٨) لأنّهم جميعًا يزعمون أنّ جسد المسيح صُلب على الخشبة رأي العيان. وكانوا مع دفعهم الوجود والعيان موجبين أنّ اللاهوت هو المصلوب على

٣. ب || ف: إذا لم يكن.
٦. ب، ف || ل: الثلث.

or gives this answer, the statement of anyone among you who claims that the crucifixion, killing and suffering all affected the Messiah in his entirety in this body – according to you, the crucifixion and killing affected his two substances together or one of his two substances – is cancelled out. This is because if it was not united to this body and was not in this body, it could not have been crucified with this body, been killed with this body or been affected by suffering in this body. There is no alternative on this matter other than these three, and each one of them invalidates one of their principles or a number of them.

213 [ii. *The crucifixion and death*]

Say to them: Tell us about the crucifixion, killing and suffering, to whom did they happen? Was it to the body of the Messiah without his divinity, to his divinity without his body, or to his body and divinity together? If they claim that this happened to the body without the divinity, they move towards the teaching of the Nestorians. We say to them also: According to you the Messiah was other than the body, because according to you the Messiah was the Word and the universal human, or the eternal hypostasis possessing two substances. And this body was individual not universal and was not the eternal hypostasis. So all these things affected someone who was not the Messiah in any respect.

214 If they say: These happened to the divinity without the body, again they abandon their teaching and set aside what is evident and what actually is as they themselves and their colleagues accept it,[48] because they all claim that the Messiah's body was crucified on the wood before people's eyes. Despite their rejection of what actually is and is evident, they are forced to accept that the divinity was crucified on

الخشبة والمطعون بالرُمح والواجد للألم والمدفون في القبر والمحاط به والمحدود وليس ذلك من قولهم.[٤٩]

٢١٥. وإن زعموا أنّ ذلك وقع باللاهوت وبالجسد جميعًا فقد زعموا أنّ اللاهوت قد صُلب مع الجسد ورُفع على الخشبة وقُتل وحلّته الألام ونالته أيدي المخلوقين وقُبر ودُفن وأحاطت به الحُفرة. ولا بُدّ من أن يكون في تلك الأحوال حيًّا أو ميّتًا: فإن كان حيًّا فهو مقتول حيّ ومدفون حيّ؛ وإن كان ميّتًا فمَن الذي أحياه بعد ذلك وأنشره، ومَن الذي أماته قبل أن يَحيا؟

٢١٦. فإن زعموا أنّ الخالق أماته فقد زعموا أنّ الخالق يُميت الخالق وأنّ الإله يُميت الإله، تعالى ربُّنا عن ذلك. وإن زعموا أنّ المخلوقين أماتوه فقد زعموا أنّ المخلوقين يميتون الخالق وأنّ المألوهين يميتون الإله، وهذا أقبح وأظهر فسادًا من الأول.

٢١٧. وإن قالوا: هو الذي أمات نفسه، قلنا: أفيجوز أن يميت الأب نفسه كما أمات الابن نفسه، وكذلك تميت الروح نفسها فيبقوا كلّهم موتى؟ وهذا كلّه تخليط ولا بُدّ لهم منه ما تمسّكوا بأصولهم، أو يرجعوا عن قولهم.

٢١٨. ويقال للذين زعموا من الملكيّة أنّ الصلب والقتل والألم كلّ ذلك نال الإله، تعالى الإله، بالتدبير لا بالحِسّ ولا بالمباشرة:[٥٠] أفتزعمون أنّ الذي ناله من ذلك ألِمَ لما ناله منه ولما حلّ به؟ فإن قالوا: نعم، فقد زعموا أنّ إلاههم يألم؛ ومَن

٨. ب || ف: ان يحيى.
١٤. ب || ف: يميت الروح نفسه.
١٨. ب || ف: تعالى.
١٩. ب || ف: فتزعموا.

the wood, was pierced by the lance, experienced the suffering, was buried in the tomb, was confined and limited by it, even though this is not their teaching.[49]

215 And if they claim that this affected the divinity and the body together, then they are claiming that the divinity was crucified with the body, was raised on the wood, was killed, the sufferings happened to him, the hands of creatures grasped him, he was entombed and buried, and the pit enclosed him. He must have been either living or dead during all these events. If he was living, then he was killed living and buried living. And if he was dead, who revived him after this and resurrected him, and who was it who made him die before he was revived?

216 If they claim that the Creator made him die, they are claiming that the Creator made the Creator die and that the Divinity made the Divinity die – may our Lord be exalted above this. And if they claim that creatures made him die, they are claiming that creatures made the Creator die and that those who are subordinate to the Divinity made the Divinity die. This is a more foul and obvious falsehood than the first.

217 If they say: It was he who made himself die, we say: Then is it possible for the Father to make himself die as the Son made himself die, and likewise for the Spirit to make itself die, so that they will all be lifeless? This is complete confusion, though it is inescapable for them as long as they hold onto their principles; or they must renounce their teachings.

218 And say to those from the Melkites who claim that the crucifixion, death and suffering affected the Divinity, may he be exalted, by control and not through sensation or directly:[50] Do you claim that the one who was affected by this suffered through what affected him and from what happened to him? If they say: Yes, they claim that their Divinity suffered. Now one who

ألم جاز عليه أن يلتذّ ويفرح ويحزَن، وهذه عندهم من صفات المحـدَثين المخلوقين. وإن قالـوا: لم يألم، فقد يجب أيضاً أن يكون لم ينله الألم لأنّه لا فرق بين «ألِمَ» و«ناله الألم». فإن قالـوا: إنّمـا ناله الألم بالتدبير لا بالحسّ ولا بالمباشـرة، قلنا: فكذلك يألم بالتدبير لا بالحسّ ولا بالمباشرة ويُسَرّ ويلتذّ وكذلك يفرح ويحزن كذلك يشمّ ويذوق كذلك. وإذا جاز أن يُصلب ويُقتل بالتدبير فوقوع جميع ما عارضناهم به من طريق التدبير هو دون القتـل والصلب في السهولة والإمكان. ولأن يفرح يحزن ويلتذّ ويألم ويشـمّ ويذوق وينـام ويسـتيقظ على أيّ وجهٍ شاؤوا إن شـاؤوا مـن طـريق المباشـرة وإن شـاؤوا من طـريق التدبير أقـرب للجـواز والإمـكان من الصـلب والقتـل والمـوت. فمـن قُتـل من طـريق التـدبير ومـات من طـريق التدبير فليس بمسـتنكر أن ينـام ويسـتيقظ من طـريق التـدبير ويفـرح ويحـزن ويلتـذ ويألم ويخـاف ويرجـو ويشمّ ويذوق من طريق التدبير إن كان للتـدبير في أصـل هذا الكـلام وجه. ثمّ يقال لهم: أيخلـوا الصـلب والقتل اللذين زعمتهم أنّهما وقعا بالأقنوم القـديم من طريق التدبير من أن تكون حقيقتهما حقيقة صلب وقتـل أو لا يكون حقيقتهما حقيقة ذلك؟ فإن لَم تكن حقيقتهـما حقيقـة صـلب ولا قتـل فإنّما علّقتم لفظًا لا على

٥. ف || ب، ل: ويلذّ.
٦. ب || ف: وإذا اختار.
٩–١٠. ب || ف: إن شاؤو ان شاو من.
١١. ب (هامش)، ف || ب (نصّ): الجواز.
١١. ب، ف || ب (هامش): ممن.
١٤. ف || ب: ويلذ.

suffers may find pleasure, be delighted and be sad. But in their view these are attributes of temporal, created beings. And if they say: He did not suffer, suffering could not have affected him, since there is no distinction between "to suffer" and "to be affected by suffering". If they say: Suffering affected him only by control not through sensation or directly, we say: In the same way he suffered by control and not through sensation or directly, and he was happy and found pleasure, was delighted and sad, smelled and tasted all in the same way. And if he could be crucified and killed by control, then it is much more likely that all these things we have argued about with them could have affected him by means of control than killing and crucifixion. If he found pleasure and was sad, was delighted and suffered, smelled and tasted, slept and woke up, by whatever way they desire, whether by direct means or by means of control, these are more possible and likely than crucifixion, killing and death. For it cannot be denied that one who is killed by control or dies by control can sleep and wake up by control, find pleasure and be sad, be delighted and suffer, be frightened and be hopeful, smell and taste by control, if in the principle of this argument there is some possibility of control.

Then say to them: Could the crucifixion and killing, which you claim affected the eternal hypostasis by control, be anything other than crucifixion and killing in reality, or were they not this in reality? If they were not in reality crucifixion and killing, then you are employing terms without

معنى وادّعيتم معاني لا حقائق لها. وإن كانت حقيقتهما حقيقة صلب وقتل فالذي وقعا به مصلوب مقتول على الحقيقة ميّت على الحقيقة ألم على الحقيقة متى ناله الألم، اعترضتم على ذلك التدبير أم لَم تعترضوا به. وذكر التدبير لا وجه له إلاّ التطريق على إبطال حقيقة وقوع الصلب والقتل، ومَن أبطل حقيقة واحدة فقاسَ قوله أبطل كلّ الحقائق وبقي بلا دين ولا عقد وسَقطَ عن أن يُكلّم أو يناظر. ويقال لهم: ما هذا التدبير الذي زعمتم أنّ الإله ناله به الصلب والقتل، وتدبير لمَن هو؟ أتدبير للإله دبّره على نفسه حتى صُلب بزعمكم وقُتل، أم تدبير دَبّره الخلق عليه؟ فأيّ ذلك ما قالوا، قيل لهم: فما في وقوع أحد هذين التدبيرين مما يُبطل المباشرة ووصول الأَذَى والألم إلى من ناله ذلك ووقع به. ثمّ يقال لهم إن زعموا أنّ ذلك تدبير الإله: كيف اِستجزتم واِستحسنتم أن تزعموا أنّ الإله دبّر قتْل نفسه وصلب نفسه؟ وإذا كان هو الذي دبّر ذلك لخلقه فلا شيء أصوب من تدبيره ولا من شيء أجري إليه تدبيره، ولا أحد من المخلوقين أصوب فعلاً ولا أحكم عملاً وتدبيرًا ممّن جرى على تدبيرٍ دبّره له الخالق وعمل عملاً أجرى للإله، تعالى، بالتدبير الذي دبّره إلى كونه وتمامه. فالذين قتلوه وصلبوه على هذا

٣. ف (هامش) || ب، ف، ل: للألم.
٧. ب، ف || ل: عن يكلّم.
١٣. ب || ف: وكيف.

meaning and purveying meanings which have no reality. And if they were in reality crucifixion and killing, then the one to whom they happened was crucified and killed in reality, was dead in reality, and suffered in reality when suffering affected him, whether you bring in control when you make your reply, or not. But there is no point in bringing in control unless it conduces to negate the reality of crucifixion and killing. And whoever negates one reality will destroy all reality by pursuing the implication of what he has said and will be left without religion or belief, and finally lose the ability to argue or debate.

And say to them: What is this control through which you claim the Divinity was affected by the crucifixion and killing, and whose control was it? Was it the Divinity's control which he exercised over himself when he was crucified, as you claim, and killed, or was it the control which humans exercised over him? Whichever of these they say, say to them: Even when these controls are in effect, there is nothing in either of them that can nullify the immediacy or nearness of injury and suffering in the one who is afflicted with and affected by this.

Then if they claim that this control is of God, say to them: How can you think it possible or right to claim that the Divinity exercised control over the killing and crucifixion of himself? And if it was he who had control of it for his creation, there can be nothing more proper than his control or to which his control is directed. And no creature can act more properly or wisely in deed or control than the one who conforms to the control which the Creator exercises over him, and carries out the deed directed at the Divinity, may he be exalted, under the control which he ordained should be put into full effect. So those who killed him and crucified him, according to this

القول مُصيبون إذًا محسنون، وصلبه وقتله كانا أولى الأشياء بهم وأصحّ تدبير دبّروه وفعل فعلوه، إن كان هو الذي دبّر ذلك وأجرى إليه حتى ناله ووقع به. وإن زعموا أنّ ذلك تدبير المخلوقين عليه لا بمشيئته ولا بتدبيره، قلنا: فهذا غير ما وهمتم بذكركم «نَيل ذلك إيّاه بالتدبير لا بالحسّ ولا بالمباشرة» وفيه أنّكم متى أنصفتم وصحّحتم على أصولكم كنتم بذلك موجبين أنّ الخلق قهروه وغلبوه وضربوه وأذلّوه وصلبوه وقتلوه وأماتوه ودفنوه. وإذا أمكن أن ينالوه ببعض هذا أمكن أن ينالوه بغيره من ضروب الأذى والمكارِه، وإن كان في بعض هذا ما كفى. وإذا جاز هذا عليه جاز عليه كلّ ما قدّمنا ذكره.

وإن كان القتل أكثر من ذلك كلّه ولكن بعض ذاك عندكم أبعد وأنتم له أشدّ كراهة وجواز هذه الأمور عليه تُدخله على أصولكم في صفات المُحْدَثين المخلوقين، تعالى إلهنا وسيّدنا عن صفات الذمّ والنقص عُلوًا كثيرًا.

٢١٩. ويقال للملكيّة جميعًا: إن كان الأقنوم القديم لا تُدركه الأبصار ولا تلمسه الأيدي، والجوهر العامّ الذي هو الإنسان الكلّي ليس بشخص قائم بذاته فتُدركه الأبصار أو تلمسه الأيدي، والمسيح عندكم هو هذان أو هو الأقنوم القديم ذو الجوهرين كما تقولون كثيرًا، فالأبصار إذًا لَم تدرك المسيح والأيدي لَم تنله. فكيف يُصلب أو يُقتل أو يُدفن مَن لا تلمسه الأيدي ولا تراه العيون ولا

١١. ب || ف، ل: بعض ذلك. ١٢. ب || ف: كراهية. ٢٠. ب،ف || ل: العيان.

teaching, were therefore correct and right, his crucifixion and killing were of utmost importance for them, the most proper control they could exercise and act they could perform, if it was he who controlled this and brought it about until it struck and affected him.

If they claim that this was the control of creatures over him, not by any will or control of his, we say: This is different from what you had in mind when you said, "He was afflicted with this through control not by sensation, nor immediately." While you can conform to your principles and remain true to them by this, you are still forced to admit that creatures defeated him, got the better of him, beat him, humbled him, crucified him, killed him, caused him to die and buried him. And if they could inflict some of these upon him, they could make him suffer other things such as injuries and calamities, though some of these are enough. If this could happen to him, then all that we have spoken about previously could happen to him. Even though death is greater than all of these, some of them, in your view, are less probable and you feel a greater aversion towards them, because allowing such things to happen to him would, according to your principles, bring him within the attributes of temporal and created beings – may our God and Lord be exalted far above attributes of weakness and limitation.

219 And say to the Melkites all together: If eyes cannot behold the eternal hypostasis nor hands touch him, and the general substance which is the universal human is not an individual being subsisting of itself whom eyes might behold and hands touch, and the Messiah, according to you, is these two things or is the eternal hypostasis possessing the two substances, as you frequently say, then eyes cannot behold the Messiah nor hands grasp him. So how could he be crucified, killed or buried, whom hands could not touch, eyes see,

يُدرك بشيءٍ من المشاعر ولا تناله الجوارح ولا الآلات؟ وإذا لَم يكن ناسوته شخصًا قائمًا بذاته يُمكن أن تدركه المشاعر وتناله الأيدي فمَن المأخوذ المصلوب المقتول المدفون؟ وما هو المسيح الذي هو عندكم أقنوم قديم وجوهر كلّي أو أقنوم قديم ذو جوهرين؟ فإن قالوا: ذلك المصلوب هو ابن أحد جوهري المسيح،(٥١) قلنا: فالمصلوب إذن هو ابن المسيح الذي هو الجوهرانِ لا المسيح بنفسه، أو ابن أحد الجوهرين المنسوبين إليه. وذاك أبعد من أن يكون هو المسيح ومن أن يكون ما ناله نال المسيح.

٢٢٠. باب آخر.(٥٢) فأمّا قول مَن قال من هذه الفرق: إنّ الاتّحاد هو امتزاج الكلمة بالجسد واختلاطها به، فأنّه قول بين الضعف والفساد من جهات، منها أن أعدل الامتزاج وأعدل الاختلاط بالجسد يوجبان أنّ الذي مازجه واختلط به في المِساحة بقدر ذلك الجسد، وأنّ أجزاء كلّ واحد منهما بإِزاء أجزاء الآخر. وهذا يُوجب الحدّ والنهاية وقِلّة المساحة للكلمة مع التبعيض والتجزّؤ أيضًا؛ والكلمة عندهم في الأصل بخلاف هذه الأوصاف.

٢٢١. وإذا أمكن ذلك في الكلمة وهي عندهم أقنوم من أقانيم الجوهر القديم أمكن ذلك في الأقنومين الآخرين، فتكون مساحة الجوهر بكمالِه مساحة ثلثة أجساد كجسد المسيح ومقداره هذا المقدار فقط وعدد أجزائه كعدد أجزاء هذه الأجساد الثلثة لا غير. وهذا معما فيه من إيجاب التجزّؤ والتبعيض والحدّ والنهاية تصغير ممّن

١. ب (هامش)، ف || ب (نص): فإنّما. ٧. ب، ف || ل: وذلك أبعد.
٤. ب || ف: عندكم أقنوم قديم ذو جوهرين؟. ١٦–١٧. ب، ف || ل: أقنوم من أقانيم، أمكن ذلك.

senses reach, or limbs and instruments grasp? And if his human nature was not an individual subsisting of itself, which senses could reach and hands hold, then who was arrested, crucified, killed and buried? And who was the Messiah, who, according to you, was the eternal hypostasis and the universal substance, or the eternal hypostasis possessing two substances? If they say: The one who was crucified was the son of one of the Messiah's two substances,[51] we say: Then the one who was crucified was son of the Messiah who was the two substances, not the Messiah himself, or son of one of the two substances belonging to him. This is less likely than that it was the Messiah or that whatever affected him affected the Messiah.

220. SECOND CHAPTER[52] [THE ARGUMENT AGAINST THEM CONCERNING THEIR MODELS OF UNITING

Metaphorical explanations of the uniting]

As for the teaching of those from these groups who say: The uniting was the mixing of the Word with the body and its mingling with it, this is a teaching which is clearly weak and wrong from many aspects. One is that the most balanced mixing and mingling with the body require that what mixes and mingles with it should have the same surface size as this body and that the parts of the two should be adjacent to one another. This imposes a limit, an end and a reduction in the size of the Word, as well as dividing and partitioning. And in their view the Word is totally unlike such descriptions.

221 If this was possible for the Word, which for them is one of the hypostases of the eternal substance, it would be possible for the two other hypostases, so that the size of the substance in its entirety would be the size of three bodies like the body of the Messiah, its area would be exactly the area of that, and the number of its parts would be like that of these three bodies without any difference. In addition to the partitioning and dividing, the limiting and the restricting imposed by this, there is the small-mindedness of the one who

قاسه أو أجازه في إله يدعيه لقدر إلهه، نعم ولو زاد في المساحة والذَرع زيادة كثيرة؛[٥٣] فهذا وجه.

٢٢٢. ووجه آخر، وهو أنّه إذا كان الاِمتزاج المعقول والاِختلاط المعقول أيضًا إنّما يكونان للأجسام[٥٤] ذوات الأجزاء المركّبة، فإذا مازح بعضها بعضًا شاعت أجزاء كلّ واحد من الجسمين بين أجزاء الجسم الآخر الذي مازجه. والكلمة ليست عندهم جسمًا؛ وإنّما هي عندهم جوهر بسيط لا تحويه الأماكن ولا تحصره الأجساد وليس بذي أجزاء مركّبة. والاِمتزاج هو أن تشيع أجزاء كلّ واحد من الشيئين الممتزجين في صاحبه كما قلنا قبل، فيتجاور ألطف المجاورة وأشدّها تقاربًا، وكذلك الاِخلاط. وإذا كانت الكلمة ليست بذات أجزاء مركّبة يجوز شياعها في الجسد فتجاور أجزاؤها أجزاء الجسد كما وصفنا لَم يجز عليها امتزاج ولا اختلاط. فإن قالوا: فإنّ ذلك الامتزاج وذلك الاختلاط خلاف هذا الامتزاج المعقول وهذا الاختلاط المعروف فيما بيننا، قلنا: فقد يجوز إذًا أن يكون الكلمة تماسّ الأجسام وتباينها خلاف هذه المماسّة وهذه المباينة المعقولتين. وكذلك تحويها الأجسام خلاف هذه الحواية المعقولة وكذلك تتحرّك وتسكن وتلذ وتألم على خلاف ما يُعقل من ذلك فيما بيّننا. وهذا أكبر وأوسع من أن نجمعه في كتاب.

٢٢٣. وكذلك يلزم الذين زعموا: أنّ الكلمة اتّخذت ذلك الجسد

١٠. ب || ف: تفاوتا.   ١٩. ب || ف: يجمعه.

gauges and judges that this is right for a Divinity and demands his Divinity to be measured, even if he were to increase the size and capacity immensely.[53] And this is one point.

222 Another point is that the mixing and mingling which can be understood are actually only of physical bodies[54] which have composite parts. So if one mixes with another, the parts of each of the two bodies spread through the parts of the other with which it is mixing. But according to them the Word is not a physical body. For them it is a simple substance which cannot be enclosed in locations or contained in bodies, and it does not have composite parts. Mixing occurs when the parts of each of the two things mixing together spread through its companion, as we have just said, to produce the most intimate adjacency and closest proximity, and it is the same with mingling. And if the Word does not have composite parts which could spread through the body so that its parts might come into adjacency with those of the body, as we have described, then mixing and mingling are not possible for it.

If they say: But this mixing and mingling were different from mixing that is understandable and mingling that is familiar among us, we say: Then it was possible for the Word to be in contact with physical bodies and be separate from them differently from the contact and separation which are understandable. In the same way its being contained by physical bodies was different from the familiar containing, and likewise it moved and was at rest, was happy and suffered differently from what can be understood about them among us. This is too huge and enormous for us to bring together in a book.

223 Likewise, those who claim that the Word took this body

هيكلاً ومحلاً، والذين قالوا: بل ادّرعت الجسد ادّراعًا. فيقال لهم: إن كان ذلك على ما يُعقل من الأجسام فقد جعلتم الكلمة جسمًا محدودًا منتقلاً يُفرّغ مكانًا ويشغل مكانًا ويُنضمّ إلى أقنومَيه الآخرين أحيانًا ويبعد عنهما أحيانًا. وإن كان ذلك على خلاف ما يعقل من الأجسام جاز أن تكون الكلمة تماسّ وتباين وتتحرّك وتسكن وتقرب من الأقنومين الآخرين وتبعد، وتلذّ وتألم على خلاف ما يعقل من الأجسام.

٢٢٤. وأمّا الذين زعموا منهم: أنّها حلّت فيه فدبّرت به وعلى يديه، فأنّا نسألهم عن قولهم «حلّت فيه» كما سألنا مَن قال «امتزجت به» ومَن قال «اتّخذته هيكلاً ومحلاً» ومَن قال «ادّرعته اِدّراعًا». فالسوأل عليهم في هذا واحد: إن كان على ما يعقل من حلول الأجسام في الأجسام فقد أثبتوها جسمًا صغيرًا محصورًا حالاً في اللحم والعظم والعصب والعروق في مجاري الدمّ ومسالك الطعام والشراب ومستقرّهما.

٢٢٥. ونسألهم عن قولهم «دبّرت به وعلى يديه» ما يُريدون به، أيُريدون أنّها جعلته آلةً وأداةً لتدبيرها كما يُقال «قطع فلان بالسيف ونجر بالفأس وكتب بالقلم» وأشباه ذلك؟ فهذا ما لا فضيلة له فيه على كثير من المخلوقين، وهو أيضًا خلاف قولهم في الاِتّحاد وخلاف زعمهم أنّه صار من الاِثنين واحد، لأنّه ليس بواجب أن يكون الإنسان والقلم شيئًا واحدًا متى كتب به، وكذلك السيف والفأس

٣. ب، ف || ل: متنقلاً.

as a habitation and dwelling, and those who say: It put on the body like a garment, are forced to accept this. And say to them: If this occurred in the way understood of physical bodies then you have made the Word into a restricted, mobile physical body which can move from a position or occupy it, can be close to its other two hypostases at times and be distant from them at others. If this occurs differently from what is understood about physical bodies, then the Word can come into contact and be separate, be moving and at rest, be close to and be distant from the other two hypostases, be happy and suffering, in ways different from what can be understood about physical bodies.

224 As for those of them who claim: It inhered in him and controlled affairs through him and by means of him, we ask them about their statement, "It inhered in him", just as we have asked the one who says, "It mixed with him", or who says, "It took him as a habitation and dwelling", or who says, "It put him on like a garment." The question against them on this is one: If it occurred in the way that is understood concerning the inhering of physical bodies in physical bodies, then they have affirmed that it was a small, contained physical body which inhered in the flesh, bone, sinew, veins in the blood vessels and passages of food and drink, and where these are found.

225 We question them about their statement, "It controlled affairs through him and by means of him", what they mean by it. Do they mean that it made him a tool and instrument for its control, as it is said, "So and so cut with the sword, chopped with the axe, wrote with the pen" and similar? But in this it had no superiority over the majority of creatures, and it is also different from their teaching about the uniting and their claim that one came from two. This is because the man and pen do not have to be one thing when he is writing with it, and similarly the sword, axe

وسائر الألات ليس بواجب متى استعمل المستعمل شيئا منها أن يكون هو وما استعمله منها شيئًا واحدًا. ولا يكون أيضًا متّحدًا بها لاِستعماله إياها واِتّخاذه إياها آلةً وأداةً كائنا ما كان الاِتّحاد. وكما يقولون «أحيا الأرض بالغيث» و«أثار السحاب بالريح» و«أنبت الزرع بالمطر» وأشباه ذلك. فإِن كانوا إلى هذا يذهبون فلا فَضل إذن لإنسان المسيح على هذه الأشياء المخلوقة التي سمّينا، وليس بواجب أن يكون الإله، تبارك وتعالى، متّحدًا بالريح لإثارته بها السحاب ولا بالمطر لإخراجه به الزرع ولا بالغيث لإحيائه الأرض به ولا لتدبيره ما دبّر بذلك.

٢٢٦. وكذلك يُسألون عن قولهم «دبّر على يديه» ما معناهم فيه. أيُريدون أنّه أظهر على يديه الأعلام والأدلّة والآيات؟ فقد فعل ذلك بالأنبياء من قبله، صلوات الله عليهم، وكانت أعلام بعضهم أعلى وأعجب من كثير من الأعلام التي ظهرت على يديه، عليه السلم وعليهم جميعًا.[٥٥] فإن كان الاِتّحاد هو ذلك فقد اِتّحد الإله إذًا بمَن لا يحصى عدده من الأنبياء ودبّر على أيديهم. وإن كانوا يُريدون أنّه «دبّر على يديه» بمعنى أنّه أمره بتدبير خلقه فمتى أمر بذلك؟ وأي خلْق مِن خلْق الله من سماء وأرض أو حيوان أو نبات أو غير ذلك تولّى المسيح تدبيره، إلاّ أن يذهبوا إلى الذي خلقه من الطين كهيئة الطير ثمّ نفخ فيه فكان بإِذن الله طائرًا؟[٥٦] فهذا يجري مجرى الآيات البديعات لا

١٠. ب || ف: دبّر به وعلى يديه.   ١٨. ب، ف || ل: وغير ذلك.

and other tools, when the user is using them they do not have to become one thing with him. Nor does he become united with them by using them or taking them as tools and instruments, whatever the uniting might be. It is also just like they say, "He revived the earth with a downpour", "He drove the clouds with the wind", "He made the seed grow with the rain", and similar. If they think in this way, there is no superiority to the human in the Messiah over these created things which we have named. For the Divinity, may he be blessed and exalted, does not have to be united with the wind in order to drive the clouds with it, or with the rain in order to make seeds appear with it, or with the downpour in order to revive the earth with it, nor for any control that he exercises in this way.

226 Likewise, they should be questioned about their statement, "He controlled through him", what sense it has for them. Do they mean that he caused signs, proofs and wonders to appear through him? But he performed this for the prophets before him, God's blessing be upon them, and the signs of some of them were more excellent and miraculous than many of the signs which appeared through him, peace be upon him and upon them all.[55] So if the uniting was this, then the Divinity united with prophets without number and controlled through them. And if they mean that he controlled through him in the sense that he ordered him to control his creation, then when was he ordered to do this? And over what part of God's creation, the heaven or the earth, animals or plants, or anything else was the Messiah given authority, unless they are thinking of what he created from clay like the shape of a bird, then he breathed into it and it flew with God's help?[56] But this conforms to extraordinary signs, not

مجرى تدبير الخلق. فإن يجاوزوا هذا ونحوه من آيات الرسل، عليهم السلم، فليس إلاّ أن يدّعوا شيئًا كان سرًّا وأمرًا مكتومًا، فهذا ما لا يعجز أحدًا ادّعاؤه. على أنّه أيضًا ليس كلّ مَن أمر بتدبير شيءٍ وجب أن يكون الله، تبارك وتعالى، متّحدًا به ولا أن يكون ذلك الأمر يوجب له العبادة من المخلوقين ولا أن يكون ربًّا للعالمين.

٢٢٧. وأمّا قول مَن قال منهم «ظهرت منه لهذا الخلق لا على الحلول ولا على المخالطة» فإنّا نسألهم عن معنى قولهم «ظهرت» ما هو؟ أهو أنّ الكلمة برزت للخلق من ذلك الجسد وانكشفت لهم فيه بعد الاستتار فعاينوها أو لمسوها؟ فهذه صفات الأجسام المحدودة التي يجوز عليها الحَصر والحواية والمِساحة. أو هو أنّها أظهرت في ذلك تدبيرًا دلّ على حكمة المدبّر وقدرته؟ فلا شيء من أجسام الخلق إلاّ ولله فيه تدبير يدلّ على حكمته وقدرته، وإن تفاضلت مقادير ذلك التدبير وتلك الدلالات. فإن كان هذا ونحوه هو معنى «ظهرت» وهو معنى «اتّحدت» فلا جسم إذن على هذه المقالة من أجسام الأنبياء ومَن هو دونهم من الناس ثمّ من سائر الحيوان ثمّ من سائر النبات ثمّ من سائر الموات والجماد إلاّ والكلمة متّحدة به ظاهرة منه للخلق. وفي هذا من القبح والخطأ ما فيه.

٢٢٨. وأمّا قول مَن قال: إنّها ظهرت فيه كما يظهر نقش الخاتم في الطينة

to control over creation. If they go beyond this and similar signs of the messengers, on whom be peace, then they can only be claiming a thing which is secret and something which is hidden, though this is something which anyone can claim. However, when he orders someone to control a thing God, blessed and exalted, does not have to be united with him, nor does the order require him to have worship from creatures or to be Lord of the worlds.

227 And as for the teaching of those of them who say, "It appeared from him to creation not by means of indwelling or mingling", we will ask them about the meaning of their statement "It appeared", what this is. Is it that the Word showed itself to the creation through this body and was disclosed to them in it after being concealed, and they saw it and touched it? But these are attributes of restricted physical bodies which can be contained, enclosed and measured. Or is it that it appeared in him as control, which indicated the wisdom and power of the controller? But there is no single physical body in the creation without God's control in it indicating his wisdom and power, even if the scope of this control and indications seem to be superior. And if this and the like is the meaning of "It appeared" and of "It united", according to this view there is no physical body of any of the prophets and other people, or indeed of other animals or plants, or of dead and inanimate beings, that the Word has not united with or appeared from it to creation. This is why it contains fallacy and faultiness all through it.

228 As for the statement of the one who says, "It appeared in him as the imprint of a seal appears in pressed

المطبوعة، فأنّا نقول لهم: ما نراكم تعدون به التمثيل بالأجسام المحدودة؟ فأجعلوا أنّا سوّغناكم هذا التمثيل. أفتزعمون أن الكلمة كانت ظاهرة في جسد المسيح مُعاينة فيه كظهور نقش الخاتم في الطينة المطبوعة متجلّيّة كتجلّي ذلك للأبصار؟ فإن قالوا: نعم، قلنا: فكلّ مَن شاهد المسيح اذاً فقد عاين الكلمة ظاهرة في جسده كمعاينتهم نقش الخاتم في الطينة المطبوعة. وفي هذا شيئان: أحدهما مكابرة الحِسّ ممَن قاله وحمل نفسه عليه والادّعاء على مشاهدات الناس ما ليس فيها؛ والثاني أنّهم يوجبون به على القديم المعاينة والحِسّ وليس ذلك من قولهم. وإن زعموا أنّ الكلمة لم تكن ظاهرة في جسد المسيح معاينةً فيه كظهور نقش الخاتم في الطينة، قلنا: فقد اسقطتم تمثيلكم وأبطلتم حجّتكم وخالفتم بين الحكمين من حيث ادّعيتم التسوية بينهما وليس بجائز لأحدٍ أن يقول «ظهر هذا كما ظهر هذا» لشيئين أحدهما مستتر غير ظاهر والآخر ظاهر للعيون والأبصار والمالامس غير مستتر عنها.

٢٢٩. وكذلك يلزم مَن زعم «أنّ الكلمة ظهرت في الجسد كما تظهر صورة الإنسان في المرآة المجلوّة النقيّة». وذلك أنّه ليس في الدنيا إنسان صحيح البصر لا آفة به ولا مانع له نظر إلى مرآة نقيّة فيها صورة ظاهرة إلاّ رأها، وعاينها معه مَن حاول النظر إليها ممّن حكمه حكمه وحاله

١. ب || ف: ما تراكم.
٥. ب، ف || ل: فان قال.
١٢. ف || ب: خالفتكم.
١٢–١٣. ب || ف: السوية وليس.
١٦. ب || ف: وذلك يلزم من قال.

clay", we say to them: Do we see you daring to compare it with restricted physical bodies? Then we will permit you this comparison. Do you claim that the Word was manifest in the body of the Messiah as something to be beheld in him, like the appearance of the imprint of a seal in imprinted clay, obvious in the way that this becomes obvious to the eyes? If they say: Yes, we say: So everyone who saw the Messiah beheld the Word apparent in his body, like their beholding of the imprint of the seal in impressed clay. There are two points in this. The first is the self-important tone of the one who says this, his seriousness about it and the claim about what people saw but was not there. And the second is that by this they require the Eternal to be seen and sensed, although their teachings do not contain this. And if they claim that the Word was not manifest in the body of the Messiah, to be beheld in him like the appearance of the seal in the clay, we say: You have made your comparison collapse, you have destroyed your proof, and you have made contradictory judgements about the two, because you have claimed they are equal, though it is not possible for anyone to say "This appears as that does" about two things one of which is hidden and not apparent and the other apparent to the sight and eyes, tangible and not at all hidden.

229 The same applies to the one who claims that the Word appeared in the bodily form like the image of a man appears in a polished, clean mirror. And this is because there is no one in the world with perfect eyesight without defect or imperfection, who could look into a polished mirror in which is a clear image and not see it. Anyone with him who fixes his gaze upon it will see the same, as long as he has the same judgement and

كحـاله؛ ولم تكـن الكلمة بمـرئية في جسد المسـيح ولا معاينة. ولا كان بين ظاهـر جسـده وباطنه، صـلّى الله عليه، وبين أجسـاد أمثاله ونظرائه في البشريّة فرق في أنّ ذلك ليس بمحسـوس فيه ولا فيهـم ولا مَرئي في جسـمه ولا في أجسـامهم. ولو جـاز أن يكـون هو ونظراؤه كذلك في الحسّ والمنظـرة وعنـد الامتحان والتفتيش عـن هذه القضـيّة منه ومنهـم، صلّى الله عليه وعلى جميع أنبياء الله ورسـله، لا تفرّق الأبصار بينهم وفي جسده دون أجسـادهم إلهُ ظـاهر فيه ظهـور نقـش الخـاتم في الطينـة وظهـور الصـورة في المـرآة، لجاز أن نقصد بأبصارنا إلى طينتين أحداهما مطبوعة والأخرى خالية فنراهما رؤيةً واحدة ونعاينهما على حالة واحدة. وكذلك نقصـد بأبصـارنا إلى مرآتين في أحـداهما صورة إنسان ناظر فيها والأخرى لا صورة فيها فلا نرى فيهمـا شيئا، فهذا ضرب من التجاهـل والعيـان يكذبه والمشـاهدة تدفعه. وإن قالـوا: فإنّ صـورة الإنسـان تُعاين وكذلك نقـش الخاتم يُرى ويُعاين والكلمـة لا تُرى ولا تُعاين، قلنـا: فلِم مثّلتـم بين ما يُعـاين وبين ما لا يُعاين في الظهور وأحدهما متى ظهر عُوين والآخر لا يُعاين بوجـهٍ من الوجوه؟ وما حقيقة الظهور الممثل بظهور نقش الخاتم وظهـور الصـورة في المرآة إذا نفيتم هذا الظهور المعقول؟ فإن قالوا: ظهوره بأفعاله أو بالدلائل عليه، فليس هذا بمشبه لظهور نقش الخاتم في الطينة ولا لظهور الصورة في المرآة، لأنّ ظهور

٣. ب || ف: ليس محسوس.

attitude. The Word was not visible in the body of the Messiah, nor could it be beheld. Between the outside and inside of his body, may God bless him, and the outside of the bodies of humans like him and equal to him there was no difference, in that it was not perceptible in him or in them, nor visible in his physical body nor in theirs. And if he and those equal to him could be like this in sense and sight, and in a test and inspection on this matter of him and them – may God bless him and all prophets and messengers of God – eyesight could not make any distinction between them, even though in his body and not in theirs the Divinity was manifest like the appearance of the imprint of the seal in the clay and the appearance of the image in the mirror, then it would be possible for us to examine with our eyes two pieces of clay, one of them impressed and the other clear, and for us to look at them with one glimpse, and see that they were in the same condition. Similarly, we could inspect two mirrors, one with the image of a human apparent and the other with no image, and yet see nothing in either. But this smacks of ignorance; our eyes belie it and what is evident rejects it.

If they say: The image of the human can be beheld and similarly the imprint of the seal can be seen and beheld, but the Word cannot be seen or beheld, we say: Then why do you compare what can be beheld with what cannot be beheld clearly, what can be beheld when it appears and what cannot be beheld at all? And what is the reality of the appearance which is comparable to the appearance of the imprint of the seal and the appearance of the image in the mirror, if you refuse to say that it is an appearance that can be understood? If they say: His appearance was in his acts or in signs about him, this is not similar to the appearance of the imprint of the seal in the clay or to the appearance of the image in the mirror. The appearance

النقش وظهور الصورة في الطينة وفي المرآة ظهور للعيان والحسّ لا ظهور فعل للنقش والصورة ولا ظهور دلالة عليهما، لأنّ معاينتهما في المرآة وفي الطينة تُغني عن الاِستدلال عليهما. وأخرى أيضًا وهي أنّه إن كان ظهور الكلمة في الجسد إنّما هو ظهورها بأفعالها أو بالدلائل عليها فهي ظاهرة في كلّ جسد إذ كان لها عندكم في كلّ جسد فعل ودليل يدلّ عليها. فإن قالوا: فإنّ الأفعال والدلائل التي ظهرت في جسد المسيح ليست في كلّ جسد ولا ظهرت من كلّ أحد، رجعنا إلى أذكارهم[٥٧] ما يقرّون بأنّه ظهر من الأنبياء المتقدّمين قبل المسيح وإلى توقيفهم على أعلامهم وأدلّتهم والعجائب التي ظهرت فيهم ولهم وعلى أيديهم. وقلنا لهم أيضًا: إنّ تَفْرِقتكم بين ما ظهر في جسد المسيح وبين ما ظهر في جسد غيره ليس نفيًا منكم للظهور وإنّما هو تفْرقة بين الظهورين وتفضيل منكم لأحد الظهورين على الآخر.[٥٨] وإلاّ فإنّ الكلمة ظاهرة بالتدبير في كلّ جسد إن كان الظهور إنّما هو التدبير. على أنّهم متى صاروا إلى هذا الموضع من الكلام فقد طرحوا تمثيلهم ذلك الأوّل بظهور النقش وظهور الصورة. ويقال لهم: مثّلتم ظهور الكلمة بظهور النقش في الطينة وبظهور الصورة في المرآة لأنّ الظاهرين مشتبهان ولأنّ الظهورين متفقان، أم مثّلتم بين ظاهرين مختلفين وظهورين ليسا بمشتبهين؟ فإن أوجبوا الاِشتباه والاتفاق فقد شبّهوا القديم بالمُحدَث في

٢. ب || ف: فعل النقش.
٣. ب || ف: عليها.
١٣. ب || ف: هي.
١٩. ب || ف: متفقين.

of the imprint and of the image in the clay and in the mirror is an appearance to the eyes and the senses, not the appearance of an action upon the imprint and the image, nor the appearance of an indication about them. To behold them in the mirror and the clay renders any requirement of proof about them unnecessary.

Further and in addition is that if the appearance of the Word in the body was only its appearance in its actions or in signs about it, then it is visible in all bodies, since according to you there are one of its actions and signs about it in every body. If they say: But the acts and signs which appeared in the body of the Messiah are not present in every body and have not appeared in every individual, we will return to their references[57] to what they claim appeared in the prophets who preceded the Messiah, and to the account they give of the signs, proofs and wonders which appeared in them and to them and through them. And we say to them as well: Your separation between what appeared in the body of the Messiah and what appeared in the body of others is not a denial of appearance by you, but only a distinction between two appearances, in which you favour one over the other.[58] From another angle, if the appearance of the Word is only by control, it appears in every body by control. But when they reach this point in the argument they have discarded their first comparison of the appearance of the imprint and of the image.

And say to them: Have you been comparing the appearance of the Word with that of the imprint in the clay and that of the image in the mirror because the two appearances are similar to one another and are alike, or have you been comparing two opposite appearances which are not similar? If they insist upon similarity and accord, they are comparing the eternal with the temporal in

النفس والفعل، وإن زعموا أنّ الظاهرين لا يشتبهان وكذلك ظهور كلّ واحد منهما لا يشبه ظهور الآخر فقد نقضوا قولهم وتمثيلهم الأوّل. فإن قالوا: يشتبهان من جهة ويختلفان من جهة أخرى، قلنا: فهل اختلفا من جهة ما اشتبها؟ فإن قالوا: نعم، ناقضوا. وإن قالو: لا، قلنا: فالكلمة إذن من تلك الجهة ليست بقديمة وظهورها من تلك الجهة ليس بظهور شيءٍ قديم لأنّها إن كانت قديمة من تلك الجهة فهي مخالفة للمُحدث الذي مثّلتموها به من جهة ما شبّهتم بينهما. وكذلك ظهورها إن كان من تلك الجهة ظهورًا لشيءٍ قديم والظهور الذي مثّلتموه به ظهور لشيءٍ مُحْدث فقد اختلفا من جهة ما مثّلتم بينهما. وإلاّ فإن حقّقتم التمثيل بينهما أو بين ظهورَيْهما من جهة من الجهات فلا بدّ من أن تُخرجوا الكلمة من تلك الجهة إلى الحدث إذ كان الحدث مشتملاً على المحدث من جميع جهاته فليس بخارج من الحدث من جهة من الجهات. أو يخرجوا ذلك المحدث من تلك الجهة إلى القدَم إذ كانت الكلمة لا توصف بالحدث من جهة من الجهات. وكذلك القول في ظهوريهما وفي فعليهما أولا. فإن جاز أن يسوّوا بينهما من جهة هما فيها مختلفان فجائز أن يخالف بينهما أو بين شيئين آخرين هما غيرهما من جهة هما فيها متفقان.

٢٣٠. القول عليهم في وصفهم المسيح. يقال للنسطوريّة: ألستم تزعمون أنّ المسيح إله وإنسان؟ فمِن قولهم:

٣. ب، ف || ل: وإن قالوا. ١٤. ب || ف: القديم.

self and act. And if they claim that the appearances are not similar to one another, and that the appearance of each does not resemble the appearance of the other, they contradict their teaching and their first comparison. If they say: The two are similar in one respect and different in another, we say: Are they different from each other in the respect in which they are similar to each other? If they say: Yes, they contradict themselves. And if they say: No, we say: Then in this respect the Word is not eternal, and its appearance in this respect is not the appearance of something eternal, because if it were eternal in this respect then it would be different from the temporal with which you compare it in the respect in which you are comparing the two. Likewise, if its appearance in this respect was the appearance of an eternal thing and the appearance with which you compare it was of a temporal thing, they would be different in the respect in which you are comparing the two.

From another angle, if you insist that the comparison between them and between their appearances was actual in any respect, then you have no alternative but to transfer the Word to temporality in this respect since temporality includes the temporal in all its respects and it cannot escape from temporality in any respect. Or they could transfer the temporal to eternity in this respect, since the Word cannot be characterised by temporality in any respect. The discussion about their appearances and about their acts or not is similar to this. But if they can make them the same in the respect in which they are different, then there could be a difference between them or two other separate things in the respect in which they are alike.

230. The declaration against them about their description of the Messiah

[1. *The argument against the Nestorians*

i. *The human nature of the Messiah*]

Say to the Nestorians: Do you not claim that the Messiah was divine and human? From their teaching

نعم. يقال لهم: أفتزعمون أنّ الإله خالق والإنسان مخلوق؟ فلا بدّ من: نعم، وكذلك يقولون. يقال لهم: أفتزعمون أنّ الخالق ربّ وأنّ المخلوق مربوب؟ فإن أبوا، سُئلوا الفرق بين «مربوب» و«مخلوق». وإن أجازوه وسوّوا بين الكلامين، قيل لهم: أفتزعمون أنّ الإنسان المربوب عبد وأنّ الربّ معبود؟ فإن أبوا، سئلوا الفرق بين «عبد» و«مربوب»، وسئلوا أيضًا الفرق بين «إنسان» و«عبد». وإن سوّوا بينهما، قلنا: فقد أوجبتهم الآن بهذا أنّ المسيح خالق ومخلوق ربّ ومربوب عبد ومعبود. فلا بدّ من ذلك ما لم ينقضوا ما أُعطوا[٥٩] وما أوجبته عليهم المسألة.

٢٣١. يقال لهم: فإذا كان المسيح عندكم موصوفًا بهاتين الصفتين، فخبرونا عمَّن أفرَد له إحداهما لا على نفي الاخرى فقال «المسيح إله» أو قال «المسيح خالق» أو قال «المسيح كلمة الله» أو قال «المسيح اِبن الله»، تعالى الله عن ذلك، أيكون مصيبًا أم مخطئًا؟ فإن قالوا: يكون مخطئًا، فقد أقرّوا على أنفسهم وأصحابهم وأسلافهم بالخطاء لأنّه ليس منهم أحد يمتنع من ذلك.

٢٣٢. وإن قالوا: يكون مصيبًا؛ قلنا: فما تقولون فيه إذا أفرد له الصفة الاخرى لا على نفي الأولى، فقال: «المسيح إنسان مخلوق عبد مربوب مملوك»، أيكون مصيبًا أم مخطئًا؟ فإن قالوا: يكون مخطئًا؛ قلنا: ولِم كان هذا مخطئًا دون الأوّل؟ فإن قالوا: لأنّه أفرد له صفة الإنسانيّة وصفة المخلوق المربوب والعبد المملوك، وليس المسيح كذلك؛ قيل لهم: فالأوّل أيضًا قد أفرد له صفة

they will reply: Yes. Say to them: Do you not claim that the Divinity is Creator and the human created? They must say: Yes, since this is what they teach. Say to them: Do you then claim that the Creator is Lord and the created is subordinate? If they reject this, they should be asked the difference between "subordinate" and "created". And if they allow it and make the two expressions equivalent, say to them: Do you then claim that the subordinate human is servant, and that the Lord is served? If they reject this, ask what is the difference between "servant" and "subordinate", and also between "human" and "servant". If they make them equivalent, we say: Then you are forced by this to accept that the Messiah was Creator and created, Lord and subordinate, servant and served. This is inescapable if they are not to contradict what they have received[59] and what the question forces upon them.

231 Say to them: If, according to you, the Messiah is characterised by these two sets of attributes, then tell us about the person who singles out one, although he does not deny the other, and says, "The Messiah is divine", or "The Messiah is Creator", or "The Messiah is the Word of God", or "The Messiah is the Son of God" – may God be exalted above this. Is he right or wrong? If they say: He is wrong, they acknowledge error against themselves, their colleagues and predecessors, because none of them reject this.

232 If they say: He is right, we say: What will you say about him if he singles out the other attribute, although he does not deny the first, and says: "The Messiah was human, created, a servant, subordinate, owned"? Is he right or wrong? If they say: He is wrong, we say: Why is this one wrong but not the first? If they say: Because he singles out his attribute of humanity and the attribute of being created and subordinate, servant and owned, and the Messiah is not like this, say to them: But the first has also singled out his attribute

القديم الخالق المعبود الذي ليس بإِنسان ولا مخلوق، وليس المسيح كذلك. فإِن كان هذا الثاني مخطئًا لأنّه أفرد له إحدى صفتيه فواجب أيضًا أن يكون ذلك الأوّل مخطئًا لأنّه أفرد له إحدى صفتيه. وإن قالوا: يكون زاعم ذلك مخطئًا لأنّه إذ أفرد له هذه الصفة لَم يبنه من سائر المخلوقين بشيء ولم يفرق بينه وبينهم، قلنا: وكذلك يكون الزاعم أنّه إله خالق مخطئًا لأنّه لم يُبنه من الإله القديم بشيء ولم يفرق بينه وبينه في هذا القول بمعنى من المعانى. ولنْ يجدوا بين هذين فرقًا فلا يقولون فيه شيئًا إلاّ أمكن الخصم أن يحتج عليهم بمثله ويُعارضهم بنظيره.

٢٣٣. ويقال لهم: وكيف يمكنكم أن تمتنعوا من إفراد هذه الصفة فتقولوا: «المسيح إنسان مخلوق عبد مربوب مملوك»، وأنتم قد تفردون له من الأسماء والأوصاف مثل هذا أو ما هو أشنع عند بعض مخالفيكم من هذا، فتقولون: المسيح اِبن داود واِبن مريم واِبن آدم ومولود من مريم وكان حملاً ثمّ مولودًا وصبيًا ثمّ ناشئًا ثمّ بالغًا، وتزعمون أنّه أكل وشرب وجاع وعطش ونام واستيقظ وصلّى وصام ودعا ربّه وهرب من عدُوّه وناله الخوف والروع والآلام؛ وتزعمون أيضًا أنّه صُلب وقُتل ودُفن. فأيّما أكبر وأعظم، إفراد هذه الصفات أو إفراد قول القائل «المسيح إنسان مخلوق وعبد لله صالح مربوب مملوك»؟

٢٣٤. وكذلك يقال لهم: إذا زعمتم أنّه ربّ من جهة لاهوته فقولوا: هو

٨. ب || ف: ولا يقولون.
٨. ب || ف: الا ما امكن.
١٤. ب || ف: حملاً مولوداً.
١٨. ب || ف: المسيح اله مخلوق.
١٩. ب || ف: وتقولوا.

of being eternal, Creator, served, who is not a human or created, and the Messiah is not like this. So if this second is wrong because he singles out one of his two attributes, then the first must also be wrong because he singles out one of his two attributes. If they say: The person who claims this is wrong because in singling out this attribute in him he does not distinguish him from the rest of creation in anything and does not make any separation between him and them, we say: In the same way the person who claims that he is divine and Creator is wrong because he does not distinguish him from the eternal Divinity in anything, and in this statement does not make any real separation between the two. They will not be able to find any separation between these two, so that they will not be able to say anything against which the opponent will not be able to argue in the same way or respond to them with anything equivalent.

233 Say to them: How can you prevent this attribute being singled out, or saying: "The Messiah was human, created, servant, subordinate, owned", while you single out names and descriptions for him that are like these, or are even more repugnant to those who are at variance with you? For you say that the Messiah is son of David, son of Mary, son of Adam, born of Mary, was a foetus and then born, was young and then grown and adult; you claim that he ate and drank, was hungry and thirsty, slept and woke up, worshipped, fasted, prayed to his Lord, and fled from his enemies, that fear, fright and suffering affected him. You also claim that he was crucified, killed and buried. So what is greater and more serious, to single out these attributes or the teaching of the one who says: "The Messiah was human, created, a pious servant of God, subordinate and owned"?

234 In the same way say to them: If you claim that he was Lord with respect to his divine nature, then say that he

عبد من جهة ناسوته. وإذا قلتم: قُتل وصُلب من جهة ناسوته، فقولوا: هو مخلوق ومربوب وعبد ومملوك من جهة ناسوته.

٢٣٥. ويقال لهم: إن كان مَن أفرد له إحدى الصفتين مخطئًا فلا يكون الواصف له إذن مصيبًا أبدًا حتى يجمع له كلّما سمّاه ببعض هذه الأسماء أو ذكره ببعض هذا الذكر هاتين الصفتين جميعًا فيقول «المسيح إله وإنسان وخالق ومخلوق وربّ ومربوب وعبد ومعبود وابن الله، تعال الله عن ذلك، وابن مريم وابن داود وابن آدم» وأشباه ذلك ممّا قدّمنا ذكره وممّا لَم نذكره ممّا في إفراد بعضه دون بعض إيقاع الشبهة. وكذلك إذا أراد مخاطب أن يخاطبه قال له «يا إله وإنسان» و«يا خالق ومخلوق» و«يا ربّ ومربوب» و«يا عبد ومعبود» ويا «ابن القديم وابن المحدث». وكذا إذا ذكره ذاكر بقتل أو صلب أو ولاد قال «ولدت مريم الإله والإنسان» و«صُلب الإله والإنسان» و«قُتل الإله والإنسان»، تعالى الله عن ذلك جميعًا أبدًا، بين الإسمين والصفتين. وإذا كان هذا هكذا فكلّ نسطوري على وجه الأرض إذن على خطأ لتركهم الجمع بين هاتين الصفتين وهذين الأسمين كلّما ذكروا المسيح وسمّوه ووصفوه، ولأن ذلك لا يكاد تسمع من أحد منهم ولأنّ الجمع بين هاتين الصفتين عند أكثرهم في أكثر الأوقات في غاية من الشناعة والخطأ. ولا بدّ لهم من أن يلزموا أنفسهم ما ألزمناه من ذلك ما تمسّكوا بأصلهم.

٢٣٦. وإن زعموا أنّ مَن أفرد له هذه الصفات التي سألناهم عن إفرادها

٨. ب || ف: لم نذكره ممّا في.
٩. ب || ف: فقال له.

was servant with respect to his human nature. And if you say: He was killed and crucified with respect to his human nature, then say: He was created, subordinate, servant and owned with respect to his human nature.

235 Say to them: If the one who singles out one of his two attributes is wrong, then someone who describes him, whenever he gives him some of these names or references, will only be right if he joins both attributes together and says, "The Messiah was divine and human, Creator and created, Lord and subordinate, servant and served, Son of God (may God be exalted above this) and son of Mary, son of David and son of Adam", and similar things which we have mentioned above and not mentioned, to single out some of which and not others produces obscurity. Similarly, if someone wished to speak to him, he would say to him "Divinity and human", "Creator and created", "Lord and subordinate", "Servant and served", "Son of the eternal and son of the temporal". And similarly if someone spoke about his death, crucifixion or birth, he would say: "Mary gave birth to the Divinity and the human", "The Divinity and the human were crucified", "The Divinity and the human were killed" (may God be exalted high above all of this), using both names and both attributes. If this is so, then every Nestorian on the face of the earth is wrong, because they do not use these two sets of attributes and names in full each time they refer to the Messiah, or name him and describe him; this is hardly ever heard from any of them, and according to most of them, the combination of the two sets of attributes most of the time produces the greatest repugnance and error. But they have to force themselves to accept these things that we have made them accept, as long as they cling to their principles.

236 If they claim that one who singles out these attributes about which we have asked them

ليخبروه فقال «المسيح إنسان مخلوق مربوب عبد مملوك» لم يكن مخطئًا كما أنّه إذا أفرد له صفة الإله الخالق لم يكن مخطئًا كانوا بهذا القول قد ركّبوا شناعة عظيمة عند أنفسهم وعند أهل نحلتهم قديمًا وحديثًا، لأنّك لا تكاد تجد صاحب تثليث يسمح نفسه بأن يقول: «المسيح مخلوق مربوب مملوك». ولو سهّل ذلك عليهم أو كان من دينهم لأكثروا استعماله والتخاطب به كما يكثرون أن يقولوا «المسيح إله» و«المسيح اِبن الله»، جل الله، و«المسيح ربّنا وإلهنا»، تعالى إلهنا وسيّدنا الواحد الذي ليس كمثله شيء.

٢٣٧. ولسنا نقتصر لهم على هذه الجملة وإن كانت عندهم عظيمة شنيعة دون المسائلة لهم وإلزامهم في هذا الباب ما يلزمهم فنقول لهم: إذا جاز أن تفردوا للمسيح هذه الصفة فتقولوا: «المسيح عبد مخلوق مربوب مملوك» فعبد لمن هو؟ ومَن ربّه ومالكه وخالقه؟

٢٣٨. فإن قالوا: ليس بعبد لأحدٍ ولا نقول أنّ لَه ربًّا ولا خالقًا ولا مالكًا؛ قلنا: فكيف يكون مخلوقًا مَن لا خالق له ومربوبًا مَن لا ربّ له وعبدًا ممولكًا مَن لا مالك له؟ وإن كان هذا جائزًا فما تنكرون من أن يكون كلّ مخلوق فلا خالق له وكلّ مربوب فلا ربّ له وكلّ عبد مملوك فهذا حكمه؟ وهذا من أشدّ شيء لأصولهم وأصول غيرهم من الملل خلافًا وهم خاصّة. وذاك أنّهم يزعمون أنّ «مخلوق» مضاف إلى «خالق» و«مربوب» مضاف إلى «ربّ» و«مملوك» مضاف إلى «مالك». وأكثرهم وأكثر رؤسائهم يتجاوزون هذا إلى أن يزعموا أنّه

١٣. ب || ف: ولا يقولون. ١٥. ب || ف: فما ينكرون.

to give a view on this, and says: "The Messiah was human, created, subordinate, servant, owned", is not wrong, just as if he singled out for him the attribute of Divinity and Creator and would not be wrong, by this statement they would be amassing together great disgrace, in their own eyes and in those of the followers of their denomination old and new. This is because you will hardly find a believer in the Trinity who would allow himself to say: "The Messiah was created, subordinate, owned". If it were easy for them, and was of their religion, they would employ it frequently in their utterances, as they frequently say: "The Messiah is divine", "The Messiah is Son of God" (God is great) and "The Messiah is our Lord and Divinity", may our one Divinity and Lord be exalted, like whom there is none.

237 Even though it is extremely repugnant to them, we will not restrict ourselves in all these questions and implications which necessarily face them in this section, and we say to them: If you can single out this attribute for the Messiah and say: "The Messiah was servant, created, subordinate, owned", then whose servant was he and who was his Lord, owner and Creator?

238 If they say: He was servant to no one and we do not say that he had a Lord, Creator or owner, we say: Then how can one who has no Creator be created, or be subordinate who has no Lord, or be servant and owned who has no owner? If this is possible, why do you deny that all created beings have no Creator, and all subordinate beings have no Lord, and that the same applies to all servants and owned beings? This is a very serious thing for them in opposing their principles and for those from other denominations who do the same, though for them especially. The reason is that they claim that "created" is related to "Creator", "subordinate" to "Lord", and "owned" to "owner". Most of them and most of their leaders go further than this and claim that

لا يستحقّ الخالق أن يُسمّى خالقًا إلاّ ومخلوق ولا إلاهًا إلاّ مألوه موجود.[٦٠] فيقال لهم: إن جاز عندكم أن يكون الشيء مخلوقًا ولا خالق له ومربوبًا ولا ربّ له فلِم لا يجوز أن يكون الإله إلاهًا ولا مألوه وأن يكون الخالق خالقًا ولا مخلوق؟ والأوّل أشدّ عليهم وهو أنّه إن كان شيء واحد مخلوقًا لا خالق له جاز أن يكون كلّ مخلوق كذلك. وكذلك في قولهم عبد ومربوب ومملوك.

٢٣٩. وإن زعموا أنّه عبد لله كانوا بإطلاق ذلك وبزعمهم أنّ المسيح عبد لله أشدّ خلافًا لأصلهم في هذا الباب ولأسلافهم. وقيل لهم عند ذلك: أفعبدًا صالحًا كان أم تزعمون أنّه بخلاف ذلك؟ فليس من قولهم ولا من قولنا ولا من قول أحد تولاّه أنّه كان بخلاف صفة الصلاح، صلّى الله عليه. وإن قالوا: كان عبدًا صالحًا، ازدادوا بهذا القول من مذهبهم فيه، عليه السلم، بُعدًا. وقيل لهم: فهل يكون عبدًا صالحًا إلاّ مَن كان لِربّه مطيعًا، وهل يكون لِربّه مطيعًا إلاّ من كان مأمورًا، وهل يكون كذلك عندكم إلاّ مَن كان قادرًا على أن يكون مطيعًا وقادرًا على أن يكون عاصيًا؟ فإذا كان ذلك كذلك فهل بينه وبين سائر البشر المخلوقين المأمورين فرق في نفس الخلقة والإنسانيّة والعبوديّة ولزوم فرض الطاعة ومجانبة المعصية والرجاء والخوف لربّه والرهبة والرغبة إلى خالقه؟

٢٤٠. فإن زعموا أنّ بينه وبينهم فرقًا وهو اتّحاد الخالق بإنسانه،[٦١] قلنا: إنّما

٦. ب || ف: مربوب وعبد ومملوك.
٨. ب، ف || ل: قيل لهم.
٩. ب || ف: أفعبد.

the Creator cannot be called Creator unless there is a created being, nor Divinity unless there is a being beneath him in existence.[60] Say to them: If in your view there can be a thing created without a Creator, and a thing subordinate without a Lord, then why is it not possible for the Divinity to be a Divinity without a being under him, and for the Creator to be Creator without a created being? The first is very serious for them, because if there is one thing created without a Creator, everything can be like this. It is the same with their statement about "servant", "subordinate" and "owned".

239 If they claim that he was servant of God, in saying this while claiming that the Messiah was the servant of God they seriously differ from their principles and from their predecessors on this subject. Say to them concerning this: Was he a pious servant or do you claim that he was not? though there is nothing in their teaching or ours, or in the teaching of anyone that would favour the idea he was other than pious, may God bless him. If they say: He was a pious servant, by this statement they move further away from their teaching about him, on him be peace. Say to them: Can there be a pious servant except one who is obedient to his lord, and can there be someone obedient to his lord except one who is under orders, and in your view can there be anyone like this except one who has power to be obedient and disobedient? If the matter is like this, then is there between him and other created humans who are under orders any distinction in createdness itself, humanity and servanthood, the imposed duty to obey and to avoid disobedience, hope and fear of their Lord, and awe and longing for their Creator?

240 If they claim that there is a distinction between him and them, which is the uniting of the Creator with the human in him,[61] we say: We have only

سألناكم هل من فرق في نفس الخلقة والعبوديّة والإنسانيّة ولزوم ما يلزم العبد المخلوق، ولم نسألكم عن معنىً ثانٍ تدّعونه له ولا عن إلهيّة تضيفونها إليه، هي غير إنسانيّته وغير خلقته وغير ما أفرزتم به من عبوديّته. فإن قالوا: نعم مجيئه من غير ذَكَر؛[٦٢] قلنا: وليس عن هذا سألناكم أيضًا، ومجيئه من غير ذكر لا يخرجه عندكم من أن يكون إنسانًا مخلوقًا يجري عليه ما يجري على أمثاله. ولا يعصمكم من أن تزعموا أنّه عبد مربوب على ما ألزمناكم بدئًا. وإنّما فارق مَن جاء من ذكر بأنّه ليس له أب أدنى وأنّ لغيره أبًا أدنى. فإنّما اختلفا في تثبيت الأب للذي جاء من ذكر ونفي الأب عنه، وليس اِختلاف الإنسانين في شيء هو غيرهما يضاف إلى أحدهما ويُنفى عن الآخر باختلاف في جوهريّتهما ولا في إنسانيّتهما ولا في عبوديّتهما. وإذا كان ذلك كذلك فقد ثبت أنّه إنسان مخلوق مربوب وعبد لله صالح كنُظرائه من الأنبياء، صلوات الله عليهم.

٢٤١. ويقال لهم إذا جاز أن يفردوا له إحدى هاتين الصفتين فيقولوا: «هو إنسان مخلوق وعبد مملوك مربوب» يرجعون إلى أنّه كذلك من جهة ناسوته، فكذلك يقولون أنّه ليس بإله ولا خالق ولا اِبنًا لله ولادًا ولا كلمة لله ولا روحه قولاً مفردًا، يرجعون إلى أنّه كذلك من جهة ناسوته، ويصوّبون قول مَن قال ذلك وأظهره وكشفه وكرّر ذكره وأكثر استعماله. فإن قالوا: لا نقول ذلك ولا نُجيزه ولا نصوّب قائله؛ قلنا: ولِم لا يجوز ذلك ولِم لا

٤. ب || ف: فليس.   ٨. ب || ف: أب ادمي وأن لغيره ابا ادمي.

asked you about a distinction in createdness itself, in servanthood and humanity, and about the necessity imposed upon the created servant. We have not asked you about a second item which you claim about him, nor the divinity which you ascribe to him. That is different from his humanity and his createdness, and different from the servanthood which you treat separately. If they say: Yes, his coming was without a male,[62] we say: Neither have we asked you about this. His coming without a male does not, in your view, exclude him from being human and created, affected by the same things as those like him. Nor does it restrain you from claiming that he was a servant and subordinate, as we compelled you to say at the start. He is only distinguished from those who came from a male by not having an earthly father, while others do. The two only differ in that a father is acknowledged for someone who comes from a male, and denied for him. Any difference between the two humans in anything external to them and attributable to one of them but denied of the other is not a difference in their substantiality, humanity or servanthood. If this is so, then it is established that he was human, created, subordinate and a pious servant of God, like his equivalents among the prophets, God's blessings be upon them.

241 Say to them, if they are able to single out one of these two attributes for him and say: "He was a created human, and an owned, subordinate servant", returning to the position that he was like this with respect to his humanity, they effectively say that he was not divine or Creator or Son of God as one born or Word of God or his spirit in any unique attribution, returning to the position that he was like this with respect to his humanity. And they agree with the person who says this, discloses it, uncovers it, mentions it repeatedly, and employs it frequently. If they say: We do not say or acknowledge this, nor do we agree with the person who says it, we say: Why is it not possible and why is not

كان قائله مُصيبًا، والمسيح عندكم ليس بقديم من جهة ناسوته ولا إلاهًا ولا خالقًا؟ فإن قالوا: فإنّ الأمر وإن كان عندنا كذلك فإنّا نكره إطلاق ذلك لما فيه من إيهام الخطاء ونفي الإلهيّة عن المسيح، قلنا: وما على خصومكم في أن ألزموكم إطلاق ما يُوهم الخطاء وينفي إلاهيّة المسيح إذ قادكم الكلام إليه، وهل تدفعون ذلك بحجة أكثر من كراهتكم لما يوهم الخطاء عندكم، وبأيّ شيء تفرقون بينكم وبين مَن قال «لا أقول المسيح إنسان ولا عبد ولا مربوب ولا مخلوق، ولا أُطلق ذلك لما فيه من إيهام الخطاء والتسويّة بينه وبين غيره من الناس، ولأنّي متى أطلقت ذلك كنتُ قد وافقت في وصفه أريوس وأصحابه أو قاربتُهم في ذلك أو كنت قد أثبتُّه إنسانًا عبدًا كما أثبَته بولى السمساطي وأصحابه والمسلمون»؟[٦٣] ولا بدّ لهم من إطلاق ذلك أو الإمتناع من هذا وفي إمتناعهم من هذا نقض لِكلّ ما أعطوا.

٢٤٢. فإن هم أجازوا قول من قال «المسيح ليس بإله ولا خالق ولا ابن الله» على حسَب ما سألناهم «ولا كلمة الله ولا روحه» وصوّبوا قول مَن قاله، كانوا بإطلاقهم ذلك وبإجازته أشدّ بعداً من مذهبهم ونحلة أسلافهم وأشدّ خلافًا لما عليه أصحابهم. وقيل لهم: وكذا يجوز لكم أيضًا أن تقولوا ولغيركم أن يزعم «إنّ المسيح ليس بإنسان ولا ابن مريم ولا ابن داود ولا من ولد آدم ولا صُلب ولا قُتل ولا دُفن ولا نالته أيدي المخلوقين ولا رآه الناس ولا شاهدوه»، فيطلق

٦. ب || ف: كراهيتكم. ١١. ب || ف: السميساطي. ١٤. ب، ف || ل: ولا ابن الله.

the one who says it right, when according to you the Messiah was not eternal with respect to his humanity, nor divine or Creator?

If they say: Even though the matter is like this for us, we will not allow it to be expressed because it contains deceitful error and the denial of the Messiah's divinity, we say: So what will prevent your opponents from forcing you to express what gives a suspicion of error and denies the divinity of the Messiah, if the argument leads you to it? And can you reject it by any greater proof than your hatred for what gives a suspicion of error among you? And how can you distinguish between yourselves and the one who says, "I will not say the Messiah was human or servant or subordinate or created, and I will not express this because it gives the suspicion of error and places him on the same level as other people. If I were to say this I would be agreeing with Arius and his followers' description of him, or coming close to them, or I would be acknowledging that he was human and a slave, as Paul of Samosata and his followers and the Muslims have done"?[63] They cannot avoid either expressing this or refusing to do so, though in refusing they overturn all they have received.

242 If they allow the statement of the one who says, "The Messiah was not divine or Creator or Son of God" in the way we have asked them, "nor Word of God or his spirit", and they agree with the one who says it, then by expressing this and allowing it they are even further from their beliefs and the creed of their predecessors, and in greater disagreement with the teachings of their colleagues. Say to them: You can say this, although another can claim: "The Messiah was not human or son of Mary, son of David or a son of Adam, nor was he crucified, killed and buried, nor did the hands of created beings hold him, nor did people see him and look upon him." He may express

هذا القول إطلاقًا ويظهر إظهارًا ويكرّر ذكره ويكثر اِستعماله ويرجع من ذلك إلى أنّه كذلك من جهة لاهوته. فإن أبوا ذلك سُئلوا الفرق، ولا فرق بوجه من الوجوه. وإن سوّوا بينهما صاروا عند أنفسهم وأصحابهم إلى غاية من غايات الخطاء. ولزمهم ألاّ يكون بعض ما عبّروا به عن المسيح من هذه العبارات ووصفوه به من هذه الصفات أولى به وبالمخبر عنه من بعض حتى يكون قول مَن قال «إنّ المسيح عبد في الصحّة» عندهم على ما سئلوا عنه كقول مَن قال «المسيح ربّ» وحتى يجعلوا قول مَن قال «المسيح لا إله ولا إنسان» كقول مَن قال «المسيح إله وإنسان». وكفى بمذهب يؤدّي صاحبه إلى هذا ونحوه وإلى أن يصير به الأحتجاج إلى حال يستوي فيها عنده نفي ما اعتقده وإثباته إن شاء تحقيقًا وإن شاء إجازه قبحًا وتناقضًا. ولو كانوا يردّون هذا الحدّ من قولهم إلى قياس لقايسناهم فيه مقايسة مجرّدة، ولكنّه أوضاع لهم فبآرائهم ما يدفعها ويدلّ على فسادها، وربّنا محمود.

٢٤٣. ويُسألون من وجه آخر فيقال لهم: أخبرونا عن المسيح الذى زعمتم أنّه إله وإنسان وأنّ تلك حقيقته، هل فعل بكماله فعلاً واحدًا قطّ على الحقيقة أو هل قال قولاً واحدًا قطّ على الحقيقة؟ فإن قالوا: نعم، فقد أثبتوا فعلاً واحدًا فعله القديم والمحدث، وهذا خلاف مذهبهم لأنّ فعل الإله عندهم غير فعل الإنسان كائنا مَن كان ذلك الإنسان. فمتى زعموا أنّ المسيح الذي هو إله وإنسان فَعَل بكماله

١٠. ب || ف: يساوي.　　١٣. ب || ف: ولكنها.　　١٩. ب || ف: كائنا ما.

this statement and make it known, he may mention it repeatedly and employ it often, and in so doing return to saying that he was like this in respect of his divinity. If they deny this, they must be asked about the distinction, though there is none in any respect. If they say the two are equal, then in their own terms and in those of their colleagues they reach the uttermost limit of error.

And they are forced to accept that some of the explanations they offer about the Messiah and the attributes they give him have no more priority or significance for him than others, so that the statement of one who says, "The Messiah is servant in reality", in the way they are asked about it is for them like the statement of one who says, "The Messiah is Lord." And they will come to recognise that the statement of the one who says, "The Messiah is not divine and not human", is like the statement of the one who says, "The Messiah is divine and human". It is enough for a doctrine that leads its followers to this and similar things, and to the point that arguments about it allow it equally to be disbelieved and believed, making it true if desired and if desired allowing it to be held as vile and contradictory. If they want this summary of their teaching to be assessed logically then we will give them the most logical assessment possible, though their positions are such that they can be rejected and proved mistaken on the basis of their own ideas. May our Lord be praised!

243 [ii. *The divine and human actions of the Messiah*]

They should be questioned about another matter, so say to them: Tell us about the Messiah who you claim was divine and human and that this was him in reality, did he ever in his entirety perform one action in reality or ever say one thing in reality? If they say: Yes, they affirm one action performed by the eternal and temporal, and this is contrary to their belief, because the action of the divine for them is different from the action of the human, no matter who this human might be. So in claiming that the Messiah, who was divine and human, performed in his entirety

فعلاً واحدًا على الحقيقة، فقد نقضوا هذا الأصل ووافقوا أصحاب المخلوق وهم يستوحشون من ذلك، وموضع استيحاش لعمري![٦٤]

٢٤٤. ومتى زعموا أيضًا أنّ فعلاً واحدًا يفعله الإله والإنسان اللذان هما المسيح، قلنا: أفَرأيتم إذا قال المسيح على هذا الوجه «أنا ابن مريم» و«أنا ابن البشر»[٦٥] و«أنا من ولد آدم» ولم يكن هذا قولاً للإنسان دون الإله أفليس قد أقرّ الإله عندكم، تعالى الإله، بأنّه اِبن البشر وأنّه من ولد آدم وأنتمى إلى بنوّة داود ومريم؟ وهذا كذب لا شكّ فيه، والإله يتعالى عن ذلك. وكذلك إن قال «أنا مولود من الأب القديم»[٦٦] أو قال «أنا وأبي شئ واحد»[٦٧] كما تروون عنه، ولم يكن هذا القول قولاً للكلمة دون الإنسان، أفليس قد ادّعى إنسان المسيح أنّه مولود من الإله وأنّه والأب القديم شئ واحد؟ وهذا كذب أيضًا، وإنسان المسيح عندكم لا يكذب والمسيح، عليه السلم، لا يقول إلاّ حقًّا. فإن رجعوا إلى أن يقولوا: إنّما أراد «أنا اِبن البشر ومن ولد آدم من جهة ناسوتي وأنا مولود من الأب وأنا وأبي شئ واحد من جهة لاهوتي»، قلنا: فإذا كان ذلك القول الواحد لهما جميعًا فهما جميعًا من ولد آدم من جهة الناسوت ومولودان من الأب من جهة اللاهوت.

٢٤٥. فإن قالوا: نعم، فالقديم إذن من ولد آدم وداود ومريم واِبن البشر، والإنسان مولود من القديم.

٢٤٦. وإن قالوا: لا، فقد ألحقوهما جميعًا الكذب في الخبر.

٩. ب || ف: يرون.
١٢. ب || ف: فالمسيح.
١٣–١٤. ب || ف: إنما اراد بابن البشر.

one action in reality, they overturn this principle and agree with the supporters of a created being, although they abominate this – quite something to abominate![64]

244 And since they claim that one action could be performed by the divine and human who were the Messiah, we say: If the Messiah in this manner said, "I am the son of Mary", "I am the son of man",[65] and "I am a child of Adam", and this was not the speech of the human separate from the divine, do you not see that the Divinity attested, as you see it (may the Divinity be exalted), that he was son of man and a son of Adam and related to the sons of David and Mary? This is a lie with no doubt, and the Divinity is exalted above it. Similarly, if he said "I am begotten from the eternal Father",[66] or "I and my Father are one thing",[67] as you relate from him, and this was not the speech of the Word separate from the human, did not the human in the Messiah claim that he was begotten from the Divinity and that he and the eternal Father were one thing? And this is a lie as well, although the human in the Messiah, according to you, did not lie, and the Messiah, peace be upon him, only spoke true.

If they retreat to saying: He only meant "I am the son of man and child of Adam with respect to my humanity, and I am begotten from the Father and I and my Father are one thing with respect to my divinity", we say: If this one statement was from both of them together then they were both together children of Adam with respect to humanity, and begotten from the Father with respect to divinity.

245 If they say: Yes, then the eternal must be a child of Adam, David and Mary, and son of man, and the human must have been begotten from
246 the eternal. | And if they say: No, they attach lies to both of them together in what they report.

٢٤٧. وإن قالوا: لا يجوز أن يفعل المسيح بكماله فعلاً واحدًا ولا أن يقول قولاً واحدًا في الحقيقة، ولكن أقاويله مقسومة على جوهرَيه القديم والمُحدث. فمتى انتسب إلى ولادة القديم فذلك قول الكلمة لا قول الإنسان، ومتى انتسب إلى ولادة مريم والبشر فذلك قول الإنسان لا قول الإله، وكذلك أفعاله منقسمة على جوهرَيه ففعل القديم لا يكون فعلاً للمُحدث وفعل المحدث لا يكون فعلاً للقديم؛ قلنا: فقد صرّحتهم الآن بأنّه لا فعل للمسيح على الحقيقة وأنّ الفعل إنّما هو للجوهر القديم دون المحدث أو للمحدث دون القديم. وما كان فعلاً للقديم لا للمحدث فليس هو فعلاً للمسيح الذي هو عندكم قديم ومحدث إذ كان القديم ليس هو جوهرَين أحدهما إله قديم والآخر إنسان، وما كان فعلاً للمحدث لا للقديم فليس هو فعلاً للمسيح الذي تزعمون أنّه إله وإنسان لأن المحدث ليس هو إلاهًا وإنسانًا. فكلّ فعل وقعتم عليه فلَم يفعله المسيح وإنّما فعله مَن ليس بمسيح. وإذا لَم يمكن أن يكون للمسيح فعل على الحقيقة ولا قول على الحقيقة لَم يجز أن يُوصف بالقدرة على قول ولا فعل إلاّ أن يرجعوا إلى المجاز والتعليق الذي لا محصول له عند التحقيق؛ فيقولوا «قال المسيح وفَعَل المسيح» يُريدون «فعل الإله لا الإنسان أو الإنسان لا الإله، وقال أحدهما لا الآخر». فيلزمكم على هذا القياس أن يكون قولكم «المسيح إله وإنسان» مجاز لا حقيقة، وإلاّ فإنّه متى لَم يكن لقول «مسيح» حقيقة متى أراد تثبيت

٣. ب || ف: انتسب إلى القديم.
٦. ب || ف: صرحتوا.
٧. ب || ف: وان الفعل للقديم انما هو للجوهر القديم.
١٠. ف || ب: احدهم قديم.
١١. ب || ف: يزعمون.
١٧. ب || ف: احدهما للاخر.

247 If they say: It was not possible for the Messiah in his entirety to perform one action or to make one statement in reality. Rather, his statements were divided between his eternal and temporal substances, so when it concerns generation from the eternal this was a statement of the Word not of the human, and when it is related to the birth from Mary and man this was a statement of the human not of the divine. Similarly, his acts can be divided between his two substances, so the act of the eternal was not the act of the temporal, and the act of the temporal was not the act of the eternal; we say: So now you are making it clear that the Messiah had no action in reality, and that the action belongs only to the eternal substance separate from the temporal or the temporal separate from the eternal. And what was an action of the eternal separate from the temporal was not an action of the Messiah, who, according to you, was eternal and temporal, because the eternal was not two substances, one divine and eternal and the other human. And what was an action of the temporal and not of the eternal was not an action of the Messiah, who you claim was divine and human, because the temporal was not divine and human. So, every action that you are aware of was not performed by the Messiah, but by a being who was not him.

If it was not possible for the Messiah to have an action in reality nor any statement in reality, then it was not possible for him to be ascribed power for speech or action, unless they revert to metaphor or an explanation which does not refer to him in reality. So they might say: "The Messiah said, and the Messiah did", and mean: "The divine acted and not the human, or the human and not the divine, and one of them spoke but not the other." According to this logic your statement, "The Messiah was divine and human", necessarily becomes metaphor and not reality. And since the term "Messiah" will have no reality, when someone wants to affirm

المسيح على الحقيقة وتصحيح أمره إلاّ بأن يُثبته إلهًا وإنسانًا. وكذلك لا حقيقة لقوله «فَعَل المسيح وقال المسيح» إذا أراد التصحيح وتثبيت الفعل والقول له على الحقيقة إلاّ بأن يثبت ذلك الفعل للإله والإنسان وذلك القول للقديم والمحدث. وهذا يؤدّي إلى ما ألزمناهم قبل من اِشتراك القديم والمحدث في الفعل الواحد وفي القول الواحد وإلى تثبيت القديم مولودًا من البشر وتثبيت الإنسان مولودًا من القديم، أو إلى إضافة الكذب في الأخبار إلى من يدّعونه إلهًا ومسيحًا.

٢٤٨. ثمّ نسألهم عن وجه آخر فنقول لهم: أخبرونا عن زعمكم أنّ المسيح مشيئة واحدة، إلى أيّ شيء تذهبون بذلك، أتذهبون إلى أن مشيئة اللاهوت هي مشيئة الناسوت وأن فعل الإنسان هو فعل الإله، أو تذهبون إلى أن مشيئة الناسوت موافقة لمشيئة اللاهوت وإن كانت غيرها في الفعل؟

٢٤٩. فإن زعموا أنّهم يذهبون بذلك إلى أن مشيئة واحدة وفعلاً واحدًا لهما جميعًا، قلنا: فقد صيّرتم فعل المخلوق فعلاً للخالق وفعل الخالق فعلاً للمخلوق؛ وهذا قول أهل الإجبار ومن يزعم أن فعلاً واحدًا مِن فاعلَين.[٦٨] وإذا جاز ذلك في بعض المخلوقين جاز في جميعهم، وإذا جاز في جميعهم وجب أن يكون كلّ مخلوق خَلَق الله مشيئته التي هي فعله مسيحًا متى خلق الله مشيئته تلك؛ فيكون الناس جميعًا مُسَحَاء على هذا القياس متى خلق الله مشيئاتهم التي هي أفعالهم ويكون كلّ واحد منهم والقديم مشيئة واحدة.

١٦. ل || ب: الاحيار (الاجبار ؟)، ف: الاخبار.

the Messiah in reality and as a guarantee of who he was, he can only affirm him as a Divinity and a human. In the same way, there is no reality to his statement, "The Messiah acted and spoke", if he wants to guarantee and affirm act and speech for him in reality and not just affirm this action for the divine and human, and this speech for the eternal and temporal. This leads to what we compelled them to accept earlier, the sharing of the eternal and temporal in one action and statement, and the affirmation that the eternal was born of a human and that the human was generated from the eternal, or to ascribing to those who claim that he was divine and Messiah lies in their reports.

248 [iii. *The will of the Messiah*]

Then we question them about another aspect and say to them: Tell us about your claim that the Messiah was one will, what do you mean by this? Do you mean that the will of the divine nature was the will of the human nature, and that the action of the human was the action of the divine? Or do you mean that the will of the human nature conformed to the will of the divine although it was different from it in action?

249 If they claim that by this they mean the two both possessed one will and one action, we say: Then you make the action of the creature the action of the Creator, and the action of the Creator the action of the creature. This is the teaching of the People of Compulsion and those who claim that there can be one action from two agents.[68] If this is possible for one creature then it is possible for all. And if it is possible for all then it follows that every creature whose will, which is his action, is created by God, is a Messiah as long as God creates this will for him. So all people are Messiahs according to this logic, provided that God creates their wills which are their actions, and every one of them and the eternal are one will.

٢٥٠. ويجب أيضًا إن كانت مشيئة القديم هي مشيئة المحدث على معنى أنّ العيــن الواحــدة فعْل لهُما جميعًا أن يكون جميع ما خلقه الإله القديـم بعد الاِتّحاد فعلاً للمُحدث حتى لا يبقى جسم ولا آية ظهرت ولا عجيبة ولاشيئ من التدبير كبير ولا صغير إلاّ كان فعلاً للناسوت وللاهوت. وهذا يؤدّيهم إلى أن يجيزوا اختراع الأجسام من الإنسان(٦٩) وهو خلاف أصلهم.

٢٥١. والدلائل على فساد هذا وعلى بطلان قول من أجاز فعلاً من فاعلَين كثيرة جدًّا، والواحد منها يخزي ويكفي، والحمد لله كثيرًا.

٢٥٢. فإن ذهب ذاهب منهم إلى أن يزعم أنّ المشيئة ليست بفعل وإنّما هي صفة للمسيح في نفسه، قلنا: فذاك أفظع، وذاك أنّ قائل هذا قد جعل صفة القديم هي صفة المحدث وأثبت ما كان لنفس القديم كائنًا لنفس المحدث. وهذا يلزمه أن يحكم بأنّ نفس القديم هي نفس المحدث.

٢٥٣. وإن زعموا أنّهم يذهبون بقولهم «مشيئة واحدة» إلى الاِتفاق في الإرادة والأفعال لا إلى أنّ العين عين واحدة فَعَلها القديم والمحدث،(٧٠) قلنا: فكّل مَن وافقت مشيئته مشيئة القديم وإرادته إرادة الخالق فهو والقديم إذن مشيئة واحدة. وواجب على هذا الأصل أن يكون الخالق، تعالى، متّحدًا به فيكون متّحدًا بكلّ إنسان وافقت مشيئته مشيئة الخالق وإرادته إرادة الإله.

١–٢. ب || ف: على أن العين.
٥. ب || ف، ل: واللاهوت.
١٠. ل (هامش) || ب، ف: اقطع.
١٢–١٣. ب || ف: بأن القديم.
١٧. ب || ف: واوجب على.

250 It follows also that if the will of the eternal was the will of the temporal in the sense that the one thing was the act of both of them together, that everything the eternal Divinity created after the uniting was the action of the temporal, so that there remained no physical body or sign which appeared and no marvel and no large or small item of control which was not an action of the human and divine natures. This leads them to allow the possibility of physical bodies originating from
251 humans,[69] which is contrary to their principle. | The proofs that this is mistaken and that the teaching of anyone who thinks possible an action from two agents is false are very many, though one is enough to shame them, and all praise to God.

252 If one of them believes he can claim that the will is not action but is only an attribute of the Messiah in himself, we say: This is quite shocking, for the reason that the person who says this has made the attribute of the eternal the attribute of the temporal, and has affirmed that what is of the eternal in himself is of the temporal in himself. This forces him to treat the eternal in himself as the temporal in himself.

253 If they claim that they mean by their statement "one will" the conformity of volition and actions, and not that the thing was one thing performed by the eternal and temporal,[70] we say: Then everyone whose will conforms with that of the eternal and his volition with that of the Creator, he and the eternal are one will. According to this principle the exalted Creator must be united with him, and will be united with every human whose will conforms with that of the Creator and whose volition concurs with that of the Divinity.

٢٥٤. ويُقال لهم في هذا أيضًا: وما هذا الاِتفاق الذي كانت به المشيئة واحدة، أهو أنّ إرادة المحدث تُشبه إرادة القديم وتوافقها في الجنس أم هو أنّ القديم إذا أراد شيئًا أراده ذلك المحدث وإن لم تتفق إراداتهما في الجنس؟ أم هو أنّ المحدث أطاع الإله فيما أمَره به وأراده منه فكان بهذا موافقًا لإرادته ولمشيئته؟ فأي ذلك ما قالوا، قلنا: فكلّ إنسان وافقت إرادته إرادة القديم في الجنس أو أراد ما أراده القديم وإن لم توافق إرادته إرادة القديم في الجنس أو أطاعه فيما أمره به وأراده منه، فهو إذن والقديم مشيئة واحدة.

٢٥٥. على أنّهم إن زعموا أنّ إرادة المحدث تُشبه إرادة القديم وتوافقها في الجنس لزمهم أن يجعلوا فعل المحدث مُشبهًا لِفعل القديم وموافقًا له في الجنس. وهذان جميعًا يؤديان إلى التشبيه بين القديم والمحدث في النفس والقدرة لأنّ الفعلين المشتبهين يدلاّن على فاعل واحد أو على فاعلين مشتبهين لا فرق بينهما في النفس ولا في القدرة. وليس من دينهم التشبيه بين القديم في نفس ولا في قدرة.

٢٥٦. وإن زعموا أنّ الاِتّفاق في المشيئة هو أنّ ذلك المحدث لا تكون منه مشيئة تخالف مشيئة القديم فربّما تعلّق بعضهم بهذا الجواب؛ قلنا: ولا يكون أيّ اِتّفاق هو إنّما الاتّفاق إن كان اِتّفاق في أن يكون مشيئته توافق مشيئة القديم. وإلاّ فإنّ الحجر لا يكون منه مشيئة تُخالف مشيئة القديم

١٠. ب || ف: بالفعل.
١١. ب || ل: فموافقا.
١٤. ب، ف || ب (هامش): بين القديم والمحدث.

254 Say to them on this as well: What is this conformity by which there was one will? Was it that the volition of the temporal resembled the volition of the eternal and concurred with it in kind, or was it that when the eternal willed something the temporal did so as well, even though their volition did not conform in kind, or was it that the temporal obeyed the Divinity in what it ordered it to do and willed for it, and so in this way it concurred with its volition and will? Whichever of these they say, we say: Then every human whose volition concurs in kind with that of the divine, or who wills what the divine wills even though his volition does not concur with that of the eternal in kind, or who obeys him in what he orders him to do and wills for him, he and the eternal are one will.

255 However, if they claim that the volition of the temporal resembled the volition of the divine and concurred with it in kind, they necessarily make the action of the temporal resemble the action of the eternal and concur with it in kind. Both of these entail comparison between the eternal and temporal in self and power, because two actions which resemble one another imply one agent or two agents who resemble one another with no difference between them in self or power. In their religion there is no comparison with the eternal in self or in power.

256 If they claim that conformity in will is that this temporal being did not have any will which differed from the will of the eternal, and sometimes some of them give this answer, we say: There can be no conformity except the conformity which was his will conforming to the will of the eternal. Otherwise, there is the stone which has no will which differs from that of the eternal,

والجماد كلّه وكذلك الموات. فينبغي على قياسكم أن تزعموا أن الحجر والجماد والموات وكلّ ذلك موافق للقديم في مشيئته إذ كان ذلك كلّه لا يكون منه مشيئة تخالف مشيئة القديم، وأنّه والقديم بذلك مشيئة واحدة. تعالى ربّنا عن ذلك وعن كلّ صفة ذميمة.

٢٥٧. فإن قالوا: فأنّا إنّما نعني بقولنا «لا يكون منه مشيئة تخالف مشيئة القديم» أيّ أنّ مشيئته متى كانت وافقت مشيئة القديم لا أنّا أرادنا نفي المشيئة عنه، قلنا: فكلّ مَن وافقت مشيئته مشيئة القديم متى كانت من سائر الملائكة والناس الذين أطاعوا فلَم يعصوا ولَم يُريدوا خلاف ما أراد بهم فواجب أن يحكموا له بهذا الحكم ويُوجبوا له هذا الاِسم.

٢٥٨. فإن قالوا: فإنّا لا نُطلق له هذا الاِسم ولا نوجب له هذا الحكم بموافقة مشيئة واحدة ومشيئتين وما قارب ذلك، وإنّما نطلق هذا الاِسم ونوجب هذا الحكم لمَن وافق كلّ مشيئاته مشيئة القديم، قلنا: فهل نقضَت مشيئات المحدث كلّها في حال الاتّحاد أو ظهرت كلّها منه في تلك الحال فاستحقّ بها هذا الاِسم وجَرى له بها هذا الحكم؟ وهل يجوز أن تظهر مشيئاته كلّها حتى لا يبقى له مشيئة إلاّ ظهرت في الوقت الذي يكون بعقبة الموت أو العجز الذي لا قوّة بعده؟ وإلاّ فإنّه ما دام حيًّا مستطيعًا فإنّ مشيئاته تحدث شيئًا بعد شيء فلا ينبغي عندكم أن يكون هو

٢. ب || ل: يزعموا.
٦. ب || ف: فان قالوا إنما نعني.
٧. ب || ف: القديم أن مشيئته.
١٦. ب، ف || ل: بها بهذا.

and all inanimate objects, and also lifeless bodies. According to your comparison you must necessarily claim that the stone, the inanimate objects and the lifeless bodies, all these things, concur with the eternal in his will, since in all of these there is no will which differs from the will of the eternal, and that they and the eternal are, by this, one will. May our Lord be exalted above this, and above every objectionable attribute.

257 If they say: By our statement, "He had no will which differed from that of the eternal", we mean only that his will concurred with the will of the eternal, because we do not mean to deny he had a will, we say: Then all other beings whose will concurs with the will of the eternal, whether angels or humans who obey and do not disobey and do not will the contrary of what he wills for them, they must reckon them in the same way and give them this name.

258 If they say: But we do not use this name or impose this reckoning upon someone because of the concurrence of one will, or two wills and the like; we only use this name and impose this reckoning upon someone whose entire will conforms to that of the eternal, we say: Then was the entire will of the temporal being destroyed at the moment of the uniting or was it manifest in him at this moment, so that he could then merit this name, and this reckoning could be used for him? And could his entire will have become manifest, so that he had no will left to appear at the time when he was in the difficulty of death or weakness, when there was no more strength? Otherwise, if while he was alive and capable his will came into being little by little, then according to you, he

والقـديم مشيئة واحدة في حال الاتّحاد ولا فيما بعدها من الأحـوال إلاّ في الحـال التي تليهـا حـال الموت أو حال العجز الذي لا قوّة بعده. وإلاّ فإن جاز أن يكون مستحقًّا لهذا الاِسم ببعض المشيئات واحدة أو اِثنتين أو نحو ذلك فكلّ مَن أتى بمشيئة توافق مشيئة القديم أو بمشيئتين أو بنحو ذلك فهو إذن والقديم مشيئة واحدة كائنًا مَن كان من سائر الناس.

٢٥٩. فإن قالوا: ولسنا نُوجِب ذلك أيضًا بظهور بعض المشيئات دون إن يكون المعلوم من ذلك المحدث أنّه لا يكون منه مشيئة إلاّ كانت موافقة لمشيئة ربّه، قلنا: فكلّ إنسان كان المعلوم منه أنّه لا تكون منه مشيئة إلاّ كانت موافقة لمشيئة ربّه من سائر الأنبياء والصالحين فهذا إذن حكمه، وكذلك سائر الملائكة المقربين الذين يطيعون ولا يعصون ولا يكون منهم مشيئة إلاّ كانت موافقة لمشيئة ربّهم يلزمهم هذا الحكم ويجري لهم هذا الاِسم إذ كان المعلوم منهم ذلك. ويجب حينئذٍ أن يكون كلّ واحد منهم والقديم مشيئة واحدة وأن يكون القديم متّحدًا بجميعهم.

٢٦٠. ثمّ يُقال لهـم: هل كان ناسوت المسيح قادرًا على أن يأتي بمشيئة تخالـف مشـيئة اللاهـوت؟ فإن قالوا: لا، كانوا بين أمرين، إمّا أن يزعمـوا أنّه يجري في الموافقة على طباع وسوس لا يمكن منه خلافه، فهذا خلاف قولهم في المختارين المطيعين، أو يجعلوه مضطرًّا إلى الموافقة لا مختارًا لها بل محمولاً عليها. وإذا كان كذلك في مشيئاته

٥. ب || ف: فهو والقديم اذن. ١٨. ب (هامش): عُنصر الشيء. ١٩. ب، ف || ل: الميعين.

and the eternal could not appropriately have been one will at the moment of uniting and not at any moment after this, if not in the moment which was followed by the moment of death or of incapacity, when there was no more strength. Otherwise, if it is possible that he was worthy of this name because of some will, one or two or more, then everyone who has a will which concurs with the will of the eternal, or two wills or more, he and the eternal must be one will, whoever he may be.

259 If they say: Nor do we deduce this from the appearance of a single will, since it is recognised that this temporal being had no will that did not concur with the will of his Lord, we say: It is recognised that no human prophet or saint had a will that did not concur with the will of his Lord, so they must be reckoned the same. And likewise the attendant angels who obey and do not disobey and have no will that does not concur with the will of their Lord, they must be reckoned like this, and this name must be applied to them, since this is recognised with respect to them. So it follows that every one of them and the eternal must be one will, and that the eternal must have united with all of them.

260 Then say to them: Did the human nature of the Messiah have the ability to produce a will which differed from the will of the divine nature? If they say: No, they have two alternatives: either they must claim that the one concurred according to a nature and constitution in which differing from the other was not possible, though this differs from their teaching about those who obey through free choice; or they make him forced to concur, and not free to choose but conveyed to it. If this is the case with his wills

وإراداته خرج عندهم من أفعال الطاعات كلّها وممّا يستحقّ بها وصارت أفعاله كلّها مضافة إلى غيره. وهذه صفة غير المختار معما في ذلك من وجوه الفساد.

٢٦١. فإن زعموا أنّه كان قادراً على أن يأتي بمشيئة تخالف مشيئة اللاهوت فقد زعموا أنّه كان قادرًا على أن يكون هو والقديم مشيئتين. وفي كون ذلك إبطال الاتّحاد إذ كانا بالاتّحاد صارا مشيئة واحدة. فالناسوت قادر في قود هذا القول على أن ينقض اتّحاد اللاهوت ويبطله. وهذا فظيع من القول على أصولهم.

٢٦٢. وكذلك يقال لهم: ألستم تزعمون أنّ كلّ مأمور مُنهَى من سائر الناس فهو مستطيع ألاّ تكون منه مشيئة إلاّ كانت موافقة لمشيئة ربّه ولأمره؟ ولا بُدّ من: نعم، ما تمسّكوا بأصولهم، لأنّ المعروف من قولهم أنّه لا يُؤمر أحد بما لا يستطيعه ولا يُنهي عمّا لا يستطيعه، ومذهبهم الموافقة لأهل العدل[٧١] في ذلك. يُقال لهم: فكلّ مأمور مُنهى من سائر الناس فهو يقدر اذًا أن يكون هو والقديم مشيئة واحدة. وإذا كان ذلك من علامات الاتّحاد فكلّ مأمور مُنهى فهو يستطيع أن يكون القديم متّحداً به.

٢٦٣. ويقال لهم على الكلام الأوّل: إن كانت مشيئة اللاهوت هي مشيئة الناسوت، أفيجوز أن يكون فعل اللاهوت هو فعل الناسوت؟ فيؤدّيهم ذلك إلى ما ألزمناهم قبل، ولن يقولوا ذلك ما تمسّكوا بأصولهم.

٢٦٤. وإلاّ فإن كان فعل اللاهوت غير فعل الناسوت، وكذلك مشيئة

and volitions then, according to them, he could not have performed any acts of obedience from which he could obtain merit, and his acts would be ascribed to someone other than him. This is an attribute of those who are not free to choose, and furthermore there are points of falseness here.

261 If they claim that he was able to produce a will which differed from the will of the divine nature, then they claim that he was able to ensure that he and the eternal were two wills. When this happened the uniting was destroyed, since in the uniting they became one will. So in pursuing this idea, the human nature was able to undo the uniting of the divine nature and destroy it. This is a violation of teaching according to their principles.

262 In the same way say to them: Do you not claim that every other individual who is under command and prohibition is capable only of a will which concurs with the will and command of his Lord? They can only say: Yes, if they hold to their principles, because their known teaching is that none is commanded to do what he cannot do or prohibited from what he cannot resist: their belief concurs in this with the People of Justice.[71] Say to them: Every other individual under command and prohibition has then power to ensure that he and the eternal are one will. So if this is a sign of the uniting then everyone under command and prohibition is able to be united with the eternal.

263 Say to them according to the first argument: If the will of the divine nature was the will of the human nature, could the action of the divine nature be the action of the human nature? This leads them to what we compelled them to accept earlier, though they will never say this as long as they hold onto their principles.

264 Otherwise, if the action of the divine nature was different from the action of the human nature, then likewise the will

اللاهوت غير مشيئة الناسوت اختلف ذلك أم اتفق.

٢٦٥. ولو أنّ قائلاً قال: «المسيح محبّة واحدة أو فعل واحد» كما قالوا هم «مشيئة واحدة» لما كان بينهم وبينه فرق.

٢٦٦. وإن ذهبوا بقولهم «المسيح مشيئة واحدة» إلى تثبيت مشيئة الأقنوم الذي أثبتوه قديمًا ونفي مشيئة الأقنوم المحدث على نحو من قول الملكيّة «المسيح أقنوم واحد»، تذهب الملكيّة إلى تثبيت الأقنوم القديم وتنفي أن يكون له أقنوم محدث، قلنا لهم: فقد أبطلتم أن يكون للإنسان الذي اتّحدت به الكلمة مشيئة لشيء من الخير أو إرادة لفعل من الأفعال، وأخرجتموه من أن يكون فاعلاً لشيء من الطاعات أو من غيرها، وأدخلتموه في صفة مَن لا فعل له من الموات أو الجماد، وهذا خلاف دينكم.

٢٦٧. ويقال لهم: إذا زعمتم أنّ المسيح مشيئة واحدة، فلِم لا تقولون «هو أقنوم واحد وجوهر واحد»؟ فإن قالوا: لو كان أقنومًا واحدًا وجوهرًا واحدًا لَكان أقنوم القديم هو أقنوم المحدث وجوهر القديم هو جوهر المحدث، قلنا: ولو كان مشيئة واحدة لكانت مشيئة القديم هي مشيئة المحدث وصفة القديم هي صفة المحدث وفعل القديم هو فعل المحدث.

٢٦٨. فإن قالوا: جائز أن تكون مشيئة القديم هي مشيئة المحدث على الاِتفاق لا على أنّ العين واحدة، قلنا: وكذلك يجوز أن يكون أقنوم القديم هو أقنوم المحدث على الاتفاق والاِتّحاد لا على أنّ العين واحدة.[٧٢]

٥. ب النص: القنوم.　　١٥. ف || ب: لكان مشيئة.

of the divine nature must have been different from the will of the human nature, whether it was contrary or in conformity.

265 If someone were to say: "The Messiah was one love or one action", as they say "One will", there would be no distinction between them and him.

266 If by their statement, "The Messiah was one will", they mean to emphasise the will of the hypostasis which they acknowledge is eternal and to deny the will of the temporal hypostasis, similar to the teaching of the Melkites, "The Messiah was one hypostasis", by which the Melkites mean to emphasise the eternal hypostasis and deny that he had a temporal hypostasis, we say to them: You have abolished the existence of a will for any good, or volition for any action in the human with whom the Word united; you have excluded him from performing any act of obedience or otherwise; and you have placed him under the attribute of a being with no action, such as the lifeless and inanimate. This is contrary to your religion.

267 Say to them: If you claim that the Messiah was one will, then why do you not say that he was one hypostasis and substance? If they say: If he were one hypostasis and substance, then the hypostasis of the eternal would be the hypostasis of the temporal and the substance of the eternal would be the substance of the temporal, we say: And if he were one will, then the will of the eternal would be the will of the temporal, the attribute of the eternal would be the attribute of the temporal, and the action of the eternal would be the action of the temporal.

268 If they say: It is possible for the will of the eternal to be the will of the temporal as conformity but not as one entity, we say: In the same way it is possible for the hypostasis of the eternal to be the hypostasis of the temporal as conformity and uniting but not as one entity.[72]

٢٦٩. فإن قالوا: لا يكون القديم موافقًا للمحدث بوجه من الوجوه، قلنا: ولا تكون مشيئة القديم توافق مشيئة المحدث بوجه من الوجوه، ولا يكون فعل القديم موافقًا لفعل المحدث بوجه من الوجوه.

٢٧٠. وإن قالوا: لو كان أقنومًا واحدًا لَكان إما قديمًا لا محدثًا أو محدثًا لا قديمًا، والقديم الذي ليس بمحدث وحده ليس بمسيح، وكذلك المحدث الذي ليس بقديم وحده ليس بمسيح، لأنّ المسيح جوهرانِ ماسح وممسوح أقنومانِ قديم ومحدث؛ قلنا لهم: ولو كان مشيئةً واحدةً لكانت تلك المشيئة إمّا مشيئة قديم ليس بمحدث أو مشيئة محدث ليس بقديم، ومشيئة القديم الذي ليس بمحدث ليست مشيئة المسيح، وكذلك مشيئة المحدث الذي ليس بقديم ليست مشيئة المسيح، لأنّ المسيح عندكم قديم ومحدث. فإمّا أن تجعلوه مشيئتين كما جعلتموه جوهرين أقنومين وإمّا أن تجعلوه جوهرًا واحدًا أقنومًا واحدًا كما جعلتموه مشيئة واحدة.

٢٧١. وإن هم رجعوا إلى الاِتفاق المشتَقّ من موافقة الطاعة للأمر أو إلى أنّ المشيئتين وقعتا مشيئتين لشيء واحد إرادتين لمراد واحد، رددنا عليهم بعض الكلام الأوّل: فإن كلّ منّ أطاع الله أو أراد ما أراد الله في كثير من الأمور وقليل فقد لزمه إذًا هذا الحكم ووجب أن يكون هو والقديم مشيئة واحدة. وقيل لهم أيضًا في ذلك: قد يُريد الإنسان شيئًا ويُريد البهيمة ذلك الشيء لعينه؛ ولا يجب أن يكون الإنسان والبهيمة مشيئة واحدة، كالإنسان

٩–١١. ب || ف: الذي ليس بمحدث ليس مشيئة المسيح، لأن المسيح عندكم قديم.
١٧. ب || ف: أراد ما أراده الله. ٢٠. ب || ف: مشيئة واحدة والإنسان.

269 If they say: The eternal did not concur with the temporal in any respect, we say: Neither did the will of the eternal concur with the will of the temporal in any respect, nor did the action of the eternal concur with the action of the temporal in any respect.

270 If they say: If he were one hypostasis then he would have been either eternal and not temporal, or temporal and not eternal, though the eternal alone who is not temporal was not the Messiah, and likewise the temporal alone who was not eternal was not the Messiah, because the Messiah was two substances, Anointer and anointed, and two hypostases, eternal and temporal, we say to them: If he were one will, then this will would have been either an eternal will not temporal, or a temporal will not eternal. But an eternal will which is not temporal was not the will of the Messiah, and likewise a temporal will which is not eternal was not the will of the Messiah, because in your view the Messiah was eternal and temporal. So either you must make him two wills as you make him two substances and hypostases, or you must make him one substance and hypostasis, in the same way that you make him one will.

271 If they revert to conformity, derived from the concurrence of obedience to command, or to two wills meeting as two wills on one thing, and two volitions reaching one outcome, we respond to them with some of the first arguments: With regard to everyone who obeys God or wills what God wills in much or a little, this judgement must be made of him and he and the eternal must necessarily be one will. And say to them also about this: A man might will something and an animal might will exactly the same thing, though the human and the animal are not necessarily one will. A human may

يريد أن يُريح دابّته والدابّة يريد ذلك، وليس بواجب أن يكون الإنسان والدابّة مشيئة واحدة. وكالرجل يريد أن يعلف حماره في وقت الجوع أو يسقيه في وقت العطش والحمار يرُيد ذلك، ولا يجب أن يكون الإنسان والحمار مشيئة واحدة؛ وكذلك سائر بهائمة وغير بهائمة.

٢٧٢. ويقال لكم ولخصومكم أيضًا: إن تجعلوا الأقنومين متفقين في اِتّحاد كلّ واحد منهما بصاحبه ومُلاءمة كلّ واحدٍ منهما بصاحبه فهما بذلك أقنوم واحد وجوهر واحد، أو تأتوا بفرق. وذلك عسير معما قلتموه واعتللتم به.

٢٧٣. قد أتينا من مُساءَلة هذا الصنف في هذا الباب على جملة كافية والكلام عليهم فيه كثير جدًا، فنحن ندعُه كراهة لطوله على أنّ كثيرًا ممّا سألناهم عنه في الاتّحاد سؤال عليهم في المسيح.[٧٣]

٢٧٤. وأمّا الملكيّة فقد مرّ عليهم كلام كثير في المسيح عند مُساءَلتنا إيّاهم في الاتّحاد. ونسأل الآن أيضًا مَن اختار منهم أن يعبّر عن المسيح بذي الجوهرين وذي المشيئتين ومَن كان الأحسن الأصوب عنده أن يقول أنّ المسيح أقنوم واحد ذو جوهرين.[٧٤] فنقول لهم: أيخلو ذو الجوهرين عندكم من أن يكون هو الجوهرين أو أحدهما أو معنى غيرهما، كما قالوا في جوهر الأقانيم الثلثة أنّه غير الأقانيم؟ فإن كانوا يذهبون إلى أنّ المسيح غير الجوهرين اللذَين أحدهما عندهم قديم والآخر محدث، سألناهم عن ذلك ليثبتوه

٦. ف || ب: ويقال لهم. ٨. ب: باتوا || ل: ياتوا.

will to let his mount rest and the mount may also will this, though the human and the animal are not necessarily one will. Similarly, a man may will to feed his donkey when it is hungry and to water it when it is thirsty, and the donkey may also will this, though it does not follow that the human and the donkey are one will. It is the same with other animals and things which are not animals.

272 And we also say to you, and to your adversaries: If you make each of the two hypostases conform to its companion in uniting, and in the adaptation of each to its companion, then by this they are one hypostasis and one substance, unless you can show the distinction. But this is difficult in the light of what you have said so insistently.

273 We have interrogated this group enough in this section, and the argument against them on it is considerable. So we will cease for fear of prolonging it, though much of what we have asked them on the uniting can be put to them on the Messiah.[73]

274 [2. *The argument against the Melkites*

i. *The two substances of the Messiah*]

As for the Melkites, many arguments against them on the Messiah arose when we were questioning them about the uniting. And now we question those among them who have chosen to designate the Messiah as having two substances and two wills, and those who regard it as better and more correct to say that the Messiah was one hypostasis possessing two substances.[74] So we say to them: In your view could the possessor of the two substances be anything other than either the two substances, or one of them, or something other than them, as they say about the substance of the three hypostases that it is other than the hypostases? If they believed that the Messiah was other than the two substances one of which, according to them, was eternal and the other temporal, we will then ask them to acknowledge it

ثالثًا كما سألناهم عن جوهر الأقانيم ليثبتوه رابعًا بما تقدم في كتابنا هذا من المسائل عليهم في ذلك وبنحوها.(٧٥) ولزمهم في عاجل الأمر أن يزعموا أنّه لا إله ولا إنسان وأنّه غير الإله وغير الإنسان إذ كان غير الجوهرين اللذَين أحدهما إله والآخر هو الإنسان، كما قالوا في جوهر الأقانيم أنّه لا أب ولا اِبن ولا روح وأنّه غير الأب والاِبن والروح.

٢٧٥. وإلاّ فإن كان المسيح إلهًا وإنسانًا فقد رجعوا عن هذا المعنى وعن هذا العبارة إلى أن يقولوا: «هو جوهران مشيئتان».

٢٧٦. ومتى زعموا أيضًا أنّه غير الجوهرين فقد صرّحوا بأنّ الأقنوم القديم غير جوهره، وهذا خلاف قولهم أن الأقانيم هي الجوهر وإن كانوا مع ذلك يزعمون أنّ الجوهر غير الأقانيم ويلزمهم في كون الأب والروح غير جوهرهما مثل الذي أطلقوه في الاِبن.

٢٧٧. ومتى زعموا أيضًا أنّ ذا الجوهرين غير الجوهرين اللذَين أحدهما قديم والآخر محدث، وليس شيء عندهم معقول غير القديم والمحدث، فلم يثبتوا ذا الجوهرين شيئًا وذو الجوهرين عندهم هو المسيح. فليس المسيح على هذا القول وعند صاحب هذا الجواب شيئًا إن فُهم قوله وما يؤدّى إليه قوله، صلوات الله على المسيح وعلى أنبياء الله أجمعين.

٢٧٨. وإن زعموا أنّ ذا الجوهرين هو أحد الجوهرين، تركوا قولهم وجعلوا المسيح جوهرًا واحدًا إمّا جوهر الإله عندهم لا غير وإمّا

١. ب || ف: رابعا مما.   ١٨. ب || ف: سائر أنبياء.

as a third, just as we asked them to acknowledge the substance of the hypostases as a fourth earlier in this book in the questions against them on this and similar things.[75] They will immediately have to claim that he was neither divine nor human but other than divine and other than human, since he was other than the two substances one of which was divine and the other the human, just as they say that the substance of the hypostases was not Father, Son or Spirit, but other than the Father,
275 Son and Spirit. | Otherwise, if the Messiah was divine and human they would retreat from this meaning and explanation to saying, "He was two substances and two wills."

276 Also, in claiming that he was other than the two substances they make it clear that the eternal hypostasis was other than its substance. This is contrary to their teaching that the hypostases are the substance. If in spite of this they continue to claim that the substance was other than the hypostases, they are forced to accept that the Father and Spirit are other than their substance, similarly to what they express about the Son.

277 While they claim also that the possessor of the two substances was other than the two substances, one of which was eternal and the other temporal, then since according to them there is nothing that can be known which is not eternal or temporal, they do not acknowledge that the possessor of the two substances was a thing, though for them the possessor of the two substances was the Messiah. So the Messiah was not a thing according to this teaching and to the person making this reply, if his words and what they entail are to be understood. God's blessings be upon the Messiah and all the prophets of God.

278 If they claim that the possessor of the two substances was one of the two substances, they abandon their teaching and make the Messiah one substance, either the substance of the Divinity as they see it and nothing else, or

جوهر الإنسان لا غير. وكلّ واحد من هذين الجوهرين فليس بذي جوهرين أحدهما قديم والآخر محدث.

٢٧٩. فإن زعموا أنّ ذا الجوهرين هو الجوهران، كانوا كمن جرّد القول بأنّ المسيح جوهران، وصار قولهم «ذو جوهرين» إذا أخرجناه على أحسن وجوهه اتساعًا في العبارة لا خلافًا في المعنى. ومتى سقط ذلك الاتساع لم يخل المعنى، فيكون الكلام عليهم حينئذٍ على نحو ما ابتدأناه على مَن جرّد القول بأنّ المسيح جوهران أقنوم واحد مشيئتان.

٢٨٠. ويقال للملكيّة جميعًا: إذا زعمتم أنّ ناسوت المسيح ليس بشخص قائم بذاته فأخبرونا عن جسد المسيح المرئي الذي به كان يذهب ويجيئ ويتصرّف، أهو شخص الإله أم شخص بعض الخلق؟ فإن قالوا: شخص الإله، زعموا أنّ شخص الإله صورة كصورة الناس وأنّه جسم كأجسامهم وأنّه محدود مذروع له جلد ولحم وعظم وجميع ما لأجسام الناس. وإن قالوا: ذلك شخص المخلوقين، قلنا: فثمّ إذن شخص واحد ليس بإله، والإنسان المتّحد به أيضًا غير ذلك الشخص. فخبّرونا عن ذلك الشخص الآخر، أليس جوهرا المسيح اللّذان أحدهما عندكم جوهر الإله والآخر هو الإنسان الكلّي غيره؟ فلا بدّ من: نعم، على ما أصّلوا؛ يقال لهم: فالمسيح على قولكم غير الجسد المولود من مريم من كلّ الجهات. فلا بدّ من: نعم، ما لم ينقضوا الأصل؛

٥. ب || ف: لا اختلافًا.
١٤–١٥. ب || ف: ذلك الشخص شخص.
١٨. ب || ف: والآخر جوهر الإنسان.

the substance of the human and nothing else. But neither one of these two substances was the possessor of two substances, one eternal and the other temporal.

279 If they claim that the possessor of the two substances was the two substances, they are like those who state simply that the Messiah was two substances, and their statement, "possessor of two substances", if we give it its best interpretation, only becomes more imprecise in expression but with no difference in meaning. When this imprecision is put aside the meaning does not change, so the argument against them then becomes the same as we began with against the person who states simply that the Messiah was two substances, one hypostasis and two wills.

280 [ii. *The human body of the Messiah*]

Say to the Melkites all together: If you claim that the human nature of the Messiah was not an independent person, then tell us about the visible bodily form of the Messiah by which he went and came and behaved, was it the person of the Divinity or the person of a creature? If they say: The person of the Divinity, they claim that the person of the Divinity is a form like the form of humans, that it is a body like their bodies and that it is restricted and measurable, with skin, bones and everything which human bodies have. If they say: It was a person from among creatures, we say: So, a person which was not divine, but neither one which was the human subject of the uniting. So tell us about this other person, were not the two substances of the Messiah, one of which, in your view, was the substance of the Divinity and the other the universal human, different from it? They can only say: Yes, according to what they hold as their principle. Say to them: So the Messiah, according to what you say, was different from the body born of Mary in every respect. They can only say: Yes, if they are not to invalidate their principle.

ويقال لهم: أفحلّ المسيح بكماله في ذلك الجسد ولابسه فعُوين فيه أو به أو نالته الأيدي فيه أو به وصلب وقتل فيه أو به، أم لَم يحلل فيه ولم يلابسه؟ فإن قالوا: نعم حلّ بكماله فيه ولابسه، فقد جعلوا الأقنوم القديم عندهم والإنسان الكلّي جميعًا محصورَين في ذلك الجسد أو به محدودَين فيه أو به يحيط بهما بشبر المساحة، وهذا خلاف أصلهم. وإن زعموا أنّ المسيح لَم يحلل في ذلك الجسد ولم يلابسه فيُرى به أو فيه أو تناله الأيدي فيه أو به ويُصلب ويُقتل فيه أو به، قيل لهم: أفناله ذلك بغير ذلك الجسد أو في غير ذلك الجسد؟ فمن قولهم: لا، لأنّه لَم يتّخذ عندهم جسداً غير المولود من مريم. يُقال لهم: فالمسيح على هذا القول لَم يُعاين ولا قتل ولا صلب ولا نالته أيدي المخلوقين بذلك الجسد ولا بغيره ولا في ذلك الجسد ولا في غيره ولا على وجه من الوجوه، لأنّ ذلك كلّه إنّما وقع بذلك الجسد في المشاهدة وهو غير الجسد من جميع الجهات وغير حالٍّ في الجسد ولا ملابس له. وإلاّ فإن كان ذلك الجسد من المسيح في شيء فقد صار المسيح إذن ثلثة أشيئًا جوهرًا قديمًا والإنسان الكلّي والشخص الجزئي المولود من مريم أو يكون ذلك الجسد قد حواه وحصره وناهاه في المساحة والمقدار. وأيّ ذلك ما قالوا، أتيسّر عليهم مذهبهم؟

٢٨١. ولا بُدّ لهم مع ذلك من أن يزعموا أنّ ناسوت المسيح بنفسه

١٤. ب || ف: فهو غير.

So say to them: Did the Messiah in his entirety inhere in this body, put it on so that he was seen in it or through it, did hands grasp him in it or through it, and was he crucified and killed in it or through it, or did he not inhere in it and not put it on? If they say: Yes he inhered in it in his entirety and put it on, they have caused the eternal hypostasis, as they see it, and the universal human to be enclosed together in this body or restricted in it or by it, while it confined them within the measure of its extent. This is contrary to their principle.

If they claim that the Messiah did not inhere in this body and did not put it on to be seen through it or in it, for hands to grasp him in it or through it, to be crucified and killed in it or through it, say to them: Then did they grasp him without this body, or in another body? They will have to say: No, because they believe he did not take any body other than that born of Mary. Say to them: So according to this statement the Messiah was not seen, killed or crucified and the hands of creatures did not grasp him through this body or through another, or in this body or in another, or in any respect, because all of this only happened to this body before witnesses, and he was different from the body in every respect and was not the one who inhered in the body nor who put it on. However, if this was the Messiah's body in any respect, then the Messiah would have been three things, an eternal substance, the universal human and the individual person born of Mary, or this body would have included him, enclosed him and restrained him within its extent and measure. Whichever of these they say, will it make their belief any easier for them?

281 In addition to this they must allow that the human nature of the Messiah itself,

وعقله ومشيئته هو الناس كلّهم أو هو إنسان واحد أو هو غير الناس. فإن زعموا أنّه الناس كلّهم فقد أثبتوا الكلمة ظاهرة في الناس كلّهم، وهذه مكابرة العيان وإيجاب أنّها اتّحدت بأشخاص الناس كلّهم مؤمنهم وكافرهم. وأدنى ما يلزمهم في ذلك أن يزعموا أنّ المولود من مريم لَم يخصّ بشيء دون سائر الناس، وإذا كان ذلك كذلك لَم يستحقّ أن يُسمّى مسيحًا دون غيره من المولودين ولا أن يكون جسدًا للمسيح دون غيره من الأجساد.

٢٨٢. فإن زعموا أن ناسوت المسيح بنفسه وعقله ومشيئته إنسان واحد شخص واحد تركوا قولهم وزعموا أنّ الكلمة اِتّحدت بإنسان جزئي. وانتقض عليهم جميع ذلك الاحتجاج الذي وصفناه عنهم بدئًا.[٧٦]

٢٨٣. فإن زعموا أنّ ناسوت المسيح غير الناس كلّهم، قيل لهم: فقد اِتّحدت الكلمة إذن بغير الناس وبغير البشر، وغير الناس وغير البشر لا يكون اِبنًا لمريم ولا ابنًا لداود ولا ابنًا لآدم، ومَن لم يكن ابنًا لآدم ولا لمريم ولا من ولد آدم فليس ابنًا لمريم ولا ولدًا لها.

٢٨٤. ويقال لهم: إذا كانت الكلمة إنّما اِتّحدت بالإنسان الكلّي فبأيّ شيء خصّ ذلك الجسد المولود من مريم؟ فإن قالوا: خصّ بأنّها ظهرت فيه، قلنا: فخبّرونا عن ظهورها في ذلك الجسد، أهو الاِتّحاد أم غيره؟ فإن كان هو الاتّحاد فقد وجب أن تكون الكلمة متّحدة بالإنسان الكلّي وبالجسد جميعًا إذ كان معنى الاِتّحاد مشتملاً عليهما. وإن لا تكون إضافة ذلك المعنى الذي هو الاِتّحاد وهو الظهور إلى الكلّي بذكر الاِتّحاد أولى من إضافته إلى

its reason and will must have been either all humankind, or one human being, or other than humankind. If they claim that it was all humankind they are then acknowledging that the Word was manifest in all humankind. This is a stubborn rejection of what is evident, and it necessitates that it united with all humankind, whether believers or unbelievers. At the very least they are obliged to claim on this that the being born of Mary was no more special than other people, though if this was so he was not worthy of being called Messiah any more than others who were born, or of being the body of the Messiah any more than other bodies.

282 If they claim that the human nature of the Messiah in itself with its reason and its will were one human and one individual, they abandon their teaching and claim that the Word united with an individual human. All this flies against the arguments that we presented from them at the start.[76]

283 If they claim that the human nature of the Messiah was different from all humankind, say to them: So the Word united with one who was different from humankind and humanity, though one who was different from humankind and humanity could not have been son of Mary or son of David or son of Adam. And one who was not son of Adam or of Mary, nor a child of Adam could not have been son of Mary nor a child of hers.

284 [iii. *The appearance of the Word in the body of the Messiah*]

Say to them: If the Word united only with the universal human, then in what way was this body born of Mary special? If they say: It was special in that it appeared in it, we say: So tell us about its appearance in this body, was it the uniting or not? If it was the uniting, then it necessarily follows that the Word must have united with the universal human and the body together, since the significance of the uniting includes them both. But if this significance of the uniting and the appearance, when the uniting is referred to, does not include the universal any more specifically than it includes the

الجسد بذكر الاِتّحاد ولا سيما وليس لأحدهما فيه معنىً ليس للآخر. وإن زعموا أنّ الظهور غير الاِتّحاد لأن الاتّحاد إنّما كان بالكلّي لا بالجزئي والظهور في الجزئي لا في الكلّي، قلنا: فهي إذن متّحدة بواحدة ظاهرة في آخر ظاهرة فيما لم يتحد به متّحدة بما لم تظهر فيه، وهذا عجيب. وممّا يزيد في التعجّب منه أنّها لم تظهر فيما صارت هي وهو واحدًا بالاِتّحاد وظهرت فيما لم تصر هي وهو واحدًا ولا حلّت فيه ولا لابسته.

٢٨٥. ومع التعجّب من ذلك فإنّا نقول لهم: ما الفرق بينكم وبين من قلب هذا فقال: «الكلمة ظاهرة في الكلّي غير متّحدة به متّحدة بالجزئي غير ظاهرة فيه»؟

٢٨٦. فإن قلتم: لو كانت ظاهرةً في الكلّي لظهرت في أجساد الناس كلّهم، قيل لكم: ولو كانت متّحدة بالكلّي لكانت متّحدة بأجساد الناس كلّهم.

٢٨٧. وإن قلتم: كيف يظهر في الكلّي والكلّي ليس بشخص قائم بذاته؟ قيل لكم: وكيف يأتحد بالكلّي والكلّي ليس بشخص قائم بذاته.

٢٨٨. وإن أجبتم إلى أنّها ظاهرة في الكلّي بظهورها في ذلك الشخص الجزئي الذي هو أقنوم من أقانيم الكلّي، قيل لكم: فكذا تكون متّحدة بالكلّي باتّحادها بذلك الشخص الجزئي الذي هو أقنوم من أقانيم الكلّي. وإن أنتم أثبتموها ظاهرةً في الكلّي باتّحادها بالكلّي، قلنا: فكذا يجب أن تكون متّحدة بالجزئي بظهورها في الجزئي، وإلاّ فالفرق؟ ومتى ثبت أنّ ظهورها في الكلّي هو اتّحادها به ثبت

body, when the uniting is referred to, then neither of them has any more reality in this than the other. If they claim that the appearing was other than the uniting, because the uniting was only with the universal not with the individual, and the appearance was in the individual not in the universal, we say: Then it united with one and appeared in another, appeared in what it did not unite with and united with what it did not appear in. This is amazing. And what adds to the amazement about it is that it did not appear in what it and he became one in through the uniting, and that it did appear in what it and he did not become one in, did not inhere in and did not put on.

285 In addition to expressing amazement about it, we say to them: What is the difference between you and someone who reverses this and says, "The Word appeared in the universal without uniting with it, and united with the individual without appearing in it"?

286 If you say: If it had appeared in the universal then it would have appeared in the bodies of all humankind, we say to you: And if it had united with the universal then it would have united with the bodies of all people.

287 If you say: How could it appear in the universal when the universal is not an independent individual being?, we say to you: And how could it unite with the universal when the universal is not an independent individual being?

288 If you reply that it appeared in the universal by appearing in this individual being which was one of the hypostases of the universal, we say to you: Then it became united with the universal by being united with the individual being which was one of the hypostases of the universal. And if you acknowledge that it appeared in the universal by its uniting with the universal, we say: Then likewise it must have become united with the individual by its appearance in the individual. And if not, what is the difference?

And as long as it is acknowledged that its appearance in the universal was its uniting itself with it, it must be acknowledged

أنّ ظهورها في الجزئي اتّحاد منها به، إلاّ أن يدّعوا أيضاً أن ظهورها في الكلّي غير اتّحادها به، فيُسألوا عن فرق بينهما.

٢٨٩. ويقال لهم أيضًا: فإن كان الظهور غير الاتّحاد فما تنكرون أن يكون التأنّس غير الاتّحاد؟ وإلاّ فإن كان تأنّس الكلمة بالإنسان هو اتّحادها به، فكذلك ظهورها فيه هو اتّحادها به.

٢٩٠. وكذلك إن هم اعتلّوا لنفي الاتّحاد عن الجسد ولتثبيتهم إيّاه للإنسان الكلّي بأن يقولوا: الكلمة جوهر بسيط والإنسان الكلّي بسيط والجسد مركّب، فاتّحاد البسيط بالبسيط جائز واتّحاد البسيط بالمركّب ليس بجائز، قلنا لهم: فكذلك يلزمكم أن تزعموا أنّ ظهور البسيط في البسيط جائز وأنّ ظهور البسيط في المركّب ليس بجائز. أوْ لاَ، فإن كان ظهور البسيط في المركّب جائز فكذلك اِتّحاد البسيط بالمركّب جائز.

٢٩١. وإن هم عادوا إلى علّتهم الأولى التي ذكرناها في أوائل الكتاب[٧٧] أو إلى نظيرها فقالوا: لو كانت الكلمة اتّحدت بذلك الجسد دون غيره لكانت إنّما جاءت بخلاص ذلك الجسد دون غيره، قلنا لهم: ولو كانت إنّما ظهرت في ذلك الجسد دون غيره لكانت إنّما جاءت بخلاص ذلك الجسد دون غيره. فإن عادوا إلى أن يزعموا أنّ الكلمة قد ظهرت في الإنسان الكلّي وفي ذلك الجسد، قيل لهم: وكذلك قد اتّحدت بالإنسان الكلّي وبذلك الجسد، وإلاّ فالفرق؟

٢٩٢. وقد ينبغي لمَن طالبهم بالفرق في هذا الكلام وفي غيره ألاّ يقنع

١. ب || ف: في الجزئى هو اتحاد.
١٩. ب || ف: الجسد فالفرق.

that its appearance in the individual was its uniting with it, unless they now claim that its appearance in the universal was other than its uniting with it, in which case they should be questioned about the difference between the two.

289 Say to them also: If the appearance was other than the uniting, how can you deny that the becoming human was other than the uniting? But if the Word's becoming human through the man was its uniting with him, then its appearance in him was its uniting with him.

290 Similarly, if they try to deny the uniting with the body and to acknowledge it with the universal human by saying: The Word is a simple substance and the universal human is simple while the body was composite, so the uniting of the simple with the simple was possible, though the uniting of the simple with the composite was not possible, we say to them: Likewise, you are compelled to claim that the appearance of the simple in the simple was possible, though the appearance of the simple in the composite was not possible. Otherwise, if the appearance of the simple in the composite was possible, then the uniting of the simple with the composite was also possible.

291 If they refer back to their first reason which we mentioned at the beginning of the book,[77] or to something similar, and they say: If the Word had united with this body and no other then it would have brought salvation only to this body and no other, we say to them: And if it had appeared only in this body and no other then it would have brought salvation only to this body and no other. But if they refer back to their claim that the Word appeared in the universal human and in this body, say to them: Then similarly it united with the universal human and this body. And if not what is the difference?

292 Anyone who asks them in this argument and others about the difference, must not be satisfied

منهم بلفظ لا معنى تحته، فإنّهم من أكثر الأمم ألفاظًا لا معانى تحتها فيما يعبّرون به عن مذاهبهم هذه، وأن يطالبهم بمعانٍ تفرق بين ما قالوا وما عُورضوا به.

٢٩٣. ومتى ادّعوا أيضًا أو ادّعى منهم مدّعٍ أنّ الظهور غير الاتّحاد سُئلوا عنهما ليُفرقوا بينهما ويدلّوا على تغايرهما واختلافهما، وهذا أمر عسر عليهم تكلّفه.

٢٩٤. ويُسألون أيضًا عن الظهور، ما هو وما حقيقته؟

٢٩٥. وهل ظهرت الكلمة في ذلك الجسد للحواسّ والمشاعر أم إنّما ظهرت بالتدبير[٧٨] الذي يدّعونه؟ فإن كانت ظهرت للحواسّ والمشاعر فقد أُدركت بهما، وهذا خلاف دينكم قديمًا وحديثًا.

٢٩٦. وإن كانت إنّما ظهرت في ذلك الجسد بالتدبير فهي ظاهرة إذن في كلّ جسم بالتدبير. وإن ادّعوا ظهورًا لا يُعقل، تحكّم الخصم عليهم وادّعى ما شاء أن يدّعيه عليهم ممّا لا يُعقل.

٢٩٧. ونقول لهم أيضًا في نظير ما تقدم من الكلام عليهم: إن كان المسيح جوهرين أحدهما الإنسان الكلّي فقد أثبتم المسيح إذًا أقانيم كثيرة لأنّ الإنسان الكلّي ذو أقانيم كثيرة. وأنتم في الأصل تمنعون أن تثبتوه ذا أقنومَين لا غير، وهذا تفاوت شديد.

٢٩٨. وإن كان المسيح أقنومًا واحدًا ذا جوهرين وفسد عنه من يختار هذه العبارة قول من قال «هو جوهران»، فكيف يصحّ إضافة الأقنوم إلى جوهر غير جوهره أو إضافة الجوهر إلى غير

٣. ب || ف: وبين ما عورضوا.　　١٤. ب || ف: ما تقدمه.
١٤. ب || ف: ويقولون.

with any term from them which carries no meaning. For they of all communities have terms which carry no meaning when they explain these beliefs of theirs. He must ask them the meanings, to distinguish between what they say and what can be said in response to them.

293 Also when they or one of them claims that the appearing is different from the uniting, they should be questioned about the two, to show the difference between them, and to point out the distinctions and variations between them. This will be a trying matter for them to take on.

294 They should also be asked about the appearance, what is it in actuality?

295 Did the Word appear in this body to the senses and feelings, or did it appear only through the control[78] which they claim? If it appeared to the senses and feelings then it would have been perceived by them, though
296 this is contrary to their religion both old and new. | If it only appeared in this body through control then it appeared in every physical body through control. If they claim that it was an appearance that cannot be understood, an opponent may continue as he wishes against them, and make whatever irrational claims he likes about them.

297 We say to them also, in the same way as in the earlier argument against them: If the Messiah was two substances, one of them the universal human, then you acknowledge that the Messiah was many hypostases because the universal human possesses many hypostases. But in your principles you do refuse to acknowledge that he possessed two hypostases and no more, so this is a considerable change.

298 If the Messiah was one hypostasis possessing two substances, and according to the person who favours this explanation the statement "He was two substances" is wrong, then how could the hypostasis be connected with a substance other than

أقنومه؟ فإن قالوا: تصحّ باتّحاد أحدهما بالآخر، قلنا: فإذا اتّحد به فقد صار واحدًا بزعمكم إذ كان الاتّحاد عندكم هو أنّه صار من اِثنين واحد، وذلك الواحد في مذهبكم هو المسيح الذي بالاتّحاد كان مسيحًا. فقد عاد الأمر إلى أن المسيح هو الجوهران لا الأقنوم ذو الجوهرين لأنّ الأقنوم لم يصر في نفسه واحدًا من اِثنين فيكون بذلك مسيحًا إذ كان الأقنوم عندكم لم يزل واحدًا في نفسه قبل الاتّحاد. وإذا لزمهم بهذا الاحتجاج وبنحوه أو بغير ذلك أن يزعموا أنّ المسيح جوهران صارا بالاتّحاد مسيحًا واحدًا فسدت عبارتهم تلك التي يختارونها، أعني زعمهم أنّ المسيح أقنوم واحد ذو جوهرين، وفسد معناها. ولزمهم أن يزعموا أنّه ذو أقانيم كثيرة ومشيئات كثيرة إذ كان جوهرين أحدهما ذو أقانيم كثيرة ومشيئات كثيرة. وهذا بيّن والحمد لله.

٢٩٩. ويقال لهم: أيخلو المسيح على الحقيق عندكم من أن يكون هو الإله الماسح والإنسان الممسوح جميعًا أو يكون هو الإنسان الممسوح لا الإله الماسح أو يكون هو الإله الماسح لا الإنسان الممسوح؟

٣٠٠. فإن قلتم: هو الإله الماسح والإنسان الممسوح، فقد أثبتموه جوهرين مختلفين على التحقيق. وإذا ثبت ذلك وكان أحد ذَينك الجوهرين عندكم هو الإنسان الكلّي والإنسان الكلّي ذو أقانيم كثيرة، فقد أثبتم المسيح ذا أقانيم كثيرة كما سمّيناكم قبل.

٧. ب || ف: فاذا.
١٠. ب || ف: والزمهم.
١١. ب || ف: كان ذو جوهرين.

its own, or the substance be connected with a hypostasis not its own? If they say: It could take place through the uniting of one with the other, we say: If it united with it then it became one according to your claim, since the uniting according to you was two becoming one, and this one in your beliefs was the Messiah who was Messiah by the uniting. So the matter returns to the Messiah being the two substances not the hypostasis possessing two substances, because the hypostasis could not in itself become one from two and so be Messiah, because according to you the hypostasis in itself was always one before the uniting. If they are compelled by these arguments, or by similar or others, to claim that the Messiah was two substances which became one Messiah by the uniting, then this explanation which they have chosen is wrong. I mean their claim that the Messiah was one hypostasis which possessed two substances; it is wrong in fact. And they are forced to claim that it possessed many hypostases and many wills, because he was two substances, one of them possessing many hypostases and wills. This is clear, and thanks be to God.

299 Say to them: As you see it, could the Messiah in reality have been anything other than both the Divinity who anointed and the human who was anointed, or the human who was anointed and not the Divinity who anointed, or the Divinity who anointed and not the human who was anointed?

300 If you say: He was the Divinity who anointed and the human who was anointed, you acknowledge that he was two distinct substances in reality. If this is confirmed, and according to you one of these two substances was the universal human and the universal human is possessor of many hypostases, then you acknowledge that the Messiah was possessor of many hypostases, which we identified for you earlier.

وإذا كانت تلك الأقانيم مختلفة مُطيعة وعاصية ومؤمنة وكافرة فبعض أقانيم المسيح مطيع وبعضها عاصٍ وبعضها ولي له وبعضها عدوّ له وهي كلّها أقانيمه ومنسوبة إليه على الصحّة. وإذا كان المسيح على هذا القول لا يكون مسيحًا تامًّا إلاّ باجتماع الجوهرين له في المسيحيّة وأحد جوهريه لا يكون جوهرًا تامًّا إلاّ بأقانيمه، بل لا يكون موجودًا البتّة إلاّ بأقانيمه، فالمسيح لا يكون مسيحًا على التمام إلاّ بأقانيمه التي هي أقانيم أحدِ جوهريه وهي أقانيم الإنسان الكلّي. وأنتم تهربون من أن تجعلوه أقنومين أو ذا أقنومين، فهذا القول يُوجب أنّه ذو أقانيم كثيرة وأنّه لا يكون مسيحًا على التمام والتحقيق إلاّ بأقانيم الناس جميعًا وأشخاصهم كلّها. وإذا كانت أقانيم الإنسان الكلّي أيضًا هي الإنسان الكلّي وتلك الأقانيم هي أشخاص الناس فأشخاص الناس كلّها هي المسيح إذ كانت أحد جوهريه وهو الجوهر الذي به كان مسيحًا على الصحّة، فالمؤمن والكافر والمطيع والعاصي والمجنون والعاقل والكبير والصغير والذكر والأُنثى كلّ هؤلاء إذًا هم المسيح على الصحّة إذ كانوا أحد جوهرَيه.

٣٠١. وإن زعموا أنّ المسيح هو الإنسان الممسوح لا الإله الماسح، تركوا قولهم تركًا مكشوفًا وصاروا إلى موافقة أريوس وبولى ومَن أنكر من المسلمين وغيرهم أن يكون المسيح إلهًا أو متّحدًا به الإله. وقيل

٩. ب || ف: تجعلوه أقنومين فهذا القول.

If these hypostases were distinct in being obedient and disobedient, believing and unbelieving, then some of the Messiah's hypostases would have been obedient and some disobedient, some his supporters and others his enemies, though they were all hypostases and really related to him. And if, according to this teaching, the Messiah was only fully Messiah through the joining of his two substances in his being Messiah, and one of his substances was only fully substance through its hypostases, and in fact could only exist at all through its hypostases, then the Messiah could only be fully Messiah through his hypostases which were the hypostases of one of its two substances, the hypostases of the universal human. You refuse to make him two hypostases or the possessor of two hypostases, though this teaching requires him to be possessor of many hypostases and only to be Messiah fully and really through hypostases of humankind together and all their individual beings.

Also, if the hypostases of the universal human were the universal human, and these hypostases were the individual beings of humankind, then all the individual beings of humankind were the Messiah, since they were one of his two substances and the substance by which he was Messiah in truth. So the believer and the unbeliever, the obedient and disobedient, the demented and the rational, big and little, male and female, all of these were therefore the Messiah in truth since they were one of his two substances.

301 If they claim that the Messiah was the human who was anointed and not the Divinity who anointed, they abandon their teaching in the most obvious way and fall into agreement with Arius and Paul, and those such as Muslims and others who deny that the Messiah was divine or that the Divinity united with him. Say to them

لهم أيضاً: والإنسان الممسوح ليس هو الذي صار بالاتّحاد واحداً من اِثنين أحدهما قديم والآخر مُحْدث، والمسيح عندكم إنّما كان مسيحًا بالاِتّحاد الذي به صار واحدًا من اِثنين.

٣٠٢. وإن زعموا أن المسيح هو الإله الماسح لا الإنسان الممسوح، قلنا: فالإله أيضاً عندكم ليس هو الذي صار بالاتّحاد واحدًا من اِثنين أحدهما قديم والآخر محدث، كما قلنا لكم. قيل: كيف يكون الإله مسيحًا والمسيح إنّما صار عندكم مسيحًا بالاتّحاد الذي به صار واحدًا من اِثنين؟ على أنّه إن كان المسيح على التحقيق هو الإله الماسح لا الإنسان فالإله عندكم على التحقيق هو اِبن البشر كما تقولون في المسيح وهو ابن مريم وداود وآدم ومن ولد آدم، وهو الذي كان يرتضع ويأكل ويشرب وينام ويستيقظ وهو المصلوب المقتول الميت على التحقيق. كلّ ذلك به وقع وإليه وصل لا بالإنسان ولا إلى الإنسان مع توابع ذلك كلّها.

٣٠٣. وإذا جاز هذا على الابن الذي هو عندكم إله، جاز على الأب مثله وعلى الروح مثل ذلك. إلاّ أن يبطلوا حقائق الصلب والقتل وهذه الأمور فيتركوا دينهم ويتجاهلوا. وفي بعض هذا كفاية لمن عقل وتثبّت في نظره. وربّنا محمود على تأييده.

٣٠٤. الكلمة على اليعقوبيّة.[٧٩] وأمّا اليعقوبيّة فإنّا نقول لهم: أخبرونا عن المسيح، أقديم هو أم محدث أم ليس بقديم ولا محدث أم قديم ومحدث؟

٨–٩. ب || ف: المسيح على هو ابن البشر.   ١١. ب || ف: كان يرضع.

also: But the human who was anointed was not the one who by the uniting became one from two, one of them eternal and the other temporal. For according to you the Messiah was only Messiah by the uniting by which two became one.

302 If they claim that the Messiah was the Divinity who anointed and not the human who was anointed, we say: But nor was the Divinity, according to you, the one who through the uniting became one from two, one of them eternal and the other temporal, as we have said to you. Say: How could the Divinity be Messiah when the Messiah only became Messiah, according to you, by the uniting, by which two became one? Although if the Messiah was in truth the Divinity who anointed and not the human who was anointed, then the Divinity, according to you, was in truth the son of man, as you say about the Messiah, and son of Mary, of David and Adam, and a child of Adam. He sucked at the breast, ate, drank, slept, woke, he was the one who was crucified, killed and dead in reality. It was he whom all this affected and to whom it happened and not the human, with all the consequences.

303 If this was possible for the Son, who according to you is divine, the same was possible for the Father and the same for the Spirit. Otherwise, they overturn the realities of the cross and the killing and these events, and so they abandon their religion and fall into ignorance. Part of this alone provides enough for anyone with reason and sound discrimination. May our Lord be praised for his help.

304 [3.] *The argument against the Jacobites*[79]

[i. *The Messiah both eternal and contingent*]

As for the Jacobites, we say to them: Tell us about the Messiah, was he eternal, or temporal, or neither eternal nor temporal, or eternal and temporal?

٣٠٥. فإن قالوا: قديم، فقد أبطلوا زعمهم أنّه جوهر من جوهرَين لأنّ القديم ليس من جوهرَين وإنّما القديم عندهم جوهر واحد لَم يزل ليس معه جوهر ثانٍ.

٣٠٦. وإن زعموا أنّ المسيح محدث تركوا قولهم أيضًا أنّه جوهر من جوهرين أحدهما قديم والآخر محدث لأنّ المحدث ليس من جوهر القديم.

٣٠٧. وإن كرهوا هذين الجوابين ورجعوا إلى أن يقولوا: هو قديم اللاهوت محدث الناسوت، تركوا قولهم أنّ المسيح جوهر واحد وأثبتوه جوهرين لاهوتًا وناسوتًا أحدهما قديم والآخر حديث.

٣٠٨. ولا بُدّ للاهوت الذي أثبتوه قديمًا وللناسوت الذي أثبتوه حديثًا من أن يكونا هما المسيح أو غير المسيح أو يكون أحدهما هو المسيح والآخر ليس بمسيح.

٣٠٩. فإن زعموا أنّهما هما المسيح فقد صرّحوا بترك قولهم وأثبتوا المسيح جوهرين.

٣١٠. وإن قالوا: هما غير المسيح، قلنا: فنحن لَم نسألكم عن «غير المسيح»، إنّما سألناكم عن المسيح، أقديم هو أم محدث، فأجبتم عن غيره وهذا من أبين الظلم.

٣١١. وإن زعموا أن أحدهما هو المسيح دون الآخر فقد تركوا أيضًا قولهم، لأنّ اللاهوت وحده ليس جوهرًا من جوهرين والناسوت

٥. ب || ف: ليس هو من. ١١. ب، ف || ل: والناسوت.
٩–١٠. ب، ف || ل: والآخر محدث.

305 If they say: Eternal, they destroy their claim that he was a substance from two substances, because the eternal is not from two substances, but according to them is only one substance who has always been, with no
306 second substance in addition. | If they claim that the Messiah was temporal, they also abandon their teaching that he was a substance from two substances one of them eternal and the other temporal, because the tem-
307 poral is not substance of the eternal. | If they reject these two answers and return to saying: He was eternal in divinity and temporal in humanity, they abandon their teaching that the Messiah was one substance and affirm that he was two substances, divine and human, one eternal and the other having come into existence.

308 There is no alternative other than that the divine nature, which they claim is eternal, and the human nature, which they claim came into existence, were either the Messiah or other than the Messiah, or one of them was the Messiah and the other was not the Messiah.

309 If they claim that they were both the Messiah, they make it clear that they have abandoned their teaching and affirm that the Messiah was two
310 substances. | If they say: They were other than the Messiah, we say: We have not asked you about "Other than the Messiah", but only about whether the Messiah was eternal or temporal. So for you to answer
311 about something else is the clearest error. | If they claim that one of them was the Messiah and not the other, they also abandon their teaching because the divine nature alone was not a substance from two substances, and the human nature

وحده ليس جوهرًا من جوهرين أحدهما قديم والآخر محدث.

٣١٢. وإن زعموا أنّ المسيح ليس بقديم ولا محدث خرجوا من المعقول مع خرجهم أيضًا من أقاويل أصحابهم، وذلك أنّ ليس في أسلافهم أحد زعم أن المسيح ليس بقديم ولا محدث.

٣١٣. ومتى تجاسر على هذا متجاسر لم يدر لعَلّ جميع من يشاهده من الناس وغيرهم ليس بقديم ولا محدث.

٣١٤. ومتى كان المسيح أيضًا ليس بقديم ولا محدث فهو ليس بإله ولا مألوه ولا ربّ ولا مربوب. والدخل في هذا كثير جداًّ.

٣١٥. وإن زعموا أنّ المسيح قديم محدث، قيل لهم: والقديم عندكم هو ما لَم يزل والمحدث هو الذي لم يكن فكان، والذي لم يزل على قولكم هذا هو الذي لم يكن. وهذا هو اِختلاط في القول، وصاحب هذا الجواب لو عُورض بكلّ ضرب من ضروب الاِختلاط والمناقضات على جوابه هذا لم يجد إلى فصل سبيلاً، ولم يمكنه أن يدفع زعْم مَن زَعَم أنّ السواد بياض والجسم عَرَض والمحال جائز والصحيح فاسد وغير ذلك من ضروب المناقضة. على أنّه ليس يعارض بشيء إلاّ والذي قاله أشدّ منه تفاحشًا وأبعد من الصواب بُعْدًا.

٣١٦. وإن زعموا أنّ المسيح قديم ومحدث، تركوا قولهم «هو جوهر واحد من جوهرين» ولحقوا بالناسطوريّة الذين زعموا أنّه جوهران أحدهما قديم والآخر محدث. وقد مرّ النقض على هؤلاء.

٢. ب || ف: فان زعموا بأن.
٥. ب || ف: لعّل من يشاهده.
١٢. ب || ف: ولو.
١٥–١٦. ب || ف: أنه لم يعارض.

alone was not a substance from two substances, one eternal and the other temporal.

312 If they claim that the Messiah was neither eternal nor temporal, they depart from reason as well as from the teachings of their colleagues. This is because among their predecessors there were none who claimed that
313 the Messiah was neither eternal nor temporal. | Should anyone make this daring claim, he could not know whether any of the people he met and
314 others were neither eternal nor temporal. | Also, if the Messiah was neither eternal nor temporal he was neither divine nor had a Divinity over him, neither Lord nor subject. The implications of this are mani-
315 fold indeed. | And if they claim that the Messiah was eternal and temporal, say to them: The eternal according to you is what has always been, and the temporal is what was not and then was. So according to this statement of yours, one who has always been was one who was not. This is confusion of expression. If the person who makes this answer were confronted with similar kinds of confusion and contradiction, he would not be able to make a distinction. Nor would he be able to reject the claim of anyone who said that black is white, or the physical body is an accident, the impossible is possible, right is wrong, and other kinds of contradiction. But he could never reply with anything more deeply abominable than what he has said, or further from the truth.

316 If they claim that the Messiah was eternal and temporal, they abandon their teaching that he was one substance from two, and they come close to the Nestorians, who claim that he was two substances, one of them eternal and the other temporal. The refutation of them has been presented above.

٣١٧. ويقال لليعقوبيّة أيضًا: أخبرونا عن المولود من مريم، أإله هو أم إنسان أم ليس بإله ولا بإنسان أم إله وإنسان أم إله إنسان؟ فأي ذلك قالوا خرجوا عن أصلهم ولزمهم فيه مثل الذي لزمهم في المسألة التي قبل هذه حرفًا بحرف، وذلك أن هذه المسألة تنزل عليهم كما نزلت تلك والزيادات فيها والمعارضات متّفقة.

٣١٨. ويُسألون أيضًا عن مسألة أُخرى من هذا النحو فيقال لهم: أخبرونا عن فعل المسيح، أهو فعل قديمٍ ليس بمحدث أم فعل محدثٍ ليس بقديم أم فعل شيءٍ ليس بمحدث ولا قديم أم فعل محدث وقديم أم فعل محدث قديم؟[٨٠]

٣١٩. فإن زعموا أن فعل المسيح فعل قديم ليس بمحدث، فقد صرّحوا بأن المسيح قديم ليس بمحدث ولا بشري، وأبطلوا أن يكون المسيح جوهرًا من جوهرين لأنّ القديم الذي ليس بمحدث ليس جوهرًا من جوهرين.

٣٢٠. وإن زعموا أنّ فعله فعل محدث ليس بقديم، فهذا ترك قولهم والمصير إلى قول أريوس وإلى قول بولى وإلى قول مَن زعم من المسلمون وغيرهم أنّ المسيح محدث مخلوق.

٣٢١. وإن زعموا أنّ فعله فعل شيءٍ ثالث ليس بمحدث ولا قديم، خرجوا عن التعارف، وأوجبوا مع ذلك إنقلاب جوهر القديم وجوهر المحدث اللذين منهما عندهم كان المسيح، ويلزمهم أيضًا على هذا الجواب أن يزعموا أنّه ليس بإله ولا بإنسان كما زعموا أنّه ليس بقديم ولا محدث.

٢٠. ب || ف: الجواب أنه ليس.

317 Say also to the Jacobites: Tell us about the one born of Mary, was he divine or human, or neither divine nor human, or divine and human, or divine-human? Whichever of these they say, they depart from their basic principle, and they are forced to accept almost what they were forced to accept in the question above letter by letter. This is because this question hits them as that did, with corresponding amplifications and objections.

318 Ask them also another question which is similar to this one, and say to them: Tell us about the Messiah's action, was it the action of an eternal being who was not temporal, or the action of a temporal being who was not eternal, or of something neither temporal nor eternal, or of a temporal and eternal thing, or of a temporal-eternal thing?[80]

319 If they claim that the Messiah's action was the action of an eternal being who was not temporal, they declare that the Messiah was eternal and not temporal or human, and make it impossible for the Messiah to be a substance from two substances, because the eternal who is not temporal is not a substance from two substances.

320 If they claim that his action was the action of a temporal being who was not eternal, this is an abandonment of their teaching and a move towards the teaching of Arius and the teaching of Paul and the teaching of such others as the Muslims who claim that the Messiah was temporal and created.

321 If they claim that his action was the action of a third thing which was not temporal or eternal, they depart from what can be known. In addition, they compel there to be a transformation of the substance of the eternal and the substance of the temporal, from both of which, in their view, the Messiah came to be. Also, according to this answer they are forced to claim that he was not divine or human, just as they claim that he was not eternal or temporal.

٣٢٢. فإن قالوا: إنّ فعله فعل قديم ومحدث، أشركوا بين القديم والمحدث في الفعل وسوّوا بينهما في الصنع والتدبير. وهذا الموضع يلحق أهل الإجبار[٨١] الذين أجازوا فعلاً واحداً من فاعلين. لا بدّ لهم من ذلك ما تمسّكوا بأصلهم. ومتى قال أحد من الناس ذلك لم يفرق بين القديم والمحدث في الأفعال بل لا يمكنه أن يفرق بينهما في القوى بل لا يمكنه أن يفرق بينهما في الأنفس متى فرّع هذا الكلام عليه. وعلى أن اليعقوبيّة متى زعموا أنّ فعل المسيح فعل قديم ومحدث فقد أثبتوا المسيح شيئين مختلفين لا جوهرًا واحدًا كما يقولون.

٣٢٣. وإن زعموا أنّ فعل المسيح فعل قديم محدث، كان هذا أكثر من التسوية بين القديم والمحدث لجعلهم القديم محدثًا والمحدث قديمًا والإله مألوهًا والربّ مربوبًا، وقد قدمنا من الدلائل على فساد هذا القول ما قدمنا. فإذا فسدت هذه الخمسة الأوجه ولم يجدوا في هذا الباب سادسًا فلا فعل يمكنهم أن يثبتوا على الحقيقة ولا فاعلاً ولا مسيحًا.

٣٢٤. فإن عادوا إلى بعض ذلك التعليق فقالوا: هو قديم بإلاهيّته محدث بإنسانيّته، قلنا: فالكلام بعدُ قائم وقد زدتمونا شيئًا آخر إذا جعلتم الجوهر الواحد قديمًا محدثًا، فإن شئتم فأجعلوه كذلك من جهة واحدة وإن شئتم فمن جهتَين، إذ كانت العين القديمة هي العين المحدثة. وإذا

٢–٣. ب || ف: وهذا الفعل يلحق.
١٢. ل || ب: الدلاليل.
١٣. ب || ف: لا يجدوا.
١٦. ب، ف || ل: فقالوا: قديم.
١٧. ب || ف: إذ.

322 If they say that his action was the action of an eternal and temporal being, they associate the eternal and the temporal in action and make them equal in design and control. This position is close to the People of Compulsion,[81] who regard as possible one action from two agents. They cannot avoid this while they hold onto their principle. As long as one of these people says this, he cannot distinguish between the eternal and the temporal in actions, and is not able to distinguish between them in their power, nor is he able to distinguish between them in their selves, as long as the argument is unfolded before him. However, as long as the Jacobites claim that the action of the Messiah was the action of the eternal and temporal, they affirm that the Messiah was two different things and not one substance as they say.

323 And if they claim that the action of the Messiah was the action of an eternal-temporal being, this is more than making the eternal and temporal equal because they turn the eternal into temporal and the temporal into eternal, the Divinity into one with divinity over him and the Lord into subject. We have already discussed above the indications of where this teaching is mistaken. If these five alternatives are wrong, they will not find a sixth on this matter, so there can be no action which they can affirm in reality, and no agent and no Messiah.

324 If they go back to part of this discussion and say: He was eternal by his divinity and temporal by his humanity, we say: The argument still applies, and you add one more thing for us if you make the one substance eternal and temporal. If you prefer, make him like this in one respect or, if you prefer, in two respects; the eternal entity was still the temporal entity. And if

ثبت أن عينًا واحدة قديمة محدثة من جهة أو من جهتَين وبوجه أو بوجهَين ثبت أنّ الذي لم يزل هو الذي لم يكن والذي لم يكن هو الذي لم يزل من جهة أو من جهتَين وبوجه أو بوجهَين.

٣٢٥. ويحقّق هذا عليهم أيضًا فيقال لهم: أفي شخص المسيح إنسانيّة قائمة وإلاهيّة قائمة قصدتم إليهما بقولكم «هو قديم بإلاهيّته محدث بإنسانيّته»؟ فإن قالوا: نعم، قلنا: فقد صار المسيح إذن جوهرين وصار شخصه أقنومين مختلفين، وهذا قول النسطوريّة لا قولكم.

٣٢٦. وإن زعموا أنّه ليس في شخص المسيح إلاهيّة قائمة ولا إنسانيّة قائمة، قلنا: فهو إذن لا إله ولا إنسان، وهذا خلاف قولكم في إلاهيّته. وأذا لم يكن أيضًا فيه إلاهيّة ولا إنسانيّة سقط قولكم «هو قديم بإلاهيّته محدث بإنسانيّته».

٣٢٧. فإن قالوا: إنّما أردنا بإلاهيّته وإنسانيّته الجوهرين اللذين منهما كان جوهر المسيح لا إنّا ذهبنا أنّ ذينك الجوهرين في شخصه قائمان موجودان بعد الاتّحاد، قلنا: فإن لم يكونا موجودين قائمين في شخص المسيح وفي جوهره فهما بين حالتين، إمّا أن يكونا بطلاً أو صارا عن المسيح بمعزل. فإن قلتم: بطلاً، فقد أبطلتم القديم والمحدث، وإن قلتم: صارا عنه بمعزل، فهما غيره وهو غيرهما وهما قديم ومحدث وهو ليس بقديم ولا محدث. فما نرى قول مَن قال: المسيح قديم بإلاهيّته محدث بإنسانيّته، إلاّ وقد أدّاه قوله

٢. ب || ف: ثبت الذي.
٣. ب || ف: جهتين بوجه.
١٢. ب || ف: بإلاهيّته محدث».

it is acknowledged that the one entity was eternal and temporal in one respect or two, or in one manner or two, then it is acknowledged that the one who has always been was one who did not exist, and one who did not exist was one who has always been, in one respect or two, or one manner or two.

325 The following can also be proved true against them, so say to them: Did humanity and divinity subsist in the individual person of the Messiah, as you suggested in your statement: "He was eternal by his divinity and temporal by his humanity"? If they say: Yes, we say: Then the Messiah becomes two substances and his individual person becomes two different hypostases. This is the Nestorians' teaching, not yours.

326 If they claim that divinity and humanity did not subsist in the individual person of the Messiah, we say: Then he was neither divine nor human, which is contrary to your teaching about his divinity. And if neither divinity nor humanity were in him, then your statement, "He was eternal by his divinity and temporal by his humanity", becomes pointless.

327 If they say: By his divinity and his humanity we mean only the two substances from which came the substance of the Messiah, and we do not think that these two substances subsisted and existed in his individual person after the uniting, we say: If they did not exist or subsist in the individual person and substance of the Messiah, then they were in one of two conditions, either they were destroyed or they were withdrawn from the Messiah. If you say: "Destroyed", you destroy the eternal and the temporal, and if you say: "They were withdrawn from him", they were separate from him and he was separate from them, they were eternal and temporal and he was neither eternal nor temporal. We can only see the teachings of those who say: "The Messiah was eternal by his divinity and temporal by his humanity", leading them

على هذا السياق إلى إثباته لا قديمًا ولا محدثًا، وهذا خلاف ما حاول وضِدّه.

٣٢٨. وإن قالوا: الإلاهيّة والإنسانيّة في شخصه جوهر واحد لاِتّحاد إحداهما بالأُخرى لا جوهرين لأنّ الاتِّحاد يُسقط العدد، قلنا: فقد عاد الأمر إلى أن العين القديمة هي العين المحدثة وأنّ الذي لم يزل هو الذي لم يكن. ولا وجه بعد هذا لِذكركم الإلهيّة والإنسانيّة في هذا الباب إذ كانا قد صارا واحدًا في قولكم ولا سيما مع زعمكم أنّ الاتّحاد يسقط العدد. ومتى ذكرتم إلاهيّته وإنسانيّته فقد أحْبَبتم ذكر الجوهرين وأتَيتم بالتثنيّة وردّدتم العدد وصحّحتموه ولم تُسقطوه. فهذه أقاويلكم ينقض بعضها بعضًا نقضًا ظاهرًا.

٣٢٩. ويُسألون من وجه آخر فيقال لهم: أخبرونا عن المسيح، أليس إنّما كان مسيحًا في حال الاتّحاد؟ فلا بدّ من: نعم، على قولهم. يقال لهم: وفي حال الاتّحاد وقع الاتّحاد بإنسان جزئي من الأقنوم القديم؟ فإذا قالوا: نعم، وكذلك يقولون ولا بدّ لهم من ذلك على قولهم، يقال لهم: وفي حال الاتّحاد هو مسيح والمسيح عندكم جوهر من جوهرين أقنوم من أقنومين.(٨٢) فلا بدّ من: نعم. يقال لهم: ففي حال ما هو أقنومان متّحِد ومتّحد به هو في تلك الحال أقنوم واحد لا غير، وفي حال ما هو جوهران جوهر المتّحِد وجوهر

٩. ب، ف || ل: احببيتم.
١٣. ب || ف: فيقال.
١٦–١٧. ب || ف: عندكم هو جوهر.

along this progression to acknowledging that he was neither eternal nor temporal. This is contrary to what they are trying to achieve, in fact its opposite.

328 If they say: By the uniting of one with the other, divinity and humanity were one substance in his individual person and not two substances because the uniting put an end to number, we say: The matter comes back to the eternal entity being the temporal entity, and what has always existed being what did not. After this there is no place for your reference to divinity and humanity in this matter, because they became one in your teaching, especially with your claim that the uniting put an end to number. However, when you refer to his divinity and humanity you readily refer to two substances, you speak in the dual, you use numbers again, you say it is right, and you do not think it is pointless to do so. One part of these statements of yours invalidates the other in the most obvious way.

329 [ii. *The transformation of the divine and human in the uniting*]

We now question them on another matter, so say to them: Tell us about the Messiah, was he only Messiah at the moment of uniting? According to their teaching they can only say: Yes. Say to them: At the moment of uniting, did the uniting of the eternal hypostasis to the individual human take place? If they say: Yes, and they will, since they must according to their teachings, say to them: So at the moment of uniting he was Messiah, and the Messiah according to you was a substance from two substances and a hypostasis from two hypostases.[82] They can only say: Yes. Say to them: So at the moment when he was two hypostases, the one uniting and the other united with, at this moment he was one hypostasis and not anything else. And at the moment when he was two substances, the substance that united and the substance

المتّحد به هو فيها جوهر واحد لا غير، وفي حال ما هو إله متّحِد وإنسان متّحد به هو في تلك الحال شيء ثالث لا إله مفرد ولا إنسان مفرد ولا إله وإنسان مجتمعان. وهذه هي المناقضة البيّنة المكشوفة وهذه المسألة كافية ولو لَم يكن عليهم غيرها.

٣٣٠. وإن هربوا مما لزمهم هذا الكلام فقالوا: لَم يكن مسيحًا في حال الاتّحاد وإنّما كان مسيحًا بعد الاتّحاد، قلنا: فليس الاتّحاد أذن كان مسيحًا إذ كان الاتّحاد واقعًا وهو ليس بمسيح في وقت وقوعه، وهذا خلاف قولكم مصرّحًا.

٣٣١. وإذا جاز أن يكون متّحدًا به وقتًا من الأوقات وليس بمسيح فلِم لا يجوز أن يبقى سائر الأوقات متّحدًا وليس بمسيح؟ وهذا يؤديهم إلى الإنسلاخ من قولهم.

٣٣٢. ويسألون أيضًا فيقال لهم: أخبرونا عن الجوهر القديم هل اِنقلب عن جوهريّته لما اتّحد بالمحدث أم لم ينقلب؟ فإن زعموا أنّه اِنقلب عن جوهره، لم يعصمهم شيء من جواز انقلاب الأقنومين الأخرين اللذين هما الأب والروح عن جوهرهما إلى جوهر المحدث، وكذلك جواز اِنقلاب المحدث عن جوهره إلى جوهر القديم. وهذا هو التجاهل عين التجاهل.

٣٣٣. فيقال لهم حينئذٍ: أفهكذا تزعمون أيضًا أنّ المحدث انقلب عن جوهره لاِتّحاد القديم به؟ فإن قالوا: لا، قيل لهم: فما جعل القديم بالاِنقلاب عن جوهره للاِتّحاد أولى من المحدث؟ وإن زعموا أنّ

٤. ب || ف: المسألة الاخر الذي كافية.
٧. ب || ف: اذا كان الاتحاد.

that was united with, at this moment he was one substance and not anything else. And at the moment when he was the Divinity which united and the human who was united with, at this moment he was a third thing, neither Divinity alone nor human alone, nor Divinity and human together. This is a clear and manifest contradiction, and this matter would be quite enough even if there were no others against them.

330 If they try to avoid what they are forced to accept in this argument, and say: He was not Messiah at the moment of the uniting, but only after the uniting, we say: Then it was not at the uniting that he was Messiah, since the uniting happened and he was not Messiah when it did. This is quite definitely contrary to your teaching.

331 If it is possible that he was united at one time and was not Messiah, then why is it not possible that he remained united at other times and was not Messiah? This leads them to cast off their teaching.

332 They should also be questioned, so say to them: Tell us about the eternal substance, was it transformed from its substantiality when it united with the temporal or not? If they claim that it was transformed from its substance, then nothing can hold them back from allowing the transformation of the other two hypostases, the Father and Spirit, from their substances to the substance of the temporal, or likewise allowing the temporal to be transformed from its substance to the substance of the eternal. This is the very depth of ignorance.

333 On this say to them: Do you in the same way claim that the temporal was transformed from its substance by the uniting of the eternal with it? If they say: No, say to them: Then what makes the eternal more suitable to be transformed from its substance by the uniting than the temporal? If they claim that

المحدث أيضًا انقلب عن جوهره لاِتّحاد القديم به، قلنا: فإلى معنى المحدث انقلب القديم وإلى معنى القديم انقلب المحدث أم إلى غير ذلك؟ فإن قالوا: انقلب القديم إلى معنى المحدث والمحدث إلى معنى القديم، قلنا: فقد صار القديم إذن حديثًا والحديث قديمًا. وهذا أشدّ التجاهل والاِختلاط في القول والعقل. وإن زعموا أنّ القديم انقلب إلى غير معنى الحَدَث والمحدث اِنقلب إلى غير معنى القِدَم خرجوا من المعقول إذ ليس في المعقول شيء يخرج من الحدث والقِدم. وسألوا أيضًا عن ذلك «الغير» ليثبتوه، ولن يجدوا إلى إثبات شيء ثالث غير القديم والمحدث سبيلاً.

٣٣٤. فإن قالوا: لم ينقلب كلّ واحد منهما عن جوهره، قلنا: فهما إذن جوهران مختلفان بعد الاتّحاد كما كانا جوهرين مختلفين قبل الاتّحاد، وكذلك هما أقنومان متغايران بعد الاتّحاد كما كانا أقنومين متغايرين قبل الاتّحاد، وهذا ترك قولكم.

٣٣٥. ويقال لهم أيضًا: أيخلو الأقنوم القديم من أن يكون بطل عند الاتّحاد وحدث غيره، أو أن يكون انقلب عن جوهريّته ويغير ذاته، أو أن يكون ثابتًا لم يبطل ولم ينقلب ولم يتغيّر عن جوهريّته؟ فإن زعموا أنّه بطل وحدث جوهر آخر هو غيره، خرجوا من دينهم ودين أسلافهم، ولم يأمنوا مع ذلك أن تبطل أقانيم القديم كلّها وجوهره. وإذا بطل ذلك الأقنوم أيضًا وحدث جوهر آخر هو غيره[٨٣] فالمسيح مُحْدَث لا محالة.

٥. ب || ف: القول والفعل.
١٣. ب || ف: قولهم.
١٤. ب || ف: ويقال لهم أيحلو.

the temporal was also transformed from its substance by the uniting of the eternal with it, we say: Then did the temporal become transformed into the reality of the eternal, and did the eternal become transformed into the reality of the temporal, or into something other than this? If they say: The eternal was transformed into the reality of the temporal and the temporal into the reality of the eternal, we say: Then the eternal became a thing that came into existence, and a thing that had come into existence became eternal. This is the most serious ignorance and confusion in word and reason. If they claim that the eternal was transformed into something other than the reality of temporality, and the temporal was transformed into something other than the reality of eternity, they depart from what is reasonable, since within what is reasonable there is nothing apart from temporality and eternity. They should also be questioned about this "other", to define it, though they will not find a way to define a third thing which is other than the eternal and the temporal.

334 If they say: Neither of them was transformed from its substance, we say: Therefore they were two distinct substances after the uniting, just as they were two distinct substances before the uniting, and likewise they were two different hypostases after the uniting, just as they were two different hypostases before the uniting. This is an abandonment of your teaching.

335 Say to them also: Was there any other possibility for the eternal hypostasis at the uniting than that it was destroyed and became something other than itself, was transformed from its substantiality and had its essence changed, or that it remained fixed, was not destroyed or transformed and was not changed from its substantiality? If they claim that it was destroyed and became another substance different from itself, they abandon their religion and the religion of their predecessors, and in addition they will not be sure whether all the hypostases and the substance of the eternal might be destroyed. But if this hypostasis was destroyed and became another substance different from itself,[83] then the Messiah was undoubtedly temporal.

٣٣٦. وإن زعموا أنّ الأقنوم القديم لم يبطل ولكنّه تغيّر وانقلب عن جوهريّته، خرجوا أيضا من قولهم ودين أسلافهم جميعًا ولم يأمنوا أنّ تنقلب سائر الأقانيم عن جوهرها، وإذا لم يكن عندهم جوهر إلاّ جوهر القديم وجوهر المحدث فانقلب عن جوهريّته القديم فإنّما ينقلب إلى جوهريّة المحدث فيصير القديم مُحدَثًا. فإذا جاز أن يصير القديم محدثًا جاز أن يصير المحدث قديمًا. وهذا كالأوّل في الفساد أو قريب منه وكفى بفساد هذا فسادًا.

٣٣٧. وإن زعموا أنّه لم يبطل ولم يتغيّر، قلنا: فالأقنوم القديم إذن ثابت بعد الاتّحاد على جوهريّته الأولى وعلى أقنوميّته الأولى قبل الاتّحاد، وهذا خلاف قولكم.

٣٣٨. ثم يقال لهم: وكذلك تقولون في المحدث أنّه لم يبطل جوهره ولا أقنومه ولا تغيّر عن جنسه بالاتّحاد؟ فإن قالوا: بلى قد بطل بالاتّحاد، قلنا: فإنّما اتّحد القديم إذن بمعدوم مبطّل إذ كان وقوع الاتّحاد قد أبطل عينه. وينبغي أيضًا إن كان الأقنوم المحدث قد بطل مع وقوع الاتّحاد أن يكون المسيح من جوهر القديم وأقنومه فقط دون جوهر المحدث وأقنومه. فهذا يبطل أن يكون المسيح جوهرًا من جوهرين لأنّ جوهر القديم ليس من جوهرين وكذلك أقنومه ليس من جوهرين ولا من أقنومين.

٣٣٩. وإن قالوا: لم يبطل جوهر المحدث ولكنّه تغيّر عن جوهريّته وعن حدثه، قلنا: فقد صار إذًا قديمًا بعد أن كان محدثًا وأزليًّا بعد أن كان

٩. ب || ف: فالقنوم. ١٢. ب: نقولون؛ ف، ل: يقولون.

336 If they claim that the eternal hypostasis was not destroyed but that it changed and was transformed from its substantiality, they likewise abandon their teaching and the religion of their predecessors together, and they will not be sure whether the other hypostases might be transformed from their substance. And then if in their view there is no substance except that of the eternal and of the temporal, then the eternal could only be transformed from its substantiality into the substantiality of the temporal, so that the eternal would become temporal. But if the eternal could become temporal, the temporal could become eternal. This is just as mistaken as the former, more or less, which is quite a mistake!

337 If they claim that it was not destroyed or changed, we say: Then the eternal hypostasis remained fixed after the uniting in its initial substantiality and hypostaticity before the uniting, which is contrary to your teaching.

338 Then say to them: Do you say the same about the temporal, that its substance and hypostasis were not destroyed or changed from their kind by the uniting? If they say: On the contrary, it was destroyed by the uniting, we say: Then the eternal must have united with something which had vanished and been destroyed, if the occurrence of the uniting destroyed it completely. So it follows from this, that if the temporal hypostasis was destroyed when the uniting took place, the Messiah was from the substance and hypostasis of the eternal alone, without the substance and hypostasis of the temporal. This frustrates the notion that the Messiah was a substance from two substances, because the substance of the eternal is not from two substances nor is its hypostasis from two substances or hypostases.

339 If they say: The substance of the temporal was not destroyed, but it was changed from its substantiality and temporality, we say: Then it became eternal after being temporal and timeless after being

زمانيًّا. وحينئذٍ نردّ عليهم الكلام الأوّل في تغيُّر الجوهر القديم بالاتّحاد وكونه محدثًا بعد أن كان قديمًا ويُسألون الفصل في ذلك.

٣٤٠. وإن سوّوا بين الكلامين وقالوا: لم يتغيّر عن جوهريّته ولا عن حدثه، قيل لهم: فهما جوهران مختلفان قبل الاتّحاد وبعده وكذا هما أقنومان مختلفان اتّحدا أم لم ياتّحدا، وهذا هو الخروج عن قولهم صراحًا.

٣٤١. ويسألوا عن وجه آخر فيُقال لهم: أخبرونا عن المسيح، أليس قد كان في صورة البشر وكان صغيرًا ثم كبر وكان يأكل ويشرب ويمشي وينام ويستيقظ وتقع عليه الحواس فيُرى ويلمس، وزعمتم أنّه أُخذ فعُذّب وصُلب وقتل ودفن؟ فلا بدّ من: نعم. يقال لهم: فالذي فَعل ما وصفتم وفُعِلَ به ما ذكرتم إنسان هو أم ليس بإِنسان؟ فإِن قالوا: ليس بإِنسان، كابروا العيان عند أنفسهم وأصحابهم وعند غيرهم ممّن شاهده في أحواله، وقيل لهم: فإِنّما حلّ ذلك عندكم إذن بالإله الذي لا يُلمس ولا يحاط به إذ أضيف إليه دون الإنسان ولم يفعل شيئ من ذلك بالإنسان، فالإله إذن عندكم على هذا القول هو ابن البشر وهو ابن مريم وهو المولود جسمًا مصوّرًا وهو الذي كان يرتضع ويبكي ويضحك ويأكل ويشرب وينام ويستيقظ وهو الذي صُلب وقُتل بعد الأخذ والتعذيب وبعد الخوف والتطريد. فإِن قالوا: نعم، كذلك لم يجعلوا بين الإله والإنسان فرقًا، وهذا نقض قولهم.

٥. ب || ف: وكذلك.
١٣. ب || ف: وإنّما.
٢٠. ب (نصّ): نُقض قولهم || فوقُ: أصولهم.

temporal. On this matter we present them with the first argument on the change of the eternal substance through the uniting, and its being temporal after being eternal, and we ask them what is the difference here.

340 If they treat the two arguments equally and say: It was not changed from its substantiality or its temporality, say to them: Then they were two distinct substances before the uniting and after it, and two distinct hypostases whether they united or not. This is a definite departure from your teachings.

341 Ask them about another matter and say to them: Tell us about the Messiah, was he not in the shape of a man, being little and then big, eating, drinking and walking, sleeping and waking, being perceptible to the senses, seen and touched; and do you not claim that he was arrested and beaten, crucified, killed and buried? They can only say: Yes. Say to them: The one who did what you have described, and to whom what you have mentioned was done, was he a human or not a human? If they say: He was not a human, they deny the evidence accepted by themselves, by their colleagues, and by others who witnessed him in his various conditions. Say to them: So according to you, this happened only to a Divinity who could not be touched or restrained; it affected him and not the human, and none of this was done to the human. So the Divinity, as you see it, according to this teaching was the son of man and the son of Mary, was born as a body and shape, and he it was who sucked at his mother's breast, cried, laughed, ate, drank, slept and woke, who was crucified and killed after arrest and beating, fear and pursuit. If they say: Yes, in doing so they keep no distinction between the Divinity and the human, and this invalidates their teaching.

٣٤٢. وإن زعموا أنّ ذلك كلّه وقع بالإنسان دون الإله، تركوا قولهم أن المسيح جوهر من جوهرين أحدهما قديم والآخر محدث وصاروا إلى قول النسطوريّة أو إلى قول بعض من زعم أنّ المسيح عبد مخلوق وليس بإله.

٣٤٣. فإن زعموا أنّ ذلك لم يقع بالإله ولا بالإنسان ولكن بشيء ثالث، قيل لهم: فالشيء الثالث هو غير ذلك الإنسان الذي ولدته مريم ونشئ وأكل وشرب وأمر ونهى، وغير الكلمة القديمة. فلا بدّ من: نعم، ما تمسكوا بأنّه شيء ثالث. يقال لهم: فالمولود إذن من مريم لم ينله ولم يجر عليه شيء مما ذكرتم، وهذا خلاف النصرانيّة ودفع الوجود أيضًا ومكابرة العيان عند صنوف النصارى وعند كثير ممّن خالف النصارى. ويقال لهم أيضًا: فالمسيح إذن ليس ابن مريم ولا ابن الله، تعالى وسبحانه وتقدّس، ولا هو كلمة الله ولا هو من البشر لأنّه بزعمكم معنىً ثالث. وهذا خروج من نصرانيّتهم ومن التعارف أيضًا.

٣٤٤. فأما تمثيلهم ما مثّلوا بالفحمة والجمرة والدينار ونحو ذلك،[٨٤] فإنّهم لا يلبثون أن ينقضوا هذا التمثيل، وذلك أنّه يقال لهم: أخبرونا عن الفحمة، أتغيّرت بدخول النار عليها أم بطلت وحدث شيء آخر أم لم تبطل ولم تتغيّر؟ وكذلك المسألة في النار الداخلة على الفحمة. فان زعموا أنّها تغيّرت، قلنا: فهذا خلاف قولكم في القديم المتّحِد لأنّكم زعمتم أنّه لم يتغيّر بالاتّحاد. وإذا كانت هذه إنّما استحقّت

٨. ب || ف: ويقال في المولود إذن.
١١. ف، ل || ب: ابن امريم.
١٦. ل || ب، ف: يلبثون او.

342 If they claim that all this happened to the human and not the Divinity, they abandon their teaching that the Messiah was a substance from two substances, one of which was eternal and the other temporal, and they tend towards the teaching of the Nestorians or to the teaching of someone who claims that the Messiah was a created servant and not a Divinity.

343 If they claim that this did not happen to the Divinity or to the human, but to a third thing, say to them: This third thing is then different from this human born of Mary, who was brought up, ate, drank, commanded and prohibited, and different from the eternal Word. They can only say: Yes, if they go on accepting that he was a third thing. Say to them: Then this being who was born of Mary, none of the things you mention touched him or affected him. This is contrary to Christianity and also a rejection of what pertains and a denial of what is evident, according to the Christian sects and to many who oppose the Christians. Say to them also: So the Messiah was not the son of Mary nor the Son of God, may he be exalted, praised and most holy, nor the Word of God nor from man, because according to your claim he was a third entity. This is a departure from their Christianity, and also from what is generally known.

344 [iii. *Metaphors of the uniting*]

As for their comparison in which they compare a lump of coal with a live coal, and a dinar with its like,[84] they very quickly contradict this comparison. This is because we say to them: Tell us about the coal, when the fire surrounds it does it change, or is it destroyed and something else comes into being, or is it neither destroyed nor changed? The same question applies to the fire and its surrounding the coal. If they claim that it is changed, we say: This is contrary to your teaching about the eternal which united, because you claim that it was not changed by the uniting. If it can only properly

اِسم «الجمرة» للتغيّر الحادث وللداخل عليها، وكان الجوهر القديم عندكم لم يدخل عليه داخل ولم يتغيّر عن جوهريّته بالاتّحاد، فليس بمستحقّ لأن يسمّى بغير اسمه الأوّل ولا أن يكون معناه بعد الاتّحاد خلاف معناه قبل الاتّحاد. وإن زعموا أنّ الفحمة بطلت عند دخول النار عليها، قلنا: وهذا أيضًا خلاف قولكم في القديم وفي المحدث لأنّ القديم عندكم لم يبطل بالاتّحاد وكذلك المحدث. على أنّه متى زعم زاعم أنّ الفحمة بطلت بدخول النار عليها أكذبه العيان لأنّا نرى النار قائمة بها وأن سترت سواد الفحمة بضيائها؛ وأيضًا النار متى أُطفئت عادت الفحمة أو ما بقى منها إلى أحوالها الأولى من السواد والبرد واليبس.وأشباه ذلك من هيأتها فهذا هذا. وإن زعموا أنّ الفحمة لم تبطل ولم تتغيّر، قلنا: فإن كانت لم تتغيّر باتّحاد النار بها فهي في حال ما صارت جمرة على جوهرها الأوّل وأمرها الأوّل، وكذلك النار إذا لم يُغيّرها اتّحادها بالفحمة فهي نار على أمرها الأوّل وجوهرها. فهما في حال الاتّحاد جوهران مختلفان جوهر النار وجوهر الفحمة. فيعود هذا التمثيل الذي فزعوا إليه حينئذٍ عليهم لا لهم، ويلزمهم أن يزعموا أنّ المسيح جوهران في حال الاتّحاد، كما أنّ النار والفحمة جوهران في حال الاتّحاد إحداهما بالأُخرى. والمعروف عندنا وعند الناس، ما لم يستكره عقله منهم مستكره أو يُدخل على نفسه الشبهة مدخل، أنّ الجمرة ليست هي النار الداخلة على الحطب والفَحْم وإنّما هي الفحمة

٧. ب، ف || ل: زعم أنّ.
١٠. ف، ل || ب: الأول.
١٥–١٦. ب || ف: فزعموا إليه عليهم.

be called a live coal because of the change that has taken place and because of it being surrounded, and nothing can surround the eternal substance, according to you, and it was not changed from its substantiality by the uniting, then it cannot properly be called by any name other than the first, nor can its reality after the uniting be opposite to its reality beforehand.

If they claim that the lump of coal is destroyed when the fire surrounds it, we say: This is also contrary to your teaching about the eternal and the temporal, because according to you the eternal was not destroyed by the uniting nor was the temporal. Although if one of them claims that the lump of coal is destroyed when the fire surrounds it, observation belies him, because we see the fire on it and concealing the black of the coal with its brightness; and then when the fire dies down again the lump of coal, or what is left of it, returns to its first condition of black, cold and dry. The same happens to things with similar characteristics.

If they claim that the lump of coal is not destroyed or changed we say: If it is not changed by the uniting of the fire with it, then at the moment when it becomes a live coal it remains its original substance and condition; and similarly the fire, if its uniting with the lump of coal does not change it, it is fire in its original condition and substance. So at the moment of the uniting they are two distinct substances, the substance of the fire and the substance of the coal. Hence this comparison in which they take refuge does service against them not for them, and it forces them to claim that the Messiah was two substances at the moment of the uniting, just as the fire and the coal are two substances at the moment when the one unites with the other.

It is accepted both by us and by others – and so none of them can disdain its rationality or entertain any possibility of doubt – that the live coal is not the fire which surrounds the firewood and the coal, but only that the coal

المتلهّبة بالنار أو الحطب الذي هو كذلك. وليست الجمرة عندنا شيئين ولا جوهر من جوهرين وإنّما هي جوهر واحد اشتمل عليه جوهر آخر. وهذا كيف أدرناه فهو خلاف قولهم في المسيح. ويقال لهم: وما تقولون في النار الداخلة على الفحمة أتغيّرت عن جوهريّتها؟ فإن قالوا: نعم، قلنا: فينبغي إذن أن لا يكون مضيئة ولا حارّة، وهذا دفع الوجود لأنّها توجد حارّة وإن كانت في الجمرة أو في الحديد أو في الدينار الذي مثّلوا به ويرى ضوؤها شائعًا في ذلك كلّه. وإن قالوا: لم تتغيّر عن جوهريّتها ولم تبطل، قلنا: فهي نار ثابتة الجوهر، وإن كانت عندكم متّحدة بالفحمة فقد بطل الآن تمثيلكم ولزمكم على ذلك الأصل أن تزعموا أنّ الجمرة شيئان نار وفحمة أو نار وحطب. وهذا يؤديكم في المسيح إلى قول نسطور[٨٥] أو إلى ترك قوله وقولكم. وكذلك القول في الدينار المحمّى وفي الزبرة من الحديد وفي الزجاج المذاب وفي كلّ ما علقت به النار أن جوهره في حال علوقها به غير جوهر النار، وأن الجوهرين قائمان اجتمعا أو افترقا وأنّهما إذا فارقته عاد إلى حاله الأُولى.

٣٤٥. فأمّا استشهادهم بقول القائل «صارت الفحمة نارًا وصار الدينار نارًا» لقولهم «صار الإنسان إلهًا» وامتناعهم زعموا من أن يقولوا «صار الإله إنسانًا» كما لا يقال زعموا «صارت النار فحمة» ولا «صارت النار دينارًا»، فإنّا بمنعنا إيّاهم من جواز اتّحاد القديم بالمحدث ودفعنا

٧. ب || ف: أو في النار الذيّ. ١٨. ب (نصّ) زعم، وفوق: زعموا.

is set alight by the fire, or the wood in the same way. As we see it, the coal is not two things nor a substance from two substances, but is only one substance enveloped by another substance. However we set this out, it is contrary to their teaching about the Messiah.

Say to them: What do you say about the fire which surrounds the coal, is it changed from its substantiality? If they say: Yes, we say: Then it obviously cannot be bright or hot. But this is a rejection of reality, because it remains hot even though it is in the live coal or iron or a dinar, with which they make the comparison, and its brightness can be seen throughout them entirely. If they say: It is not changed from its substantiality and is not destroyed, we say: Then it is fire fixed as substance, and if it unites with the coal, as you say, then your comparison with the coal is now destroyed, and according to this principle you must claim that the live coal is two things, fire and the lump of coal, or fire and wood. And with respect to the Messiah, this brings you to the teaching of Nestorius,[85] or to abandon his teaching and yours. It is the same with the teaching about the heated dinar, the piece of iron, the molten glass, and everything on which fire takes hold, that at the moment it takes hold on its substance it is different from the substance of the fire, and that the two substances exist either together or separate, and that when it separates from it it returns to its original condition.

345 As for their use of the statement, "The lump of coal became fire and the dinar became fire", to support their statement, "The human became divine", and their rejection, so they claim, of saying, "The Divinity became human", just as it is not said, they claim, "The fire became a lump of coal", or, "The fire became a dinar", since we have prevented them from claiming that the uniting of the eternal and the temporal was possible, and have rejected

قولهم في ذلك بما تقدّم في كتابنا هذا ما قد اسقطنا عن أنفسنا مؤونة مناظرتهم في هذه الدعوى والاحتجاج عليهم في هذا التمثيل وفي سائر هذه التعليقات التي لا محصول لها إذا رُدّوا إلى الأصل. وإذا فسدت عليهم تلك الأصول فسدت فروعها. ولكنّا مع ذلك لا ندع أن نُريهم بالحجّة الواضحة فساد ما تعلّقوا به من هذه الشبهة التي أوردوها على أنفسهم، لئلا يبقي لهم شيء تعلّقوا به من وجه من الوجوه، والله المعين على كلّ خير تبارك وتعالى. فنقول لهم: أخبرونا عن قول القائل «صارت الفحمة ناراً وكذلك الدينار»، أيخلو هذا القائل من أن يكون قصد إلى أن يجعل الفحمة نارًا في الحقيقة، أو إلى الاتّساع في العبارة، أو إلى استغراق الصفة والتمثيل، كما يقول القائل عند اشتداد الحرّ «ما الدنيا إلاّ ناراً» و«قد صارت الأرض جمرة» وأشباه ذلك مما يقصدون به إلى المبالغة في الصفة والتمثيل؟ فإن زعموا أن القائل «صارت الفحمة ناراً» إنّما قصد تصييرها ناراً في الحقيقة، قلنا لهم: فقائل هذا كاذب لا شكّ فيه ولا خلاف عند أحد من الناس، لأنّ النار حقيقةً ملتهبة متصاعدة والجمرة ثقيلة سافلة، ولو أرسلها مُرسل لانِحدرت حتى تجد ما يقلها ويمسكها، ولها جِرم كثيف والنار ليست كذلك. وجهات مخالفتها للنار كثيرة جدًّا. واتّفاق الناس على ذلك بالحجّة لا بالاصطلاح يُغنينا عن الإطالة فيه. وإذا كان قائل هذا كاذبًا سقط الاحتجاج به وبقوله وكان كلّ من امتثل قوله وسلك

١. ب || ف: ذلك ما تقدم.

their teaching about this, according to what we have already said in this book, we have now eliminated the inconvenience of disputing with them on this claim, or of finding arguments against them on this comparison and all the related details which have no outcome, if they are referred back to the principle. If these principles are proved wrong against them, then their repercussions are also proved wrong. Despite this, we will not omit to show them with a clear demonstration the errors to which they cling connected with this vague notion which they cite against themselves, so that nothing of any kind at all will remain for them to cling to, and God the blessed and exalted is a help in all that is good.

So we say to them: Tell us about the statement, "The lump of coal became fire, and also the dinar", can the person who makes it have any other intention than either to make the lump of coal fire in reality, or to give a more general explanation, or to make the description and comparison more vivid, in the same way that someone says about the fierceness of heat, "The world is nothing but fire", or, "The world has become a glowing coal", and similar things, in which the description and comparison are intentionally exaggerated? If they claim that the person who says, "The lump of coal became fire", intends to make it fire in reality, we say to them: This person is a liar, and nobody would doubt this or differ over it, because fire in reality bursts into flames and moves upwards, while the lump of coal is heavy and solid, so that if it is released it drops, to be found, carried away and stored. It has a dense mass, while fire is not like this, and there are a great many ways in which it is different from fire. People agree on this because of proof, not simply convention, and there is no need to go on about it. And if the person who says this is lying, then any argument from him and his speaking will be ineffective, and everyone who copies what he says and follows

سبيله كاذبًا مثله. وإن زعموا أنّ قائل هذا إنّما قصد إلى استغراق الوصف والتمثيل وإلى الاتساع في العبارة لا إلى تصيير الفحمة والدينار نارًا في الحقيقة، قلنا: فإذا كان ذلك كذلك فليس ينبغي لكم أن تجعلوا الاستعارة والاتساع في العبارة أصلاً للأمور القياسيّة وللمقايسات الحقيقية، لأنّ الأمور القياسيّة على حقائقها اتسعت العبارة أم ضاقت لا تتغيّر ولا تنقلب حقائقها. والأمور التي يتكلم فيها على استعارة الأسماء والاتساع في العبارة إن لم يستعمل ذلك فيها وردّت من الألفاظ والأسماء إلى مقدار استحقاقها لا إلى ما يتسع به في العبارة عنها نقضت صفاتها وتغيرت أسماءوها، كقول القائل على طريق الاتساع في العبارة «صارت الأرض جمرة» فهو إذا أسقط هذا الاتساع وردّ الأمر إلى الواجب قال «صارت الأرض حارّة» أو قال «شديدة الحرارة» فيسقط ذلك الاسم وتذهب تلك الصفة المستغرقة. فأمّا الجمرة التي مثل بها الأرض واستعار لها صفتها فهي الجمرة الحقيقة وهي جمرة اتسعت العبارة أم ضاقت.

فإذا كان القائل «صارت الفحمة والدينار نارًا» إنّما هو بمنزلة من قال «صارت الأرض جمرة» لا لأنّ الفحمة والدينار نار في الحقيقة كما أن الأرض ليست جمرة في الحقيقة وكان هذا عندهم نظيرًا لقولهم «صار الإنسان إلهًا»، فقد علمنا عند التحقيق أنّ الإنسان لم يصر إلهًا في الحقيقة كما أنّ الفحمة لم تصر نارًا على الحقيقة وكما أنّ الدينار لم يصر نارًا على الصحّة وكما أن الأرض

١٨–١٩. ب || ف: علمنا أنه لم يصر.

his method will be a liar like him.

If they claim that the person who says this means only to make the description and comparison more vivid and the explanation more general, not to make the lump of coal or the dinar into fire in reality, we say: If this is so, then you should not employ the use of metaphors or generalised explanation as a principle in matters of logic and in true logical comparing. This is because matters of logic remain true to their natures and do not change or alter, whether the explanation is generalised or straightforward.

If issues which are discussed in metaphorical terms and generalised explanations are not treated like this, and they are restored from the terms and names to their appropriate dimensions and not to the generalised explanations given them, their descriptions disappear and their names are changed. For example, if the person who says in an effort to generalise an explanation, "The earth has become a glowing coal", abandons this generalisation and restores the whole thing to its essential form, saying, "The earth has become hot", or "The heat is fierce", the terminology drops away and this exaggerated attribute vanishes. As for the live coal to which he compares the earth and whose attribute it is given in metaphor, it is a live coal in reality and a live coal whether the explanation is generalised or straightforward.

If the person who said, "The lump of coal and the dinar became fire", was treated on the same level as someone who said, "The earth has become a live coal", because the lump of coal and the dinar are not fire in reality and the world is not a live coal in reality, and in their view this was similar to their statement, "The human became divine", then we would know in truth that the human did not become divine in reality, just as the lump of coal did not become fire in reality nor the dinar fire in actuality, and just as the earth

ليست جمرة في الحقيقة. وإذا ثبت أنّ الإنسان لم يصر إلهًا فهو على ما كان عليه من إنسانيّته وإذا كان الإله لم يصر إنسانًا فهما إله وإنسان بعد الاتّحاد هذا، لو صحّ الاتّحاد، كما كانا إلهًا وإنسانا قبل الاتّحاد، وهما جوهران بعد ذلك كما كانا جوهرين قبل ذلك. وهذا قول بيّن الفساد واضح الانتقاض وإنّ عجبي ليكثر من قوم يفرحون ويعبّرون بهذا المقدار من تعليق الألفاظ والأسماء التي لا حقائق لها ولا معنى تحتها. ولو أنّنا بعد ذلك كلّه حققنا لهم دعواهم في أنّ الفحمة صارت نارًا وكذلك الدينار وسلّمنا لهم ذلك على غاية ما يحبون، لَما كان هذا مشبهًا لأدّعائهم أنّ الإنسان صار إلهًا. وذلك أنّ الفحمة لا تصير نارًا على ما عبّروا إلاّ بمخالطة النار إيّاها وحُلولها فيها وشياعها في أجزائها، ولا تكون كذلك إلاّ والفحمة شاغلة لأجزاء النار الحالة فيها عن غيرها ومانعة لها من الحلول في شئ سواها في حال ما هي حالّة فيها، والنار في تلك الحال أيضًا محدودة بها. وليس بجائز عندهم أن يخالط القديم ناسوت المسيح ولا يشيع في أجزائه ولا يشغله ذلك الناسوت شغل الفحمة ما حلّ فيها من النار. ولا يجوز أيضًا أن يحدّه جسم من الأجسام عندهم ولا يشتمل عليه. فكيف يصير هو وناسوت المسيح واحدًا؟ وكيف اتّحد أحدهما بصاحبه حتى يصير ذلك الإنسان إلهًا؟ تعالى الإله الواحد الذي ليس كمثله شئ وهو السميع البصير.[٨٦] (تمّ الكتاب على النسطوريّة والملكيّة ومَن وصفنا قوله من اليعقوبيّة.

١٣. ب || ف: عن الحلول.

is not a live coal in reality. If it is acknowledged that the human did not become divine then he remained in his humanity, and if the Divinity did not become human then they were Divinity and human after this uniting, granted that the uniting happened, just as they were divine and human before the uniting. And they were two substances after this just as they were two substances before it. This is a statement which is evidently wrong and clearly contradictory, although it is amazing how many people, when they give an explanation, merrily employ terms and names which have no reality or meaning behind them.

If after all this we were to allow the correctness of their claim about the lump of coal becoming fire and about the dinar, and we conceded this to them as far as they would like, it would still not be like their claim that the human became divine. This is because the lump of coal only becomes fire, according to the way they explain, when the fire mingles with it, inheres within it and spreads through its parts. But this happens only when the lump of coal restrains the parts of the fire which inhere within it from other things, and prevents it from inhering in separate things as long as it inheres within it, during which time the fire is also restricted by it. But as they see it, the eternal could not mingle with the humanity of the Messiah and spread through his parts, nor could the humanity restrain it in the way that the lump of coal restrains the fire which inheres within it. Further, in their view no body could restrict it or restrain it. So how could it and the humanity of the Messiah become one? And how could one of them unite with its companion so that this human might become divine? Exalted is God the One, like whom there is nothing, and he is the all-hearing, all-seeing.[86]

(The book against the Nestorians, the Melkites and those from the Jacobites whose teachings we have described is complete.

والحمد لله ربّ العلمين كثيرًا.

ونحن مبتدئون في النقض على من أضيف إلى اليعقوبيّة كالأليانيّة وأصحاب أوطاخي[٨٨] ـ وسائر ما يتلو ذلك إلى آخر ما في هذه النسخة موجود في النسخة المختارة.[٨٩]

قال يحيى: من أول هذا الموضع إلى الموضع الذي عليه هذه العلامة + لم يوجد في النسخة الصحيحة المختارة.)

٣٤٦. انقضى الكلام+ على اليعقوبيّة،[٩٠] ويقال لهذه الفرق الثلث: مَن خلق ناسوت المسيح، المسيح أو غيره؟

٣٤٧. فإن قالوا: المسيح، قلنا: فقد كان المسيح إذن قبل الناس وقبل الخلق جميعًا. وهذا يبطل قولهم أنّ المسيح إله وإنسان جوهران وذو جوهرين وجوهر من جوهرين، لأن القديم قبل الخلق ليس بإله وإنسان ولا بجوهران ولا بذي جوهرين ولا بجوهر من جوهرين.

٣٤٨. وإن زعموا أنّ الذي خلق ناسوت المسيح غير المسيح، أقرّوا بأن الخالق هو غير المسيح وجعلوا المسيح محدثًا.

٣٤٩. ويقال لهم: خبّرونا، هل يجوز عندكم أن يلامس النساء فيولد له ويكون أبًا لبعض البشر كما كان اِبنًا لبعض البشر؟ فإن قالوا: لا يجوز ذلك، قلنا: وما الفرق بين أن يُولَد وبين ألاّ يُولِد، وكيف يجوز أن يكون اِبنًا لبعض الناس ولا يجوز أن يكون أبًا لبعض الناس؟

٣٥٠. وإن قالوا: قد كان ذلك جائزًا، قلنا: فلو وَلَدَ كان يكون وَلَدُه إلهًا ومسيحًا. فقد أوجبوا التناسل للإله وأجازوا أن يكون إله ابن إله أبدًا ما تناسلوا ومسيح بن مسيح أبدًا كذلك، فيكون المسيح مرّة

All praise to God the Lord of the worlds.[87]

Now we begin the refutation of those who are connected to the Jacobites such as the Julianists, the followers of Eutyches[88] – and the rest that follows this to the end of what is in this copy is contained in the preferred copy.[89]

Yaḥyā said: From the start of this passage to the passage above which is this sign ∻ is not found in the preferred correct copy.)

346 [CONCLUDING ARGUMENTS AGAINST THE THREE SECTS]

The argu∻ment against the Jacobites is complete,[90] so say to these three sects: Who created the humanity of the Messiah, the Messiah or another?

347 If they say: The Messiah, we say: Then the Messiah was before humankind and before the entire creation. This destroys their teaching that the Messiah was divine and human, two substances, possessing two substances, and a substance from two substances, because the eternal one before creation was not divine and human, or two substances, or the possessor of two substances, or a substance from two substances.

348 If they claim that the one who created the humanity of the Messiah was other than the Messiah, they acknowledge that the Creator is other than the Messiah, and they make the Messiah temporal.

349 Say to them: Tell us, could he, in your view, have had intercourse with a woman so that a child was born to him, and have become father to a man just as he was son to a man? If they say: This is not possible, we say: Then what is the difference between being born and not having a child, and why could he be son of a man but not father to a man?

350 If they say: This was possible, we say: If he had a child, then his child would be divine and Messiah. So they would then implicate the Divinity in reproduction, and allow there to be a Divinity who was son of the Divinity for ever, as long as they reproduced, and similarly Messiah son of Messiah for ever. So the Messiah would be

مسيحًا بالاتّحاد ومرّة بالولادة، وهذا غاية من الاختلاط. وإن قالوا: كان يكون ولدُه لا إلهًا ولا مسيحًا؛ قلنا: وما الفرق بين هذا وبين أن يكون ولد الإنسان لا إنسان وولد البهيمة لا بهيمة؟ وإن جاز أن يكون ولد الإله عندكم ليس بإله وولد المسيح ليس بمسيح فما تنكرون أن يكون ولد المسيح ليس بإنسان؟ وإذا جاز أن يكون ولد الإله ليس بإله، فما تنكرون أن تكون الكلمة المتولّدة عندكم من الإله ليست بإله؟ وهذا كلّه تخليط من قائليه وموصّليه.

٣٥١. ويقال لهم: أليس لو لامس المسيح عندكم النساء فأولد، كان يكون ذلك الولد عندكم اِبن اِبن الله، تعالى الله وسبحانه، وكان الإله القديم عندكم جدّ ولدِ المسيح كما أنّ مريم التي هي أمّ المسيح جدّة ولدِ المسيح متى أولد؟[٩١] فإن قالوا: لا، خرجوا من المعقول وجعلوا الأب ليس بجدّ، فيلزمهم أن تكون الأمّ ليست بجدّة، وهذا ضرْب من التجاهل. وإن أثبتوا الإله، سبحانه وتعالى، جدّاً لولدِ المسيح أوقعوا الإنسان بين القديم والمحدث وأوجبوا التناسل من حيث كرهوا. وهذا الكلام، وإن كان مفسّداً لأقاويل هذه الفرق الثلثة، فإنّه على اليعقوبيّة والملكيّة أشدّ ولهم ألزم، سبحان الله الواحد الصمد الذي ليس كمثله شيءٌ

لم يلد ولم يولد ولم يكن له كفوًا أحد.[٩٢]

٣٥٢. (قال يحيى: ووجدتُ في آخر بعض نسخ هذا الكتاب بعد تمام الكتاب وانقضائه ما هذه نسخته، فأثبتُ ذلك هاهنا وهذه حكاية

٨. ب || ف: وأولد.
١٣–١٤. ب || ف: الاله تعالى جداً.

Messiah by uniting at one time and at another by generation. This is extreme confusion. If they say: His son would not have been divine or Messiah, we say: What is the distinction between this and the child of a human not being human or the offspring of an animal not being an animal? And if in your view a child of the Divinity need not have been a Divinity, and a child of the Messiah not Messiah, then why do you deny that a child of the Messiah would not have been human? If the child of the Divinity need not have been a Divinity, then why do you deny that the Word, which according to you is generated from the Divinity, is not the Divinity? All this is confusion from those who say it, and who pass it on.

351 Say to them: In your view, if the Messiah had had intercourse with a woman and had a child born, would not this child have been, in your view, the son of the Son of God, may God be exalted and praised, and would not the eternal Divinity, in your view, have been the grandfather of the Messiah's child, and Mary, the Messiah's mother, the grandmother of the Messiah's child, since he had a child?[91] If they say: No, they abandon what is reasonable and make the Father not a grandfather, and are forced to make the mother not a grandmother, which smacks of ignorance. If they acknowledge that the Divinity, praised and exalted may he be, was grandfather to the Messiah's child, they place the human between the eternal and the temporal and are forced to accept reproduction, even though they loathe it. This argument, though it shows the errors in the teachings of all three sects, is most serious and compelling against the Jacobites and Melkites. God the one, the self-subsistent be praised, nothing resembles him,

> who has never begotten nor been begotten, none is like him.[92]

352 (Yaḥyā said; I have found something at the end of some copies of this book, after its conclusion and close, of which this is a copy. I have recorded it here, and these are its very

ذلك:) ونحن مبتدئون في النقض على من أضيف إلى اليعقوبيّة كالأليانيّة وأصحاب أوطاخي، وعلى باقي صنوف النصارى كالمارونيّة والسباليّة والأجريغارية وأصحاب مقدونيوس وأصحاب بلنارس والأريوسيّة وأصحاب أوناميوس وأصحاب فوطينس والبولية أصحاب بولى السمُساطي[٩٣] في كتاب مفرد إن شاء الله تعالى، ولا قوّة إلاّ بالله العلي العظيم.[٩٤]

(قال يحيى بن عدي رحمه الله: وقد كنا كتبنا هذا الكتاب نسخة قبل هذه ثم رأينا تغيير بعض ما فيه فغيّرنا وزدنا زيادات لم تكن فيه ونقلناه إلى هذه النسخة. فمَن صارت إليه تلك النسخة فأحسن أن يتخيّر ما فيها من الصواب والمحاسن ويترك ما سوى ذلك فشانه فذلك. فإنّما كثيرة المحاسن وإن كنا قد اخترنا هذه عليها لأنّها أصحّ وأشدّ إحكامًا وأحسن تأليفًا وإن لم يكن ممن يحسن تخيّر ذلك ولا تمييزه فليترك تلك وليعمل على ما في هذه فأنها أجمع لما يحبّ ويلتمس ومن انتسخ كتابنا هذا فليلحق هذا الفصل في آخره ليعرفه ويعمل عليه من قرأه إن شاء الله. عورض بكلام أبي عيسى في هذا الجزء النسخة الصحيحة وصحّح بحسبها بقدر الطاقة. ولله الحمد شكرًا دائمًا كثيراً كاستحقاقه. آمين.)

٣. ل || ب: مقدرنيوس، ف: مقدانيوس.
٤. ب || ف: بلناريوس.
٤. ل || ب: نوطينس، ف: نوطينوس.
١٠–١١. ب || ف: فسانه وذلك.
١٢. ب || ف: يختار.
١٧. ب || ف: كاستحقاقه.

words:)

We shall start to refute those who are connected with the Jacobites, such as the Julianists and the followers of Eutyches, and other Christian divisions, such as the Maronites, the Sabellians, the Gregorians, the followers of Macedonius, the followers of Apollinaris, the Arians, the followers of Eunomius, the followers of Photinus, and the Paulicians, the followers of Paul of Samosata,[93] in a separate work, if God the exalted wills. There is no strength except by God the most high, the most great.[94]

NOTES

Notes to Chapter 1

1 W. M. Watt, *The Formative Period of Islamic Thought*, Edinburgh, 1973, p. 186 and references.

2 D. Thomas, "Two Muslim–Christian Debates from the Early Shīʿite Tradition", *Journal of Semitic Studies* 33, 1988, p. 55, trans. from Abū Jaʿfar Muḥammad Ibn Bābawayh, *Kitāb al-tawḥīd*, ed. H. al-Ḥusaynī al-Ṭihrānī, Tehran, 1387, p. 271.

3 Thomas, "Two Muslim–Christian Debates", pp. 60–5.

4 For accounts of Christians under Muslim rule at this time, see C.E. Bosworth, "The Concept of *Dhimma* in early Islam", in B. Braude and B. Lewis, eds., *Christians and Jews in the Ottoman Empire*, New York and London, 1982, vol. I, pp. 37–51; H. Goddard, *A History of Christian–Muslim Relations*, Edinburgh, 2000, pp. 34–78.

5 H. Cheikho, *Dialectique du langage sur Dieu, lettre de Timothée I (728–823) à Serge*, Rome, 1983, pp. 187f.

6 A. Mingana, "The Apology of Timothy the Patriarch before the Caliph Mahdi", *Bulletin of the John Rylands Library* 12, 1928, pp. 137–298.

7 See e.g. Thomas, "Two Muslim–Christian Debates", pp. 65–75, for an example from a debate in which the Imām ʿAlī al-Riḍā was set against a number of opponents in the presence of al-Maʾmūn (see also on this D.J. Wasserstein, "The 'Majlis of al-Riḍā': a Religious Debate in the Court of the Caliph al-Maʾmūn as Represented in a Shīʿī Hagiographical Work about the Eighth Imām ʿAlī ibn Mūsā al-Riḍā", in H. Lazarus-Yafeh, M. R. Cohen, S. Somekh, S. H. Griffith, eds., *The Majlis, Interreligious Encounters in Medieval Islam*, Wiesbaden, 1999, pp. 108–19); S. H. Griffith, "The Monk in the Emir's *Majlis*: Reflections on a Popular Genre of Christian Literary Apologetics in Arabic in the Early Islamic Period", in Lazarus-Yafeh, *Majlis*, pp. 13–65.

8 In addition to Griffith, "The Monk in the Emir's *Majlis*", see also A. Abel, "Masques et visages dans la polémique islamo-chrétienne", *Tavola rotunda sul tema: Christianesimo e Islamismo, Roma, 17–18 Aprile, 1972*, Rome, 1974, pp. 85–131.

9 See S.H. Griffith, "The Prophet Muḥammad, his Scripture and his Message according to the Syriac Apologies in Arabic and Syriac from the First Abbasid Century", in T. Fahd, ed., *La vie du prophète Mahomet*, Paris, 1983 (repr. in S.H. Griffith, *Arabic Christianity in the Monasteries of Ninth Century Palestine*, Aldershot, 1992, no. I), pp. 105–8, for a summary of the position. G. Tartar,

Dialogue islamo-chrétien sous le calife al-Ma'mûn (813–834), les épîtres d'al-Hashimî et d'al-Kindî, Paris, 1985, pp. 59–76, argues in favour of an early date, while S. Stroumsa, *Freethinkers of Medieval Islam, Ibn al-Rāwandī, Abū Bakr al-Rāzī, and their Impact on Islamic Thought*, Leiden, 1999, pp. 193–8, argues in favour of a late date, though neither finally resolves the matter.

10 A. Tien, *Risālat ʿAbdallah Ibn Ismāʿīl al-Hāshimī ilā ʿAbd al-Masīḥ Ibn Isḥāq al-Kindī*, London, 1880, p. 8.9–12, trans. Tartar, *Dialogue islamo-chrétien*, pp. 92f.

11 J. Troupeau, "Les couvents chrétiens dans la littérature arabe", *La Nouvelle Revue du Caire* 1, 1975, pp. 265–79 (repr. in J. Troupeau, *Etudes sur le Christianisme arabe au Moyen Age*, Aldershot, 1995, no. XX); H. Kilpatrick, "Representations of Social Intercourse between Muslims and non-Muslims in some Medieval *Adab* Works", in J. Waardenburg, ed., *Muslim Perceptions of Other Religions, a Historical Survey*, Oxford, 1999, pp. 218f.

12 See *EI*², vol. X, pp. 17f., art. "Al-Ṭabarī, ʿAlī b. Rabban".

13 *Al-Radd ʿalā al-Naṣārā*, ed. J. Finkel, *Thalāth rasāʾil li-Abī ʿUthmān . . . al-Jāḥiẓ*, Cairo, 1926, p. 17.14f.

14 L. Massignon, "La politique islamo-chrétienne des scribes nestoriens de Deïr Qunnā à la cour de Baghdad au IXe siècle de notre ère", *Vivre et Penser* 2nd series 2, 1942, pp. 7–14 (repr. in *Opera Minora*, Beirut, 1963, vol. I, pp. 250–7).

15 *EI*², vol. I, p. 1298, art. "Bukhtīshūʿ"; D. Gutas, *Greek Thought, Arabic Culture*, London and New York, 1998, p. 118.

16 *EI*², vol. I, p. 1141, art. "Bayt al-Ḥikma"; Gutas, *Greek Thought, Arabic Culture*, ch. 6.

17 This is related in S.K. Samir, "The Christian Communities, Active Members of Arab Society throughout History", in A. Pacini, ed., *Christian Communities in the Arab Middle East*, Oxford, 1998, p. 79.

18 Al-Jāḥiẓ, *Radd*, pp. 19.20–20.4; see the English translation by J. Finkel, "A Risāla of al-Jāḥiẓ", *Journal of the American Oriental Society* 47, 1927, p. 331, and the French translation by I.S. Allouche, "Un traité de polémique christiano-musulmane au IXe siècle", *Hesperis* 26, 1939, p. 137.

19 Al-Jāḥiẓ, *Radd*, p. 18.14–16.

20 *Ibid*., p. 18.6–14; Finkel, "A Risāla of al-Jāḥiẓ", pp. 328f.

21 The fullest discussion of the development of the "Covenant of ʿUmar" is by A.S. Tritton, *The Caliphs and their Non-Muslim Subjects*, London, 1930, pp. 5–17; see also A. Fattal, *Le statut légal des non-musulmans en pays d'Islam*, Beirut, 1958, pp. 60–9. For a translation of the text of al-Ṭurṭūshī, *Sirāj al-mulūk*, see N. Stillman, *The Jews of Arab Lands*, Philadelphia, 1979, pp. 157f.

22 Abū Jaʿfar al-Ṭabarī, *Taʾrīkh al-rusul wa-al-mulūk*, ed. M.J. de Goeje *et al*., Leiden, 1879–1901, vol. III, pp. 712f.; trans. C.E. Bosworth, *The ʿAbbasid Caliphate in Equilibrium* (*The History of al-Ṭabarī*, vol. XXX), Albany, 1989, p. 268.

23 Al-Ṭabarī, *Taʾrīkh*, vol. III, pp. 1389ff.; trans. J. Kraemer, *Incipient Decline* (*The History of al-Ṭabarī*, vol. XXXIV), Albany, 1989, pp. 89ff.

24 D. J. Sahas, *John of Damascus on Islam, the "Heresy of the Ishmaelites"*, Leiden, 1972; R. Hoyland, *Seeing Islam as Others Saw It*, Princeton, 1997, pp. 480–4.

25 Hoyland, *Seeing Islam*, p. 489; the Greek text and an English translation of the *Disputatio* is given in Sahas, *John of Damascus*, pp. 142–55.

26 Sahas, *John of Damascus*, pp. 142–9.

27 See the exchange of letters about free will and predestination between the Umayyad Caliph ʿAbd al-Malik and al-Ḥasan al-Baṣrī (d. 110/728), in H. Ritter, "Studien zur Geschichte der islamischen Frommigkeit: I. Ḥasan al-Baṣrī ", *Der Islam* 21, 1933, pp. 1–83; partial trans. in A. Rippin and J. Knappert, *Textual Sources for the Study of Islam*, Chicago, 1989, pp. 115–21.
28 Watt, *Formative Period*, pp. 94–107.
29 See S. Rissanen, *Theological Encounter of Oriental Christians with Islam during Abbasid Rule*, Åbo, Finland, 1993, pp. 127–31, for a summary of the various positions. H.A. Wolfson, *The Philosophy of the Kalām*, Harvard, 1976, pp. 58–64, 112–32, supports the view that Islamic theological thinking is heavily indebted to Christianity, while J. van Ess, "The Beginnings of Islamic Theology", in J. E. Murdoch and E. D. Sylla, eds., *The Cultural Context of Medieval Learning*, Dordrecht and Boston, 1973, pp. 87–111, favours the view that it developed according to its own internal logic and that interreligious encounters acted mainly as stimuli.
30 Watt, *Formative Period*, pp. 178f.
31 *Ibid.*, pp. 182–6.
32 R. M. Frank, *The Metaphysics of Created Being according to Abū l-Hudhayl al-ʿAllāf*, Istanbul, 1966, esp. pp. 39–44.
33 M.Fakhry, *Islamic Occasionalism*, London, 1958, pp. 33ff.
34 D. Thomas, "Islamic Understanding of the Trinity during the Abbasid era", in L. Ridgeon, ed., *Islamic Interpretations of Christianity*, Richmond, 2000, pp. 86–8.
35 S. Griffith, "The Concept of *al-Uqnūm* in ʿAmmār al-Baṣrī's Apology for the Doctrine of the Trinity", in S. K. Samir, ed., *Actes du premier congrès international d'études arabes chrétiennes*, Rome, 1982, pp. 169–91.
36 Translated from M. Hayek, *ʿAmmār al-Baṣrī, apologie et controverses*, Beirut, 1977, pp. 46.16–47.3.
37 *Ibid.*, p. 52.13; cf. Tien, *Risāla*, pp. 33.9–35.11, trans. Tartar, *Dialogue islamo-chrétien*, pp. 125–7, where ʿAbd al-Masīḥ al-Kindī strives to maintain the same distinction.
38 See Thomas, "Islamic Understanding of the Trinity", p. 90–5.
39 Al-Jāḥiẓ, *Radd*, p. 25.2–5; see D. Thomas, "The Question better not Asked", in T. Gabriel, ed., *Islam in the Contemporary World*, New Delhi, 2000, pp. 20–41.
40 See, e.g., Q 4.171, 6.101, 17.111, 19.35.
41 Sahas, *John of Damascus*, pp. 132–41.
42 See *EI²*, vol. I, pp. 922f., art. "Baḥīrā".
43 See n. 9 above.
44 Tien, *Risāla*, p. 50.1–3, trans. Tartar, *Dialogue islamo-chrétien*, pp. 148f.
45 J.-M. Gaudeul, *La correspondance de ʿUmar et Léon (vers 900)*, Rome, 1995, pp. iiif. (dating) and 71ff. See also the forthright remarks about Islam made by the contemporary Abraham of Tiberias before the emir ʿAbd al-Raḥmān al-Hāshimī, summarised in Griffith, "The Monk in the Emir's *Majlis*", pp. 22–37.
46 S. Griffith, "Faith and Reason in Christian Kalām: Theodore Abū Qurrah on Discerning the True Religion", in S. K. Samir and J. S. Nielsen, eds., *Christian Arab Apologetics during the Abbasid Period (750–1258)*, Leiden, 1994, esp. pp. 26–35.
47 Hayek, *ʿAmmār*, pp. 24–41, sections 2 and 3; also S. Griffith, "ʿAmmār al-Baṣrī's *Kitāb al-Burhān*: Christian Kalām in the First Abbasid Century", *Le Muséon* 96, 1983, pp. 161–5.

48 See n. 6 above.
49 Mingana, "Apology", respectively, pp. 158–63 and 198–219; 153–8, 167–8 and 176–83; 168–75 and 183–8.
50 See Hoyland, *Seeing Islam*, p. 474.
51 Ibn al-Nadīm, *Kitāb al-fihrist*, ed. M. Riḍā-Tajaddud, Tehran, 1971, pp. 215.9, 230.2, 185.1.
52 ʿAbd al-Jabbār, *Tathbīt dalāʾil al-nubuwwa*, ed. ʿA.-K. ʿUthmān, Beirut, 1966, p. 148.1; cf. al-Jāḥiẓ, *Radd*, pp. 29.21–30.8.
53 ʿAbd al-Jabbār, *Tathbīt*, pp. 148.6, 198.13. For brief excerpts from this attack quoted in later authors, see P. Sbath, *Vingt traités philosophiques et apologétiques d'auteurs arabes chrétiens*, Cairo, 1929, pp. 65.7–10, 66.14–67.1.
54 Ibn al-Nadīm, *Fihrist*, p. 207.6.
55 *Ibid.*, p. 204.21f. Hayek, *ʿAmmār*, pp. 18–20, suggests the connection between the two.
56 See A. Périer, "Un traité de Yaḥyā ben ʿAdī", *Revue de l'Orient Chrétien* 22, 1920–1, pp. 3–21, which contains al-Kindī's arguments and the replies of the same Christian theologian who replies to Abū ʿĪsā al-Warrāq. For a fuller discussion of his arguments see D. Thomas, *Anti-Christian Polemic in Early Islam*, Cambridge, 1992, pp. 35–7.
57 Ed. I.-A. Khalifé and W. Kutsch, "Ar-Radd ʿalā-n-Naṣārā de ʿAlī aṭ-Ṭabarī", *Mélanges de l'Université Saint Joseph* 36, 1959, pp. 113–48; trans. J.-M. Gaudeul, *Riposte aux Chrétiens par ʿAlī al-Ṭabarī*, Rome, 1995.
58 Ed. A. Mingana, *Kitāb al-dīn wa-al-dawla*, Manchester, 1923; trans. A. Mingana, *The Book of Religion and Empire*, Manchester, 1922.
59 I. di Matteo, "Confutazione contro i Cristiani dello zaydita al-Qāsim b. Ibrāhīm", *Rivista degli Studi Orientali* 9, 1921–2, pp. 301–64.
60 See Thomas, *Polemic*, p. 33.
61 *Ibid.*, pp. 33–5.
62 See D. Thomas, "The Bible in Early Muslim Anti-Christian Polemic", *Islam and Christian-Muslim Relations* 7, 1996, pp. 32–7.
63 See Thomas, *Polemic*, pp. 38–41.
64 ʿAbd al-Jabbār, *Al-mughnī*, vol.V, ed. M.M. al-Khuḍayrī, Cairo, 1960, pp. 80–151.
65 The works mentioned below are listed in G. Monnot, "Les écrits musulmans sur les religions non-bibliques", *Mélanges de l'Institut Dominicain d'Etudes Orientales* 11, 1972, pp. 5–48; repr. in G. Monnot, *Islam et religions*, Paris, 1986, pp. 39–82; see esp. pp. 50–7.
66 Another work of his, the *Kitāb al-aṣnām*, (*The Book of Idols*) is extant, ed. A. Zakī, Cairo, 1924. In his edition and French translation of this work, W. Atallah, *Les Idoles de Hichām Ibn al-Kalbī*, Paris, 1969, pp. LIVf., observes, "toute idée d'apologie ou de polémique nous paraît absente de son livre . . . Ibn al-Kalbi paraît avoir dans cet ouvrage le détachement de l'éridit soucieux d'informer, de consigner par écrit et de classer tout ce qui se rapportait à l'antiquité arabe à laquelle l'attachaient tant de liens".
67 G. Monnot, *Penseurs musulmans et religions iraniennes*, Paris, 1974, p. 59.
68 Monnot, *Islam et religions*, p. 56; and see al-Bīrūnī, *Taḥqīq mā li-al-Hind*, ed. E. Sachau, London, 1887, p. 4.3–8.
69 Monnot, *Islam et religions*, p. 44.
70 See p. 90.1–2 below for Abū ʿĪsā's reference to this in the *Radd*; and see also D.

Thomas, "Abū ʿĪsā al-Warrāq and the History of Religions", *Journal of Semitic Studies* 41, 1996, pp. 275–90, on which the following discussion is based.

71 See Thomas, "History of Religions", pp. 278–82.
72 *Ibid.*, p. 277.
73 *Ibid.*, pp. 276f.
74 *Ibid.*, pp. 282f.
75 *Ibid.*, p. 282.
76 See pp. 86–95 below.
77 Thomas, "History of Religions", pp. 286–9; and see the list of Abū ʿĪsā's works given at the end of Chapter 2, pp. 33–5, below.
77 Samir, "Christian Communities", p. 74, makes similar comments on this relationship.

Notes to Chapter 2

1 See discussion in Thomas, *Polemic*, pp. 9–16; J. van Ess, *Theologie und Gesellschaft im 2. und 3. Jahrhundert Hidschra, eine Geschichte des religiösen Denkens im frühen Islam*, vol. IV, Berlin/New York, 1997, pp. 289–94; D. Urvoy, *Les penseurs libres dans l'Islam classique*, Paris, 1996, pp. 102–17.
2 See Stroumsa, *Freethinkers of Medieval Islam*, esp. pp. 40–6.
3 *Kitāb al-intiṣār*, ed. and trans. A. Nader, Beirut, 1957, pp. 73.10ff., 111.24.
4 *Ibid.*, pp. 110.2f., 108.13, 108.2 and 12, 110.6, 111.24ff.
5 Quoted by ʿAbd al-Jabbār; see A. al-Aʿasam, *History of Ibn ar-Rīwandī, the Heretic*, Beirut, 1975, p. 98.
6 Al-Ashʿarī, *Kitāb maqālāt al-Islāmiyyīn*, ed. H. Ritter, Istanbul, 1930 (repr. Wiesbaden 1980), pp. 64.1f., 33.11f., 34.11f., 349.12–15. Further to this question, W. Madelung, "Bemerkungen zur imamitischen Firaq-Literatur", *Der Islam* 43, 1967, p. 48, and M.J. McDermott, "Abū ʿĪsā al-Warrāq on the *Dahriyya*", *Mélanges de l'Université St Joseph* 50, 1984, p. 387, show that al-Ashʿarī made more extensive use of Abū ʿĪsā's works than he divulges.
7 Al-Masʿūdī, *Murūj al-dhahab*, ed. and trans. (French) C. Barbier de Meynard and Pavet de Courteille, Paris, 1861–77, vols. V, pp. 473f., VI, pp. 56ff., VII, pp. 234–7.
8 Ibn al-Nadīm, *Fihrist*, pp. 216.7–12, 401.20.
9 ʿAbd al-Jabbār, *Tathbīt*, pp. 128.5, 129.11, 414.10, 508.20, 225.13, 528.22ff., 407.9f., 371.9f., 374.10f.
10 Al-Sharīf al-Murtaḍā, *Al-shāfī fī al-Imāma*, ed. ʿA.-Z. Ḥusaynī, Tehran, 1986, vol. I, pp. 89f.; excerpted in Aʿasam, *History*, p. 102.
11 Al-Najāshī, *Kitāb al-rijāl*, Bombay, 1317/1898–9, pp. 23.12, 47.16.
12 Al-Ṭūsī, *Fihrist*, ed. A. Sprenger *et al.*, Calcutta, 1853–5, pp. 263.4ff., and see also pp. 586ff., 99.5.
13 Al-Shahrastānī, *Kitab al-milal wa-al-niḥal*, ed. W. Cureton, London, 1846, p. 188.14.
14 Ibn al-Jawzī, *Al-muntaẓam fī taʾrīkh al-mulūk wa-al-umam*, Hyderabad, 1357/1938, vol. VI, p. 102.3ff.
15 Al-Ashʿarī, *Maqālāt*, p. 33.11f.
16 W. Madelung, *EI²*, vol. III, pp. 496–8, favours this against later dates; also Watt, *The Formative Period*, pp. 161 and 348 n. 37, argues for a date between 186/803 and 199/814–15.

17 See M. Chokr, *Zandaqa et Zindīqs en Islam au second siècle de l'héjire*, Damascus, 1993, p. 216 and n. 52.
18 Al-Khayyāṭ, *Intiṣār*, pp. 73 (they were both Ibn al-Rāwandī's teachers), 108.
19 Al-Masʿūdī, *Murūj al-dhahab*, vol. VII, p. 236.
20 The suggestion made in Thomas, *Polemic*, p. 11, that a possible polemical exchange with al-Jāḥiẓ is also relevant to dating must now be withdrawn since it is based on inaccurate information; see van Ess, *Theologie*, vol. IV, pp. 294f. n. 58.
21 Ibn al-Jawzī, *Muntaẓam*, vol. VI, p. 102.3ff.
22 ʿAbd al-Raḥīm al-ʿAbbāsī, *Kitāb maʿāhid al-tanṣīṣ*, ed. M. M. ʿAbd al-Ḥamīd, Cairo, 1947–8, vol. I. p. 158.11–22.
23 Al-Shahrastānī, *Milal*, pp. 188–92; see S. M. Stern's reference to this in *EI*^{2}, vol. I, p. 130, art. "Abū ʿĪsā al Warrāḳ".
24 ʿAbd al-Jabbār, *Mughnī*, vol. V, p. 15, and al-Shahrastānī, *Milal*, p. 192. W. Madelung, "Abū ʿĪsā al-Warrāq über die Bardesaniten, Marcioniten und Kantäer", in A.R. Roemer and A. Noth, *Studien zur Geschichte und Kultur des Vorderen Orients*, Leiden, 1981, p. 210, n. 4 (repr. in W. Madelung, *Religious Schools and Sects in Early Islam*, Aldershot, 1985, no. XX) suggests that al-Nawbakhtī may have been responsible for the passage containing the date. But in that case ʿAbd al-Jabbār, who acknowledges al-Nawbakhtī as the intermediary from whom he takes Abū ʿĪsā's account, would have had to remove it.
25 Madelung, "Firaq-Literatur", pp. 47f. The passage occurs in MS or. Leiden 2584, f. 21b; see P. Voorhoeve, *Handlist of Arabic MSS in the Library of the University of Leiden and other Collections in the Netherlands*, Leiden (2nd edn), 1980, p. 395.
26 Al-Ashʿarī, *Maqālāt*, p. 67.12–16.
27 *Ibid.*, pp. 79, 82, 84.
28 Al-Ṭabarī, *Taʾrīkh*, pp. 1520f.; trans. G. Saliba, *The Crisis of the ʿAbbasid Caliphate* (*The History of al-Ṭabarī*, vol. XXXV), Albany, 1985, pp. 18f.
29 Al-Ashʿarī, *Maqālāt*, p. 64.1.
30 Al-Masʿūdī, *Murūj*, vol. V, p. 474.
31 Al-Ashʿarī, *Maqālāt*, p. 84.3–5; al-Masʿūdī, *Murūj*, vol. VII, pp. 330f.
32 Al-Ashʿarī, *Maqālāt*, pp. 64.1f., 349.12–15.
33 Al-Masʿūdī, *Murūj*, vols. VI, pp. 56ff., VII, pp. 234–7.
34 Al-Sharīf al-Murtaḍā, *Shāfī*, pp. 89f. (Aʿasam, *History*, p. 102).
35 Al-Najāshī, *Rijāl*, p. 263.4ff.
36 Al-Khayyāṭ, *Intiṣār*, e.g., pp. 110.2ff., 108.2, 12f.
37 This is given on the authority of ʿAbd al-Jabbār by al-Sharīf al-Murtaḍā in *Shāfī*, quoted in Aʿasam, *History*, p. 98.
38 Ibn al-Nadīm, *Fihrist*, p. 401.20.
39 ʿAbd al-Jabbār, *Tathbīt*, e.g., pp. 128.5, 129.11, 414.10, 508.20.
40 Ibn al-Jawzī, *Muntaẓam*, vol. VI, p. 100.2.
41 Al-Shahrastānī, *Milal*, p. 188.14. B. Abrahamov, *Islamic Theology, Traditionalism and Rationalism*, Edinburgh, 1998, p. 28 and n. 65, adduces evidence to show that in this period this particular accusation was not infrequently levelled at both supporters of divine omnipotence and supporters of human responsibility.
42 See e.g. al-Khayyāṭ, *Intiṣār*, pp. 73.10f., 108.2, 110.2, 111.24.
43 Abū Manṣūr al-Māturīdī, *Kitāb al-tawḥīd*, ed. F. Kholeif, Beirut, 1970, pp. 197.1–4, 199.17–20.

44 Al-Khayyāṭ, *Intiṣār*, pp. 111.24–112.2; see also al-Sharīf al-Murtaḍā in Aʿasam, *History*, pp. 98f.
45 See the list of Abū ʿĪsā's works on pp. 34f. below.
46 Al-Khayyāṭ wrote the *Kitāb al-intiṣār* as a refutation of his *Kitāb faḍīḥa al-Muʿtazila*, and Abū ʿAlī al-Jubbāʾī wrote a refutation of his *Kitāb al-dāmigh* (see ʿAbd al-Jabbār, *Mughnī*, vol. XVI, ed. A. al-Khulī, Cairo, 1960, p. 389.11f., and Ibn al-Jawzī, *Muntaẓam*, vol. VI, p. 99.20f.).
47 Al-Māturīdī, *Tawḥīd*, pp. 197.1–4, 199.17–20.
48 Al-Sharīf al-Murtaḍā, *Shāfī*, p. 89 (Aʿasam, *History*, p. 102); al-Māturīdī, *Tawḥīd*, e.g. p. 187.9–15, also gives an instance of Ibn al-Rāwandī arguing against Abū ʿĪsā.
49 Ibn al-Jawzī, *Muntaẓam*, vol. VI, p. 100.2f.
50 See Thomas, *Polemic*, pp. 24f.
51 See U. Rudolph, *Al-Māturīdī und die sunnitische Theologie in Samarkand,* Leiden, 1997, pp. 177f. Stroumsa, *Freethinkers of Medieval Islam*, esp. pp. 71–6, suggests rather differently that Ibn al-Rāwandī and Abū ʿĪsā actually collaborated over these arguments, and that they only appear to disagree because of the dialogue form employed in composition. Her arguments are attractive but are built upon conjectures that cannot in the last analysis be sustained with certainty.
52 See Thomas, "History of Religions", pp. 278–82, and also Thomas, *Polemic*, p. 188, n. 71.
53 Al-Sharīf al-Murtaḍā, *Shāfī*, p. 89 (Aʿasam, *History*, p. 102).
54 Al-Māturīdī, *Tawḥīd*, pp. 197.1–4 (and see Thomas, *Polemic*, pp. 26 and 189, nn. 86 and 87), 199.17–20. On the first of these points, Christians at about this time argued in a similar way, that although the Qurʾan imputed to them the belief that Mary was divine and to the Jews the belief that Ezra (ʿUzayr) was the son of God, and recounted the miracle of Jesus speaking as a baby in the cradle, neither they nor any other major religion acknowledged such ideas, and the majority must be right; see al-Jāḥiẓ, *Radd*, pp. 10.9–11.3, 12.4–13.4.
55 Stroumsa, *Freethinkers of Medieval Islam*, pp. 40–4. This is a resumption of the argument which she originally presents in "The *Barāhima* in Early Kalām", *Jerusalem Studies in Arabic and Islam* 6, 1985, pp. 230f. n. 5, on which see Thomas, *Polemic*, p. 21.
56 Stroumsa, *Freethinkers of Medieval Islam*, e.g. p. 70.
57 See Thomas, *Polemic*, pp. 24–30 for a full discussion, and partly based upon this Urvoy, *Penseurs libres*, pp. 113–14. In what follows, the discussion is restricted to the explicit references to statements by Abū ʿĪsā recorded in al-Māturīdī, *Tawḥīd*. Stroumsa, *Freethinkers of Medieval Islam*, pp. 51–64, also discusses some of these references and gives useful translations of key passages.
58 Al-Māturīdī, *Tawḥīd*, pp. 186.10–14, 198.15f.
59 *Ibid.*, pp. 195.17f., 196.8–10.
60 *Ibid.*, pp. 191.16–192.2. R.C. Martin, "The Role of the Baṣrah Muʿtazilah in Formulating the Doctrine of the Prophetic Miracle", *Journal of Near Eastern Studies* 39, 1980, pp. 175–89, discusses third-/ninth and fourth-/tenth-century opinions about the Qurʾan as prophetic miracle, and depicts the intellectual context in which these polemical jibes may have been made.
61 *Ibid.*, p. 200.14–16.
62 *Ibid.*, pp. 187.19–188.4; for the subject of the opening *wa-qāla* see p. 186.10.

63 *Ibid.*, p. 197.1f.
64 *Ibid.*, p. 201.1–4.
65 See Thomas, *Polemic*, pp. 24f., for what may have been the complicated literary origin of these fragments.
66 Al-Māturīdī, *Tawḥīd*, p. 199.1f.
67 *Ibid.*, p. 199.11f.
68 See Thomas, "History of Religions", pp. 275–90, for a detailed investigation of the contents and possible intention of the *Maqālāt*, and also Chapter 1, pp. 19f. above.
69 Thomas, "History of Religions", pp. 279–82.
70 Al-Sharīf al-Murtaḍā, *Shāfī*, p. 89 (Aʿasam, *History*, p. 102).
71 See Abū ʿĪsā's Introduction to the *Radd*, para. 12, pp. 88.25–90.2 below.
72 See the list of Abū ʿĪsā's works at the end of this chapter.
73 The suggestion that Abū ʿĪsā was not merely a cynic about intellectual matters is lent support by a rather simple story attributed to him by the sixth-/twelfth-century Ibāḍī author Abū ʿAmmār ʿAbd al-Kāfī. In this he crisply relates how a Sophist abandoned his doubts about knowing anything for certain when his enemies hid his mule and, contrary to his own principles, he was driven to insist that he truly knew he had ridden on it when he came to dispute against them (*Al-muzaj*, ed. ʿA. Ṭālbī, *Ārāʾ al-Khawārij al-kalāmiyya*, Algiers, 1978, pp. 281–3, on which see Urvoy, *Penseurs libres*, p. 114, though he mistakenly includes Abū ʿĪsā as a participant in the story rather than the narrator). ʿAbd al-Kāfī gives no details about the origins of this intriguing excerpt.
74 See *EI*[2], vol. VIII, pp. 386–9, art. "al-Rāfiḍa".
75 Al-Ashʿarī, *Maqālāt*, pp. 31–5, 36–9, 47f., 48f., 49f.
76 Thomas, *Polemic*, p. 22.
77 *Ibid.*, p. 23, although al-Najāshī contested his authorship of this work.
78 ʿAbd al-Jabbār, *Tathbīt*, p. 371.
79 Al-Ashʿarī, *Maqālāt*, pp. 64.1f., 33.11–13.
80 *Ibid.*, p. 471.9.
81 *Ibid.*, p. 50.4–10. It may be that the fragments of arguments in which Abū ʿĪsā discredits the transmission of the Qurʾan by a single authority in its first stages, al-Māturīdī, *Tawḥīd*, pp. 196.14–17, 198.15f., reflect this position.
82 Al-Khayyāṭ, *Intiṣār*, pp. 111.24–112.2; also Abū ʿAlī al-Jubbāʾī, quoted by al-Sharīf al-Murtaḍā from ʿAbd al-Jabbār, in Aʿasam, *History*, pp. 98f.: *kāna ʿinda al-khalwati rubbamā qāla.*
83 See below, e.g. paras. 159, 166, 231, 255, 260, 262, 295, 325, 340 and 343.
84 Thomas, *Polemic*, pp. 22–4; see also van Ess, *Theologie*, vol. IV, pp. 430–2.
85 Thomas, "History of Religions", esp. pp. 275–82.
86 This was certainly the case with the *Radd ʿalā al-Naṣārā*, as Abū ʿĪsā himself acknowledges; Thomas, *Polemic*, p. 70.
87 See H. Modarressi, "Early Debates on the Integrity of the Qurʾan, a brief survey", *Studia Islamica* 77, 1993, p. 27.
88 Stroumsa, *Freethinkers of Medieval Islam*, pp. 76f., 84f.
89 Al-Sharīf al-Murtaḍā, *Shāfī*, pp. 89f.
90 *Ibid.*
91 This occurs on f. 21b at the start of the brief account of the Jārūdiyya given in Abū ʿĪsā's name. It reads: *Abū ʿĪsā al-Warrāq lahu kitāb yusammā al-nawḥ ʿalā al-*

bahā'im li-istinkār amr al-Shāriʿ bi-dhabḥihā, "Abū ʿĪsā al-Warrāq: he has a book entitled *The Lament over Animals*, an expression of loathing for the Lawgiver's command to slaughter." This note must have been added after 608/1211–12 when the MS was copied (Voorhoeve, *Handlist*, p. 395), and it indicates that, at least in the mind of the person responsible, the book was a diatribe against Islamic sacrificial practices; see Thomas, *Polemic*, pp. 19f. for further references to Abū ʿĪsā's views on this subject.

92 See Stroumsa, *Freethinkers of Medieval Islam*, p. 84, and also the marginal gloss in al-Jushamī referred to in the preceding note.

Notes to Chapter 3

1 See Chapter 1 above, p. 16.
2 Ibn al-Nadīm, *Fihrist*, p. 207.6.
3 *Ibid.*, p. 204.21f.
4 Mingana, "Apology", pp. 153, 167, 176.
5 *Ibid.*, pp. 155f.
6 Al-Qāsim, *Radd*, p. 309.3–12.
7 *Ibid.*, pp. 311.8–312.6.
8 *Ibid.*, pp. 314.23–316.3.
9 *Ibid.*, pp. 316.3–318.8.
10 *Ibid.*, p. 319.13–15.
11 *Ibid.*, pp. 319.28–321.8.
12 *Ibid.*, pp. 321.8–322.18.
13 See Thomas, "The Bible in Early Muslim Anti-Christian Polemic", pp. 32–6.
14 *Ibid.*
15 See EI^2, vol. X, pp. 17f., art. "Al-Ṭabarī, ʿAlī b. Rabban".
16 S. K. Samir, "La réponse d'al-Ṣafī Ibn al-ʿAssāl à la Réfutation des Chrétiens de ʿAlī al-Ṭabarī", *Parole de l'Orient* 11, 1983, pp. 290–2, suggests on the basis of the title of Ibn al-ʿAssāl's refutation, *Al-ṣaḥa'iḥ fī jawāb al-naṣā'iḥ*, that the original title of al-Ṭabarī's work was *Kitāb al-naṣā'iḥ*. This is not supported by al-Ṭabarī himself, who in his *Kitāb al-dīn wa-al-dawla* refers to this work variously as *Al-radd ʿalā aṣnāf al-Naṣārā* (p. 86.7) and *Al-radd ʿalā al-Naṣārā* (p. 93.2).
17 ʿAlī al-Ṭabarī, *Radd*, p. 122.12–17.
18 *Ibid.*, p. 126.6–18.
19 See Samir, "Réponse", pp. 284–6.
20 ʿAlī al-Ṭabarī, *Radd*, p. 138.17–20.
21 ʿAlī al-Ṭabarī's twelve principles of agreed belief about the nature of God, *Radd*, pp. 128.19–129.4, are equivalent to al-Qāsim's arguments about God at the opening of his *Radd*, pp. 304–305.21.
22 See Finkel, "A Risāla of al-Jāḥiẓ", pp. 312f.
23 See pp. 13f. above.
24 Al-Jāḥiẓ, *Radd*, pp. 29.21–30.8.
25 *Ibid.*, p. 25.5–22.
26 *Ibid.*, p. 26.1f.
27 *Ibid.*, pp. 29.21–30.8.
28 *Ibid.*, pp. 30.8–32.14.
29 *Ibid.*, pp. 26.6–27.2.

30 For later developments in the discussion raised by this question, see Thomas, "The Question better not Asked".
31 Of course, we cannot know whether there were more arguments of a doctrinal nature in the lost parts of the *Radd*.
32 Al-Jāḥiẓ, *Radd*, pp. 37.18–38.10.
33 Ed. and trans. (German) J. van Ess, *Frühe muʿtazilitische Häresiographie*, Beirut, 1971, pp. 71–127 (Arabic), 61–121 (German).
34 Al-Nāshiʾ, *Awsaṭ*, pp. 76.17–77.17.
35 See van Ess, *Häresiographie*, p. 67 (German).
36 Al-Nāshiʾ, *Awsaṭ*, pp. 77.21–82.6.
37 *Ibid.*, pp. 82.13–83.6.
38 *Ibid.*, pp. 83.7–84.13.
39 See below, e.g. paras. 176, 215, 231, 235.
40 ʿAbd al-Jabbār, *Tathbīt*, p. 198.14.
41 A rationalist (and rationalising) explanation of the denial of Jesus' crucifixion in Q 4.157 preserved from Abū ʿAlī's lost *tafsīr* illustrates the kind of approach he favoured. He says that when the Jews came to arrest Jesus he had already been raised up to God, so they took another person out of fear that people would come to believe in Jesus because of his miraculous ascension. The Jews crucified this man on a hillock where people could not see him clearly, and after his death his features were distorted and made him unrecognisable; see D. Gimaret, *Une lecture muʿtazilite du Coran*, Louvain–Paris, 1994, pp. 252f. This account shows economically how a substitute was crucified without people finding out, and why the Jews did this. So there is no divine involvement, except for the miracle of the ascension which directly involved a messenger of God.
42 See Thomas, *Polemic*, pp. 38–41.
43 ʿAbd al-Jabbār, *Mughnī*, vol. V, p. 80.8–12.
44 *Ibid.*, pp. 106.5–107.16, reading *al-bunuwwa* instead of *al-nubuwwa* on p. 107.13. It is unclear whether all this is Abū ʿAlī's argument, though it preserves his main point.
45 See the point quoted from "our masters" on p. 109.7–11, that *ibn* can only be used metaphorically when referring to human relationships.
46 *Ibid.*, pp. 111.17–112.4.
47 *Ibid.*, pp. 140.12–141.4.
48 See pp. 96–103 below.
49 See Thomas, *Polemic*, pp. 39f.
50 Al-Nāshiʾ, *Awsaṭ*, p. 83.13.
51 Al-Jāḥiẓ, *Radd*, p. 22.4–14, and ʿAbd al-Jabbār, *Mughnī*, vol. V, pp. 80.16–81.2, agree on the difficulty of rationally grasping Christian doctrines.
52 See D. Thomas, "The Miracles of Jesus in Early Islamic Polemic", *Journal of Semitic Studies* 39, 1994, pp. 221–43; supplemented by *idem*, "Abū Manṣūr al-Māturīdī on the Divinity of Jesus Christ", *Islamochristiana* 23, 1997, pp. 60f., n. 15.
53 F. Nau, "Un colloque du Patriarche Jean avec l'Emir des Agaréens", *Journal Asiatique* onzième série 5, 1915, pp. 225–71; see R. Hoyland, *Seeing Islam as Others Saw It*, Princeton, 1997, pp. 459–65, for a full account of the debate, its date and the period in which the report of it was written.
54 Nau, "Colloque", pp. 257–60. Griffith, "Prophet Muḥammad", p. 100, sums up

the discussion as "a miniature catechism of Christian beliefs, designed to furnish the reader with ready answers to the customary questions raised by Muslims". The question of its historicity does not affect the point that it is framing Christian beliefs for Muslims.

55 This last point is also made in the attack on Christianity attributed to the Caliph ʿUmar II but probably written at some time towards the end of the third/ninth century; see D. Sourdel, "Un pamphlet musulman anonyme d'époque ʿabbaside contre les Chrétiens", *Revue des Etudes Islamiques* 34, 1966, p. 27; also Gaudeul, *Correspondance de ʿUmar et Leon*, pp. iiif.

56 Mingana, "Apology", p. 220 n. 3; see also H. Putman, *L'Eglise et l'Islam sous Timothée I (780–823)*, Beirut, 1975, pp. 184f., and Hoyland, *Seeing Islam*, pp. 472–5.

57 John 20.17. In addition to its obvious meaning when singled out from its context, the closeness of part of this verse to Q 19.36 may explain why this became the single most popular proof-text among Muslim polemicists.

58 Mingana, "Apology", pp. 153–7.

59 The same emphasis upon the possibility rather than the manner of Incarnation is evident in his letter no. 40 (ed. (Syriac) and trans. (French) Cheikho, *Dialectique du langage sur Dieu*), where the major issues are divine limitation, the worship of Christ's humanity, the involvement of one member of the Trinity rather than all three (this is the subject of Abū ʿĪsā's first set of arguments, and appears in other works of the period, see below pp. 69–71), and the implication of the divine in the suffering and death of the Messiah (pp. 255–67, for the French translation, pp. 317–26 for the Syriac text). This letter, written in or just before 165/781 to Timothy's friend Sarjis, is the account of the fictional meeting with a Muslim who was "well instructed in the thought of Aristotle" (Cheikho, pp. 54–7) mentioned in Chapter 1. Timothy again employs metaphors here with the same ingenuity as with the Caliph.

60 See J. P. Migne, *Patrologia Graeca*, vol. XCIV, Paris, 1860, cols. 521–1228; trans. F. A. Chase, *Saint John of Damascus, Writings* (*The Fathers of the Church, a New Translation*, vol. 37), Washington DC, 1958.

61 Sahas, *John of Damascus on Islam*, text and translation on pp. 132–41.

62 The few divisions in which the work now appears were made later and do not conform to indications in the text; see Chase, *John of Damascus*, p. xxxii, and S.D.F. Salmond, *John of Damascus, Exposition of the Orthodox Faith* (*A Select Library of the Nicene and post-Nicene Fathers of the Christian Church*, second series vol. 9/2), Oxford and New York, 1889, p. viii.

63 Chase, *John of Damascus*, p. 268, ch. 45, cf. pp. 337f.

64 I. Dick, "Deux écrits inédits de Théodore Abuqurra", *Le Muséon* 72, 1959, pp. 56–9 text, 60–2 French translation.

65 See I. Dick, *Théodore Abuqurra, Traité de l'existence du Créateur et de la vraie religion* (*Patrimoine arabe chrétien* 3), Jounieh and Rome, 1982, pp. 39–58/XI-XIII, though the fullest account of Theodore's life and activities is given in S. Griffith, "Reflections on the Biography of Theodore Abū Qurrah", *Parole de l'Orient* 18, 1993, pp. 143–70.

66 He says nothing about dating in the original article but makes this suggestion in *Théodore Abuqurra*, pp. 64/XVI.

67 In the edition the exposition of the Trinity takes just over a page, while the Incarnation takes about three pages.

68 Dick, "Deux écrits", p. 57.3–6.

69 Another work by Theodore that comes into this category is his letter to his Jacobite friend (C. Bacha, *Les Œuvres arabes de Théodore Aboucara*, Beirut, 1904, pp. 104–39) in which he expounds his own Chalcedonian Christology and criticises the Monophysite alternative. There are also the three accounts of their belief in Christ which the Nestorian ʿAbd Īshūʿ, the Melkite Theodore Abū Qurra and the Jacobite Abū Rāʾiṭa were asked to outline for a *wazīr* (G. Graf, *Die Schriften des Jacobiten Ḥabīb Ibn Ḫidma Abū Rāʾiṭa* (*Corpus Scriptorum Christianorum Orientalium* 130), Louvain, 1951, pp. 163–5) in which each describes his own conception of how the two natures relate to each other.

70 Bacha, *Œuvres*, pp. 180–6; trans. G. Graf, *Die arabischen Schriften des Theodor Abū Qurra*, Paderborn, 1910, pp. 178–84.

71 See also Graf, *Abū Rāʾiṭa*, pp. 45–6, where the Jacobite also makes use of the reference to God being seated on the throne, and Abū Bakr al-Bāqillānī, *Kitāb al-tamhīd*, ed. R. J. McCarthy, Beirut, 1957, pp. 88.3–6 and 90.10–15, where an anonymous Christian is reported making exactly the same comparison.

72 Bacha, *Œuvres*, p. 80.13.

73 *Ibid.*, pp. 75–82; Graf, *Arabischen Schriften*, pp. 160–8.

74 Bacha, *Œuvres*, pp. 91–104; Graf, *Arabischen Schriften*, pp. 184–98.

75 Dick, *Traité*, pp. 224–8.

76 *Ibid.*, pp. 120f./XXXVIIIf.

77 See the fragment of his *Awāʾil al-adilla fī uṣūl al-dīn*, preserved by ʿĪsā b. Isḥāq Ibn Zurʿa, in Sbath, *Vingt traités philosophiques*, p. 60.14–16.

78 See his *Mughnī*, vol. V, pp. 144.11–145.2. It is not unreasonable to suppose that the early third-/ninth-century Muʿtazilī ʿĪsā b. Ṣubayḥ al-Murdār's attack on Theodore, which is mentioned by Ibn al-Nadīm (see n. 2 above) was also against these arguments.

79 It is possible to imagine that al-Qāsim Ibn Ibrāhīm, whom we have discussed above (pp. 17, 39f.), was reacting to precisely this kind of argument in the opening parts of his *Radd ʿalā al-Naṣārā* where he mentions that the majesty and godliness of God would be impugned by his having to share with another being like himself. As we have indicated, al-Qāsim probably wrote this work soon after a period of stay in Egypt between 100/815 and 211/826 (Madelung, *Der Imam al-Qāsim Ibn Ibrāhīm*, pp. 89f.), where he would have been able to acquaint himself fully with Christian teachings.

80 This new awareness appears to be absent from the anonymous *Fī tathlīth Allāh al-wāḥid*, which dates from the middle of the second/eighth century (for arguments about its precise date see S. K. Samir, "The Earliest Arab Apology for Christianity (*c.* 750)", in Samir and Nielsen, *Christian Arabic Apologetics during the Abbasid Period (750–1258)*, pp. 61–4; S. Griffith, "The View of Islam from the Monasteries of Palestine", *Islam and Christian–Muslim Relations* 7, 1996, p. 11 and notes; and Hoyland, *Seeing Islam*, pp. 502f.), where the whole history of redemption is related in terms of God becoming man, but with no more explanation of the Incarnation than that the Messiah was God and man (see Samir, "Arab Apology", pp. 84–96, esp. sentences 239, 240, 310, 311, superseding at this point the incomplete text and translation of M. D. Gibson in *Studia Siniatica* 7, London, 1899).

81 See Hayek, *ʿAmmār*, introduction, and Griffith, "Concept of *al-Uqnūm*", p. 170.

82 See n. 3 above, and also Hayek, *ʿAmmār*, p. 19. See also Griffith, "*Kitāb al-Burhān*", pp. 147f.
83 See Griffith, "Concept of *al-Uqnūm*", pp. 169–91; Griffith, "*Kitāb al-Burhān*", pp. 168–74.
84 See Griffith, "*Kitāb al-Burhān*", pp. 149–59.
85 Hayek, *ʿAmmār*, pp. 56.13–60.9; and see Griffith, "*Kitāb al-Burhān*", pp. 172f.
86 Hayek, *ʿAmmār*, pp. 60.10–62.14; Griffith, "*Kitāb al-Burhān*", pp. 173f.
87 Hayek, *ʿAmmār*, pp. 62.16–69.15; Griffith, "*Kitāb al-Burhān*", pp. 174–6.
88 See al-Qāsim Ibn Ibrāhīm, *Radd*, pp. 317.8–318.6; *Fī tathlīth Allāh al-wāḥid* in Samir, "Arab Apology", pp. 84–97.
89 Hayek, *ʿAmmār*, pp. 71.13, 72.2; and see Griffith, "*Kitāb al-Burhān*", pp. 157f. Abū ʿĪsā refers to this Christological model in the Introduction to his *Radd*, see below, p. 88.7f., para. 11.
90 Hayek, *ʿAmmār*, p. 70.21f.
91 *Ibid.*, pp. 78.19–79.4.
92 The questions are usually introduced with the simple words *fa-in qāla:*, though earlier in the work there is the slightly less bald *in saʾala sāʾil min al-mukhālifīn, fa-qāla:* (p. 148.14).
93 This question has not survived in full (Hayek, *ʿAmmār*, p. 178) though its gist is clear.
94 Hayek, *ʿAmmār*, pp. 178–215.
95 See below pp. 96–107, sections 151–60.
96 Graf, *Abū Rāʾiṭa*, pp. 27ff., paras. 2–7; see also pp. 96–9, paras. 151–6 below.
97 Hayek, *ʿAmmār*, pp. 188.1–191.15.
98 But see J. M. Fiey, "Ḥabib Abū Rāʾiṭa n'était pas évêque de Takrit", in *Actes du deuxième congrès international d'études arabes chrétiennes (Oosterhesselen, 1984)*, Rome 1986, pp. 211–14.
99 Graf, *Abū Rāʾiṭa*, pp. IIf.; see also S. Griffith, "Ḥabīb ibn Ḫidmah Abī Rāʾiṭah, a Christian *mutakallim* of the First Abbasid Century", *Oriens Christianus* 64, 1980, pp. 161–201.
100 Graf, *Abū Rāʾiṭa*, pp. 27–64.
101 *Ibid.*, p. 27.12, also pp. 1.13, 3.7. It is further indicated in the reference to "our belief that God is in the heavens and on the throne" on p. 46.6f. See Griffith, "Prophet Muḥammad", pp. 126f., for the suggestion that this name results from Christians witnessing Muslims turning south towards Mecca in prayer.
102 Graf, *Abū Rāʾiṭa*, pp. 31.19–32.2.

Notes to Chapter 4

1 See pp. 25–8 above, and also Thomas, "History of Religions", pp. 275–86.
2 For the example of his account of dualist beliefs being employed by a succession of later authors, see Madelung, "Abū ʿĪsā al-Warrāq über die Bardesoniten, Marcioniten und Kantäer".
3 Abel, *Réfutation*, pp. vi–xi.
4 See, among many examples, para. 274, referring back to the arguments against Melkite teachings about the divine substance in paras. 65f. (Thomas, *Polemic*, pp. 102–9, though the whole section is concerned with this issue); para. 291, referring to the explanation given in para. 10 (Thomas, *Polemic*, p. 68) as to why the Word

united with the universal human (Platti, *Incarnation*, trans., p. 128 n. 1, is mistaken in saying the reference is to para. 208).

5 See G. Endress, *The Works of Yaḥyā Ibn ʿAdī*, Wiesbaden, 1977, p. 99, for alternative versions of this title.

6 MS Paris 167 f. 207a; Platti, *Incarnation*, text, p. 132.9f.

7 This sign, which is written as a dot within two concentric circles, is one of the signs used in MS P167 to indicate sections and subsections in the argument, the other being a dot within a single circle. The dot within two circles usually indicates the end of a major section.

8 See below pp. 270.20f., and also 88.16ff.

9 Platti, *Incarnation*, text, p. 203 n. 17, gives a different explanation, that the passage referred to by Yaḥyā as not being included in the superior MS begins at the point marked by the cross, which is at the beginning of para. 346, and probably continues to the end of the work. But this seems to ignore Yaḥyā's words that this particular passage ends at the cross mark, *ilā al-mawḍiʿ alladhī ʿalayhi hādhihī al-ʿalāma*.

10 Platti, *Incarnation*, text, p. 203 n. 14, trans., p. 172 n. 195, adopts a similar view.

11 This might suggest that an equivalent *bāb awwal* has been omitted from the beginning of the first part at para. 151, or maybe para. 161.

12 In view of Yaḥyā's Jacobite beliefs, it is possible that this is his addition.

13 E.g. paras. 273, 274.

14 See Platti, *Incarnation*, trans., pp. 193, XIVf.

15 See Thomas, *Polemic*, pp. 112.18, 126.1, 154.13, 162.15 for indications of the start of new arguments, like para. 230, but not of decisive new directions.

16 See al-Qāsim, *Radd*, pp. 316.3–318.6.

17 See above pp. 25f.

18 Yaḥyā as a Jacobite might be expected to have made some comment about this work if he knew of its existence.

19 See Thomas, "History of Religions", and pp. 19f. above.

20 See pp. 88.26–90.2 below, para. 12.

21 *Ibid.*

22 See Thomas, "History of Religions", pp. 278–82.

23 See further the remarks in Thomas, *Polemic*, pp. 57f.

24 See Thomas, "Miracles", and further Thomas, "Abū Manṣur al-Māturīdī on the Divinity of Jesus Christ", pp. 60f., n. 15.

25 There is a further reference in para. 229.

26 See p. 57 above. Platti, *Incarnation*, trans., p. 2 n. 1, notes this correspondence.

27 Graf, *Abū Rāʾiṭa*, p. 27.12, and see p. 46.6ff. where a reference to the Qurʾan makes this plain. Abū Raʾiṭa's favourite name for his opponents is Ahl al-Tayman, e.g. p. 1.13.

28 Graf, *Abū Rāʾiṭa*, p. 27.12–15.

29 See pp. 102–5 below, paras. 158–9.

30 Graf, *Abū Rāʾiṭa*, text, p. 29.1–6.

31 See pp. 96–9 below, paras. 151–6.

32 See Hayek, *ʿAmmār*, p. 205.

33 See Cheikho, *Dialectique du langage sur Dieu*, paras. 275–9 (pp. 263–5 in the French translation); also Mingana, "Apology", pp. 162f.

34 ʿAbd al-Jabbār, *Mughnī*, vol. V, p. 141.1–4.

35 See Thomas, *Polemic*, p. 57. A reference in para. 256 below, to Christians offering a particular reply, suggests some evidence of direct engagement.
36 See Thomas, *Polemic*, p. 56, referring to para. 130 where Abū ʿĪsā suggests that other Muslims may fill in the outlines he provides.
37 Paras. 15 and 186 below.
38 Para. 291 below.
39 E.g. paras. 182–6, 213–19 below.
40 See Urvoy, *Penseurs libres*, p. 107, who observes that the consequence of Abū ʿĪsā's rigorously logical approach "est d'évacuer tout ce qui relève de la sensibilité et que seule la totalité de la doctrine, vécue comme un ensemble, peut donner. C'est ce qui va être la source des principles faiblesses de la partie critique de l'œuvre."
41 Para. 13 below.
42 See Thomas, *Polemic*, pp. 66f., para. 6.
43 See the list at the end of Chapter 2, pp. 33–5 above, and Thomas, *Polemic*, pp. 22ff., title nos. 7 and 12–16 for bibliographical details.
44 See Thomas, "History of Religions", *passim*.
45 *Ibid*., p. 283.
46 P. 90.1f., para. 12 below, where the *Maqālāt* is mentioned.
47 See Thomas, *Polemic*, pp. 29f., for suggestions that Abū ʿĪsā was independent in his strict monotheistic principles; van Ess, *Theologie* vol. IV, p. 289, calls him simply a rationalist.
48 Thomas, *Polemic*, pp. 24–9, and Chapter 2 above, pp. 28f.
49 See *ibid*., pp. 31–42 for mentions of the known works.
50 See Sbath, *Vingt traités philosophiques*, pp. 64, 66.
51 See Thomas, *Polemic*, p. 41 nn. 55–9 for references to these works. The so-called Letter of ʿUmar II, supposedly written by the Umayyad caliph to the Byzantine emperor Leo III, can also be included in this period; see Sourdel, "Pamphlet musulman", pp. 2–3 (though see Hoyland, *Seeing Islam*, pp. 490–501, for arguments in favour of a date earlier in the third/ninth century). According to the reconstruction of this work by J.-M. Gaudeul, *La correspondance de ʿUmar et Léon (vers 900)*, the original contained a number of arguments against the Incarnation, pp. 9–20, though none of these resembles anything in Abū ʿĪsā's work.
52 Al-Nāshiʾ, *Awsaṭ*, pp. 76–84, paras. 17–47 (Arabic).
53 *Ibid*., pp. 81ff. (German).
54 ʿAbd al-Jabbār, *Tathbīt*, p. 198.14. On his arguments against the Trinity preserved by ʿAbd al-Jabbār, see Thomas, *Polemic*, pp. 38–41.
55 ʿAbd al-Jabbār, *Mughnī*, vol. V, p. 80.9–15; and see al-Jāḥiẓ, *Radd*, p. 37.18–20.
56 ʿAbd al-Jabbār, *Mughnī*, vol. V, pp. 106.5–107.16; and see al-Jāḥiẓ, *Radd*, p. 25.2ff.
57 ʿAbd al-Jabbār, *Mughnī*, vol. V, p. 111.15f. Abū ʿAlī's view about the interpretation of Q 5.116 is given on p. 141.6–10.
58 *Ibid*., p. 140.12–20, in line 20 following the reading in MS *mīm* rather than the version given in the text which is *qadara al-lāhūt bi-qudrati ka-al-nāsūt*.
59 *Ibid*., p. 141.1–5.
60 Abū ʿĪsā, *Radd*, e.g. paras. 243, 322f.
61 *Ibid*., paras. 155f.
62 See Thomas, *Polemic*, pp. 41f., for references to known works on Christianity by Muslim authors of this period.

63 *Ibid.*, pp. 42–50, for a demonstration of their dependence on Abū ʿĪsā in the arguments they adduce against the Trinity.
64 See M. Allard, *Le problème des attributs divins dans la doctine d'al-Ashʿarī et de ses premiers grands disciples*, Beirut, 1965, pp. 290–5; *EI*[2], vol. I, p. 958, art. "al-Bāḳillānī".
65 Ed. R. J. McCarthy, Beirut, 1957.
66 A. Abel, "Le Chapitre sur le Christianisme dans le 'Tamhīd' d'al-Bāqillānī", in *Etudes d'Orientalisme dédiées à la mémoire de Lévi-Provençal*, vol. I, Paris, 1962, pp. 1–11, esp. pp. 9–10. W. Z. Haddad, "A Tenth-Century Speculative Theologian's Refutation of the Basic Doctrines of Christianity: al-Bāqillānī (d. A.D. 1013)", in Y. Y. Haddad and W. Z. Haddad, eds., *Christian–Muslim Encounters*, Gainsville, 1995, pp. 82–94, describes al-Bāqillānī's arguments without referring to Abū ʿĪsā.
67 *Tamhīd*, pp. 87–103, paras. 154–83, of which pp. 87–98, paras. 154–73, are related to Abū ʿĪsā's *Radd*.
68 *Ibid.*, pp. 87f., paras. 154f.
69 See p. 88.12–15 below, para.11.
70 See Bacha, *Œuvres*, pp. 180–6, esp. pp. 182.11–183.2, where Theodore argues that just as God can be seated on the throne in heaven, so he can inhere in the human body.
71 Other possibilities are that al-Bāqillānī was employing Abū ʿĪsā's *Maqālāt al-nās* or a hypothetical source used by Abū ʿĪsā. In either of these cases we would have to accept that Abū ʿĪsā omitted detailed identifications of Christian groups when he incorporated the analogies into the *Radd*. A third possibility is that he used an unknown intermediary source based upon the *Radd*.
72 *Tamhīd*, paras. 157–63.
73 *Ibid.*, para. 158.
74 Para. 220 below.
75 *Tamhīd*, paras. 165f.
76 *Tamhīd*, p. 93.14–18, and compare Abū ʿAlī al-Jubbāʾī's identical point in ʿAbd al-Jabbār, *Mughnī*, vol. V, p. 141.11–13, employing the term *al-tamānuʿ*. Neither author acknowledges Q 21.22 as a source of inspiration.
77 Paras. 151–6 below.
78 Para. 154 below.
79 *Tamhīd*, para. 172, cf. *Radd*, para. 188.
80 *Tamhīd*, para. 173, cf. *Radd*, paras. 176–8.
81 See Thomas, *Polemic*, p. 46.
82 See J. R. T. M. Peters, *God's Created Speech*, Leiden, 1976, pp. 8ff.; *EI*[2], vol. I, p. 59, art. "ʿAbd al-Djabbār b. Aḥmad"; R. C. Martin *et al.*, *Defenders of Reason in Islam*, Oxford, 1997, pp. 49ff.
83 See Thomas, *Polemic*, pp. 48–50.
84 See Thomas, "History of Religions", pp. 278–80.
85 *Mughnī*, vol. V, pp. 81.15f., 82.19–83.2.
86 P. 90.21–3, para. 14 and p. 86.19–23, para. 10 below.
87 *Mughnī*, vol. V, p. 83.3–6.
88 He uses *Malkiyya* and *Malkāniyya* at various places without any apparent distinction, e.g. pp. 81.4 and 19, 96.3 and 11.
89 Below, p. 92.8–19, para. 14.

90 *Mughnī*, vol. V, p. 83.7–13, in line 10 reading *ḥallat fīhi fa-dabbarat bihi wa-ʿalā yadīh*, following Abū ʿĪsā; see p. 88.8, para. 11, below.
91 P. 88.4–15, para. 11 below.
92 E.g. *Mughnī*, vol. V, pp. 83.20–84.1 and p. 86.12f. below, *Mughnī*, vol. V, p. 84.6–10 and pp. 92.20–94.13 below.
93 *Mughnī*, vol. V, pp. 114–51; there are mistakes in the titles on pp. 121, 123 and 126.
94 *Ibid.*, p. 114.6–9; in l. 9 it makes better sense to read *aw yajʿalū al-khāliq al-ilāh huwa al-ab, alladhī al-kalima ibnuhu, dūna al-ibn* rather than *ibnuhu, dūna al-ab.*
95 Paras. 151ff. below,
96 *Mughnī*, vol. V, p. 124.3f.
97 Paras. 226, 227, 229 below.
98 See Thomas, *Polemic*, p. 12.
99 See para. 362 below.
100 For references to detailed descriptions of the major MSS, see Thomas, *Polemic*, pp. 51f., and also Platti, *Incarnation* text, pp. VIII–XIV.
101 There is a stain on the folio over parts of this name (Platti, *Incarnation*, text, p. X), though on the microfilm copy it can be read with certainty.
102 Thomas, *Polemic*, p. 52.
103 See Platti, *Incarnation*, text, p. XI and n. 6.
104 Thomas, *Polemic*, p. 53.
105 Platti, *Incarnation*, text, p. XV.
106 See Thomas, *Polemic*, pp. 68–77.

Notes to the text and translation

1 In addition to the text and English translation of this Introduction in Thomas, *Polemic*, pp. 66–77, it is also published with a French translation by E. Platti, "La doctrine des Chrétiens d'après Abū ʿĪsā al-Warrāq dans sa traité sur la Trinité", *Mélanges de l'Institut Dominicain d'Etudes Orientales* 20, 1991, pp. 7–30.

Throughout the first part of the *Tabyīn*, on the Trinity, Yaḥyā employs the formula "Then the enemy of the Christians said", *thumma qāla khaṣm al-Naṣārā*, to introduce each quotation from Abū ʿĪsā. In the second part, on the Uniting, he changes to the less charged "Then Abū ʿĪsā said", *thumma qāla Abū ʿĪsā* (though for no apparent reason, in MS V113 at para. 163 the first formula reappears).

In paras. 1–8 (Thomas, *Polemic*, pp. 66–9), Abū ʿĪsā summarises the three sects' teachings about the Trinity.

2 The archaic forms in which this verb and its derivations appear in the MSS, *iytaḥada, iytiḥād* and *muwtaḥid*, have been modernised.

3 These forms appear in all MSS as *a.t.w.ḥ.d* and *a.t.w.ḥ.ā.d*, and in V113 and V114 with *tashdīd* as *a.t.w.ḥ.ḥ.d* and *a.t.w.ḥ.ḥ.ā.d*. Their morphological irregularity is difficult to explain satisfactorily, but given the context they may originally have been the fifth verbal forms *tawaḥḥada* and *tawaḥḥud*, which an early copyist who did not recognise them changed to resemble the more common eighth form. The form *tawaḥḥud* is also used in precisely this context by ʿAmmār al-Baṣrī (Hayek, *ʿAmmār*, p. 71.2 and see also 51.3, 70 ult. and note) and al-Shahrastānī (*Milal*, p. 172.3). On its occurrence in al-Shahrastānī see W. M. Watt, "Ash-Shahrastānī's Account of Christian Doctrine", *Islamochristiana* 9, 1983, p. 250, n. 2, and also D. Gimaret and G. Monnot, eds., *Livre des religions et des sectes* 1, Louvain, 1986,

p. 613, n. 5. The latter suggest that the term is used to designate the reuniting of the incarnate Word with the Godhead, but this seems strained. The word is certainly odd in the context, but its form and position are best explained, as Watt suggests, by the need to find a suitable term to balance *tajassud* in the previous clause.

4 See ʿAbd al-Jabbār, *Mughnī*, vol. V, pp. 82.19–83.2. These synonyms were common among Arab Christian authors at this time.

5 Many of the metaphors that follow were used by Christians from early times to explain the Incarnation. Although some were favoured by particular denominations, most were employed with different interpretations of meaning by writers from all denominations.

ʿAbd al-Jabbār almost certainly makes use of this passage in *Mughnī*, vol. V, p. 83.7–13 (see G. Monnot, "Les doctrines des Chrétiens dans le 'Moghnī' de ʿAbd al-Jabbār", *Mélanges de l'Institut Dominicain d'Etudes Orientales* 16, 1983, pp. 9–30), and it probably forms the basis of al-Bāqillānī's list in *Tamhīd*, pp. 87.4–88.10.

6 The metaphors of the habitation and clothing were particularly preferred by Nestorian theologians at this time. Both Timothy I (Mingana, "Apology", p. 163) and ʿAmmār al-Baṣrī (Hayek, *ʿAmmār*, pp. 194.6–16, 196.13–16) made use of them. See also Yaḥyā Ibn ʿAdī in his letter to the Nestorian Abū al-Ḥasan al-Qāsim Ibn Ḥabīb, ed. E. Platti, *La grande polémique antinestorienne de Yaḥyā b. ʿAdī* (*Corpus Scriptorum Christianorum Orientalium* 427, 428 text; 437, 438 trans.), Louvain. 1981–2, text pp. 7.12f., 30.13ff.

7 Abū ʿĪsā employs the term *uqnūm*, transliterated from the Syriac *qnōmā*, which was commonly used at the time for an individual Person of the Godhead, and any identifiably individual being; see Hayek, *ʿAmmār*, pp. 50.1–4, 51.5–6 (in the variant form *qunūm*); al-Qāsim Ibn Ibrāhīm, *Radd*, p. 315.23–5 (identifying *uqnūm* as *shakhṣ*).

8 See Yaḥyā, *Polémique antinestorienne* text, pp. 6.9–7.7, giving a Jacobite account of the uniting that fully agrees with this statement.

9 This list of Christian sects corresponds closely to the one given at the end of the *Radd*, para. 352, where Abū ʿĪsā signals his intention to begin a refutation of these minority groups. The list he gives there contains these five groups together with six more.

10 An implication of this clear statement, coming after the reference to the minority groups, is that even as he began the *Radd* Abū ʿĪsā was aware that a full refutation of Christian doctrines would have to include these other groups. Hence his planned work against them, which he anticipates at the very end.

11 This is a reference to Abū ʿĪsā's major work on religions which is usually referred to by other authors as *Kitāb maqālāt al-nās* or simply *Kitāb al-maqālāt*. It contained descriptive accounts of the main beliefs prevalent in the Islamic world in the early ʿAbbasid period, and was clearly a source of information for the *Radd ʿalā al-Naṣārā*; see Thomas, "History of Religions", and pp. 30f. above.

12 E. Platti says that this explanation of phonetic distinctions is a later copyist's interpolation ("Doctrine des Chrétiens d'après Abū ʿĪsā al-Warrāq", p. 27, n. 1 to para. 13 of the Arabic text) though there seems no reason to agree. Abū ʿĪsā was as capable as anyone else of going into this degree of explanatory detail, and there are indications in the *Radd* that he personally heard Christians presenting their

arguments (para. 256, p. 206 below, where he mentions that some Melkites sometimes offer a particular answer, and Thomas, *Polemic*, p. 96.16, where he refers to *ajwibathum al-masmūʿa minhum*). The two sounds he attempts to distinguish are apparently a quiescent "v" in the case of *Sabāliyya* (it has disappeared completely in the form given by al-Qaḥṭabī in the list of sects from his work by Ibn al-Nadīm, *Fihrist*, p. 402.15, where it appears as *Sāliyya*), and a "p" in the case of *Bawliyya* (see van Ess, *Häresiographie*, p. 83, n. 2).

13 This is a reference to the Council of Nicea, which met in 325 with the main purpose of condemning the Christological teachings of Arius.

14 This version of the Creed is unlike any known from other sources, its main distinguishing features being the detailed description of the triune Godhead, and the restriction to articles on the Godhead and person of Christ. Since these are the two subjects of the *Radd*, it might follow that Abū ʿĪsā himself composed it, especially since the first article resembles his general account in the Introduction of the relationship between the Persons (Thomas, *Polemic*, p. 66.13–15). But some of its features argue against this. Firstly, the reference to the Spirit proceeding from both the Father and the Son, *wa-rūḥan munbathiqan baynahumā*, disagrees with explicit statements elsewhere in the *Radd* that it proceeds from the Father alone (Thomas, *Polemic*, pp. 66.15, 174.21–176.2 though in a passage which corresponds almost *verbatim* with the first of these and is probably based upon it or its source, ʿAbd al-Jabbār, *Mughnī*, vol. V, p. 81.12, gives this statement as *wa-lam tazul al-rūḥ fāʾidan min al-ab wa-al-ibn* = Abū ʿĪsā, *Radd*, *wa-lam yazul al-rūḥ munbathiqan min al-ab, wa-rubbamā jaʿalū makān "munbathiq" "fāʾidan"*, raising the possibility of textual alteration). And secondly, the reference to the Son clothing himself in the human body, *fa-tadarraʿa bihi*, recalls a Nestorian metaphor of the Incarnation (see n. 6 above).

But there are also difficulties which prevent an easy attribution to a Christian source. Firstly, no informed Christian would have acknowledged this as the Creed of Nicea, as Abū ʿĪsā so clearly assumes. Secondly, its intriguing reference to the doctrine of the double procession of the Holy Spirit has always been rejected by the Eastern churches, so its inclusion in a compilation that would derive from an eastern source is surprising (though it was not unknown in Muslim circles; al-Bāqillānī, *Tamhīd*, p. 86.15, mentions it without comment). And thirdly, references to clothing metaphors are absent from known versions of the Creed including Nestorian (see Gaudeul, *Riposte aux Chrétiens par ʿAlī al-Ṭabarī*, pp. V–X, quoting the Creed of Theodore of Mopsuestia and the version given in Arabic by ʿAlī al-Ṭabarī himself).

There is no doubt that the Creed is compatible with Christian beliefs, and it seems to be incompatible with what Abū ʿĪsā says about the Spirit elsewhere. So it may have originated among some Nestorians who maintained their own credal principles. But what remains surprising (whatever its origins) is that, whereas he shows such care elsewhere, Abū ʿĪsā should accept this as the Nicene Creed.

15 Having summarised views about the mode of uniting in the Messiah, in this paragraph Abū ʿĪsā presents views about the divine and human elements in his composite make-up. These form the basis of the second major section of the refutation against the Incarnation, paras. 230ff.

16 The origin of the comparison with the coal and the fire goes back at least to the fifth-century reflections upon the glowing coal in the vision of the prophet Isaiah,

Is. 6.6–7, in which it was employed to show how the humanity of Jesus was united so inextricably with the divine that it became incorruptible (A. Grillmeier, *Christ in Christian Tradition* 2/2, London, 1995, pp. 82–7). The reference to the *dinār* indicates that Monophysite Christians in the Islamic world had updated the image. Evidence that the coal metaphor was ecumenical in interpretation is shown in its use by both the Jacobite Abū Rāʾiṭa (Graf, *Abū Rāʾiṭa*, text, p. 33.13ff.), and the Nestorian ʿAmmār al-Baṣrī (Hayek, *ʿAmmār*, pp. 179 ult.–180.3), the latter following the precedent of Nestorius himself (Grillmeier, *Christ in Christian Tradition* 1, London, 1975, pp. 516f.).

17 For a fuller discussion of Abū ʿĪsā's understanding of the term *tadbīr*, see para. 218 and n. 50 below.

18 This is one of the handful of references in the *Radd* which show that Abū ʿĪsā was aware of the Christian meaning of the crucifixion. He does not comment on it in his refutation.

19 He now continues with the first part of his attack, against the doctrine of the Trinity, paras. 16–150.

20 This is one of the few structural markers visible in the work. See also paras. 220, 230, 304, and further 161, 187, 242 and 274.

21 Abū ʿĪsā frequently employs passive forms to introduce the Muslim question or rejoinder; here the Arabic is *yuqālu lahum*. In order to avoid clumsy English constructions, these have nearly always been translated with active forms or imperatives.

22 As shown in the discussion above, pp. 69–71, this was evidently a question which was familiar within Muslim–Christian debate in this period. It is clear from Abū ʿĪsā's formulation of it here that he, like other Muslims, understood the hypostases as separate entities capable of individual action. The word he employs, *uqnūm*, which is transliterated from the Syriac *qnōmā* (the variant *qunūm* also appears), was the most familiar Arabic term for the Greek *hypostasis* at this time.

23 Although Abū ʿĪsā does not acknowledge it, there is an echo here of Q 21.22, which was the origin of the proof of there being only one God based on the argument of mutual hindrance between two or more deities; see R. J. McCarthy, *The Theology of al-Ashʿarī*, Beirut, 1953, pp. 9f. and p. 10 n. 8.

24 In his Introduction, para. 2 (Thomas, *Polemic*, pp. 66f.), Abū ʿĪsā summarises the Melkite teaching on the Trinity as follows: "The Eternal One is one substance which possesses three hypostases: the hypostases are the substance but the substance is other than the hypostases." Al-Nāshiʾ al-Akbar attributes this interpretation specifically to a sub-group of the Melkites; van Ess, *Häresiographie*, p. 80.1–8, and see his discussion on pp. 76f. (German). The word employed for substance, *jawhar*, was becoming the most usual translation of *ousia* at this time.

25 See Abū ʿĪsā's description of the Melkite Christology in para. 14: "The Messiah was two substances and one hypostasis . . . an eternal hypostasis, the Word, and nothing more." This accurately summarises the Chalcedonian Definition which states that Christ was two distinct natures brought together "into one Person and one hypostasis . . . one and the same Son and only begotten God the Word".

26 Abū ʿĪsā may be acknowledging here that he has some knowledge of the contents of Christian scripture. He also reveals his awareness of the dangers in arguing from scriptural texts, since what can be claimed from one can be refuted from another.

27 This Melkite doctrine is summarised in the Introduction to the *Radd*, para. 10, see p. 86.11–15 above.
28 That is, from God's power. Abū ʿĪsā is consistently careful to avoid referring to the Christian Divinity as Allah. This impersonal usage conceals his assumption that the true God from whom power issues is the One whom both Muslims and Christians recognise, though differently, while it provides a means for him to get around saying directly that the true God is involved in this Melkite construction with a human.
29 See Theodore Abū Qurra, in Bacha, *Œuvres*, e.g. p. 183.3, 7 and 17, for the same idiom.
30 The terms *lāhūt* and *nāsūt* are commonly used by Arab Christian authors in this period, e.g. Theodore Abū Qurra in Bacha, *Œuvres*, pp. 183.13, 184.11; Abū Rāʾiṭa in Graf, *Abū Rāʾiṭa*, p. 51.7.
31 This and the other metaphorical explanations rejected in this paragraph refer back to Abū ʿĪsā's Introduction, para. 11, p. 88.5–15 above.
32 This recalls the quotation from Isaiah 7.14 in Matthew 1.23: "A virgin will conceive and bear a son, and he shall be called Emmanuel, a name which means 'God is with us'." The intentional use of the present tense, *talidu*, both here and in the repetition in para. 170 suggests that Abū ʿĪsā had some direct awareness of the Biblical wording of this prophecy.
33 This is because while the Jacobites can argue that the Messiah, who was a simple nature and hypostasis, experienced death as an individual even though only his humanity was affected, the Nestorians must concede that since the two natures and hypostases remained distinct, a part of the Messiah remained unaffected.
34 The order of these events recalls Q 4.157: "They did not kill him and did not crucify him."
35 This comment reflects Abū ʿĪsā's sense of distaste rather than his reaction to any real Christological explanations. He lists the theoretical possibilities as he sees them, though without reference to actual Melkite beliefs.
36 Abū ʿĪsā's conception of the term *jism*, "physical body", as a finite concrete entity, resembles that of contemporary Muʿtazilī thinking, in which despite variations it was always defined in material, spatial terms; see al-Ashʿarī, *Maqālāt*, pp. 301–6. See further nn. 47 and 54.
37 This is obviously a reversal of the normal relationship. ʿAmmār al-Baṣrī, in Hayek, *ʿAmmār*, p. 51.21f., demonstrates the same thinking in his clarifying statement: "Substance . . . encompasses many hypostases, as the substance of the human, *al-insān*, encompasses all the hypostases of humankind, *jamīʿ aqānīm al-ins.*"
38 Abū ʿĪsā's point here is that even if Mary gave birth to the universal human in the form of the individual child, as the Melkites maintain, rather than as the universal human substance itself, she must nevertheless have given birth to two sons. Here, as throughout the *Radd*, he equates a named reality, in this case the universal human, with a discrete entity.
39 If through the different activities and moral attitudes of its individual beings the human universal can be said to be involved in opposite and contradictory actions, it may simultaneously both obey and disobey divine commands. With respect to an omnipotent and omniscient God, this means that he has imposed requirements which he knows cannot be fulfilled and appears as unjust and intolerant.

This implication, which in the next sentence Abū ʿĪsā concedes is something his Christian opponents have not drawn, recalls brief statements quoted from his lost *Al-gharīb al-mashriqī* by the fourth-/tenth-century author Abū Ḥayyān al-Tawḥīdī in his *Kitāb al-imtāʿ wa-al-muʾānasa*, ed. A. Amīn and A. al-Zayn, Cairo, 1939–44, vol. III, p. 192.4–6, 9–12. There Abū ʿĪsā contends that since someone who issues a command in the knowledge that it cannot be carried out is foolish, *safīh*, and since God knows that unbelievers will not believe, it follows that there cannot be any logical reason to command them to believe (see Thomas, *Polemic*, p. 27 and n. 92; Urvoy, *Libres penseurs*, p. 114). If his intention in this syllogism is to undermine Muslims' certainties about a just and wise God who also imposes the demand that all must believe in him or be punished, he appears to be applying its implications to the arguments of his Melkite opponents, and leading them to see that their concept of the universal human threatens the coherence of their belief in God.

40 Both Christians and Muslims would agree that such experiences are inappropriate for either the divine nature or the universal human.

41 Abū ʿĪsā presses the logic of the Melkite interpretation to its limit. Since they agree that in the uniting the divine and human became one, then it must follow that the divine and the universal human became one. But as he shows in paras. 189 on, it is impossible to explain this without giving the universal the attributes of an individual. So, if the universal cannot unite, the act of uniting must have taken place between the divine nature and individual human nature, which is identical with the teaching of the Nestorians and Jacobites.

42 See Abū ʿĪsā's Introduction to the *Radd*, para. 5, in Thomas, *Polemic*, pp. 66–7.

43 This is the Nestorian interpretation of the uniting, which Chalcedonians would condemn.

44 I.e. the universal human and the individual human.

45 The distinction between the two forms Yasūʿ and ʿĪsā suggests that Abū ʿĪsā may be reproducing a brief Christian statement he knows in which the name has intentionally been preserved in its non-Qurʾanic Arabic form in order to distinguish the figure of Christian belief from the ʿĪsā of the Qurʾan. The convert ʿAlī al-Ṭabarī customarily uses the form Yasūʿ when referring to Christian teachings about Jesus, *Radd ʿalā al-Naṣārā*, e.g., pp. 121.7, 123.8, 131.6, 134.14, but pointedly uses ʿĪsā when referring to Jesus as one of the line of prophets, *Radd*, e.g., pp. 120.22, 121.2, 130.14.

46 This is one of the rare explanations of Abū ʿĪsā's method in the *Radd*. He concedes that he has gone beyond the precise statements of his opponents, but defends himself by pointing out that he wants to refute all possible variants of the Melkite interpretation in order to remove any grounds for defence. This approach suggests that he intended the work as a source or handbook for actual debates; see Thomas, *Polemic*, pp. 56f., for indications of the same general intention in the first part of the *Radd*.

47 When referring to the human body of the Messiah, Abū ʿĪsā uses *jasad* in contrast to *jism*, by which he designates one of the fundamental units of temporal being; see n. 36 above.

48 Abū ʿĪsā again reveals his comprehensive, if rather artificial, method as he examines this docetic alternative for purely theoretical purposes.

49 These details of Christ's passion, and particularly the allusion to Jesus' side being

pierced after his death, referred to in John 19.34 (it also appears after Matthew 27.49 in some Gospel witnesses), suggest the extent of Abū ʿĪsā's knowledge of the details of Christian teachings.

50 See Abū ʿĪsā's Introduction, para. 15, p. 94.10–12 above, where it is given as a teaching held by many of the Melkites. Their use of *tadbīr*, which is a translation of the Greek *oikonomia* (Griffith, "*Kitāb al-Burhān*", p. 157; Platti, *Incarnation*, trans., pp. XVIII, 63 n. 1), as the opposite of physical sensation is apparently intended to explain how the Word was really involved in the Passion without actually undergoing human experiences. Elsewhere in the *Radd* Abū ʿĪsā quotes it in Christian usage in two alternative metaphors of the Incarnation: "[The Word] inhered in it [the body] and controlled though it and by means of it", *ḥallat fīhi fa-dabbarat bihi wa-ʿalā yadīh*; "it did not inhere in it but it controlled by means of it and appeared through it to creation", *lam taḥlul fīhi wa-lakinnahā dabbarat ʿalā yadīh wa ẓaharat minhu li-hādhā al-khalq* (para.11, p. 88.8f. above). And the Nestorian ʿAmmār al-Baṣrī employs it with the same meaning: "He resided in a body from us by control in order to be near his creation, but without being confined or contained by it", *sakana bi-al-tadbīr fī jasadinā li-yataqarraba min khalqihi bi-ghayri taḥdīdi wa-lā iḥāṭati bihi* (Hayek, *ʿAmmār*, p. 72.2f; see also p. 71.9f). These instances suggest that Arab Christians employed the term to mean that the Word overshadowed or influenced the being and actions of the Messiah without losing its divine attributes or being restricted by the human body. But despite their efforts Abū ʿĪsā in his habitual manner denies the subtlety of their distinction and argues that the Word must nevertheless have entered into the human experiences of the Messiah. He himself employs the term in para. 182, p. 120.6 below, in a more ordinary sense to indicate the Messiah's conscious control over himself.

51 This appears to be a way of saying that it was the human individual, who in Melkite theology would be a single hypostasis of the universal human substance and so might be referred to as its "son".

52 This heading is the only one of its kind remaining in the work. Its presence indicates that Abū ʿĪsā's original may have contained many more structural markers.

53 The distaste evident in this remark about the restriction imposed upon the Godhead reflects Abū ʿĪsā's basic preoccupation with removing any limits at all from him; on this see pp. 31–3 above, and Thomas, *Polemic*, pp. 29f.

54 As he moves from attacking the idea of mingling between the divinity and human body, *jasad*, of the Messiah to a more general consideration of this physical process, Abū ʿĪsā employs the technical term *jism*, on which see n. 36.

55 In this comparison between the miracles of Jesus and those of other prophets Abū ʿĪsā makes use of a motif which formed an important element in many Muslim polemical works; see pp. 68f. above. Where other authors often list a series of miracles of Jesus and other prophets, he in typical fashion simply alludes to the principle in the comparison.

56 This is an allusion to Jesus' miracle mentioned in Q 3.49 and 5.110, of which it is more or less a quotation. Abū ʿĪsā's point is that his Christian opponents may be attaching weight to Jesus' act of creating birds, *idh takhluqu min al-ṭīni ka-hay'atī al-ṭayr*, as an indication that he had been delegated creative power and so could be said to have "control", *tadbīr*. But he rejects the claim without any discussion, on the grounds that the miracle is only a sign of Jesus' prophetic status and no more. But he may not represent the whole of contemporary thinking in this, since

a disciple of al-Naẓẓām, Aḥmad Ibn Ḥā'iṭ (died *c.* 230/845), is known to have argued on the basis of this Qur'anic miracle that Jesus was a second creator (al-Shahrastānī, *Milal*, pp. 42.2–14, 44.2–13; and see Thomas, *Polemic*, pp. 5–8). Abū ʿĪsā's airy rejection of this possibility may thus refer to a much wider and more profound debate going on in the early third/ninth century.

57 See n. 55 above. He intimates here that he knows actual comparisons of individual miracles performed by Jesus and the Hebrew prophets.

58 Abū ʿĪsā's contention is that the distinction made by the Christians is arbitrary, since there was no unique distinguishing sign in the actions of the Messiah that singled him out from the prophets or indeed other people. Thus they have no cogent reason for preferring the appearance of God in the actions of Jesus over his appearance in the actions of anyone else.

Al-Māturīdī tersely makes the same point when he replies to a Christian opponent who is attempting to maintain that God was uniquely present in Christ: "He will say, Because God made miracles appear through him; say: He made them appear through Moses, so say he is another son"; Thomas, "Abū Manṣūr al-Māturīdī", p. 52.22.

59 I.e. the cumulative tradition of Christian teaching.

60 This recalls the argument in one of the Melkite Theodore Abū Qurra's short works, that since God is logically head, *ra'īs*, in eternity, he must have an eternal relationship with another being, *mar'ūs*, who can only be a son of his own nature; Bacha, *Œuvres*, pp. 91–104. ʿAbd al-Jabbār knew that this argument came from Theodore, and rejected it, *Mughnī*, vol. V, pp. 144.11–145.7. If Abū ʿĪsā's reference to a number of scholars employing an argument like this is accurate, it appears that Theodore's version is only one among many.

The necessary relationship between God and created things to which Abū ʿĪsā draws attention here was avoided at all costs by Muslim theologians at this time. The solution favoured by most of them was that creating was not an essential attribute of God, and so he did not have to be Creator eternally; see al-Ashʿarī, *Maqālāt*, e.g., p. 505.5ff.

61 The distinction between the Messiah and other human beings does not depend upon any quality in his human nature but upon the fact that it was with him that the divine nature chose to unite.

62 Here and in the argument that follows, the differences between Christian and Muslim understandings of the virgin birth are exposed. While Christians would adduce the miracle as evidence of Jesus' divine sonship, following Matthew 1.18–25 and Luke 1.26–38, Muslims see it only as evidence of God's power to create in any way he wills, following Q 2.117, 3.47.

63 Again Abū ʿĪsā displays his detailed knowledge of the differing Christological positions. His argument in this paragraph and the whole section on the Nestorian Christology so far is an attempt to probe into the sharp distinction they make between the divine and human natures in Christ; as he relates in the Introduction, para. 14, pp. 90.22–92.1 above, they acknowledge two hypostases and substances united only in volition, *mashī'a*.

64 In this exclamation that it is outrageous to object to the idea that the Messiah was human, Abū ʿĪsā reveals his staunch loyalty to the radical distinction between the one, single God and all other beings. His argument implies that if the Nestorians acknowledge that Christ could act as a single individual they are virtually agree-

ing with the view of Muslims that the Messiah and all created beings acted under the guidance and influence of God.

65 The epithet *ibn al-bashar* could be a literal translation of the enigmatic title *ho huios tou anthrōpou*, which Jesus uses of himself in the Gospels and by which he appears to indicate his own unique part in the coming of the Kingdom of God. But if the title has come to Abū ʿĪsā from Christian sources (and his aside in para. 302, *kamā taqūlūna fī al-Masīḥ*, suggests that it has) he ignores its resonance entirely and employs it simply as evidence of Jesus' humanity. See also para. 341.

66 See e.g. John 1.14, 1.18, and also the Nicene Creed, "eternally begotten of the Father".

67 See John 10.30, and also 17.11, 17.22.

68 Platti's reading of *Ahl al-Ijbār* (*Incarnation*, text, p. 113, trans., p. 98) for what the Christian copyists of the MSS found incomprehensible, seems obviously correct. Abū ʿĪsā also refers to this group in the part of his *Radd* against the Trinity; Thomas, *Polemic*, p. 170.10, and n. 71 (p. 206). Known also as the Mujbira and Jabriyya, they were credited with the teaching that all human actions were determined and therefore compelled by God; see *EI*[2] vol. II, p. 365, art. "Djabriyya".

69 Abū ʿĪsā employs the term *ajsām* here, indicating that he means concrete units of temporal reality (rather than human bodies, *ajsād*; see nn. 47 and 54). His implication is that in this Christian argument humans become creators.

70 The Nestorians attempt to draw a distinction between the divine and human wills coalescing into one, and agreeing as two on the one action. Abū ʿĪsā proceeds to investigate this in detail in the following paragraphs.

71 He presumably means the Muʿtazila, who were known as the People of Unity and Justice. His own insistence that God must act in a reasonable and just way and that any claim that impugns this must be flawed, which is exhibited vividly in the brief statements quoted from him by Abu Hayyan al-Tawḥīdī (see n. 39 above), seems to underlie his argument at this point.

72 Abū ʿĪsā neatly forces his Nestorian opponents to accept that in the same way as they talk about conformity of divine and human wills into one, they must concede the possibility of conformity of divine and human natures into one. Even though this is not a joining of the two into one individual, which would be similar to the Jacobite Christology, it threatens the Nestorian insistence upon two distinct natures and individual beings.

73 Abū ʿĪsā refers back to the first major part of his attack on the Incarnation. His arguments there against the Nestorians on the act of uniting are also relevant here.

74 The distinction between these two views is brought out more clearly in para. 298, pp. 232–5 below, where Abū ʿĪsā indicates that the first is equivalent to saying that the Messiah was actually two substances.

75 See Thomas, *Polemic*, p. 66, para. 2, for Abū ʿĪsā's summary of the Melkite Trinitarian formula, and pp. 98–113, paras. 60–9, for his demonstration that if the divine substance is distinct from the three hypostases it must be a fourth constituent of the Godhead.

76 See Abū ʿĪsā's Introduction, para. 10, p. 86.11f. above.

77 See Abū ʿĪsā's Introduction, para. 10, p. 86.12–15 above.

78 This refers back to the earlier argument about *tadbīr* in paras. 226f.

79 This surviving subtitle indicates that there may have been many more in the original work.

80 As the ensuing argument shows, the distinction Abū ʿĪsā has in mind between the two alternatives *muḥdath wa-qadīm* and *muḥdath qadīm* is that according to the former the two natures acted in concert, while according to the latter they acted as one agent and became fused together.

81 See n. 68 to para. 249 above.

82 See Abū ʿĪsā's Introduction, para. 12, p. 88.16–19 above.

83 By combining with the human into one entity the hypostasis of the divine Word would cease to participate in the divine substance and would come to participate in the substance of humanity.

84 See Abū ʿĪsā's Introduction, para. 14, p. 92.13–19 above, and n. 16.

85 I.e. that the Word and human remained distinct as hypostases and natures.

86 See Q 42.11. As one of the very few quotations from the Qurʾan which appear in the *Radd*, this was presumably chosen with great care. By means of it Abū ʿĪsā may have intended tacitly to indicate that there was no need for God to be either trinitarian or incarnate to enjoy a full relationship with his creation. In later centuries Ibn ʿArabī cited the verse as a prime example of the paradox of God-in-himself and God-for-us (*Kitāb al-jalāl wa-al-jamāl*, in *Rasāʾil Ibn ʿArabī*, Hyderabad, 1948, vol. II, pp. 5f.) which exactly amplifies this point. One of the markers which usually indicate the end of an argument from Abū ʿĪsā or a reply from Yaḥyā, appearing as a dot within two concentric circles (as opposed to the dot within one circle which indicates a lesser division within an argument) is inserted at the end of this quotation.

87 This may have been the conclusion of the first version of the *Radd*; see pp. 62–3 above. If so, the long attack against the Jacobites, which itself forms the third part of the second section which began at para. 230, ended with nothing more than a single pious exclamation (just like the end of the attack against the Melkites in this section, para. 303), and the whole *Radd* was brought to a close with just one sentence and the quotation of Q 1.2. But since the opening *khuṭba* is also barely more than a sentence long (see para.1, p. 86.4–6 above, though as it survives in summarised form, its original length is difficult to gauge exactly), this is perhaps only to be expected.

88 Abū ʿĪsā intimates at the very beginning of the *Radd* that he will not discuss minor sects: "Among the Jacobites there are other divisions which differ from these [the majority of the Jacobites] over the uniting and who the Messiah was. They have other names, but we shall not state these nor discuss their views in this book, nor the views of other Christian divisions such as the Maronites, the Julianists, the Sabellians, the Arians, the Paulicians, or any other of their sects. For we have written this book specifically about the majority of these three sects and not others" (para.12, p. 88.20–5 above). He now states his intention to go on to refute these sects, revealing that all along he has had in mind a complete refutation of all forms of Christian teaching.

89 Yaḥyā cuts Abū ʿĪsā's declaration short, maybe because in the middle of copying this version he has come across another, which he regards as superior, *al-nuskha al-mukhtāra*, and in which he has found the brief arguments against all three Christian sects that follow.

90 The end of "this passage ", *hādhā al-mawḍiʿ*, is clearly marked, and since its beginning is not indicated in any special way it must presumably begin at the marker which concludes the argument in para. 345, referred to in n. 86 above.

91 See al-Jāḥiẓ, *Radd*, p. 26.6–17, drawing similar implications from the proposition that Jesus may have been God's adopted Son.

92 This is a free quotation of Q 112.2–4. It marks the conclusion of the longer, second version of the *Radd*, and apt as it is at this point, its brevity and abruptness may result not only from Abū ʿĪsā's normal practice (see n. 87 above), but also from his urgent desire to move on to lesser Christian sects. At the start of the *Radd* (para.12, p. 88.24f. above) he states that in this work he is concentrating only on the Nestorians, Melkites and the majority of the Jacobites (see n. 88). But he clearly means now to complement it with a further study.

93 Abū ʿĪsā lists the Maronites, Julianists, Sabellians, Arians and Paulicians at the beginning of the *Radd* (see n. 88 above), where he informs the reader: "We have previously given descriptions of the Christian divisions, their titles and names, and reported some of the reasons for the distinctions between their beliefs and the proofs employed by each group, in the book in which we have described the views of people and the differences between them, *maqālāt al-nās wa-ikhtilāfihim*" (pp. 88.25–90.2 above). It is reasonable to assume that he drew upon the information he had gathered there for his projected work. But did he ever write it? We may suppose that if Yaḥyā knew it he would have given some idea about its contents, so his silence suggests he did not.

Scanty evidence from the little-known early fourth-/tenth-century Muslim, Aḥmad b. Muḥammad al-Qaḥṭabī, points to the possibility that the work did appear and had some limited circulation. For in the list of Christian sects that is preserved from this author's lost *Radd ʿalā al-Naṣārā* by Ibn al-Nadīm, all the sects mentioned by Abū ʿĪsā are presented, and in the same order and form as here (see Thomas, *Polemic*, p. 42). J. van Ess has suggested that this similarity can be explained by al-Qaḥṭabī having incorporated Abū ʿĪsā's list into his own (*Häresiographie*, pp. 82f. German). This raises the possibility that he may have taken it from Abū ʿĪsā's projected work, though since he could also have found it here, or in Abū ʿĪsā's *Maqālāt*, or indeed in Abū ʿĪsā's putative original source, it does not provide more than a possibility that the work on subsidiary sects appeared.

The same applies to ʿAbd al-Jabbār (*Mughnī*, vol. V, pp. 84.19ff., 146.12ff. and 146.9–11), and al-Shahrastānī (*Milal*, p. 173.12f.), who may also have been dependent upon Abū ʿĪsā (*Häresiographie*, p. 84, German). The only solid evidence would be actual arguments against these Christian sects surviving in a number of later Muslim authors, and attributable to the same original.

94 See Q 2.255, 42.4.

BIBLIOGRAPHY

al-Aʿasam, A., *History of Ibn ar-Rīwandī, the Heretic*, Beirut, 1975

al-ʿAbbāsī, ʿAbd al-Raḥīm, *Kitāb maʿāhid al-tanṣīṣ*, ed. M. M. ʿAbd al-Ḥamīd, Cairo, 1947–8, vol. I, p. 158.11–22

ʿAbd al-Jabbār, Abū al-Ḥasan b. Muḥammad, *Al-mughnī fī abwāb al-tawḥīd wa-al-ʿadl*, Cairo, 1958–65 (*Mughni*)

Tathbīt dalāʾil al-nubuwwa, ed. ʿA.-K. ʿUthmān, Beirut, 1966 (*Tathbīt*)

Abel, A., *Le livre pour la réfutation des trois sectes chrétiennes*, Brussels, 1949 (duplicated)

"Le Chapitre sur le Christianisme dans le 'Tamhīd' d'al-Bāqillānī", in *Etudes d'Orientalisme dédiées à la mémoire de Lévi-Provençal*, vol. I, Paris, 1962, pp. 1–11

"Masques et visages dans la polémique islamo-chrétienne", *Tavola rotonda sul tema: Christianesimo e Islamismo, Roma, 17–18 Aprile, 1972*, Rome, 1974, pp. 85–131

Abrahamov, B., *Islamic Theology, Traditionalism and Rationalism*, Edinburgh, 1998

Abū Rāʾiṭa, see Graf, *Abū Rāʾiṭa*

Allard, M., *Le problème des attributs divins dans la doctine d'al-Ashʿarī et de ses premiers grands disciples*, Beirut, 1965

ʿAmmār al-Baṣrī, see Hayek, *ʿAmmār*

al-Ashʿarī, Abū al-Ḥasan, *Maqālāt al-Islamiyyīn*, ed. H. Ritter, Istanbul, 1930 (repr. Wiesbaden, 1980)

Atallah, W., *Les Idoles de Hichām Ibn al-Kalbī*, Paris, 1969

Bacha, C., *Les Œuvres arabes de Théodore Aboucara*, Beirut, 1904 (*Œuvres*)

al-Bāqillānī, Abū Bakr, *Kitāb al-tamhīd*, ed. R. J. McCarthy, Beirut, 1957 (*Tamhīd*)

al-Bīrūnī, Abū Rayhan, *Taḥqīq mā li-al-Hind*, ed. E. Sachau, London, 1887

Bosworth, C. E., "The Concept of *Dhimma* in Early Islam", in B. Braude and B. Lewis, eds., *Christians and Jews in the Ottoman Empire*, New York and London, 1982, vol. I, pp. 37–51

Calder, N., "The Barāhima: Literary Construct and Historical Reality", *Bulletin of the School of Oriental and African Studies* 57, 1994, pp. 40–51

Charfī, A., "La fonction historique de la polémique islamochrétienne à l'époque abbaside", in S. K. Samir and J. Nielsen, *Christian Arabic Apologetics during the Abbasid Period (750–1258)*, Leiden, 1994, pp. 44–56

Cheikho, H. P., *Dialectique du langage sur Dieu, lettre de Timothée I (728–823) à Serge*, Rome, 1983

Chokr, M., *Zandaqa et Zindīqs en Islam au second siècle de l'héjire*, Damascus, 1993

Coope, J., *The Martyrs of Córdoba*, Lincoln and London, 1995

Dick, I., "Deux écrits inédits de Théodore Abuqurra", *Le Muséon* 72, 1959, pp. 53–67

"Un continuateur arabe de saint Jean Damascène; Théodore Abuqurra, évêque melkite de Harran", *Proche-Orient Chrétien* 12, 1962, pp. 209–23, 319–31, 13, 1963, pp. 114–29

Théodore Abuqurra, Traité de l'existence du Créateur et de la vraie religion (*Patrimoine arabe chrétien* 3), Jounieh and Rome, 1982

Encyclopaedia of Islam, new edition, Leiden and London, 1960 continuing (*EI*²)

Endress, G., *The Works of Yaḥyā Ibn ʿAdī*, Wiesbaden, 1977

Ess, J. van, *Frühe muʿtazilitische Häresiographie*, Beirut, 1971, ed. and trans. al-Nāshiʾ al-Akbar, *Kitāb al-awsaṭ fī al-maqālāt* (*Häresiographie*)

"The Beginnings of Islamic Theology", in J. E. Murdoch and E. D. Sylla, eds., *The Cultural Context of Medieval Learning*, Dordrecht and Boston, 1973, pp. 87–111

Theologie und Gesellschaft im 2. und 3. Jahrhundert Hidschra, eine Geschichte des religiösen Denkens im frühen Islam, Berlin/New York, 1991–7

Fakhry, M., *Islamic Occasionalism*, London, 1958

Fattal, A., *Le statut légal des non-musulmans en pays d'Islam*, Beirut, 1958

Fiey, J. M., "Ḥabib Abū Rāʾiṭa n'était pas évêque de Takrit", in *Actes du deuxième congrès international d'études arabes Chrétiennes, (Oosterhesselen, 1984)*, Rome, 1986, pp. 211–14

Finkel, J., "A Risāla of al-Jāḥiẓ", *Journal of the American Oriental Society* 47, 1927, pp. 311–34

Frank, R. M., *The Metaphysics of Created Being according to Abū l-Hudhayl al-ʿAllāf*, Istanbul, 1966

Gaudeul, J.-M., *Riposte aux Chrétiens par ʿAlī al-Ṭabarī*, Rome, 1995; see ʿAlī b. Rabban al-Ṭabarī

La correspondance de ʿUmar et Léon (vers 900), Rome, 1995

Gimaret, D., *Une lecture muʿtazilite du Coran*, Louvain–Paris, 1994

Gimaret, D., and Monnot, G., eds., *Livre des religions et des sectes*, vol. I, Louvain, 1986

Goddard, H., *A History of Christian–Muslim Relations*, Edinburgh, 2000

Graf, G., *Die arabischen Schriften des Theodor Abū Qurra*, Paderborn, 1910, German trans. (*Arabischen Schriften*)

Die Schriften des Jacobiten Ḥabīb Ibn Ḫidma Abū Rāʾiṭa (*Corpus Scriptorum Christianorum Orientalium* 130 text, 131 trans.), Louvain, 1951 (*Abū Rāʾiṭa*)

Griffith, S., "Ḥabīb ibn Ḫidmah Abū Rāʾiṭah, a Christian *mutakallim* of the First Abbasid Century", *Oriens Christianus* 64, 1980, pp. 161–201

"The Concept of *al-Uqnūm* in ʿAmmār al-Baṣrī's Apology for the Doctrine of the Trinity", in K. Samir, ed., *Actes du premier congrès international d'études arabes chrétiennes (Goslar, Septembre 1980)*, Rome, 1982, pp. 169–91

"ʿAmmār al-Baṣrī's *Kitāb al-Burhān*: Christian *Kalām* in the first Abbasid Century", *Le Muséon* 96, 1983, pp. 145–81

"The Prophet Muḥammad, his Scripture and his Message according to the Christian Apologies in Arabic and Syriac from the First Abbasid Century", in T. Fahd, ed., *La vie du prophète Mahomet, Colloque de Strasbourg 1980*, Paris, 1983, pp. 99–146, repr. in S. H. Griffith, *Arabic Christianity in the Monasteries of Ninth-Century Palestine*, Aldershot, 1992, no. I

"Faith and Reason in Christian Kalām: Theodore Abū Qurrah on Discerning the True Religion", in S. K. Samir and J. S. Nielsen, eds., *Christian Arab Apologetics during the Abbasid Period (750–1258)*, Leiden, 1994, pp. 1–43

"The Monks of Palestine and the Growth of Christian Literature in Arabic", *The Muslim World* 78, 1988, pp. 1–28

"Reflections on the Biography of Theodore Abū Qurrah", *Parole de l'Orient* 18, 1993, pp. 143–70

"The View of Islam from the Monasteries of Palestine", *Islam and Christian–Muslim Relations* 7, 1996, pp. 9–28

"The Monk in the Emir's *Majlis*: Reflections on a Popular Genre of Christian Literary Apologetics in Arabic in the Early Islamic Period", in H. Lazarus-Yafeh, M. R. Cohen, S. Somekh, S. H. Griffith, eds., *The Majlis, Interreligious Encounters in Medieval Islam*, Wiesbaden, 1999, pp. 13–65

Grillmeier, A., *Christ in Christian Tradition*, London, 1975–95

Gutas, D., *Greek Thought, Arabic Culture*, London and New York, 1998

Haddad, W. Z., "A Tenth-Century Speculative Theologian's Refutation of the Basic Doctrines of Christianity: al-Bāqillānī (d. A.D. 1013)", in Y. Y. Haddad and W. Z. Haddad, eds., *Christian–Muslim Encounters*, Gainsville, 1995, pp. 82–94

al-Ḥasan al-Baṣrī, see Ritter, "Studien"

Hayek, M., *ʿAmmār al-Baṣrī, théologie et controverses*, Beirut, 1977, ed. and trans., *Kitāb al-burhān, Kitāb masāʾil wa-ajwiba* (*ʿAmmār*)

Hoyland, R., *Seeing Islam as Others Saw It*, Princeton, 1997

Ibn al-Jawzī, Abū al-Faraj, *Al-muntaẓam fī tārīkh al-mulūk wa-al-umam*, Hyderabad, 1357/1938

Ibn al-Nadīm, Abū al-Faraj, *Kitāb al-Fihrist*, ed. M. Riḍā-Tajaddud, Tehran, 1971 (*Fihrist*)

al-Jāḥiẓ, Abū ʿUthmān, *Al-Radd ʿalā al-Naṣārā*, ed. J. Finkel, *Thalāth rasāʾil li-Abi ʿUthmān . . . al-Jāḥiẓ*, Cairo, 1926, trans. I.S. Allouche, "Un traité de polémique christiano-musulmane au IXe siècle", *Hesperis* 26, 1939, pp. 123–55; see also Finkel, "A Risāla of al-Jāḥiẓ" (*Radd*)

Kitāb al-ḥayawān, ed. ʿA.-S. Hārūn, Cairo, 1965–9

John of Damascus, *The Fount of Knowledge*, ed. J. P. Migne, *Patrologia Graeca* XCIV, Paris, 1860, cols. 521–1228; trans. S.D.F. Salmond, *John of Damascus, Exposition of the Orthodox Faith* (*A Select Library of the Nicene and post-Nicene Fathers of the Christian Church*, second series vol. 9/2), Oxford and New York, 1889; F.A. Chase, *Saint John of Damascus, Writings* (*The Fathers of the Church, a New Translation* vol. 37), Washington DC, 1958

al-Khayyāṭ, Abū al-Ḥusayn, *Kitāb al-intiṣār*, ed. and trans. A. Nader, Beirut, 1957

Kilpatrick, H., "Representations of Social Intercourse between Muslims and non-Muslims in some Medieval *Adab* Works", in J. Waardenburg, ed., *Muslim Perceptions of Other Religions, a Historical Survey*, Oxford, 1999, pp. 213–24

Lewis, B., *The Jews of Islam*, Princeton, 1984

McCarthy, R. J., *The Theology of al-Ashʿarī*, Beirut, 1953

McDermott, M. J., "Abū ʿĪsā al Warrāq on the *Dahriyya*", *Mélanges de l'Université St Joseph* 50, 1984, p. 387

Madelung, W., *Der Imam al-Qāsim Ibn Ibrāhīm und die Glaubenslehre der Zaiditen*, Berlin, 1965

"Bemerkungen zur imamitischen Firaq-Literatur" *Der Islam* 43, 1967, pp. 37–52

"Abū ʿĪsā al-Warrāq über die Bardesaniten, Marcioniten und Kantäer", in A. R. Roemer and A. Noth, *Studien zur Geschichte und Kultur des Vorderen Orients*, Leiden, 1981, pp. 210–24, reprinted in W. Madelung, *Religious Schools and Sects in Early Islam*, London, 1985, no. XX

Martin, R. C., "The Role of the Baṣrah Muʿtazilah in Formulating the Doctrine of the Prophetic Miracle", *Journal of Near Eastern Studies* 39, 1980, pp. 175–89

Martin, R. C. *et al.*, *Defenders of Reason in Islam*, Oxford, 1997

Massignon, L., "La politique islamo-chrétienne des scribes nestoriens de Deïr Qunnā à la cour de Baghdad au IXe siècle de notre ère", *Vivre et Penser* 2nd series 2, 1942, pp. 7–14, reprinted in *Opera Minora*, Beirut, 1963, vol. I, pp. 250–7

al-Masʿūdī, Abū al-Ḥasan, *Murūj al-dhahab*, ed. and trans. C. Barbier de Meynard and Pavet de Courteille, Paris, 1861–77

al-Māturīdī, Abū Manṣūr, *Kitāb al-tawḥīd*, ed. F. Kholeif, Beirut, 1970

Mingana, A., "The Apology of Timothy the Patriarch before the Caliph Mahdi, Woodbrooke Studies 3", *Bulletin of the John Rylands Library* 12, 1928, pp. 137–292 ("Apology")

Modarressi, H., "Early Debates on the Integrity of the Qurʾan. A brief survey", *Studia Islamica* 77, 1993, pp. 5–39

Monnot, G., *Penseurs musulmans et religions iraniennes*, Paris, 1974

"Les doctrines des Chrétiens dans le 'Moghnī' de ʿAbd al-Jabbār", *Mélanges de l'Institut Dominicain d'Etudes Orientales* 16, 1983, pp. 9–30

Islam et religions, Paris, 1986

"Abū Qurra et la pluralité des religions", *Revue de l'Histoire des Religions* 208, 1991, pp. 49–71

al-Najāshī, Aḥmad b. ʿAlī, *Kitāb al-rijāl*, Bombay, 1317/1898–9

al-Nāshiʾ al-Akbar, Abū al-ʿAbbās, *Awsaṭ*, see van Ess, *Häresiographie*

Nau, F., "Un colloque du Patriarche Jean avec l'Emir des Agaréens", *Journal Asiatique* onzième série 5, 1915, pp. 225–71

Périer, A., "Un traité de Yaḥyā ben ʿAdī", *Revue de l'Orient Chrétien* 22, 1920–1, pp. 3–21

Peters, J.R.T.M., *God's Created Speech*, Leiden, 1976

Platti, E., *La grande polémique antinestorienne de Yaḥyā b. ʿAdī* (*Corpus Scriptorum Christianorum Orientalium* 427, 428 text; 437, 438 trans.), Louvain, 1981–2

Abū ʿĪsā al-Warrāq, Yaḥyā Ibn ʿAdī, de l'Incarnation (*Corpus Scriptorum Christianorum Orientalium*, 490 text, 491 trans.), Louvain, 1987

"La doctrine des Chrétiens d'après Abū ʿĪsā al-Warrāq dans sa traité sur la Trinité", *Mélanges de l'Institut Dominicain d'Etudes Orientales* 20, 1991, pp. 7–30

Putman, H., *L'Eglise et l'Islam sous Timothée I (780–823)*, Beirut, 1975

al-Qāsim b. Ibrāhīm al-Ḥasanī, *Al-radd ʿalā al-Naṣārā*, ed. I. di Matteo, "Confutazione contro i Cristiani dello zaydita al-Qāsim b. Ibrāhīm", *Rivista degli Studi Orientali* 9, 1921–2, pp. 301–64 (*Radd*)

Rissanen, S., *Theological Encounter of Oriental Christians with Islam during Abbasid Rule*, Åbo, Finland, 1993

Ritter, H., "Studien zur Geschichte der islamischen Frommigkeit: I. Ḥasan al-Baṣrī", *Der Islam* 21, 1933, pp. 1–83; partial trans. in A. Rippin and J. Knappert, *Textual Sources for the Study of Islam*, Chicago, 1989, pp. 115–21

Rozemund, K., *La christologie de Saint Jean Damascène*, Ettal, 1959

Rudolph, U., *Al-Māturīdī und die sunnitische Theologie in Samarkand*, Leiden, 1997

Sahas, D. J., *John of Damascus on Islam, the "Heresy of the Ishmaelites"*, Leiden, 1972

Samir, S. K., "La réponse d'al-Safī Ibn al-ʿAssāl à la Réfutation des Chrétiens de ʿAlī al-Ṭabarī", *Parole de l'Orient* 11, 1983, pp. 281–328

"The Earliest Arab Apology for Christianity (*c.* 750)" in S. K. Samir and J. Nielsen, *Christian Arabic Apologetics during the Abbasid Period (750–1258)*, Leiden, 1994, pp. 57–114

"The Role of Christians in the Fatimid Government services of Egypt to the Reign of al-Ḥāfiẓ", *Medieval Encounters* 2, 1996, pp. 177–92

"The Christian Communities, Active Members of Arab Society throughout History", in A. Pacini, ed., *Christian Communities in the Arab Middle East*, Oxford, 1998, pp. 67–91

Sbath, P., *Vingt traités philosophiques et apologétiques d'auteurs arabes chrétiens*, Cairo, 1929

al-Shahrastānī, Abū al-Fatḥ, *Kitāb al-milal wa-al-niḥal*, ed. W. Cureton, London, 1846

al-Sharīf al-Murtaḍā, *Al-Shāfī fī al-Imāma*, ed. ʿA. Z. al-Ḥusaynī, Tehran, 1986

Sourdel, D., "Un pamphlet musulman anonyme d'époque ʿabbaside contre les Chrétiens", *Revue des Etudes Islamiques* 34, 1966, pp. 1–33

Stillman, N., *The Jews of Arab Lands*, Philadelphia, 1979

Stroumsa, S., "The *Barāhima* in Early Kalām", *Jerusalem Studies in Arabic and Islam* 6, 1985, pp. 229–41

Freethinkers of Medieval Islam, Ibn al-Rāwandī, Abū Bakr al-Rāzī, and their Impact on Islamic Thought, Leiden, 1999.

al-Ṭabarī, Abū Jaʿfar, *Taʾrīkh al-rusul wa-al-mulūk*, ed. M.J. de Goeje *et al.*, Leiden, 1879–1901

al-Ṭabarī, ʿAlī b. Rabban, *Kitāb al-dīn wa-al-dawla*, ed. A. Mingana, Manchester, 1923; trans. A.Mingana, *The Book of Religion and Empire*, Manchester, 1922

Al-radd ʿalā al-Naṣārā, ed. I.-A. Khalifé and W. Kutsch, "Ar-Radd ʿalā-n-Naṣārā de ʿAlī aṭ-Ṭabarī", *Mélanges de l'Université Saint Joseph* 36, 1959, pp. 113–48; trans. J.-M. Gaudeul, *Riposte aux Chrétiens par ʿAlī al-Ṭabarī*, Rome, 1995

Tartar, G., *Dialogue islamo-chrétien sous le calife al-Maʾmûn (813–834), les épîtres d'al-Hashimî et d'al-Kindî*, Paris, 1985; see Tien, *Risāla*

al-Ṭawhīdī, Abū Ḥayyān, *Kitāb al-imtāʿ wa-al-muʾānasa*, ed. A. Amīn and A. al-Zayn, Cairo, 1939–44

Theodore Abū Qurra, see Bacha, *Œuvres*; Graf, *Arabischen Schriften*

Thomas, D., "Two Muslim–Christian Debates from the Early Shīʿite Tradition", *Journal of Semitic Studies* 33, 1988, pp. 53–80

Anti-Christian Polemic in Early Islam, Abū ʿĪsā al-Warrāq's "Against the Trinity" (University of Cambridge Oriental Publications 45), Cambridge, 1992

"The Miracles of Jesus in Early Islamic Polemic", *Journal of Semitic Studies* 39, 1994, pp. 221–43

"Abū ʿĪsā al-Warrāq and the History of Religions", *Journal of Semitic Studies* 41, 1996, pp. 275–90

"The Bible in Early Muslim Anti-Christian Polemic", *Islam and Christian–Muslim Relations* 7, 1996, pp. 29–38

"Abū Manṣūr al-Māturīdī on the Divinity of Jesus Christ", *Islamochristiana* 23, 1997, pp. 43–64

"The Question better not Asked", in Theodore Gabriel, ed., *Islam in the Contemporary World*, New Delhi, 2000, pp. 20–41

"Islamic Understanding of the Trinity during the Abbasid era", in L. Ridgeon, ed., *Islamic Interpretations of Christianity*, Richmond, 2000, pp. 78–98

Tien, A., *Risāla ʿAbdallah Ibn Ismāʿīl al-Hāshimī ilā ʿAbd al-Masīḥ Ibn Isḥāq al-Kindī*, London, 1880

Timothy I, see Cheikho, *Dialectique du langage sur Dieu*; Mingana, "Apology"

Tritton, A.S., *The Caliphs and their Non-Muslim Subjects*, London, 1930

Troupeau, G., "Les couvents chrétiens dans la littérature arabe", *La Nouvelle Revue du Caire* 1, Cairo, 1975, pp. 265–79, repr. in G. Troupeau, *Etudes sur le christianisme arabe au Moyen Age*, Aldershot, 1995, no. XX

Urvoy, D., *Les penseurs libres dans l'Islam classique*, Paris, 1996

Voorhoeve, P., *Handlist of Arabic Manuscripts in the Library of the University of Leiden and other Collections in the Netherlands*, Leiden (2nd ed.), 1980

Wasserstein, D.J., "The 'Majlis of al-Riḍā': a Religious Debate in the Court of the Caliph al-Maʾmūn as Represented in a Shīʿī Hagiographical Work about the Eighth Imām ʿAlī ibn Mūsā al-Riḍā", in H. Lazarus-Yafeh, M.R. Cohen, S. Somekh, S.H. Griffith, eds., *The Majlis, Interreligious Encounters in Medieval Islam*, Wiesbaden, 1999, pp. 108–19

Watt, W. M., *The Formative Period of Islamic Thought*, Edinburgh, 1973

"Ash-Shahrastānī's Account of Christian Doctrine", *Islamochristiana* 9, 1983, pp. 249–59

Wolfson, H. A., *The Philosophy of the Kalām*, Harvard, 1976

Yaḥyā Ibn ʿAdī, see Platti

Yāqūt, Yaʿqūb b. ʿAbdallah, *Kitāb irshād al-arīb ilā maʿrifat al-adīb*, ed. D. S. Margoliouth, Leiden and London, 1907–26

INDEX

UNIVERSITY OF CAMBRIDGE
ORIENTAL PUBLICATIONS PUBLISHED FOR THE
FACULTY OF ORIENTAL STUDIES

45 *Anti-Christian polemic in Early Islam: Abū ʿĪsā al-Warrāq's "Against the Trinity"*, by David Thomas
46 *Devotional literature in South Asia: current research, 1985–8. Papers of the fourth conference on devotional literature in New indo-Aryan languages*, edited by R. S. McGregor
47 *Genizah research after ninety years: the case of Judaeo-Arabic. Papers read at the third congress of the Society for Judaeo-Arabic Studies*, edited by Joshua Blau and Stefan C. Reif
48 *Divination, mythology and monarchy in Han China*, by Michael Loewe
49 *The Arabian epic: heroic and oral storytelling*, volumes I–III, by M. C. Lyons
50 *Religion in Japan: arrows to heaven and earth*, edited by P. F. Kornicki and I. J. McMullen
51 *Kingship and political practice in colonial India*, by Pamela G. Price
52 *Hebrew manuscripts at Cambridge University Library: a description and introduction*, by Stefan C. Reif
53 *Selected letters by Rabindranath Tagore*, edited by Krishna Dutta and Andrew Robinson
54 *State and court ritual in China*, edited by Joseph P. McDermott
55 *Indian semantic analysis: the* nirvacana *tradition*, by Eivind Kahrs
56 *The Syraic version of the Old Testament: an introduction*, by M. P. Weitzman
57 *The cult of Asharah in ancient Israel and Judah: evidence for a Hebrew goddess*, by Judith M. Hadley
58 *The transformation of nomadic society in the Arab East*, edited by Martha Mundy and Basim Musallam